Preliminary Edition

INTRODUCTION TO
ACCOUNTING

A USER PERSPECTIVE

Kumen H. Jones

Jean B. Price

with

Martha S. Doran

PRENTICE HALL, Englewood Cliffs, New Jersey 07632

Production Editor: *Cathleen Profitko*
Manufacturing Buyer: *Patrice Fraccio*
Acquisitions Editor: *Rob Dewey*
Development Editor: *David Cohen*
Assistant Editor: *Diane DeCastro*
Editorial Assistant: *Amy Hinton*

Printed in the United States of America

10 9 8 7 6 5 4 3 2

ISBN 013-182031-1

Prentice-Hall International (UK) Limited, *London*
Prentice-Hall of Australia Pty. Limited, *Sydney*
Prentice-Hall Canada Inc., *Toronto*
Prentice-Hall Hispanoamericana, S.A., *Mexico*
Prentice-Hall of India Private Limited, *New Delhi*
Prentice-Hall of Japan, Inc., *Tokyo*
Simon & Schuster Asia Pte. Ltd., *Singapore*
Editora Prentice-Hall do Brasil, Ltda., *Rio de Janeiro*

TO THE READER:

As the cover indicates, this is a ***preliminary edition*** of <u>Introduction to Accounting: A User Perspective</u>. The final book will be published in the summer of 1995.

We are providing this early edition of our work to the market because there has been a significant demand for a text like ours. The approach we have adopted is to focus on the ***uses*** of accounting information, rather than the preparation.

This preliminary edition will provide you an opportunity to learn about the judgment and decision-making aspects of accounting. The finished product will actually include additional features that you won't see here. Primarily, these will be photographs and illustrations, and our "Think About It" boxes. These boxes will provide short vignettes from the business world that help the reader see the relevance of each topic in the text.

In the final edition, the Activities Book will be published as a separate supplement. In this edition, all the activities are included in the back of the text.

Because we wish to create a book that meets the needs of both students and professors, we are very interested in your feedback. You are encouraged to send your comments and suggestions to:

Rob Dewey
Accounting Editor
Prentice Hall
113 Sylvan Avenue
Englewood Cliffs, NJ 07632

PREFACE

As the 21st century approaches, it is time to assess the preparations we have made for the business world of the future. Clearly, technological advances have affected the skills required in today's world. As computers and machines take over many of the more repetitive tasks, business people are depended on to do all the things that only people can do — in particular, communicating, thinking, and decision making. The philosophy embraced as this book was developed focuses on these skills.

As you work with this text, you will find that it focuses heavily on the uses of accounting information rather than the preparation of the information. Decision making is a critical skill in today's business world, and is a primary focus of this text. We support the recommendations made by the Accounting Education Change Commission in its Position Statement No. Two: *The First Course In Accounting*. We think the course should be a broad introduction *to* accounting, rather than introductory accounting as it has been traditionally taught. It should be taught from the perspective of the user, not the preparer. It should emphasize WHAT accounting information is, WHY it is important, and HOW it is used by economic decision makers.

We have offered a logical approach to the material covered in the text. As you work your way through the material in this book, you will go through a series of discovery experiences. First, you will discover a need for information. Second, you will discover the accounting information developed to address that need. Third, you will discover complications and/or limitations associated with the information, which in itself creates a new need, and the process begins again. Each subject presented is driven by the subject preceding it. The purpose of this approach is to present accounting information in context. That is, not just as something that exists, but as something that exists in response to specific needs.

Along with the new approach to the subject matter itself, we offer a new approach to the presentation of the material and the learning process. Throughout the text, you will find *Discussion Questions (DQ's)*. These should not be overlooked. They can serve both the student and the professor. These questions may be used as a basis for classroom discussion, written assignments, or group work. However, even if they are not formally used as part of the required work for this course, they should not be ignored. You will gain a greater understanding of the issues discussed if you will take the time to ponder each discussion question as you reach it in your reading.

At the end of each chapter, you will find **KEY TERMS DEFINED** and **REVIEW THE FACTS**. These features will help you to assess your understanding of the main ideas presented.

The **APPLY WHAT YOU HAVE LEARNED** section includes a variety of assignments. You will find matching problems, short answer questions, and calculations. This section also includes assignments that require critical thinking and writing, as well as some problems dealing directly with financial statements.

In the back of this book, you will find **ACTIVITIES** for each chapter. These are creative assignments that work well to support cooperative and interactive learning. Traditional accounting texts included nothing quite like these. An instructor's manual will be available to accompany this preliminary edition, and its most important function will be to aid the instructor with the operation of the activities. Even if the activities are not required in this course, you will benefit by looking them over. They will broaden your thoughts about the topics addressed in the text.

One feature which is clearly missing when this text is compared to traditional accounting texts is the coverage of bookkeeping. We believe that it should be up to the individual program to determine the appropriate timing and amount of coverage needed on this topic. Our focus is on preparing the students to be wise users of accounting information. Clearly, we have chosen to omit all coverage of bookkeeping skills. Currently, we suggest a tutorial package developed by Ivy software as a way to introduce debits and credits if that is necessary. Eventually, a product specifically designed to accompany this text will be available in both a manual and a computerized form.

Overall, each part of this book was created to stimulate robust and invigorating interchange between instructor and student as together they grapple with accounting issues. We hope that students and teachers alike benefit from the use of this book, and actually enjoy the work necessary to explore the world of accounting.

BRIEF CONTENTS

TABLE OF CONTENTS

CHAPTER BRIDGE: Regardless of the form of organization or the business activity involved, success and even survival depends on making wise decisions.

CHAPTER BRIDGE: Decision making is an important activity in the business world. Economic decision making relies heavily on accounting information. Therefore, it is important that the accounting information provided meets the needs of economic decision makers.

CHAPTER BRIDGE: As we examine various steps in the operation of a business, you will see how important decision making really is. Remember, accounting information is a major input into the decision making process. Accounting information is made available to decision makers in the form of financial statements; these financial statements are valuable tools of the trade.

CHAPTER BRIDGE: Often, businesses need even more funding than is available through investments by their owners. Another source of funds is borrowing.

CHAPTER BRIDGE: The balance sheet is a financial tool that helps decision makers evaluate the present financial condition of a business. Now, we will introduce two financial tools that help decision makers evaluate past performance — the income statement and the statement of owners' equity.

CHAPTER BRIDGE: The three statements introduced thus far rely on measurements of economic activity. But from what perspective have these measurements been made? Before relying on accounting information, decision makers must know what basis of economic measurement was in place when the information was compiled.

CHAPTER BRIDGE: Revenue recognition and expense recognition as prescribed under accrual accounting require that expenses be recognized in the same income statement period as the revenues that they helped to generate. This matching principle results in several situations requiring special treatment under accrual accounting. One such situation is the allocation of the costs of long-lived assets, which is the focus of the next chapter.

CHAPTER BRIDGE: In addition to the variations allowed regarding depreciation, accrual accounting allows a variety of methods for tracking the costs of inventory. In the next chapter, we explore the issues surrounding merchandise inventory and cost of goods sold and the variations among companies' financial statements with regards to this issue.

CHAPTER BRIDGE: Thus far, we have introduced three financial
statements used as tools to help economic decision makers. In
addition, we have explored in some detail the results of using
accrual accounting as a basis of economic measurement. The most
striking weakness of the accrual basis is the fact that it takes the
accounting information user's eye off of cash. In the next chapter,
we introduce the statement of cash flows, a financial statement that
helps to bring the user's focus back to cash.

CHAPTER BRIDGE: Economic decision makers rely on the information provided in the financial statements. For this information to be truly useful, the external decision makers must be assured that the statements were prepared under a consistently applied set of guidelines. The guidelines are called generally accepted accounting principles (GAAP), and the assurance is provided through the audit process.

CHAPTER BRIDGE: With assurance from the auditor in hand, economic decision makers can proceed with confidence in their further uses of the accounting information. The in-depth examination of relationships between and among financial statement items is called financial statement analysis. These analytical techniques can provide valuable insight to decision makers.

CHAPTER 1

INTRODUCTION TO BUSINESS IN THE UNITED STATES

The business of America is business.

> - Calvin Coolidge,
> 30th President of the United States

The word **business** means different things to different people. For some, the word conjures up dreams of excitement and opportunity. For others, it represents a nightmare of greed and exploitation. But regardless of whether our view of it is positive or negative, each of us is touched every day by what goes on in business.

The dictionary has several definitions of the word business, including: 1. One's work or occupation; 2. A special task or duty; 3. A matter or affair; 4. Commerce or trade; 5. A commercial or industrial establishment.

As you can see, not only can people have different impressions of what "business" means, but the word itself can actually mean different things in different contexts. The last two definitions in the previous paragraph, though, are particularly important for this book. It is important for you to understand that at times "business" is used to describe the entirety of commerce and trade, and at other times it is used to describe an individual company. In fact, please note that in the economic world, the words "company" and "business" are often used interchangeably. This situation holds true for books about the world of business, as well, including this one. So, when you see the word "business", make sure you understand the context in which it is used.

This chapter is intended to serve as a brief introduction to business in general and the way in which it is conducted in the United States. The information in this chapter should provide you with the background necessary to put the accounting concepts presented in this text into the proper business context. After all, accounting information is the key ingredient for making wise business decisions.

When you have completed your work on this chapter, you should be able to:

1.   Describe the four factors of production.

2.   Distinguish between a planned economy and a market economy.

3.   Explain the basic concepts of capitalism and how they relate to the profit motive.

4.   Compare and contrast the distinctions between the sympathetic and mercenary societies as described by Adam Smith.

5. Explain the basic issues surrounding the debate as to whether or not businesses have a social responsibility.

6. Distinguish among the three basic forms of business organization: proprietorships, partnerships and corporations; describe the advantages and disadvantages of each.

7. Distinguish among the three major types of business activities and define hybrid type businesses.

8. Explain the basic need for and complications of international business trade.

WHAT IS BUSINESS?

Essentially, business is the process of producing (manufacturing) goods (products) and services and then distributing (selling) them to those who desire or need them. It sounds simple enough, but it is actually an amazingly complex process, and few people ever gain a complete understanding of its many aspects.

While we cannot even begin to present an in-depth study of the many aspects of business, there are a few basics we must talk about if we are to present accounting in its proper context. We will begin with what are called the **factors of production**.

Factors of Production

Several key ingredients are needed to support economic activity; these items are called the factors of production. Economists have broken the factors of production into four categories:

1. **Natural Resources.** These include land and the things that come from the land, such as timber, mineral deposits, oil deposits, and water.

2. **Labor.** This is sometimes called the **human resource factor**. It encompasses the mental and physical efforts of all workers, regardless of skill or education, who perform the many tasks required to produce and sell goods and services.

3. **Capital.** This factor includes the buildings, machinery, and tools used to produce goods and services. Unfortunately, the word "capital" is used rather loosely. Sometimes it is used to refer to the money that buys the buildings, machinery, and tools used in production. This can be confusing, so whenever you see the word, whether in this book or elsewhere, be careful to understand the context in which it is being used.

4. **Entrepreneurship.** This is the factor of production that brings the first three together. **Entrepreneurs** are people willing to accept the opportunities and risks of starting and

running businesses. They acquire the capital, assemble the labor force, and utilize available natural resources to produce and sell goods and services.

How these four factors of production are combined to produce goods and services depends on the type of economic system utilized by a society.

Planned and Market Economies

In a **planned economy**, a strong, centralized government controls all or most of the natural resources, labor, and capital used to produce goods and services. In other words, the government replaces the entrepreneur as the fourth factor of production. **Communism** and, to a lesser extent, **socialism** are examples of planned economies. Some people may argue that Communism is dying out and soon will be nonexistent; however, at least for the time being, this system is alive and well in Cuba. Socialism, in varying degrees, can be found in several countries; Sweden operates under one of the purest forms of socialism.

A **market economy** relies on competition in the marketplace to determine the most efficient way to allocate the resources of the economy. In a market economy, all or most of the factors of production are privately owned and controlled, and the government does not attempt to coordinate economic activity. **Capitalism** is an example of a market economy. Capitalism is also known as the free enterprise, free market, or private enterprise system and is the economic system used to conduct business in the United States.

The concept of capitalism is most often traced to the writings of Adam Smith (1723-1790). In his book <u>An Inquiry into the Nature and Causes of the Wealth of Nations</u> (usually referred to simply as <u>Wealth of Nations</u>), published in 1776, Smith said that if individuals are free to promote their own self-interests, an "invisible hand" of competition will lead to the production of the best possible products at the lowest possible price. The market system developed by this invisible hand of competition would not allow unsafe or poor quality products to flourish because people would not buy them. And while environmental issues were not directly addressed in 1776, the market envisioned by Smith would also presumably adjust to prevent damage to the environment.

The Profit Motive

The self-interests discussed by Adam Smith can be broadly summed up as the **profit motive**. Basically, the idea behind the profit motive is that a person will do something only if the benefit derived from doing it is greater than the sacrifice required by doing it. A rational person desires the greatest benefit derived from the least sacrifice. When this natural desire in one person is pitted against the same desire in another person, the result is competition.

To illustrate the profit motive, let's say Marty needs a new pair of shoes. Because he is a rational person, Marty desires the best pair of shoes he can buy for the least amount of money spent. Ralph owns a shoe store. Because he is a rational person, Ralph desires to sell his shoes for the highest price he can. Marty goes to Ralph's shoe store and looks at a pair of shoes Ralph has priced at $100. Assuming he likes the shoes and can afford to pay $100, Marty will buy them if he feels they provide him with the most benefit for the least sacrifice.

Now let's add one other ingredient. Enter Elizabeth, who also owns a shoe store. She sells shoes identical to the pair Marty is considering buying at Ralph's. The difference is, she is selling them for $90.

```
┌─────────────────────────────────────────────────────────────┐
│                                                               │
│                    Discussion Questions                      │
│                                                               │
│                                                               │
│      1-1.  What do you think caused Ralph and Elizabeth to    │
│            establish different selling prices for an          │
│            identical pair of shoes?                           │
│                                                               │
│                                                               │
│      1-2.  Assuming Marty decides to buy the shoes, what      │
│            do you think will determine where he buys them?    │
│                                                               │
│                                                               │
└─────────────────────────────────────────────────────────────┘
```

In this example, Marty's self-interest pits the self-interests of
Ralph and Elizabeth against one another because Marty's desire to
pay the lowest price possible for the shoes will make Ralph and
Elizabeth compete for his business. If Ralph loses enough sales to
Elizabeth because she sells shoes for less than he does, he will be
forced to lower his selling price. In fact, he may want to reduce
his selling price for the shoes to $85, thus attracting sales away
from Elizabeth. She will then be forced to lower her selling
price. This is Adam Smith's invisible hand at work. No one makes
Ralph and Elizabeth lower their prices; the force comes from
competition in the market.

There comes a point, of course, below which the selling price
cannot go. If Ralph and Elizabeth pay $55 for the shoes they buy
for resale, they obviously cannot sell those shoes for less than

that, or it makes no sense to even bother. In order to make a **profit**, they must sell the shoes for more than they paid for them. Profit is the excess of benefit over sacrifice, thus if Marty buys the shoes from Ralph for $100, Ralph's profit can be calculated as:

        Amount received from Marty (BENEFIT)...............$100
        Less what Ralph paid for the shoes (SACRIFICE)..... 55
        Equals GROSS PROFIT on the sale of shoes...........$ 45

While this $45 represents the profit Ralph earned on the sale of this one pair of shoes, it is usually called **gross profit** because it does not represent his actual profit from operating his shoe store. He has other costs, such as rent on the store, utilities, wages paid to employees, and so on. All these items must be taken into account before he can calculate his real profit, which is usually called **net profit** or **net income**.

If Ralph does not earn a sufficient profit on his shoe store business, he will have to close it and go into another line of work. The same, of course, is true for Elizabeth. And what is true for Ralph and Elizabeth in their shoe stores is also true for the society as a whole if it operates within a capitalistic economy. If businesses do not earn profits, they cease to exist. Once again, this is Adam Smith's "invisible hand" at work. Only those companies that are profitable will be allowed by the market to stay in business; those that are not profitable will be forced out of business.

Profits vs. Social Responsibility

Some people feel that "profit" is a dirty word and that we would be better off if companies were motivated by something other than the almighty dollar. These individuals feel that American business should strike a balance between profit and social responsibility. On the other hand, there are others who believe that business has no obligation beyond earning profits. That is, companies have no social responsibility.

We live in a world that seems to measure success by whether someone "beat" someone else. It's what has been described as a zero-sum game, meaning that for every winner there must be a loser. So on the surface, the following quotation from Vince Lombardi (former football coach of the Green Bay Packers), seems to more accurately capture our modern world than the one by Grantland Rice (well-known sportswriter).

>   Winning is not everything, it is the only thing!
>   - Vince Lombardi

>   It matters not whether you win or lose, but
>   how you play the game.
>   - Grantland Rice

In recent years, however, there has been renewed concern over how the game of business is played. An increasing number of investors, creditors, and other economic decision makers have become interested not only in "the bottom line" (making money), but how companies conduct themselves as citizens in the community, as well. In other words, business can be viewed as a win/win situation rather than win/lose.

Many of those opposed to the profit motive have attacked Adam Smith's Wealth of Nations (and capitalism in general) as nothing more than a justification of greed and the exploitation of people and the environment, while many proponents of capitalism seem to think the "invisible hand" spoken of by Smith will automatically protect society from unsafe or poor quality products. In truth, very few people have actually read Wealth of Nations. They talk about it, pro or con, and have read what others have written about the book, but they have not read it themselves. This is unfortunate because there is, in fact, nothing in the book to support either of the positions we described. This is especially true if the work is placed in the context of Adam Smith's philosophy.

As stated earlier, Wealth of Nations was published in 1776. Seventeen years earlier, in 1759, Smith published The Theory of Moral Sentiments. In it, Smith describes what he calls the optimal society, where all affairs - social, economic, and political - are conducted with the love of others in mind:

> It is thus that man, who can subsist only in society, was fitted by nature to that situation for which he was made. All the members of human society stand in need of each other's assistance, and are likewise exposed to mutual injuries. Where the necessary assistance is reciprocally afforded from love, from gratitude, from friendship, and esteem, the society flourishes and is happy. All the different members of it are bound together by the agreeable bands of love and affection, and are, as it were, drawn to one common centre of mutual good offices.

This was the optimal society, also called the **sympathetic society**, as envisioned by Adam Smith, the "Father of Capitalism." Smith did, in fact, recognize that humans often fail to act on that innate sympathy, the result being a suboptimal society:

> But though the necessary assistance should not be afforded from such generous and disinterested motives, though among the different members of the society there should be no mutual love and affection, the society, though less happy and agreeable, will not necessarily be dissolved. Society may subsist among different men, as among different merchants, from a sense of its utility, without any mutual love or affection; and though no man in it should owe any obligation, or be bound in gratitude to any other, it may still be upheld by a mercenary exchange of good offices according to an agreed valuation.

This suboptimal society has also been referred to as **the mercenary society**. The "invisible hand" still works in this society, but all

12

members must be constantly on their guard, because each member is supposedly trying to get ahead by taking advantage of everyone else. Basically, it is a society based on mutual distrust.

The real questions we all must ask are: (1) What kind of society do we want?, and (2) If we are living in a mercenary society and want to create a more sympathetic society, how do we go about making the necessary changes? These are questions that transcend this class, and indeed, they transcend all the other courses you will take while you are in college.

```
┌─────────────────────────────────────────────────────────┐
│                   Discussion Questions                   │
│                                                          │
│    1-3. In what ways do you think the optimal            │
│         (sympathetic) and the suboptimal (mercenary)     │
│         societies differ?                                │
│                                                          │
│    1-4. Which of the two societies (sympathetic or       │
│         mercenary) do you think best describes our own?  │
│         Provide an example to support your position.     │
│                                                          │
│    1-5. If you think that we are living in a mercenary    │
│         society and that a sympathetic society would be  │
│         better, what do you think is the best way to     │
│         move from the one to the other?                  │
└─────────────────────────────────────────────────────────┘
```

Social Responsibility In Business Today

Recently, there has been a renewed interest in whether or not business is conducted in a socially responsible manner. A growing number of people are refusing to do business with companies they feel are insensitive to social and environmental concerns. In response to this concern, a great many companies are making an effort to communicate their commitment to responsible and ethical business practices.

A word coined in the past few years to describe anyone to whom a company owes a responsibility is **stakeholder**. A stakeholder is anyone who is affected by the way a company conducts its business. The idea behind stakeholders is that many people and other companies are affected by the decisions a company makes and the manner in which it conducts its affairs. That is, they have a stake in the way a company is run. The trick is determining just exactly who all the stakeholders are and just what a company's responsibilities are to each of them.

In the past couple of years, annual reports of certain companies have included information directed at parties deemed by the company to be stakeholders. This is an example of what we were talking about earlier when we said many companies are taking great pains to demonstrate their commitment to responsible conduct.

Whether this trend toward socially conscious business behavior is mere "public relations" or a real commitment remains to be seen. In any event, the days when a company could conduct its business without regard to anything but making a profit are very likely gone forever. In a way, it could be said that Adam Smith's invisible hand is moving once again, sweeping companies unwilling to respond to the pressure to act responsibly out of the marketplace.

Discussion Questions

1-6. Make a list of those to whom you think a company owes responsibility. What are the specific responsibilities it has to each? How do you think it could best go about fulfilling each of those responsibilities?

1-7. Can you think of any companies that have fulfilled the responsibilities you outlined in your answer to the Discussion Question above, and yet have been profitable, as well?

FORMS OF BUSINESS ORGANIZATION

Generally speaking, there are three forms of business organization in the United States: **sole proprietorships, partnerships,** and **corporations.** Each of the three has certain advantages in relation to the others, and each has certain disadvantages.

Sole Proprietorships

A sole proprietorship, also called a **proprietorship,** is a business owned by a single individual. A common misconception about this form of business is that it is always a small business. While the vast majority of sole proprietorships are small, the classification has nothing to do with the size of the business, only with the fact that it has a single owner.

Advantages of sole proprietorships

1. *Easy and inexpensive to set up.* Except for obtaining the necessary government permits (all of which are state and local), there are no special legal requirements associated with starting a sole proprietorship. All a person has to do is decide what kind of business he or she wants to establish and obtain those licenses and permits, and that person is in business.

2. *No sharing of profits.* When there is a single owner, there is no such thing as sharing of profits (except with the government, of course, in the form of taxes). Whatever the business earns belongs solely to the owner.

3. *Owner has total control.* This is probably the number one reason why a person starts his or her own business. Virtually everyone who works for someone else feels stifled by having to "answer to the boss." The sole proprietor answers to no one when it comes to decisions as to how to run the business (so long as it's legal).

4. *Independence.* This is closely related to having total control. We have listed it separately as an advantage because it is broader than simply being in a position to control how the company is run. This one can actually be thought of as the ability to choose one's lifestyle. There is no accumulation of "vacation days" for sole proprietors. On the other hand, they are free to take days off whenever they want to, if they feel they can spare the time.

5. *Few government regulations.* We already touched on this one when we talked about how easy it is to start a sole proprietorship. Corporations face even more government regulations once they are organized. This is not true for proprietorships. So long as the owner pays his or her taxes and does not engage in illegal activities, a proprietorship is reasonably free from government regulation.

6. *No special income taxes.* From a legal standpoint, a sole proprietorship is simply an extension of its owner. Therefore, a proprietorship pays no income tax. The earnings of the company are considered the earnings of the owner and become a part of his or her taxable income.

7. *Easy and inexpensive to dissolve.* Sole proprietorships are about as easy to end as they are to start. If the owner decides to shut the company down, all he or she must do is notify the appropriate licensing agent for state and local government and pay off remaining debts, and the business is no longer a business.

Disadvantages of sole proprietorships

1. *Unlimited liability.* Earlier, we stated that from a legal standpoint, a sole proprietorship is simply an extension of its owner. For this reason, all obligations incurred by the business are considered legal obligations of the owner. What this means is that if the company goes into debt and cannot pay its bills (regardless of the reason), the folks to whom the business owes the money can sue for the owner's personal property, such as his or her house, car, or boat.

2. *Limited access to capital (money).* All businesses, regardless of form (proprietorship, partnership, corporation), must have money to operate. This is often referred to as capital. The amount of capital available to a sole proprietorship is limited to the amount of his or her own money the owner can put into the business, or the amount the owner can borrow on a personal loan. Remember that legally this form of business is the same as the owner, therefore, whenever the business borrows money, the owner is actually borrowing.

3. *Limited management expertise.* We have already mentioned that one of the advantages of the proprietorship form is total control. While this can certainly be considered a positive, it does have a negative side to it. No one is an expert in everything (although we're sure you know people who think they are), and a sole proprietor is limited to whatever management expertise he or she possesses. Many proprietorships get into trouble because the owner lacks skills in areas critical to the survival of the company.

4. *Personal time commitment.* Running a business is hard work, and most sole proprietors work very long hours — probably longer hours than they would have to if they were employees of someone else. However, because they are working for their own benefit and not someone else's, most sole proprietors consider the time well spent. But make no mistake about it, it takes a tremendous amount of time to run your own business.

5. *Often have limited lives.* As we shall see when we discuss the other two business forms, partnerships and corporations tend to have longer lives than sole proprietorships. The reason

18

for this is fairly simple: Unless the company is sold to someone else (another sole proprietor) or passed on to the owner's heirs, the life of the business is no longer than the life of the owner.

Notwithstanding the disadvantages of proprietorship, it is the dream of many Americans to own their own business, and nearly 71 percent of companies in the United States are sole proprietorships. Because most of them are small businesses, only about 6 percent of all business revenues come from this form of business.

Partnerships

Think of a partnership as a proprietorship with two or more owners. This is a bit simplistic because there are actually several different types of partnerships; however, for our purposes here, thinking of a partnership as a proprietorship with two or more owners is appropriate. As was the case with the sole proprietorship form, there is a common misconception that all partnerships are small businesses. In fact, some partnerships are quite large. Most public accounting firms are partnerships, and some of them have as many as 2,000 partners and 20,000 employees.

Advantages of partnerships

1. *Easy to form.* From a legal standpoint, partnerships are not much more complicated to form than are proprietorships. Once the appropriate licenses and permits are obtained, a partnership is in business.

2.   *Increased management expertise.* Partnerships are often formed because one person has skills in a specific area of business and another person possesses expertise in a different area. So, by combining those areas of expertise into a partnership, the possibilities of a successful business are enhanced.

3.   *Access to more capital (money).* When more than one person is involved in the ownership of the business, there usually exists greater access to capital. In fact, many partnerships are formed for this very reason.

4.   *Few government regulations.* As was the case with sole proprietorships, partnerships are subject to relatively few government regulations. So long as the partners pay their taxes and the partnership does not engage in illegal activities, there is not much government interference.

5.   *No special income taxes.* Partnerships are not legally separate from their owners. Therefore, partnerships do not pay income taxes. Rather, any profits earned by a partnership are considered personal income of the partners and the partners pay tax on the earnings as part of their personal tax returns.

6.   *Greater business continuity.* Because there are more people involved, partnerships tend to have longer lives than do sole proprietorships. When a partner dies or withdraws from the partnership, the legal life of the partnership ends. For all practical purposes, however, the business generally does not need to stop its operations. The partnership agreement may allow the remaining partner or partners to either continue with one less partner, or admit another partner to the firm.

Disadvantages of partnerships

1.   *Unlimited liability.* Because partnerships are legally no different than the owners, the partners are personally liable for all obligations of the business. In fact, in most instances, each partner is personally liable for all the obligations of the partnership. This means if any partner

20

makes a decision that obligates the partnership, all the partners are liable, even if they had known nothing about the decision.

2. *Must share profits.* When a partnership is formed, there is an agreement prepared outlining how any profits of the company are to be divided. Usually this is based on how much each partner invested in the partnership. Regardless of whether or not such an agreement is fair and equitable, the fact remains that once a partnership is formed, there will be a sharing of profits with others.

3. *Potential conflicts between partners.* Suppose one partner wants the company to begin selling a new product, and another partner disagrees. If the two partners have equal power, they have entered what it has become fashionable to call "gridlock." The basis for conflicts among partners may range from personal habits to overall business philosphy, and there may be no solution other than dissolving the partnership to resolve them.

4. *Often difficult to dissolve.* Ending a partnership can be very nasty. When a partnership is formed, everybody is happy and the future looks bright. Unfortunately, people and circumstances change. So, when partnerships are dissolved, it is often because someone has become dissatisfied with the way the partnership is being run. Accusations and counter-accusations are made, friends become enemies, and often the result is litigation (lawsuits). If they are wise, individuals forming a partnership will include provisions for dissolution in the original partnership agreement, while everyone is still friends. You might think of it as the business version of a pre-nuptial agreement where the parties forming the business agree on how the business marriage is to be ended.

Frankly, while there are advantages to the partnership form, many people feel those advantages are far outweighed by the disadvantages. Only about 1 percent of the businesses in the

United States are partnerships, and they account for only about 4 percent of all business revenues.

Corporations

From a record keeping and accounting standpoint, proprietorships, partnerships, and corporations are all considered to be completely separate from their owner or owners. This means that all information pertaining to the financial affairs of a company are carefully separated from those of the owners, regardless of the organizational form of the company. This distinction between companies and their owners only holds true for accounting purposes. As we mentioned before, both proprietorships and partnerships are considered to be the same as their owners legally. Of the three forms of business organization, only the corporate form is legally considered a separate entity from its owners.

Way back in 1819, Chief Justice John Marshall of the United States Supreme Court made this statement:

> A corporation is an artificial being, invisible, intangible, and existing only in contemplation of law.

This ruling changed the course of business in the United States forever. As a separate legal entity, a corporation has many of the rights and obligations of a person. These include the right to enter into contracts and the right to buy, own, and sell property. A corporation is required by law to discharge its obligations lawfully, and it can be sued if it does not. A corporation can be taken to court if it breaks the law, and it is obligated to pay taxes, just like an actual person. In addition to the legal obligations of corporations, the moral obligation of corporations to be socially responsible has been a topic of widespread discussion in recent years. The fact that corporations are separate legal entities leads to several distinct advantages and disadvantages of this business form.

Advantages of corporations

1. *Limited Liability.* Because a corporation is a separate legal entity from its owners (stockholders), the owners are not liable for the corporation's obligations. The maximum amount a **stockholder** can lose is the amount of his or her investment.

2. *Greater Access to Capital.* By dividing ownership into relatively low-cost shares of stock, corporations can attract a great number of investors. Some corporations in the United States have in excess of a million different stockholders.

3. *Easy Transferability of Ownership.* Because shares of ownership in corporations are usually relatively low-cost, they can be purchased or sold by individual investors much more easily than an ownership interest in either of the other two forms of business.

4. *Continuity of Life.* Because a corporation is legally separate and distinct from its owner or owners, it continues to exist even when there is a complete change in ownership. The transfer of shares of stock has no effect on a corporation.

Disadvantages of corporations

1. *Greater Tax Burden.* All businesses, regardless of form, must pay property taxes and payroll taxes. In addition to these taxes, corporations must pay federal income tax and in many states they are also required to pay state and even local income taxes. Part of the after-tax profit is distributed to the owners in the form of dividends. These dividends are considered personal income to the owners and are taxed again. This is what is referred to as **double taxation**, and it has been the subject of fierce debate for many years in the United States.

2. *Greater Government Regulation.* Corporations are subject to significantly more government control than are either sole proprietorships or partnerships. Some corporations are required to file reports with both federal and state regulatory bodies. Filing these reports is time consuming and costly.

3. *Absentee Ownership.* In almost all proprietorships and in most partnerships, the owners also manage the business. They are assured, therefore, that the company is being operated according to their wishes. In many corporations, the vast majority of the stockholders have no involvement in the day to day operation of the business. Professional managers sometimes operate the company in their own interests, rather than for the benefit of the owners.

Although corporations represent a relatively small percentage of the total number of businesses in the United States, they transact roughly six times as much business as all proprietorships and partnerships combined, and corporations control the vast majority of business resources in the United States.

TYPES OF BUSINESSES

In addition to the organizational form a company takes
(proprietorship, partnership, or corporation), companies in the
United States can also be classified as to the type of business
activity in which they are engaged. The three broad
classifications are **manufacturing**, **merchandising**, and **service**.
While a single company can actually be involved in all three of
these business activities, usually one of the three constitutes the
majority of the company's interests.

Manufacturing Companies

The standard definition of a manufacturing company is a company
that purchases raw materials and converts them into some tangible,
physical product. We often think of these raw materials as the

25

completely unprocessed natural resources discussed earlier as one of the factors of production. While these natural resources certainly describe raw materials used in the manufacture of some products, raw materials often include completely finished products manufactured by others. For example, a company that manufactures household appliances may purchase many items, such as coils and generators used in the production of refrigerators. These coils and generators, while raw materials to the refrigerator manufacturer, are manufactured finished products for another company.

The distinguishing characteristic of a manufacturing type business is that it takes the raw materials it purchases and creates essentially a different product from them. As examples of manufactured products, take a look around you wherever you are as you read this. With the exception of the items provided by Mother Nature, all the tangible items you see were made by somebody. Examples of well-known manufacturing companies are: Bethlehem Steel, Intel (producer of computer components), The Boeing Company, and McDonnell Douglas Corporation.

The economic might of the United States was built on its manufacturing base. For many years, the country enjoyed almost total domination of manufacturing in the world. While this situation has changed somewhat over the past 50 years, manufacturing is still an important part of the American economy.

Roughly 22 percent of American jobs are offered by companies classified primarily as manufacturers.

Merchandising Companies

Like manufacturers, merchandising companies sell tangible, physical products as their major business activity. The difference is they buy the product they sell in a finished form rather than manufacturing it. This tangible, physical product is also called merchandise, hence the designation for this type of company.

There are two kinds of merchandisers:

- **Wholesale Merchandiser.** A wholesaler is a company that buys its product from the manufacturer (or another wholesaler) and then sells the product to the company that eventually sells the product to the end consumer. Examples of wholesale merchandisers include A. L. Lewis, a well-known grocery wholesaler, and W. W. Grainger, a major wholesale merchandiser of tools. These names may not be familiar to you because, as a consumer, you most often deal with a retailer rather than dealing directly with a wholesaler.

- **Retail Merchandiser.** A retailer is a company that buys its product from a wholesaler (or in some instances, directly from the manufacturer of the product) and then sells the product to the end consumer. We are all familiar with major retail operations such as Sears, Wal-Mart, and K-Mart. Other retail chains have focused on establishing themselves in specific regions of the country. Companies such as Target and Rose's have taken this approach. Many successful retailers are individual operations, rather than being part of a chain. Gift shops, clothing stores, and shoe stores are often individually-owned retail operations.

A wholesaler is what has traditionally been referred to as "the middleman" in American business. There are those who feel that wholesalers add nothing to the process and the economy would be better off without them. In fact, you will often see advertising in which a retailer claims he or she can sell you products for a lower price because he or she has "cut out the middleman." This concept has spurred the growth of many popular factory outlets. The increase in operations promoting "warehouse shopping" is also a result of an attempt to reduce prices by eliminating the middleman. This type of store provides only limited customer service and sales assistance, but promises lower prices in exchange for customers' willingness to accept "no frills shopping". While there are surely instances in which eliminating the middleman may result in lower prices, the wholesale merchandiser serves an important purpose in the American economy. By dealing in very high volume, wholesale merchandisers play an important role in the distribution process and often help to make the products purchased by consumers actually less expensive.

As an example of how the manufacturing and distribution process works, let's follow a pair of shoes as they go from the manufacturer, to the wholesaler, to the retailer, and ultimately into the hands of the consumer.

The manufacturer purchases leather, thread, and the other raw materials necessary to manufacture shoes. When these raw materials have been converted into a pair of shoes, the manufacturer sells them to a wholesaler for $30. In setting this selling price the manufacturer is considering all the costs associated with producing the shoes, plus a profit. The wholesaler then sells the pair of shoes to a retailer for $55. In setting this selling price the wholesaler is considering its cost for the shoes ($30), the cost of running its own business, plus a profit.

We have already discussed the part of the process from the wholesaler to the retailer to the ultimate consumer. Remember Marty, Ralph and Elizabeth? We talked about them earlier in the chapter when we were discussing the profit motive. Ralph or Elizabeth buys the pair of shoes for $55 from the wholesaler and Marty buys the shoes from one of them for the price dictated by market pressure.

The whole manufacturing and distribution process is very simple in concept, but extremely complicated in application. It is not a process that was planned, but rather one that has evolved over several hundred years. Although there are many problems associated with this system, it is one that has proven to be remarkably efficient. Merchandising operations provide approximately 28 percent of all jobs in the United States. This proportion has been stable since 1975 and is expected to remain so as the turn of the century approaches.

Service Companies

The last of the three broad types of companies in the United States is the service company. These are companies that do not deal in tangible products. Rather, as the name implies, they perform some sort of service as their major business activity. Doctors, lawyers, and accountants are examples of those who provide services instead of products. Another example would be the freight companies that transported the shoes in our previous example from the manufacturer to the wholesaler and from the wholesaler to the retailer.

The service industry is the fastest growing part of the U.S. economy. From 1975 to 1989, the percentage of total jobs in the United States provided by companies classified primarily as service companies rose from 21 percent to 30 percent. This percentage is expected to continue rising during the next decade.

Hybrid Companies

Earlier we stated that although businesses could be broadly classified by their type of operation (manufacturing, merchandising, service), some actually are involved in more than one type of activity. These are known as **hybrid companies**. For example, General Motors Corporation manufactures automobiles and trucks and is therefore classified as a manufacturer. In recent years, however, GM has become involved in activities that are classified as service. General Motors Acceptance Corporation (GMAC) was created specifically to provide financing for the customers of GM purchasing cars and trucks. Ford Motor Company has done the same thing with its Ford Motor Credit Company. Even more recently, these companies have begun to issue credit cards (Visa and Master Card). In the near future, we can expect the distinction among manufacturing, merchandising, and service companies to become even more blurred. As the struggle for survival in the world of business becomes even more intense, many companies will find it beneficial to involve themselves in a wide variety of business activities. This will be particularly true as the trend toward a global marketplace becomes more pronounced. American businesses simply must be prepared to view the world of business in a different light than ever before.

```
+------------------------------------------------------------------+
|                     Discussion Questions                         |
|                                                                  |
|                                                                  |
|    1-9. In what type of business activity                        |
|                                                                  |
|         (manufacturing, merchandising, or service)               |
|                                                                  |
|         would you like to be involved?  Describe in              |
|                                                                  |
|         detail the type of operation which most                  |
|                                                                  |
|         interests you.  What characteristics of this             |
|                                                                  |
|         type of business do you find appealing?                  |
|                                                                  |
|                                                                  |
+------------------------------------------------------------------+
```

THE GLOBAL NATURE OF BUSINESS IN THE 1990'S AND BEYOND

There are those in the United States who long for "the good old days," when everything sold in the U.S.A. was made in the U.S.A. Well, those days are gone forever. American businesses simply cannot produce all the goods and services demanded in the American marketplace. On the other hand, there are certain items produced in the United States that either have no market here or that are produced in greater quantities than can be sold here. The result is international business. When goods produced outside the United States are brought into the country and sold, they are called **imports**. When goods produced in the United States are sold in some other country, they are called **exports**.

There are complications caused by conducting business across national borders. While there are several specific complications we could discuss, they can all be thought of broadly as either economic or political complications (and even these two categories are not truly separate).

Economic Complications

Earlier in the chapter we touched on the major economic systems existing in the world today (communism, socialism, and capitalism). Whenever a company located in a country that is under one of these economic systems does business with a company located in a country with a different economic system, there are bound to be difficulties involved. Companies in capitalistic economies are motivated by profits. This motivation is not the driving force behind companies in communistic and socialistic economies. Rather, the movement of goods and services in these types of economies is part of some social plan.

Another economic complication results from the use of different currencies by different countries. For example, the fact that the United States uses dollars, England uses pounds, France uses francs, Japan uses yen, and many other countries have their own form of currency, causes international trading to be very complicated. As business is conducted between companies in the United States and companies in other countries of the world, the results of business transactions must be translated into dollars before an American company can know if those transactions have been profitable. **Translation** means converting the currency of one country (pounds, for example) into its equivalent in another country's currency (dollars, for example). This process would be quite simple if it were not for one problem — the currency exchange rates change constantly. Banks and other financial institutions often operate on a daily quotation of the exchange rate. In reality, however, the rate of exchange between dollars and pounds, yen, or any other foreign currency may change minute-to-minute.

Political Complications

The economic system employed by a particular country is usually an outgrowth of the political system employed by that country (or vice versa). There are, therefore, tremendous political implications involved with the type of economic system used by a country. Political complications, however, go beyond the issues of the type of economic system in place.

Two countries with the same type of economic system would still experience difficulties in dealing with one another. This is because every country, regardless of its economic system, must protect what it views as its own self-interest. In the area of international trade, this self-interest usually focuses on the comparison of import levels and export levels. It is usually considered bad for a country to import a larger quantity of products than it is exporting. As an extreme example of what we are talking about, assume the merchandising type businesses in a certain country began to import all the products sold in that country because they cost less than the same products produced by manufacturing companies within the country. Before long, all the manufacturing companies in the country would go out of business. All the jobs associated with manufacturing would disappear, and an essential part of the country's economic base would cease to exist. To provide protection for their own economic bases, countries create trade agreements amongst themselves.

These agreements are formal treaties between and among countries and are designed to control the relationship between imports and exports. Trade agreements generally establish quotas and/or tariffs on imported products. **Quotas** limit the quantities in which particular items can be imported. For example, a limit may be placed on the number of Japanese cars that can be brought in and sold in the United States. **Tariffs** are taxes that raise the price of imported products so they cost about the same as products produced within the country. Trade agreements are usually very complicated and sometimes take years to negotiate. One of the largest of these treaties is the General Agreement on Tariffs and Trade, which was signed by 92 countries shortly after World War II. Other treaties that have been in the news in recent years are the United States - Canada Free Trade Pact of 1989, which eliminated most trade barriers between those two countries, and the North American Free Trade Agreement (NAFTA) among the United States, Canada, and Mexico.

The problem with all these international trade agreements is the same as the problem with all treaties — getting the parties involved to abide by them. Even after the agreements are made, there is really nothing but good faith on the part of the treaty members to ensure compliance.

BUSINESS AND ACCOUNTING

Business is about making decisions: decisions about what business form to take (proprietorship, partnership, corporation); decisions about what type of business activity to engage in (manufacturing, merchandising, service), and decisions about whether or not to engage in international business. Accounting information, in one form or another, plays a significant role in all these decisions.

This is an accounting text. Its emphasis, however, is not so much on how accounting information is prepared, but rather on how accounting information is used. To illustrate the relationship between accounting and business decisions, let's return to the example involving Ralph, Marty and Elizabeth.

Remember that Ralph paid $55 for the pair of shoes he later sold to Marty for $100. We calculated the gross profit on the sale of these shoes as:

Amount received from Marty (BENEFIT)............... $100

Less what Ralph paid for the shoes (SACRIFICE)..... _ 55_

Equals GROSS PROFIT on the sale of shoes.......... _$ 45_

We pointed out that the $45 does not actually represent profit because Ralph has other costs associated with his shoe store that must be taken into account before he can calculate his real profit. Think about the phrase "taken into account." This is accounting. The function of accounting is to provide information to Ralph, Elizabeth, and the two shoe manufacturers to be used in making business decisions.

```
                    Discussion Questions


    1-10. If rent and other costs associated with the

          shoe store amount to $3,000 a month, how many

          pairs of shoes must Ralph sell at $100 a pair

          before he earns a profit?  $45 profit


    1-11. What should Ralph do if Elizabeth (remember

          her?) begins to take sales away by selling

          identical pairs of shoes for $90?


    1-12. What if Ralph finds out he can buy the

          identical pair of shoes from a manufacturer in

          Mexico for $40?


    1-13. What should the U.S. shoe manufacturer do if

          it begins to lose sales to the Mexican shoe

          manufacturer that is selling these identical

          shoes at the cheaper price?
```

We live in what is known as the information age.   Advances in
computer and telecommunication technology allow us to have access
to a great deal of information about almost any subject of
interest.   Not only do we have access to more information, but we

can have it quicker than at any time in the history of the world. One of the drawbacks, however, is that we are now flooded with information. Finding information specific to your needs can be like standing on the beach and trying to catch the incoming tide with your mouth. Quite simply, it's easy to drown in all the information that hits you.

The purpose of this book is to provide you with the knowledge and skills you need to sift through and use the information available to you. Specifically, we will provide you with a set of tools you can use as you make decisions involving accounting information.

CHAPTER SUMMARY

Business may have several meanings, but in this context, business is either commerce or trade as a whole or a specific company involved in commerce or trade. All economic activity revolves around the four factors of production: (1) natural resources, (2) labor, (3) capital, and (4) entrepreneurship. These four factors of production are handled differently in various types of economies. In a planned economy, a strong, centralized government controls most or all of the factors. In a market economy, most of the factors of production are privately owned.

Capitalism is the market economy within which American business is operated. This system relies on each participant's concern about his or her self-interests to create competition. Capitalism relies on the profit motive and its resulting competition to allocate resources and force businesses to operate efficiently.

Adam Smith described two basic types of societies: sympathetic and mercenary. An issue resulting from a study of his philosophy is whether business has a social responsibility to its stakeholders. Adam Smith's writings offer thought-provoking views of how societies operate and how they should operate.

The three basic forms of business organization are: proprietorships, partnerships and corporations. Each form has its own advantages and disadvantages as compared to the other two.

Most business activity can be categorized as either manufacturing, merchandising, or service. Hybrid businesses are those which conduct more than one of these types of activities.

In today's market, business must see the world as a global economy and a global market. International trade is here to stay. Conducting business with other countries is not without complications. Economic complications include those resulting from the interaction of countries with different types of economies and those with different types of currency. Political complications are a result of the fact that each country is concerned about its own self-interests; these complications are simply worsened when the countries involved operate within different types of economies.

This overview of American business was provided as a basis for understanding the context within which accounting operates. Accounting provides information critical to making business decisions, and this book will provide you with an understanding of how to use accounting information.

KEY TERMS DEFINED

Business. Depending on the usage, the word may represent the area of commerce or trade or an individual company.

Capital. A factor of production which includes the buildings, machinery and tools used to produce goods and services. Also, sometimes used to refer to the money used to provide those items.

Capitalism. A type of market economy. The economic system in place in the United States.

Communism. An example of a planned economy.

Corporation. One of the three forms of business organizations. The only one that is considered to be a legal entity separate from its owners.

Double taxation. The tax imposed on the after-tax profits which have been distributed to the stockholders of a corporation in the form of dividends.

Entrepreneurs. People willing to accept the opportunities and risks of starting and running businesses.

Entrepreneurship. The factor of production that brings the natural resources, labor, and capital together to form a business.

Exports. Goods that are produced in one country yet sold in another country.

Factors of production. The four major items needed to support economic activity: natural resources, labor, capital, and entrepreneurship.

Gross profit. The excess of benefit received over the sacrifice made to complete a sale. Gross profit considers only the cost of the item sold; other costs of operations are not considered.

Human resource factor. The mental and physical efforts of all workers performing tasks required to produce and sell goods and services. Another name for the factor of production, labor.

Hybrid companies. Those companies involved in more than one type of activity (manufacturing, merchandising, service).

Imports. Goods that are produced outside the country in which they are sold.

Labor. Equivalent to the human resource factor. One of the factors of production.

Manufacturing. The business activity that converts purchased raw materials into some tangible, physical product.

Market economy. A type of economy that relies on competition in the marketplace to determine the most efficient way to allocate the resources of the economy.

Mercenary society. A society based on mutual distrust in which members must be constantly on their guard.

Merchandising. The business activity involving the selling of finished goods produced by other businesses.

Natural resources. Land and the materials that come from the land, such as timber, mineral deposits, oil deposits, and water. One of the factors of production.

Net income. The amount of profit that remains after all other costs have been taken out of gross profit.

Net profit. Equivalent to net income.

Partnership. The business form similar to a proprietorship, but having two or more owners.

Planned economy. An economy where a strong, centralized government controls all or most of the natural resources, labor, and capital used to produce goods and services.

Profit. The excess of benefit over sacrifice remaining after all operating costs are considered; same as net profit or net income.

Profit motive. The motivational factor that drives a person to do something when the benefit derived from doing it is greater than the sacrifice required by doing it.

Proprietorship. A business that is owned by a single individual.

Quotas. A quantity limitation placed on imported goods.

Retail merchandiser. A company that buys its product from a wholesaler or manufacturer and then sells the product to the end consumer.

Service. A business activity that does not deal with tangible products, but rather provides some sort of service as its major operation.

Socialism. A type of planned economy.

Sole proprietorship. Equivalent to a proprietorship.

Stakeholder. Anyone who is affected by the way a company conducts its business.

Stockholder. A person who owns shares of stock in a corporation.

Sympathetic society. A society where all affairs are conducted with the love of others in mind.

Tariff. Taxes which raise the price of imported products so they cost about the same as products produced within the country.

Translation. The conversion of the currency of one country into its equivalent in another country's currency.

Wholesale merchandiser. A company that buys its product from the manufacturer (or another wholesaler) and then sells the product to a retail merchandiser.

REVIEW THE FACTS

1. What are the four factors of production? Define each.

2. Describe the primary difference between a planned economy and a market economy. Provide an example of systems that operate under each type of economy.

3. Explain what is meant by the profit motive.

benefit greater than sacrifice

4. Define gross profit and net profit.

5. Contrast the two societies described by Adam Smith — the sympathetic society and the mercenary society.

6. Explain the meaning of the word stakeholder.

anyone affected by company business

7. Name and describe the three basic forms of business organization.

proprietorship, partnership, corporation

8. Describe several advantages and disadvantages of each form of business organization referred to above.

9. Name and describe the three major classifications of business activity.

manufacturing, merchandising, service

10. What are the two types of merchandisers and how do they differ?

wholesaler, retailer

11. What is a hybrid company?

12. Give two examples of the complications that arise as a result of doing business with companies in other countries.

economic (system + currency)
political (system + trade

13. Define quotas and tariffs. Explain the purpose of each.

Prevent economic collapse bcy of international competition

14. Describe the relationship between business and accounting.

accounting helps in making business decisions

Chapter 1
APPLY WHAT YOU HAVE LEARNED

A1-1. Presented below are the three basic forms of business in the United States, followed by some of the advantages relating to those forms of business:

    a.   Sole Proprietorship.
    b.   Partnership.
    c.   Corporation.

1.____ Owner has total control.

2.____ Greater business continuity.

3.____ Easy transfer of ownership.

4.____ Limited liability.

5.____ Greater access to capital.

6.____ Easy and inexpensive to establish.

7.____ Few government regulations.

8.____ Easy to dissolve.

9.____ No special income taxes.

10.____ No sharing of profits.

11.____ Greater management expertise.

REQUIRED:

Match the letter next to each form of business with the appropriate advantage. Each letter will be used more than once and it is possible that a particular advantage may apply to more than one of the business forms.

A1-2. Presented below are the three basic forms of business in the United States, followed by some of the disadvantages relating to those forms of business:

    a.   Sole Proprietorship.
    b.   Partnership.
    c.   Corporation.

1. _A_ Usually has less access to capital than the other two forms.

2. _C_ Greater tax burden.

3. _A_ Limited management expertise.

4. _A_ Unlimited liability.

5. _C_ Absentee ownership.

6. _B_ Must share profits.

7. _C_ Greater government regulation.

8. _B_ Often difficult to dissolve.

9. _B_ Potential ownership conflicts.

REQUIRED:

Match the letter next to each form of business with the appropriate disadvantage. Each letter will be used more than once and it is possible that a particular disadvantage may apply to more than one of the business forms.

A1-3. Suzanne Weiser owns and operates a jewelry store. During the past month she sold a necklace to a customer for $1,500. Suzanne paid $1,000 for the necklace.

REQUIRED:

a. What type of business does Suzanne own (manufacturer, wholesaler, retailer, etc.)? Explain how you determined your response.

She runs a retail business because she is selling the merchandise directly to the customer.

b. Calculate Suzanne's gross profit on the sale of the necklace.

$500

c. Identify four costs besides the $1,000 cost of the necklace that Suzanne might incur in the operation of her jewelry store.

rent
utilities
employee wages
security system

A1-4. Explain the concept behind the word *stakeholder* and contrast it with the definition of the word *stockholder*.

A1-5. The chapter discussed five types of business in the United States. They were:

1) Manufacturer.
2) Wholesale merchandiser.
3) Retail merchandiser.
4) Service.
5) Hybrid.

REQUIRED:

a. Explain in your own words the characteristics of each type of business.

b. Discuss how each of these five different types of business is different from the other four.

c. Give two examples of each type of business (do not use any examples given in the chapter) and explain how you determined your answers.

A1-6.   Presented below are items relating some of the concepts presented in this chapter followed by the definitions of those items in a scrambled order:

a.   Entrepreneurship.
b.   Capitalism.
c.   Planned economy.
d.   Exports.
e.   Factors of production.
f.   Manufacturing company.
g.   Merchandising company.
h.   Mercenary society.
i.   Translation.

1. _D_ Goods produced in one country yet sold in another country.

2. _F_ A business that converts purchased raw materials into some tangible, physical product.

3. _A_ The factor of production that brings all the other factors of production together.

4. _G_ Either a wholesaler or a retailer.

5. _B_ A type of market economy.

6. _E_ The four major items need to support economic activity.

7. _I_ The conversion of the currency of one country into its equivalent in another country's currency.

8. _C_ A strong, centralized government controls all or most of the factors of production.

9. _H_ Based on mutual distrust, where all members must be constantly on their guard.

REQUIRED:

Match the letter next to each item on the list with the appropriate definition. Each letter will be used only once.

CHAPTER 2

INTRODUCTION TO DECISION MAKING

What time did you get up this morning? Why did you get up when you did? Did the time you went to bed last night influence what time you got up this morning? What time did you go to bed last night? Why did you go to bed when you did? How would you answer if we asked why you enrolled in this course? OK, it's required. But, why did you take it this term and not next? What course did you not take because you decided to take this one?

As the questions posed above illustrate, life is a never-ending sequence of decisions, some very complex, and others relatively simple. Most of these decisions then lead to, or at least influence, other decisions that must be made. The problem with making decisions, regardless of their complexity, is that they almost certainly must be made using incomplete information about the outcome. Because we cannot know the future, about the best we can hope for in any given decision situation is to reduce uncertainty by assembling as much information as we can before we have to make the decision.

The purpose of this chapter is to present the decision-making process in a way you may not have thought of it before. It has been designed to help you make decision making a more cognitive process. By cognitive, we mean that you should be able to take a logical, thinking approach to making decisions rather than just reacting to the pressures of the moment.

Decision making is usually considered a topic more appropriately covered in management or psychology classes. So why is it being presented in an accounting class? The answer can be found in the subtitle of this book, A USER PERSPECTIVE. What *is* accounting information used for? To make decisions, of course. In fact, accounting is of no use whatsoever unless it can be used by people in making decisions. Therefore, it is appropriate, before we present how accounting information is used, to spend some time on the general subject of decision making.

When you have completed your work on this chapter, you should be able to do the following:

1. Explain the concepts of extrinsic and intrinsic rewards, sacrifices, and opportunity costs as they pertain to decision making.

2. Differentiate between routine and nonroutine decision situations.

3. Describe the different information processing styles used in making decisions.

4. Use a general problem-solving model to make decisions.

5. Explain the importance of creativity in the decision making process.

6. Describe the role of values in decision making.

7. Differentiate between two distinctly different views of ethics.

8. Describe the advantages and disadvantages of individual and group decision making.

WHAT IS DECISION MAKING ANYWAY?

Decision making is the process of identifying alternative courses of action and selecting an appropriate alternative in a given decision situation. That's as good a textbook definition as any other, but there are a couple of things we should emphasize before we proceed. First, the phrase *identifying alternative courses of action* does not mean the ideal solution will present itself if we just look hard enough. The ideal solution may not be apparent given the available information. In fact, the ideal solution may not even be possible given the circumstances at the time the decision must be made. Second, the phrase *selecting an appropriate alternative in a given decision situation* implies that there may be

54

other appropriate alternatives and also that inappropriate alternatives were evaluated and rejected. Thus, judgment is fundamental to decision making.

Another concept implicit in our definition of decision making is that of choice. If the ability to choose is missing, there is no decision to be made. Fortunately, we always have a choice. We may not like the alternatives available to us, but we are never left without choices.

```
┌─────────────────────────────────────────────────────────────┐
│                    Discussion Questions                       │
│                                                               │
│                                                               │
│     2-1. Do you believe that you always have a choice?        │
│                                                               │
│                                                               │
│     2-2. Can you identify any instances in your own life      │
│           where you were truly powerless to make a            │
│           choice?                                             │
│                                                               │
└─────────────────────────────────────────────────────────────┘
```

Rewards & Sacrifices — The Trade-Off

In general, the aim of all decisions is to obtain some **reward**. That reward may be money or almost anything else, but there is always a desired reward. To obtain that reward, there will always be **sacrifice**. When you made the decision to attend college, for example, you certainly desired a reward for doing so. So, what was the sacrifice? If you are paying for your own education it won't take you long to answer that question. But what if your employer or your parents are paying the bills? What if you are on a full scholarship? Does that mean there is no sacrifice? No, there are still sacrifices you are making.

Discussion Questions

2-3. What reward or rewards do you hope to obtain by attending college?

2-4. What sacrifices are you personally making to attend college?

In answering the second of the two discussion questions above, you should have thought of some things you can't do because you are going to college. Some of these sacrifices cannot be measured in dollars (such as the major loss of sleep, the lack of home-cooked meals and the loss of leisure time). Some, however, can be measured. Suppose that instead of attending college you could work full time and earn $15,000 a year. In a very real sense, then, it is costing you $15,000 a year to attend college, in addition to what it costs you for tuition, books, and so on. That $15,000 could be called an **opportunity cost** of making the decision to attend college. An opportunity cost is the cost of what is foregone (given up) because a particular alternative is chosen. It is the amount of benefit that *would* have been received if a different choice had been made. Opportunity costs are just one type of sacrifice that a decision may involve.

If every decision involves sacrifice, what we really desire as decision makers is that the reward (benefit) derived from making a decision be greater than the sacrifice (cost) required to attain it. Examining the relationship between rewards and sacrifices is known as **cost/benefit analysis**. In a condition of absolute certainty, determining the cost/benefit of any decision is a breeze. Unfortunately, absolute certainty rarely, if ever, exists.

The examples we use in describing the trade-off between rewards and sacrifices almost always involve money as the reward. However, money often is not the reward we truly desire. Money is what is known as an **extrinsic reward**, meaning simply that it comes from outside ourselves and is only a material object we may acquire. An **intrinsic reward**, on the other hand, is one that comes from "doing" rather than "getting." When you have worked hard and accomplished a difficult task, the sense of satisfaction you feel is an example of an intrinsic reward. The reward comes from within, and you feel the same sense of satisfaction whether or not there is an extrinsic reward involved. While money may be very important, it is not necessarily the most important thing in life.

One final comment to consider about rewards and sacrifices is the old adage that says "the best things in life are free." Not so! Anything worth having requires sacrifice. What the saying really means is money cannot buy happiness, and most of us (once we get past our lust for toys) would agree. Even those who do not agree will very likely come to believe it at some point in their lives. While many of the best things in life do not involve money, all involve sacrifice.

ANYTHING WORTH HAVING WILL REQUIRE SACRIFICE.

Any reward (intrinsic or extrinsic) you seek will require some sort of sacrifice.

Discussion Questions

2-5. Can you think of something you genuinely desire
in life that will not require a sacrifice of
some kind?

2-6. What is the one thing you desire most out of
life? What sacrifices do you think will be
required to obtain it?

Coping With Uncertainty and Risk

Uncertainty in any given decision situation increases the chance of making the wrong choice. The higher the degree of uncertainty, the greater the **risk** of making the wrong choice. Unfortunately, because we cannot know the future, uncertainty will always exist. Therefore, good decision making does not lie in the elimination of uncertainty, but in learning to cope with it.

It may surprise you to learn that there has been a significant amount of research into how people cope with uncertainty in decision situations. Most of it merely confirms what you probably already know. That is, that as the uncertainty of outcome increases, the confidence of the decision maker decreases.

So how can you cope with uncertainty, given that it can never be entirely eliminated? You do so by compiling as much relevant information as you can in a given decision situation, thereby reducing the amount of risk involved and increasing your level of comfort in making the decision. This strategy is a valuable approach no matter what type of decision you are facing.

Routine and Nonroutine Decisions

The number of times a particular decision needs to be made varies greatly from situation to situation. Some situations recur so frequently that the decision alternative is selected automatically. These kinds of decisions are known as **routine decisions**. The basis of routine decision making is that recurring problems need only be solved once, and that decision then becomes a rule, or standard. Whenever the situation recurs, the rule is simply implemented.

It is too easy to fall into the trap of thinking that routine decisions are related only to simple situations. In reality, whether a decision is routine or not is dependent not on its complexity, but rather on whether the situation recurs, and some very complicated problems must be routinely faced.

Nonroutine decisions are those that must be made in new and unfamiliar circumstances. While the problems presented in these situations are often intricate, once again, decisions are determined to be nonroutine by their frequency — or rather their infrequency — not their complexity.

All of us face both routine and nonroutine decision situations. It is important that we learn to identify which type of decision we are facing.

2-7. Think of a decision situation in your life that you consider to be routine. Can you remember the first time you had to make that particular decision? How did you go about making the decision?

2-8. Can you think of a situation in your life in which you faced a nonroutine decision? How did you go about making the decision?

2-9. Describe a situation in which you (or someone else) applied a decision rule developed for a routine decision to a nonroutine situation and experienced unexpected results.

HOW WE MAKE DECISIONS

Thinking is something we do constantly, yet we rarely stop to analyze our own thinking in a methodical, orderly way. It may sound silly, but we really should spend some time thinking about the way we think, because the quality of the decisions we make is directly related to the way we process information. It is very easy, if we are not careful, to allow our thinking to get into an unproductive rut. Our brains are amazing things and will run on automatic pilot if we let them.

Information Processing Styles

As is the case with determining how people cope with uncertainty, there has been a great deal of research devoted to finding out how people use their brains to process information. This research has identified two general information processing styles, which we will refer to as the **intuitive style** and the **systematic style.**[1]

People who possess the intuitive processing style prefer to solve problems by looking at the overall situation, exploring many possible solutions, and finally making a decision based on intuition (hunches). These people are not content with working on problems that arise repeatedly and require the same solution each time; they enjoy a rapidly changing environment, dealing with broad issues and general policy options. These are "big picture" people.

Conversely, people who possess the systematic style are more comfortable solving problems by breaking them down into parts and then approaching them systematically. They prefer working in a slower-paced environment that allows them to be methodical in their problem solving. These are "detail" people.

62

One style of information processing is not better than the other. Sometimes the intuitive style is more effective in a given situation, and sometimes the systematic style is more effective. Also, nobody uses one style exclusively. We all use both styles to some degree, but we all tend toward one or the other.

Discussion Questions

2-10. To which careers do you think people using the intuitive style are most attracted?

2-11. To which careers do you think people using the systematic style are most attracted?

2-12. Which of the two information processing styles do you believe you use most often?

2-13. Can you think of a situation in your life in which you were forced to work with someone who used a different processing style than your own?

2-14. What kinds of problems could arise when you are forced to work with someone using a different information processing style?

Reasoned Decision Making

Reasoned decision making, also called cognitive, or rational decision making, involves considering various aspects of a situation before deciding on a course of action. This approach to decision making can be used with both intuitive and systematic information processing. The existence of reasoned choices implies there are unreasoned choices, as indeed there are. Remember, the brain will run on automatic pilot if we allow it to, which leads to unreasoned choices.

Reasoned decision making can be described as a seven step process:

Step #1: Determine the real decision to be made.
The key to reasoned decision making is determining what decision needs to be made. In other words, you must make sure you understand what the real problem is. Too often, when confronted with a decision, we treat a symptom of the problem and not the problem itself. It is critical that the real decision is determined, and that it is correctly identified as either a routine or nonroutine decision.

Step #2: Identify alternative courses of action.
The approach to this step is determined by whether the situation is routine or nonroutine. If the decision to be made is routine, you simply apply the appropriate decision rule. In this case, Steps #3

64

and #4 of this decision model can be skipped. If, however, the decision is nonroutine, identifying alternative solutions becomes an important part of the decision making process. Some alternatives will emerge quickly, but these are rarely anything more than stopgap measures (meaning they treat symptoms, not problems). Good decision making requires creativity. We are much more comfortable choosing obvious courses of action, which explains why so few of us are really good at making difficult decisions. Sherlock Holmes, the great master sleuth, offered this explanation as to why Dr. Watson had been unable to unravel a particular mystery:

> Once again, Watson, you have confused the impossible with the improbable.

This quotation describes **creative decision making** perfectly. The way to solve a problem is to make sure you eliminate only the impossible as a potential solution and consider everything else, however improbable. This was easy for Holmes, because he was a fictional character. He could make all the right decisions because the author (who knew how everything would turn out in the end) wanted him to. In real life, it is much easier said than done; however, our decision making abilities would be greatly improved if we would open our eyes to more alternative solutions. Creative decision making is an important topic, and following this presentation of the decision making process, we will discuss it in greater detail.

65

Step #3:   Analyze each alternative critically.

If anything, this step is even more difficult than the previous one because it requires the decision maker to attempt to trace the alternatives into the future and to consider all the possible outcomes of each.   This is not really possible with any degree of accuracy because there are too many variables in the future. Instead you must choose a very few (probably no more than two or three) critical factors to be considered and then see how each of the alternatives under consideration affect those factors.   The critical factors to consider depend on the circumstances of the situation.   Some examples of these factors are: (1) how much each alternative will cost, (2) how much time each alternative will require, and (3) how much risk is associated with each alternative.

Step #4:   Select the best alternative in the circumstances.

A noted scholar in the field of problem solving, Russell Ackoff, has identified three types of alternatives available in any given decision situation: those that will *resolve* the problem, those that will *solve* the problem, and those that will *dissolve* the problem.[2] Resolving a problem means finding an alternative that is acceptable.   Solving means finding the absolutely A-number one best solution.   Dissolving means changing the circumstances that caused the problem, thereby not only eliminating the problem, but ensuring it will not happen again.   Ideally, the results of this decision making process will produce an alternative that dissolves the problem, but realistically that occurs only occasionally.   In fact,

Ackoff suggests that most decisions we make are of the first type, meaning we resolve problems by finding acceptable (usually stopgap) solutions. For this reason, one decision may eventually create the need for other decisions to be made.

Step #5: Implement the chosen alternative.

On the surface, this appears to be the easiest of all the steps in this process. You might think that once an alternative has been selected, implementation would be easy. Not so. Often times, activity stops after an alternative is chosen or a decision is made. The hesitation that occurs before the chosen alternative is implemented is caused by what is known as **cognitive dissonance**,[3] and even if you've never heard of it, you have probably experienced it. In common language, we call it "having second thoughts." It doesn't matter how methodical and analytical you have been in your approach to making a decision, you still feel you have not considered everything. Much that affects the outcome lies in the future and is unknown. Therefore, there is always at least some chance you have made a poor choice. When cognitive dissonance sets in, all the alternatives you have rejected begin to look better and better. There is no easy answer as to how to overcome such hesitation. There does come a point, however, when you must simply take a deep breath and charge ahead by implementing the chosen alternative.

Step #6: Reevaluate the decision as new information becomes available.

This step is often skipped, because once you have overcome those "second thoughts" spoken of in Step #5, you will tend to become very committed to the decision you have made. In fact, most of us will go out of our way to avoid new information. Why? Because it puts us back in the position of questioning the soundness of our decision — and that makes us extremely uncomfortable. It may sound crazy, but if you really want to become good at making tough decisions, you must become comfortable with being uncomfortable. You must not be afraid to continue analyzing your decision in the light of new and better information, even after your decision has been implemented.

Step #7: Evaluate the final outcome.

This step is very difficult because it may be a long time before the results of a decision are known. Thus, it may be a long time before you can determine whether the decision was a good one. Moreover, you don't make decisions in a vacuum. The decisions of others, over which you have no control, may influence the outcome of the decision you have made. Nevertheless, this is an important step in the process if you are to continue refining your decision making skills.

This decision model, in one form or another, is found in numerous texts for various classes. Our model is not the only "right" way to make decisions. However, it is important that you begin to take a reasoned, cognitive approach to decision making. By way of review, the steps of the decision making model are presented below:

SEVEN STEPS OF DECISION MAKING

Step #1: *Determine the real decision to be made.*

Step #2: *Identify alternative courses of action.*

Step #3: *Analyze each alternative critically.*

Step #4: *Select the best alternative in the circumstances.*

Step #5: *Implement the chosen alternative.*

Step #6: *Reevaluate the decision as new information becomes available.*

Step #7: *Evaluate the final outcome.*

```
                    Discussion Questions


  2-15. Some might argue this seven-step process of
        decision making is too rigid.  How would you
        respond?


  2-16. Think back to your decision to choose the
        college you attend.  If you had used this
        decision model, would you have made the same
        choice?  Explain.


  2-17. Think again about your decision to choose the
        college you attend.  At what point will you be
        able to apply Step #7 to your decision?
```

Creative Decision Making

The second step of the decision making model in the previous section stressed the importance of being creative in identifying possible courses of action. This means going beyond the obvious alternatives. Being creative and considering a greater number of possible alternatives reduces the chance that the best possible solution may be overlooked.

Notwithstanding the difficulties involved, you *can* become more creative in your approach to making decisions. While it has been traditionally thought (and therefore taught) that people are either inherently creative or they're not, there is convincing evidence that the art of creativity can be learned. Sidney J. Parnes, a professor of creative studies at Buffalo State University, has stated that creativity is increased if a problem solver progresses from "what is" (which refers to being aware of the facts surrounding the present situation), to "what might be" (implying a free-thinking consideration of many possible alternatives), to "what can be" (weeding out impossible and unacceptable alternatives), to "what will be" (choosing the best alternative in the circumstances), and finally to an action that creates a new "what is".[4]

For an example of this approach to being creative, consider the simple act of getting the oil changed in your car. There was a time when getting an oil change took at least a whole day (unless you changed it yourself, which many of us were either too lazy or too inept to do). You called the local garage and made an appointment (usually for two or three days later if the garage was busy). When the big day came, you dropped your car off at the garage and found some way to get where you had to be that day. Late in the afternoon, you called to see if the car was done. If it was, you found some way to get back to the garage and pick up your car. If it wasn't (which was often the case), you were without your car for a second day. All this just to get your oil changed. Does anybody go through all this inconvenience to get their oil changed anymore? Why not? Because somebody went through the creative problem solving process. The result was a new "what is": oil changes in less than 30 minutes.

A word of caution before we leave this section on creative decision making: Creativity is very hard for most of us. Did you know that in the late 1800's, the director of the U.S. Patent Office recommended to Congress that the patent office be shut down permanently because everything had been invented? You may feel this fellow was extremely shortsighted, but in fact he was not all that much different from the rest of us. What he lacked was the ability to envision better ways of doing things. The late Senator Robert Kennedy once said,

> Some men see things as they are and ask,
> "Why?"; I dream of things that never were and
> ask, "Why not?".

What he meant was that we must never become satisfied with things as they are. We must constantly force ourselves to reevaluate the present "what is" and find creative ways to improve.

```
                    Discussion Questions


    2-18. Try to recreate the development of the 30

          minute oil change using Professor Parnes'

          creative process.  How many alternatives did

          you come up with under "what might be"?  Was it

          difficult to think of any?  If so, why do you

          think it was?


    2-19. You have recently gone through the

          registration process at your school.  That

          certainly qualifies as a "what is."  Are you

          satisfied with the procedure?  If not, what

          creative suggestions do you have to improve it?


    2-20. If you could change just one other "what is"

          into a new "what is," what would it be?  How

          would you do it?
```

PERSONAL VALUES AND DECISION MAKING

The most important influence on the decisions we make is the set of
personal values we hold. Some of you are now saying to yourselves
"Oh boy, here it comes. They're about to preach a sermon on what

I should believe and how I should live my life." Well, we are not about to do any such thing. Personal values are just that, *personal* values. Yours are different (even if only slightly) than those of every other person. We would not be so presumptuous as to try and tell you what is "right" or what is "wrong."

What is important in relation to personal values and decision making is that each of us examine critically what is truly important to ourselves.

> An unexamined life is not worth living.
>   - Socrates

Because life is so hectic, we all have a tendency to become complacent about defining those things we hold dear. If we do not stop periodically to take an inventory of what we believe, we run the risk of waking up one day and realizing that the decisions we have made run counter to what we thought we valued. And this one thing is absolutely true:

THE COMPROMISE OF PERSONAL VALUES IS A PROCESS, NOT AN EVENT.

It happens a little bit here and a little bit there, until you have become a different person altogether. The halls of history are littered with the remains of men and women who spent a lifetime climbing a ladder only to find it was leaning in the wrong window.

74

As we tried to make clear in our discussion, you should examine your life from time to time and determine what your priorities are.

> It is better to be Socrates dissatisfied than
> a pig satisfied.
> — John Stuart Mill

You may not like what the examination reveals, but it is better to examine your life and be dissatisfied than to drift along and be satisfied. What you believe is not as important as knowing and understanding exactly what it is you believe and how those beliefs impact the decisions you make.

Discussion Questions

2-21. What has been the most important single influence in the development of your personal values?

2-22. Provide an example of conflicts that can arise as you deal with others whose personal values differ from your own.

2-23. Do you think it is possible to reach a compromise with someone having different values without compromising your own values? Explain.

Ethics and Personal Values

There is no hotter topic in American business today than **ethics**. Universities across the country are experiencing an increased demand for courses in ethics. Major corporations are stepping up their training in this area in an attempt to improve the "ethical behavior" of their officers and managers. Virtually every new textbook in accounting, finance, marketing, and other business subjects comes with supplements and helpful hints on teaching students how to react to situations in which they might be tempted to act "unethically."

There are two very different approaches to ethics.[5] The first is known as **virtues ethics** or **character ethics**. It is also sometimes called classical ethics because its historical roots are in ancient Greece, most notably in the teachings of Socrates, Plato, and Aristotle. This approach could be described as an "inward out" approach, meaning that power and direction come from inside the individual and are manifested outward in dealings with others. It requires a person to spend a good deal of time determining what kind of person he or she wants to be. Once the virtues and character traits required to be that kind of person have been identified, they predetermine the reaction to *any* situation. Virtues ethics is the basis for the famous warning by William Shakespeare:

> Above all, to thine own self be true, and it
> shall follow as night the day, Thou cans't
> not then be false to any man.

The second approach is called **rules ethics** or **quandary ethics** (quandary means predicament or dilemma). This approach is also sometimes referred to as modern ethics and has its roots in organized religion. Quandary ethics could be described as an "outward in" approach, meaning that power and direction come from outside the individual in the form of rules that dictate how that person should react to a given quandary or dilemma. Under this approach, a person confronted by a difficult situation searches until the appropriate rule is found and then applies it to the problem at hand. The key difference between rules ethics and character ethics is that the individual goes "outside himself" to find the rule.

We are not trying to suggest that one of these two approaches is superior to the other. There are, however, potential problems with each of them that we should discuss. First, virtues ethics can lead to disastrous results if a person confuses it with selfishness. The highest perversion of this approach is self-centered, egoistic greed. The necessary presumption behind virtues ethics is that the virtues and character traits identified will include respect for others. Rules ethics, on the other hand, is absolutely dependent on: (1) the ability to determine the appropriate rule in a given situation, and (2) how much confidence a person has in the rules (and those who establish them). An inability to determine the appropriate rule or a loss of respect for the rules (or rule-makers) leads to confusion and uncertainty.

If we do not have our own sense of power and direction, we must get it from someone or something outside ourselves. The real danger lies in not being aware of where our power and direction are coming from. This concern brings us back to our original discussion of personal values and our statement that *what you believe is not nearly as important as knowing and understanding what it is that you believe*. More important still is the need for each of us to be alert and aware of how our personal values necessarily influence our decision making. As a decision is made, we will see it supported by our values, or we will see our decision conflict with our values. As you make important decisions in you life, you should be able to determine if each decision and your personal values are in harmony.

2-24. Ponder your own personal values. Are these
values determined from outside yourself or from
inside yourself? Have any of your values
started as external and become internal?

2-25. How much do your personal values influence
your decisions? Do you ever find yourself
making a different decision if others will know .
your decision than you would if no one would
ever know what you have decided? What do you
think this means in terms of "inward out"
versus "outward in" ethics?

INDIVIDUAL VERSUS GROUP DECISION MAKING

Thus far we have discussed the problems in decision making caused
by uncertainty, different information processing styles, routine
versus nonroutine decision situations, the need for creativity, and
the influence of personal values on the process. We will now
complicate the process even further by considering **individual
decision making** versus **group decision making.**

There is an old saying that two heads (or more) are better than one, meaning that the more people involved in the decision process, the better your chances are of making the right decision. That may not always be true, but we all find ourselves in group decision making situations from time to time. Some situations are so personal that no one outside of ourselves can be involved in the decision process even if we wanted them to be. On the other hand, there are times when we are required to work in groups, even when we might prefer to make decisions by ourselves. Thus it is essential that you understand the advantages and disadvantages of both individual and group decision making.[6]

Individual decision making has some distinct advantages over group decision making. For one thing, you don't have to find a time and place everyone in the group can meet. You also don't have to listen to group members make comments and suggestions you know for a fact are no good. Finally, compromise is unnecessary because your point of view is the only one to be considered. However, your decision will be only as good as your individual judgment and grasp of the circumstances. Therein lies the single most significant drawback to making decisions by yourself. This limitation is the reason that when we make important, nonroutine decisions by ourselves, most of us desire to bounce the decision off someone else. We know, or at least fear, that there may be things of importance we have not considered.

80

Group decision making has several advantages over making decisions by yourself. Groups bring a greater knowledge base to the process because more people are involved. The problem at hand will usually be viewed from more than one legitimate perspective. Viewing the problem at hand from various perspectives almost certainly leads to more alternative solutions being considered. An additional advantage is that groups tend to be less apprehensive about whether the alternative chosen is at least reasonable; somehow, there seems to be safety in numbers.

On the surface it would seem that group decision making is superior to individual decision making. There are, however, some serious problems associated with working in groups. Some of them have to do with the actual functioning of groups, and others with the quality of decisions made by groups.

- *Information processing styles.* If all members of the group are intuitive types, the group may have a lot of grandiose ideas, but wind up short on specifics. If all members are systematic types, the group may never get past deciding on a seating arrangement at the first meeting. Ideally, there should be a mix of the two types. But they must work together, utilizing the best aspects of each style, or the group can become paralyzed.

- *Domineering members.* The quality of group decision making usually suffers if some members of the group begin to "cave in" to other members simply because those other members can talk louder and longer.

- *Social pressure.* The pressure to conform to the views of other members of the group, coupled with the natural desire not to look foolish, can stifle an individual's creative contributions.

- *Goal replacement.* The goal of the group should always be to accomplish whatever it was formed to do. Secondary considerations, such as winning an argument, proving a point, or taking revenge on a fellow group member, sometimes become more important to some members of the group.

- *Differing personal values.* Each member of the group will bring a different set of personal values to the process. From time to time those values may conflict, and resolution is often difficult and sometimes impossible.

- *Unequal effort.* In order for a group to succeed, all members of the group must do their share of the work. If any member of the group slacks off in his or her efforts, not only will the quality of work suffer, but the morale of other group members will probably be affected.

- *Groupthink.* This is considered by many to be the most dangerous threat to good group decision making. In a group setting, people are often tempted to ignore their own sound judgments in evaluating alternatives in order to achieve concensus. A group member may not feel good about the decision being made but thinks everyone else in the group does, and so he or she goes along with the decision. Remember, the fact that everybody agrees on an alternative does not mean it is a good or even acceptable alternative.

```
                        Discussion Questions

    2-26. Which of the seven items listed as potential
          problems of group decision making would you
          consider least likely to occur in a group
          formed in a business environment?


    2-27. Which of the seven items listed as potential
          problems of group decision making would you
          consider the most serious in a group formed as
          part of a class at your school?


    2-28. If you were the instructor of this course,
          what policies would you institute to make
          certain all members of assigned groups worked
          for the common good of the group?
```

Decision making is important in many aspects of life. Now that you
have a basic understanding of the decision making process, we can
explore particular decisions involving the business world. Chapter
3 provides insight into economic decision making and useful
accounting information.

CHAPTER SUMMARY

Life is a sequence of decision situations, some complex, others simple. Regardless of complexity, virtually all decisions must be made using incomplete information because they deal with the future, which is unknown.

In general, the aim of all decisions is to obtain some type of reward, either extrinsic or intrinsic. To obtain that reward, certain sacrifices must be made. Good decisions are made when a reasonable balance is found between the sacrifice and the reward in the context of uncertainty.

Decisions can be classified as either routine or nonroutine. Routine decisions are recurring, whereas nonroutine decisions are those that must be made in new and unfamiliar circumstances. A real key to good decision making is the ability to distinguish between routine and nonroutine decisions.

Besides the uncertainty of the future, the way people process information has a great influence on their decision making process. There are two general information processing styles: the intuitive style and the systematic style. Each has advantages over the other, and one is not necessarily better than the other.

Another key to good decision making is establishing some sort of

85

reasoned (cognitive) approach to the decision process. A seven-step model for making decisions was presented as a guideline.

Still another key to making good decisions is the development of a more creative approach to the process. The most important part of this approach is the ability to consider alternatives that are not readily apparent.

The personal values each of us holds exert a tremendous influence on the decisions we make. Erosion of our values is a process, not an event. To prevent this erosion, we must take stock of what we believe from time to time. The personal values we hold form the basis of our system of ethics.

There are two general approaches to ethics. They are virtues (character) ethics and rules (quandary) ethics. While these approaches are different, either of them can serve you well. The question is not which approach to take, but which approach you are taking.

Finally, we discussed individual versus group decision making. Each has advantages and disadvantages in relation to the other, but all of us participate in both at some point in our lives.

KEY TERMS DEFINED

Character ethics. Another name for virtues ethics. Sometimes called classical ethics.

Cognitive dissonance. The hesitation that sets in after an alternative has been chosen, but before it has been implemented. Having "second thoughts".

Cost/benefit analysis. Deals with the trade-off between the rewards of selecting a given alternative and the sacrifices required to obtain those rewards.

Creative decision making. Allowing (forcing) one's self to consider more than just the obvious alternatives in a decision situation.

Decision making. The process of identifying alternative courses of action and selecting an appropriate alternative in a given decision situation.

Ethics. A system of standards of conduct and moral judgment.

Extrinsic reward. Any reward that comes from outside the decision maker. The money earned for fulfilling job responsibilities is an example of an extrinsic reward.

Group decision making. Two or more persons working together to solve a problem.

Individual decision making. One person working alone to solve a problem.

Intrinsic reward. Any reward that comes from within the decision maker. The sense of satisfaction that comes from doing a job well is an example of an intrinsic reward.

Intuitive style. A style of processing information in which decisions are based on hunches after considering the big picture and brainstorming as to possible solutions.

Nonroutine decisions. Decisions that must be made in new and unfamiliar circumstances.

Opportunity cost. The benefit or benefits foregone by not selecting a particular alternative. Once an alternative is selected in a decision situation, the benefits of all rejected alternatives become part of the opportunity cost of the alternative selected. *like the $ you could make if you weren't in college*

Personal values. The system of beliefs that guides an individual in determining what is right and what is wrong in the decision making process.

Quandary ethics. Another name for rules ethics. Sometimes called modern ethics.

Reasoned decision making. An approach to decision making where the decision maker attempts to consider all aspects of a situation before deciding on a course of action.

Reward. The benefit or benefits attained by selecting an alternative in a decision situation.

Risk. The probability that an alternative selected in a decision situation will yield unsatisfactory results.

Routine decisions. Recurring decision situations in which an appropriate solution need be found only once. That decision becomes the rule, or standard, and whenever the situation recurs, the rule is implemented.

Rules ethics. A system of ethics in which the rules of conduct come from outside the individual. When a situation occurs, the individual determines the appropriate rule of conduct and applies it to the decision required by the situation. Also called quandary ethics.

Sacrifice. Something given up in order to attain a desired reward.

Systematic style.   A style of processing information in which decisions are made after breaking a problem down into parts and methodically approaching each part.

Uncertainty.   A lack of complete information about the future. This is closely related to risk.   The greater the degree of uncertainty, the greater the risk of selecting unacceptable alternatives.

Virtues ethics. A system of ethics in which the individual decides what kind of person he or she desires to be, thereby establishing a code of conduct that can be applied to any situation.   Also called character ethics.

REFERENCES

1. Weston H. Agor, "Managing Brain Skills: The Last Frontier," _Personnel Administrator_ (October 1987): 55-56.

2. Russell L. Ackoff, "The Art and Science of Mess Management," _Interfaces_ 11 No. 1 (February 1981): 20-21.

3. Leon Festinger, _A Theory of Cognitive Dissonance_ (Stanford, Calif: Stanford University Press, 1975).

4. Sidney J. Parnes, "Learning Creative Behavior," _The Futurist_ (August 1984): 30.

5. Our treatment of this subject is light. If you are interested in a more indepth coverage, begin by reading one or more of the following books:

    a. John Kekes, _The Examined Life_ (Totowa, NJ: Rowan & Littlefield, 1988).

    b. Alasdair MacIntyre, _After Virtue_ (South Bend, IN: University of Notre Dame Press, 1981).

    c. David L. Norton, _Personal Destinies_ (Princeton, NJ: Princeton University Press, 1976).

    d. Edmund Pincoffs, _Quandaries and Virtues_ (Lawrence, KS: University of Kansas Press, 1986,.

    e. Richard Taylor, _Ethics, Faith, and Reason_ (Englewood Cliffs, NJ: Prentice Hall, 1985).

6. For a very interesting and enlightening discussion of individual versus group decision making, see Gayle W. Hill, "Group Versus Individual Performance: Are N + 1 Heads Better Than One?" _Psychological Bulletin_ 91, No. 3 (1982): 517-539.

REVIEW THE FACTS

1. Provide two examples of rewards and sacrifices that may be involved when a decision is being made.

    money, education. ge...

2. What is an opportunity cost?

3. Define cost/benefit analysis.

4. Describe the difference between an extrinsic reward and an intrinsic reward.

5. How are uncertainty and risk related?

6. What is the difference between routine and nonroutine decisions?

7. Describe the two major information processing styles.

8. Explain the term reasoned decision making.

9. Describe the seven steps of the decision model presented in this chapter.

10. Why is creative decision making important?

11. What is the role of personal values in the decision making process?

12. Name and describe the two different approaches to ethics.

13. Describe the advantages and disadvantages of both individual and group decision making.

Chapter 2
APPLY WHAT YOU HAVE LEARNED

A2-1. Presented below are the disadvantages of group decision making as presented in the chapter, followed by the definitions of those disadvantages in a scrambled order:

a. Different information processing styles.
b. Domineering members of the group.
c. Social pressure.
d. Goal replacement.
e. Differing personal values.
f. Unequal effort.
g. Groupthink.

1.____ Some members of the group may not work as hard as others.

2.____ Not everyone believes the same way.

3.____ The group may contain both intuitive types and systematic types.

4.____ The natural desire not to look foolish may stifle a group member's creative contribution.

5.____ Group members are often tempted to ignore their own judgment in order to achieve consensus.

6.____ Winning an argument, proving a point, or taking revenge becomes more important than accomplishing the task at hand.

7.____ The work of the group suffers simply because some members can talk louder and longer than others.

REQUIRED:

Match the letter next to each disadvantage with the appropriate definition. Each letter will be used only once.

A2-2. Bob Sturges, a college sophmore, has just gotten a job working with mentally handicapped children. He will make $5.00 per hour. Working with these children is something Bob has always wanted to do. He even thinks it may be something he wants to pursue as a career.
REQUIRED:
a. From the facts given in the problem, what would you consider to be the extrinsic and intrinsic rewards Bob will receive from his new job?

b. Which do you think will be more valuable to Bob, the extrinsic rewards or the intrinsic rewards? Explain your reasoning.

A2-3. Vicki Carlisle is in trouble! She has been in New York on business for the past week, and this morning she was supposed to fly to Los Angeles for a very important dinner meeting to be held at 6:00 p.m. Unfortunately, Vicki has overslept and missed her flight. As she hurries to shower and get dressed, she is trying to decide what to do next. "If only I had not slept through my alarm," she says to herself over and over, "that's the real problem."
REQUIRED:

a. Do you think Vicki has determined her real problem? If not, help her identify the real problem.

b. Now that the real problem has been determined, identify two alternative courses of action Vicki might take to solve her problem. Then, analyze each of them critically for her.

A2-4. Clarence Oddbody, an employee of Barnstorm, Inc. has been on business in Bedford Falls, New York for the past two weeks. Bedford Falls happens to be his hometown, and Clarence has stayed the entire two weeks with his mother. Orville Potter (Clarence's boyhood chum) owns the local hotel and has offered to provide Clarence with receipts for a two week stay at the hotel. Clarence would then submit the receipts and be reimbursed. Barnstorm, Inc. would really not be out anything, because it is company policy to reimburse employees for out-of-town lodging.
REQUIRED:

a. Explain how Clarence would approach this decision situation under virtues or character ethics.

b. Explain how Clarence would approach this decision situation under quandary or rules ethics.

c. Which approach do you think would serve Clarence better in all such decision situations? Explain your reasoning.

A2-5. Presented below are items relating to concepts presented in this chapter, followed by the definitions of those items in a scrambled order:

a. Cost/benefit.
b. Ethics.
c. Intuitive information processing style.
d. Opportunity cost.
e. Systematic information processing style.
f. Risk.
g. Uncertainty.

1. ___ Decisions are made after breaking a problem down into parts and methodically evaluating each part.

2. ___ Decisions are based on hunches after considering the big picture and brainstorming.

3. ___ The probability that an alternative selected will yield unsatisfactory results.

4. ___ The rewards of selecting a given alternative in relation to the sacrifices required to obtain those rewards.

5. ___ The benefit foregone by not selecting a particular alternative.

6. ___ A system of standards of conduct and moral judgment.

7. ___ Lack of complete information about the future.

REQUIRED:

Match the letter next to each item with the appropriate definition. Each letter will be used only once.

CHAPTER 3

ECONOMIC DECISION MAKING & USEFUL ACCOUNTING INFORMATION

In Chapter 1, we had a brief introduction to business in the United States, and in Chapter 2, decision making was discussed in a very general sense. In this chapter, we turn our attention to **economic decision making**, which will require us to draw upon what was learned from the first two chapters. Economic decision making simply refers to those decisions involving money, and for this class, that means business decisions involving money. Everything discussed in Chapter 2 about decision making applies to the subject of economic decision making.

All economic decisions of any consequence include the use of some sort of accounting information. Often, accounting information is made available in the form of financial reports. The relationship between accounting information and the decision makers who use it can be described this way:

> Financial reporting should provide information that is useful to present and potential investors and creditors and other users in making rational investment, credit, and similar *decisions*. The information should be comprehensible to those who have a *reasonable understanding of business and economic activities and are willing to study the information with reasonable diligence*.
>
> - Statement of Financial Accounting Concepts #1, Financial Accounting Standards Board, 1986 pp. 39-40 (Emphasis added)

Those who would use accounting information to make economic decisions must understand the business and economic environment in which accounting information is generated, and they must also be willing to devote the time and energy required to make sense of the accounting reports. In this chapter, we will explore economic decision making and the role of useful accounting information in that process.

When you have completed your work on this chapter, you should be able to do the following:

1. Describe the two types of economic decision makers.

2. Explain the basic differences between managerial accounting and financial accounting.

3. List the three questions all economic decision makers are attempting to answer and explain why these are so important.

4. Describe the concept of cash as the ultimate measurement of business success or failure.

5. Define accounting information and explain its distinction from data.

6. Name the primary characteristics of useful accounting information and describe each one in your own words.

7. Name the secondary characteristics of useful accounting information and describe each one in your own words.

ECONOMIC DECISION MAKING

Because today's world seems to revolve around economic issues, each of us finds that economic decision making impacts our daily lives. We will be better equipped to deal with these impacts if we have a better understanding of the economic decision making process and the information that affects it. First, let's take a look at the people making economic decisions.

Economic decision makers can be divided into two broad categories: those internal to a company and those external to a company. **Internal decision makers** are individuals within a company who make decisions on behalf of the company, while **external decision makers** are individuals or organizations outside a company who make decisions that affect that company.

Internal Decision Makers

The first characteristic of internal decision makers is they make decisions *for* the company. In other words, they are acting on behalf of the company. They decide such things as whether the company should sell a particular product, whether the company should enter a certain market, whether to hire or fire employees, and similar matters. Note that in all of the examples given, the responsible internal party is not making the decision for herself or himself, but rather for the company.

The second characteristic of internal decision makers is they have greater access to the financial information of the company than do those outside the company. Depending on their particular position within the company, internal decision makers may have access to much or even all of the company's financial information. Don't be misled — this does not mean that these folks have complete information. Remember that because these decisions always relate somehow to the future, they always involve unknowns.

External Decision Makers

The first characteristic of external decision makers is they make decisions *about* a company. In other words, their decisions are not made on behalf of the company, but they affect the company nonetheless. External decision makers decide such things as whether to invest in the company, whether to sell to the company, whether to buy from the company, whether to lend money to the company, and other similar matters.

The second characteristic of external decision makers is they have limited access to the financial information of the company about which they are attempting to make decisions. In fact, they are limited to what the company gives them, which in most cases, will not be everything it possesses.

Discussion Questions

3-1. With regard to a particular company, who do you think are considered internal economic decision makers?

3-2. With regard to a particular company, who do you think are considered external economic decision makers?

3-3. What reasons can you think of that would cause a company to withhold certain financial information from external parties?

The decisions made by internal and external decision makers are similar in some ways, but in many instances are very different. So different, in fact, that over time a different branch of accounting has developed to meet the needs of each category of user. The accounting information generated specifically for use by internal decision makers is the product of what is called **managerial accounting,** while the accounting information used by external parties is the product of what is called financial **accounting.**

What All Economic Decision Makers Want to Know

Although internal and external parties face different decision situations, these decision makers are identical in at least one respect. Both are trying to predict the future, as are all decision makers. Specifically, economic decision makers, whether internal or external, are attempting to predict the future of **cash flow,** the movement of cash in and out of a company. As explained below, one of the objectives of financial reporting is to provide information that would be helpful to those trying to predict cash flows.

> Thus, financial reporting should provide information to help investors, creditors, and others assess the *amounts, timing, and uncertainty* of prospective net cash inflows to the related enterprise.
>
> — Statement of Financial Accounting Concepts #1, Financial Accounting Standards Board, 1986 p.40 (Emphasis added)

The difference between cash inflows and cash outflows is known as **net cash flow.** A positive net cash flow indicates that the amount of cash flowing in exceeded the amount flowing out during a particular period. If cash outflows exceed cash inflows during a period, a negative net cash flow results. All economic decisions are wrapped up in attempting to predict the future of cash flows by searching for the answers to the following three questions:

1. Will I be paid?

    This question refers to the <u>uncertainty</u> of cash flows.

2. When will I be paid?

    This question refers to the <u>timing</u> of cash flows.

3. How much will I be paid?

    This question refers to the <u>amounts</u> of cash flows.

There are a couple of things you need to be clear on concerning the answers to these questions. First, we are talking about *CASH!* Of all the words in the English language, cash is one you do not need to have defined. You know what it means (you may not have any, but you know it when you see it). Second, the answer to each question contains two parts: return <u>on</u> investment and return <u>of</u> investment. For example, let's assume you are considering buying a $1,000 Certificate of Deposit (CD) at your bank, which will earn 10 percent annual interest (paid to you every three months). If you buy this CD, you must hold it for two years, after which the bank will return your $1,000. Before you make this economic decision, you must attempt to answer the three questions:

1. *Will you be paid?* We are back to the <u>uncertainty</u> of the future discussed in Chapter 2. Because it is impossible to know the future, there is *always* a risk in making an economic decision. However, assuming the economy doesn't collapse and the bank stays in business, you very likely will be paid both your return <u>on</u> investment and your return <u>of</u> investment.

2. *When will you be paid?* Now, the focus is on the <u>timing</u> of future cash flows. Presuming you will be paid (see question #1), you will receive an interest payment every three months for two years (return <u>on</u> investment), and then you will receive your initial $1,000 back (return <u>of</u> investment).

3. *How much will you be paid?* This question refers to the <u>amount</u> of future cash flows. The return <u>on</u> your investment is the $200 interest you receive ($1,000 X 10 percent X 2 years), and the return <u>of</u> your investment is the $1,000 the bank gives you back.

Don't get the wrong impression about the last two questions. In this example, the answer was very explicit once you satisfied yourself concerning the first question. In the vast majority of economic decision situations, the answers to the second and third questions are much less certain than we have presented here. A major purpose of this text is to show how accounting information is

used to answer the three questions in various economic decision
situations.

Discussion Questions

3-4. Consider the most recent economic decision you
     made. Can you reduce it to the three
     questions? Explain.

3-5. Can you think of any economic decision
     situation that cannot be reduced to the three
     questions? Explain.

3-6. Can you apply the seven-step decision model
     presented in Chapter 2 to the example of the
     Certificate of Deposit? Explain.

Cash is the "Ball" of Business

Does the title above make sense to you? Probably not. Well, it
should when you finish reading the discussion that follows. We
hope so, anyway, because the concept discussed here is among the
most important you will ever cover in this or any other business
class.

Let's talk about the game of golf for a minute and then try to relate it to business. If you've ever played the game, you know it is impossible to play well consistently unless you keep your eye on the ball. You may hit a decent shot from time to time even if you do look up during your swing, but in the long run you are doomed if you don't learn to keep your head down and your eye on the ball. What's strange is that even once you have learned to keep your eye on the ball, the tendency is not to. Well, in business cash is the ball, and anyone hoping to be successful in the game of business had better learn the importance of keeping his or her eye on it. Unfortunately, because this game is so complex, it is very easy to become distracted and confuse other things with cash. In your business classes in college and throughout your life, whether you become an investor or an entrepreneur, or you become interested in the financial situation of the company you work for, you will hear about the importance of many different measures of performance. You may be asked to focus on various items such as profits, net income, net worth, equity, as well as other measures of financial performance. Just remember — these things are important and are desirable, *BUT THEY ARE NOT CASH!*

Well, there you have it. Cash is cash and everything else is something else. It's a simple enough concept, but an amazing number of people lose sight of it. Even those of us who think we really understand it have a tendency to divert our attention from it. Make no mistake: businesses die because they run out of cash, and many of them run out of cash because their management becomes too concerned with something else, such as profits, net worth, net income, or other measures of performance.

Before we leave this topic, it is important that you are aware that the accounting profession has played a part in distracting financial information users, causing them to take their eye off the ball (cash). Unfortunately, some methods used to account for business and economic activity in the United States measure performance in something other than cash. While there are sound reasons for doing so, the accounting reports generated using such measurement criteria can be misleading to those who do not understand those criteria. It is important that you understand the reasons for and the limitations of those criteria. If you work hard to understand the ideas presented in this text and in this class, you will become aware of the impact of these limitations on the usefulness of accounting information. You will become a very "street smart" user of accounting information.

WHAT EXACTLY IS ACCOUNTING INFORMATION?

Our focus thus far in this chapter has been solely on economic decision making; we must now turn our attention to the accounting information used in making those decisions. The dictionary defines accounting as a reckoning of financial matters, and information as knowledge, or news. Putting the two together, **accounting**

information can be defined as knowledge or news about a reckoning of financial matters. The accounting profession's own definition of accounting provides some insight:

> Accounting is a service activity. Its function is to provide *quantitative information, primarily financial in nature, about economic entities that is intended to be useful in making economic decisions.*
>
>   - Statement of the Accounting Principles Board #4,
>   1970 p. 6

Quantitative means numbers (as in quantity), and financial means having to do with money. Thus, accounting information involves the numbers (primarily those dealing with money) used to make economic decisions.

But what do the numbers represent, and where do they come from? Well, whenever a company or person has a transaction involving money, accounting data are generated. Think of your own life for a minute. You have transactions involving money. You may pay your rent, buy groceries, make car payments, lend money to a friend, and so on. Each time you have one of these economic transactions, accounting data are generated. If you think about it, the number of transactions you can have is almost infinite. This is true for you personally, and it's true for companies, as well. The sheer volume of these data can be staggering.

Data vs. Information

In the previous paragraph, we used the phrase accounting **data** rather than accounting **information**. This change was not for the sake of variety. Data, which are the raw results of transactions, become information only when they are put into some useful form.

Consider this example:

Carol Brown, vice-president of sales for Balloo Industries, noticed that the amount spent by the sales force on gasoline for company cars over the last few months seemed extremely high. She was concerned that salespersons could be using the company cars for personal use. When each car is brought in for monthly maintenance, odometer readings are made; therefore, Ms. Brown knew she could find out how many miles each member of the sales force put on each car on a monthly basis. She hoped that gathering this information would help her to determine if the cars were being misused. Ms. Brown notified Jack Parsons, the sales supervisor, of her concerns. He agreed to prepare a report to provide the necessary information.

The report compiled by Mr. Parsons consisted of 6 columns of data: (1) salesperson's name, (2) make and model of his or her company car, (3) date the car was issued to salesperson, (4) odometer reading on date of issue, (5) date of most recent maintenance work, (6) odometer reading at time of most recent maintenance.

When Ms. Brown reviewed the report, she quickly concluded that it contained very little useful information. Mr. Parsons was reminded of the purpose of the report — to help Ms. Brown determine if any members of the sales force were using company cars for personal activities. Mr. Parsons retreated to his office to try again.

The second version of Mr. Parson's report consisted of all six columns that had been included in the original report and five additional columns: (7) sales region covered, (8) serial number of the vehicle, (9) how long the salesperson had been with the company, (10) total sales generated by each salesperson this year, and (11) current odometer reading of each vehicle.

Mr. Parsons had gone to considerable trouble to gather this additional data. Was Ms. Brown pleased? NO! Mr. Parsons provided additional DATA, but no additional INFORMATION.

Discussion Questions

3-7. Which of the data items (1 - 11) provided by Mr. Parsons were useful to Ms. Brown? Were any items of NO value to her? Evaluate the usefulness of each item offered by Mr. Parsons. Would the items you found to be of no help to Ms. Brown be of importance in a different setting?

3-8. Mr. Parsons has not been able to provide useful information to Ms. Brown. Design a report that you feel would be most helpful to Ms. Brown as she tries to decide if salespersons are misusing the company cars. You may gather any data that the company would reasonably have available. Provide Ms. Brown simple instructions on how to use the information you have provided.

3-9. What economic transactions have you had in the past month that generated accounting data?

3-10. What criteria would you use to determine if an item is data or information?

Useful Accounting Information

In the first part of this chapter, we established that the users of accounting information must have an understanding of business and, further, that they must be willing to study the information if they hope to make sound economic decisions. However, it is equally true that to be useful to the economic decision maker, accounting information must be presented in such a way that those users can make sense of it. Accountants have been roundly criticized in recent years for failing to provide information understandable to anyone but other accountants.

The criticism leveled at the accounting profession is not without some merit. As business and economic activities have become more complex, the accounting profession has responded with more and more complex rules, many of which serve to make accounting information less understandable to those who do not spend their lives studying those rules. But regardless of the complexity of environment or rules, there are certain characteristics any information (including accounting) must possess in order to be considered useful. Once you understand the characteristics of useful accounting information, you will have a much easier time making sense of the reports based on that information.

Who Decides What is Useful Accounting Information?

There are really two answers to that question. One is that the users themselves must decide what accounting information is useful and what is not. It is a grave mistake on the part of economic decision makers to leave this to the "experts." If the accounting profession is not providing the information needed, or is not preparing it in a way that makes sense, the users must demand a change. A second answer is that the accounting profession itself decides what accounting information is useful and what is not. However, the information provided by accountants should always be in response to the needs of those who will be using the information.

Currently, the organization principally responsible for establishing accounting guidelines and rules is the **Financial Accounting Standards Board (FASB)**. In 1976, it issued a mammoth three-part Discussion Memorandum entitled *Conceptual Framework for Financial Accounting and Reporting: Elements of Financial Statements and Their Measurement*. It was different from any statement previously made by the accounting profession in the United States because it described not only what accounting is presently, but what it ought to be as well. In the 19 years since the *Conceptual Framework* was published, the FASB has issued six *Statements of Financial Accounting Concepts* related to financial reporting. The remaining discussion in this section of the chapter is based on the *Conceptual Framework* and the six subsequent *Statements of Concepts*. We will focus on what the FASB called the **qualitative characteristics** of useful accounting information. The word qualitative refers to the qualities possessed by useful accounting information.

There is one other matter to be addressed before we proceed. Earlier we stated that a separate branch of accounting has evolved to meet the needs of internal and external decision makers. Managerial accounting generates information specifically for internal users, and financial accounting provides the information used by external parties. As its name implies, the Financial Accounting Standards Board is a part of the financial accounting branch and does not concern itself directly with the needs of internal users. Therefore, the concepts and ideas contained in the *Conceptual Framework* and the six subsequent *Statements of Concepts* are intended to apply to financial accounting. Most of the characteristics of useful accounting information discussed in those statements, however, apply equally well to managerial accounting. As we go through the discussion, we will point out those characteristics that do not apply to information used by internal parties and the reasons why they don't.

Remember that all economic decision makers are trying to determine whether they will be paid, when they will be paid, and how much they will be paid. In other words, they are attempting to predict

113

the amounts and timing of future cash flows. To be of value in this decision process, accounting information must possess certain qualitative characteristics. These are divided into two categories: primary and secondary qualities.

PRIMARY QUALITIES OF USEFUL ACCOUNTING INFORMATION

The two primary qualities that distinguish useful accounting information are **relevance** and **reliability**. If either of these qualities is missing, accounting information will not be useful.

Relevance

To be considered relevant, accounting information must have a bearing on a particular decision situation. In other words: Does the information make a difference? Does it matter? Does it relate? The accuracy of information isn't important if it is not capable of making a difference in a decision. Relevant accounting information possesses at least two characteristics:

- **Timeliness.** Regardless of the quality of accounting information, it is useless if it arrives too late to influence a decision. It may sound bizarre, but timeliness is more important than total accuracy. In an attempt to produce extremely accurate reports, providers of the information often make the information available too late to be of any value.

If accounting information is not timely, it is of no value. Timeliness alone, however, is not enough. In order for accounting information to be relevant, it must also possess at least one of the following characteristics:

- **Predictive Value.** Before economic decision makers commit resources to one alternative over another, they must be able to satisfy themselves that there is a reasonable expectation of a return on investment and a return of investment. Accounting information that helps reduce the uncertainty of that prediction is said to have predictive value.

OR

- **Feedback Value.** After an investment decision has been made, information must be available to assess the progress of that investment. Think back to the seven-step decision model presented in Chapter 2. Step #6 is a reevaluation of the decision as new information becomes available, and Step #7 is an evaluation of the final outcome of the decision. If accounting information provides input for those evaluations, it is said to have feedback value.

Reliability

To be considered reliable, accounting information must possess three qualities:

- **Verifiability**. Accounting information is considered verifiable if several qualified persons, working independently of one another, would arrive at similar conclusions using the same data. In other words, if there would be consensus among several individuals about the measurement of an item, that measurement information is considered verifiable.

- **Representational Faithfulness**. There must be agreement between what the accounting information says and what really happened. If a company's accounting information reports sales revenue of $1,000, and the company really had sales revenue of $1,000, the accounting information is representationally faithful. However, if a company's accounting information reports sales revenue of $1,000, and the company really had sales revenue of $800, the accounting information lacks representational faithfulness.

- **Neutrality**. To be useful, accounting information must be free of bias. That means it should not leave things out simply because they are unpleasant. We have stressed how difficult it is to make good decisions, and the problem becomes even

116

worse when information is suppressed or slanted in some way, either good or bad. The necessity to remain neutral presents one of the most difficult challenges facing the accounting profession. Accountants, both managerial and financial, are under constant pressure by interested parties to "cook the books" or practice "creative accounting." In other words, they are often asked to make the accounting information present a more favorable picture than really exists.

There are those who feel the importance of the characteristic of reliability (and its implied qualities of verifiability, representational faithfulness, and neutrality) applies only to information provided to external users (financial accounting), but not to information provided to internal parties (managerial accounting). They base that position on the essential difference between the information available to each type of user. Remember that internal parties may have access to all the accounting information available within the company, whereas the external users are limited to whatever information the company provides. The external users *must* have assurance that the information they receive is reliable. Although we do not disagree as to the importance of reliability to the external users, we think it is just as important to internal decision makers.

```
┌─────────────────────────────────────────────────────────────┐
│                                                               │
│  │                   Discussion Questions                   │ │
│  │                                                          │ │
│  │                                                          │ │
│  │  3-11. Think back to the seven-step decision model       │ │
│  │                                                          │ │
│  │        presented in Chapter 2.  How would the absence    │ │
│  │                                                          │ │
│  │        of these primary qualities of useful accounting   │ │
│  │                                                          │ │
│  │        information affect Step #3 and Step #4?           │ │
│  │                                                          │ │
│  │                                                          │ │
│  │                                                          │ │
│  │  3-12. Do you think these primary qualities apply to     │ │
│  │                                                          │ │
│  │        information other than financial information?     │ │
│  │                                                          │ │
│  │        Explain.                                          │ │
│  │                                                          │ │
└─────────────────────────────────────────────────────────────┘
```

SECONDARY QUALITIES OF USEFUL ACCOUNTING INFORMATION

Use of the term "secondary qualities" does not mean these characteristics are of lesser importance than the primary qualities we just discussed; in some decision making settings, these characteristics are crucial. However, if a secondary quality of accounting information is missing, the information is not necessarily useless. This is the distinction between primary and secondary qualities. The secondary qualities of useful accounting information are **comparability** and **consistency**. Although these qualities have some relevance to managerial accounting, they really are more applicable to financial accounting.

Comparability

Economic decision making involves the evaluation of alternatives. In order to be useful in such an evaluation, the accounting information for one alternative must be comparable to the accounting information for the other alternative(s). For example, assume you intended to make an investment and were considering two companies as investment alternatives. If the two companies use totally different accounting methods, a comparison would be very difficult. Comparability is an important quality of accounting information in many decision making settings.

Let's look at comparability in a setting with which you may be more familiar. Joshua is a high school junior who always achieves 93% averages in his classes. For 2 1/2 years now, he has attended a school which operates on a 10-point grading scale, where 90-100% earns an "A". Midway through Joshua's junior year, his mother received a job transfer and the family moved to another part of the state. In spite of the disruption caused by the move, Joshua maintained his 93% average in all his classes. This achievement should have been something to be proud of; however, the new school uses a 6-point scale. Only performance at 94% and above earns an "A". After being a straight-A student for 2 1/2 years, Joshua received all B's on his report card.

To an outsider, it appears that Joshua's performance has dropped, but it has not. This is an example of the consequences of using information that is not comparable. The meaning of an "A" at the old school is not comparable to the meaning of that grade at the new school.

Consistency

Extending the example of Joshua's grades, we can examine the characteristic of consistency. Suppose that Joshua's mother never received a job transfer and the family never moved. Instead, Joshua remained at his original high school for all four years. Again, his performance level was always 93%. After Joshua's junior year, the school's administrators instituted new policies to improve education. Beginning in Joshua's senior year, the school required a 94% level of performance to earn an "A". This resulted in Joshua receiving three years of straight-A's and one year of B's. Is it fair to conclude that Joshua's performance fell in his senior year? No, Joshua is a victim of information that lacks consistency.

Now consider the concept of consistency as it relates to economic decision making. Imagine how difficult it would be to assess the progress of an investment if, through the years, different accounting treatments were applied to similar events. Consistency in the application of measurement methods over periods of time

120

increases the usefulness of the accounting information provided about a company or an investment alternative.

Comparability and consistency (or lack thereof) often have similar effects on the decision making process. Basically, comparability relates to a comparison between information from different entities or alternatives. Consistency relates to the use of information from the same source over time. Both factors are important and can have major impacts on economic decision making.

Discussion Questions

3-13. Think back to the seven-step decision model. How would the absence of these secondary qualities of useful accounting information affect Step #4 and Step #6?

Now that you understand the qualities necessary to make accounting information useful, you can appreciate the fact that not all the information produced will meet these criteria. As a decision maker and user of accounting information, you must evaluate the qualities of the information available and assess its usefulness. The following story reflects the concerns of some frustrated users of accounting information:

There was a guy who wanted more than anything to take a hot-air balloon ride. So, he bought a balloon, filled it with hot air, and set out on a journey from Philadelphia to Pittsburgh to fulfill his lifelong dream. The trip was everything he had imagined it would be. From high in the air, he could look down and see people going about their business. The only time they stopped was to look up at him and his balloon floating gracefully through the sky. He knew how envious they were, because he had felt that way many times himself.

Everything was going along smoothly until he had traveled about 75 miles. Then, he ran into rough weather. He faced just a few clouds at first, but then came those awful winds. Next, the brave balloonist faced rain, with thunder and lightning. Before long, he was hopelessly lost, having been blown way off course. To make matters worse, his balloon began to lose air and for the first time the man began to fear for his life. He did not crash, however, because as his balloon fell to earth, its ropes became caught in the branches of a huge tree — his fall had been broken.

So there he was, sitting in his balloon basket, hanging in a tree, without the slightest idea where he was. Just then, he spotted a man walking along the road below. "Pardon me", said the man in the tree, "can you tell me where I am?" "Certainly," said the man walking on the road, "you are in a basket, in a tree." The man in the tree thought about that for a moment and then said, "You must be an accountant!" The man on the road beamed with pride that his professionalism was showing. "Why yes, I am", he said "but how did you know?" "Because", answered the guy in the tree, "your information is totally accurate and absolutely worthless."

As you work your way through this book, you should become comfortable with your ability to determine what information you need and how to get it. As an experienced accounting information user, you will know how to gather useful accounting information, and avoid the frustration of the man in the tree.

DECISION MAKERS AND UNDERSTANDABILITY

Although the characteristics of useful accounting information discussed in this chapter are important, none of them means a thing unless the users can understand the information. As the FASB said in *Statement of Financial Accounting Concepts #1*, accounting information should be understandable to those who have a reasonable understanding of business and are willing to devote the effort required to gain that understanding. There is persuasive evidence in the world today to indicate that there is a real communication gap between those who prepare accounting information and those who use it.

The accounting profession itself may be at least partially responsible for this problem. However, the users also bear some responsibility. We live in a complex world, and accounting for the events and transactions of that world is also complex. To expect accountants to provide information which can be understood without effort is foolish. The information itself cannot be understood without an understanding of the basis upon which it is prepared.

Economic decision makers must also understand that what they receive from accountants constitutes only a part of the information they need in making economic decisions. It is an important part, to be sure, but only a part. The reports generated from accounting information can be thought of as the tools of the accounting trade. Those attempting to use them must have a thorough understanding of what the tools can do and what they cannot be expected to do. As each financial tool is introduced and discussed throughout the rest of this text, keep in mind that each has limitations and imperfections. However, after working with the material provided, you should be able to use each financial tool to its fullest potential.

CHAPTER SUMMARY

Economic decisions are those decisions involving money. For our purposes, they are decisions within the context of American business. These economic decisions are made by two distinctly different types of decision makers. Internal decision makers are individuals within a company. They have access to much, if not all, the financial information available concerning the company, and they make decisions on behalf of the organization. External decision makers are individuals or organizations outside a company. They are limited to the information provided to them by the company, and they make decisions about the organization.

Because there are essential differences between the kinds of decisions made by internal and external parties, a different branch of accounting has developed over time to provide information to the two types of users. Managerial accounting information is the information prepared for use by internal parties, and financial accounting information is the information prepared for use by external parties.

Both internal and external parties are attempting to predict the future and timing of cash flows. Essentially, they are all trying to determine whether they will be paid, when they will be paid, and how much they will be paid.

As suggested by the concerns of economic decision makers, cash is of utmost importance. When evaluating business success or failure, cash is the ultimate measurement criterion.

Accounting information is a key ingredient to good decision making. Business activity produces data. This data is of no value to decision makers until it is put into a useful form. At that point, data is transformed into information.

To be useful to economic decision makers in their attempt to predict the future and timing of cash flows, accounting information must possess certain qualitative characteristics. The primary qualitative characteristics of useful accounting information are: (1) relevance, requiring timeliness and either predictive value or feedback value; and (2) reliability, requiring verifiability, representational faithfulness and neutrality.

Useful accounting information should also possess the secondary characteristics of comparability and consistency. In addition, in order to be useful, accounting information must be understandable.

KEY TERMS DEFINED

Accounting information. Raw data that have resulted from transactions and that have been transformed into a form that can be used by economic decision makers.

Cash flow. The movement of cash in and out of a company.

Comparability. One of the two secondary qualitative characteristics of useful accounting information. It means reports generated for one entity may be compared with the reports generated for other entities.

Consistency. One of the two secondary qualitative characteristics of useful accounting information. It means an entity consistently uses the same accounting methods and procedures from period to period.

Data. The raw results of transactions and events. Data are of little use to decision makers because they do not differentiate between transactions of relatively different importance.

Economic decision making. The process of making decisions involving money. For our purposes, decision making that takes place in the course of business transactions.

External decision makers. Economic decision makers outside a company. They make decisions about the company. The accounting information they use to make those decisions is limited to what the company provides them.

Feedback value. Part of the primary qualitative characteristic of relevance. To be useful, accounting must provide decision makers information to assess the progress of an investment.

Financial Accounting. The branch of accounting developed to meet the informational needs of external decision makers.

Financial Accounting Standards Board (FASB). The organization principally responsible for establishing accounting guidelines and rules in the United States.

Information. Raw data that have been transformed so that they are useful in the decision making process.

Internal decision makers. Economic decision makers within a company. They make decisions for the company. They have unlimited access to the accounting information of the company.

Managerial Accounting. The branch of accounting developed to meet the informational needs of internal decision makers.

Net cash flow. The difference between cash inflows and cash outflows; can be either positive or negative.

Neutrality. Part of the primary characteristic of reliability. To be useful, accounting information must be free of bias.

Predictive value. Part of the primary characteristic of relevance. To be useful, accounting must provide information to decision makers that can be used to predict the future and timing of cash flows.

Qualitative characteristics. These are characteristics accounting information must possess in order to be useful. They include the primary characteristics of relevance (predictive value, feedback value, and timeliness) and reliability (verifiability, representational faithfulness, and neutrality), and the secondary characteristics of comparability and consistency.

Relevance. One of the two primary qualitative characteristics of useful accounting information. It means the information must have a bearing on a particular decision situation.

Reliability. One of the two primary qualitative characteristics of useful accounting information. It means the information must be reasonably accurate.

Representational Faithfulness. Part of the primary characteristic of reliability. To be useful, accounting information must reasonably report what actually happened.

Timeliness. Part of the primary characteristic of relevance. To be useful, accounting information must be provided in time to influence a particular decision.

Verifiability. Part of the primary characteristic of reliability. Information is considered verifiable if several individuals, working independently, would determine the same amount.

REVIEW THE FACTS

1. What is economic decision making?

2. There are two broad categories of economic decision makers. Name them and explain their differences.

3. What are the two major branches of accounting and how do they differ?

4. List the three major questions asked by economic decision makers.

5. What is accounting information?

6. Explain the difference between data and information.

7. What is the name of the organization principally responsible for the establishment of accounting guidelines?

8. Name the two primary qualitative characteristics of useful accounting information.

9. What characteristics are necessary in order for accounting information to be relevant?

10. List the characteristics necessary in order for accounting information to be reliable.

11. Explain the difference between primary and secondary qualities of useful accounting information.

12. What are the secondary qualities of useful accounting information?

13. Explain the responsibility of both the accounting profession and the user as it relates to the understandability of accounting information.

Chapter 3
APPLY WHAT YOU HAVE LEARNED

A3-1.   Dave Cavazos is a commercial artist. His business entails painting signs of various types for businesses. He has received a $10,000 order from Steve Demmon & Company for 1,000 signs to be displayed in Demmon's retail outlets. While Dave is excited about the prospect of doing the job, he is a little concerned, because he estimates it will take him a month working full time to complete the signs and Demmon proposes to pay him the contract amount 30 days after he delivers the signs. These are Demmon's standard payment terms, although Dave did a small job for them last year ($500), and he received payment 45 days after completing the work.

Dave figures the materials for the job (poster board, paint, brushes, etc.) will cost $5,500, which he can buy on credit from Long's Art Supply Company (30 day terms).

Having taken the accounting course in which you are now enrolled, Dave remembers that any economic decision entails attempting to answer the following three questions:

- Will I be paid?

- When will I be paid?

- How much will I be paid?

REQUIRED:

a.   Presuming Dave can satisfy himself as to the first question (Will I be paid?), what are the answers to the other two questions? Remember the last question (How much?) has two parts.

b.   The problem states that Dave is concerned. What do you think is really troubling him about the order from Demmon & Company?

c.   Based on your answer to the previous requirement, identify three things Dave could do to lessen his anxiety and explain how they might help him feel more at ease.

132

A3-2. Presented below are the qualitative characteristics of useful accounting information as presented in the chapter, followed by definitions of those items in a scrambled order:

1. Relevance. ___
2. Timeliness. ___
3. Predictive Value. ___
4. Feedback Value. ___
5. Reliability. ___
6. Verifiability. ___
7. Representational Faithfulness. ___
8. Neutrality. ___
9. Comparability. ___
10. Consistency. ___

a. The same measurement application methods are used over time.

b. The accounting information is free of bias.

c. The information provides input to evaluate a previously made decision.

d. The information allows the evaluation of one alternative against another alternative.

e. In assessing the information, qualified persons working independently would arrive at similar conclusions.

f. The information helps reduce the uncertainty of the future.

g. The information has a bearing on a particular decision situation.

h. The information is available soon enough to be of value.

i. The information can be depended upon.

j. There must be agreement between what the information says and what really happened.

REQUIRED:

Write the letter of the appropriate definition in the space after each qualitative characteristic. Each letter will be used only once.

A3-3. Claudia Peel is the Controller (chief accountant) of Holesapple Company. She is trying to decide whether to extend credit to Mower Company, a new customer. Holesapple does most of its business on credit, but is very strict in granting credit terms. Mike Mower, the owner and president of Mower Company has sent the following items for Claudia to look at as she performs her evaluation:

1. All the company bank statements for the past five years (a total of 60 bank statements).

2. A detailed analysis showing the amount of sales the company expects to have in the coming year and its estimated profit.

3. Another, less detailed analysis, outlining projected company growth over the next 20 years.

4. A biographical sketch of each of the company's officers and a description of the function each performs in the company.

5. Ten letters of reference from close friends and relatives of the company's officers.

6. A report of the company's credit history prepared by the company on Mower Company letterhead.

7. A letter signed by all company officers expressing their willingness to personally guarantee the credit Holesapple extends to Mower. (You may assume this is a legally binding document.)

REQUIRED:

a. As she evaluates Mower Company's application for credit, is Claudia Peel an *internal* decision maker or an *external* decision maker? Explain your reasoning.

b. Analyze each item Mower sent in light of the primary qualitative characteristics of relevance (including timeliness, predictive value & feedback value) and reliability (including verifiability, representational faithfulness & neutrality). Explain how each item either possesses or does not possess these characteristics.

A3-4. Exactly two weeks from today you must take the mid-term exam for this class. You feel you are in trouble because you can't seem to grasp exactly how you should prepare for the exam. As you are walking across campus, you see the following notice pinned to a bulletin board:

```
+---------------------------------------------------------------+
|                                                               |
|         WORRIED ABOUT THE ACCOUNTING MID-TERM???              |
|                                                               |
|                     I CAN HELP!!!                             |
|                                                               |
|               I GUARANTEE AN "A" OR "B"                       |
|                                                               |
|              WILL TUTOR FOR $10 PER HOUR                      |
|                                                               |
|   Qualifications:                                             |
|   1.   Got an "A" in the course myself.                       |
|   2.   Have outlines of all chapters of the text.             |
|   3.   Over 140 satisfied customers from previous             |
|        semesters.                                             |
|   4.   Know the Professor personally.                         |
|   5.   Know the authors of the text personally.               |
|   6.   Working on a graduate degree in Biology.               |
|                                                               |
|          CALL JOE DOKES AT 555-5555                           |
|                                                               |
+---------------------------------------------------------------+
```

REQUIRED:

Evaluate each of Joe's claimed qualifications in relation to the primary characteristics of:

a. Relevance (including timeliness and predictive value or feedback value).

b. Reliability (including verifiability, representational faithfulness and neutrality).

CHAPTER 4

TOOLS OF THE TRADE PART I — THE BALANCE SHEET:

INITIAL FINANCING — INVESTMENTS BY OWNERS

Tools are invented to solve problems. They are responses to specific needs. If a tool is adequate and is properly used, it will produce satisfactory results, but if it is inadequate, or improperly used, difficulties and even disaster may result. Consider the following:

> THE PROBLEM developed. So, somebody analyzed THE PROBLEM and, having figured out what needed to be done to solve it, invented THE TOOL. Soon, many people began using THE TOOL to solve THE PROBLEM. Eventually, no one would even consider using anything else.

> For many years THE TOOL was used with great success. There came a time, however, when it no longer solved THE PROBLEM, but nobody realized it. Whenever confronted with THE PROBLEM, folks instinctively reached for THE TOOL. Even with people dying (THE PROBLEM was a very dangerous one), no one ever questioned the use of THE TOOL.

There are at least three possible explanations as to what happened in the situation described above:

1. The nature of THE PROBLEM had changed. If this were the case, it would be no wonder THE TOOL ceased to provide the desired results.

2. Those using THE TOOL only thought they were applying it to THE PROBLEM. In fact, they were using it to try to solve ANOTHER PROBLEM, which, on the surface, looked like THE PROBLEM.

3. THE TOOL never really did solve THE PROBLEM, but merely appeared to, and reality finally caught up with it.

What probably happened is a routine solution had been applied to a nonroutine situation. Recall that the key to reasoned decision making, step #1 of the decision making process discussed in Chapter 2, is determining the real problem to be solved. Similarly, determining the real problem is of paramount importance in using a tool. Once the real problem has been determined, the appropriate tool can be applied to solve it. If the appropriate tool does not exist, one can then be developed.

Financial statements should be thought of as tools for solving economic problems. As with all tools, they have been developed in response to specific needs. If these financial tools are adequate and are properly used, they will produce satisfactory results. If they are inadequate, or improperly used, difficulties and even disaster may result. In this chapter, we will discuss only one financial statement — the balance sheet. There are several others that will be discussed as we proceed through this text.

When you have completed your work on this chapter, you should be able to do the following:

1. Identify and explain the accounting elements contained in the balance sheet.

2. State in your own words how the balance sheet provides information about the financial position of a business.

3. Compare and contrast the balance sheets of proprietorships, partnerships, and corporations.

4. Describe the basic organizational structure of a corporation.

5. Differentiate between common stock and preferred (preference) stock.

6. Describe the components of stockholders' equity and understand the meaning of treasury stock.

7. Explain what information is available on a corporate balance sheet and what information is not.

8. Explain the basic process operating in the primary and secondary stock markets.

THE FIRST TOOL: INTRODUCTION TO THE BALANCE SHEET

We took great pains, in Chapter 3, to define the real problem facing those who must make economic decisions. As these people evaluate alternative investment opportunities, they are trying to determine whether they will be paid, and if so, when the payment will occur and how much it will be. We also stated that this evaluation begins with an assessment of an alternative's present condition and its past performance. Keep in mind that the present and the past are useful only if they can be used to reasonably predict the future. Over time, financial tools have been developed to convey information about the present condition and past performance of an entity. The financial tool that focuses on the present condition of a business is the **balance sheet.**

4-1. When Aunt Hattie was alive, she was always a
joker. Now she has passed on and left you and
your cousin Igor (whom you can't stand) the two
businesses she owned. You get first choice.
Aunt Hattie's will stipulates that you may ask
ten questions in order to determine the present
condition of each company. Lawyers for the
estate will provide the answers. Provide your
list of ten questions.

4-2. You are locked in a room that has no windows
and only one door. In order to get out of the
room, you must request one tool and explain how
you will use it to get through the door. You
may not request a key or any lock-picking
equipment. Choose the one tool you request and
describe its features. Then, explain in detail
how you will use it to get out of the room.

The Accounting Elements

Before we talk about the balance sheet, we should spend some time talking about the **accounting elements**. The dictionary defines the word "element" as a component, part, or ingredient. The results of every economic transaction or event experienced by a company can be classified into one or more of those elements. We will introduce you to three of the accounting elements in this chapter. Others will be presented later in the text, as circumstances warrant. As we discuss these elements, we will give you both the actual FASB wording in italics and a less technical explanation. The three elements that are components of a balance sheet are:

1. **Assets.** *Probable future economic benefits obtained or controlled by a particular entity as a result of past transactions or events.* Assets are the "things" a company has. Cash is the item that most clearly fits the definition of an asset.

2. **Liabilities.** *Probable future sacrifices of economic benefits arising from present obligations of a particular entity to transfer assets or provide services to other entities in the future as a result of past transactions or events.* Liabilities are the debts a company has — what they owe. A company may have an obligation to transfer assets to someone (pay off a debt) or provide services (if they received payment

141

in advance). Liabilities are the result of past transactions and will require settlement some time in the future.

3.   **Equity.** *The residual interest in the assets of an entity that remains after deducting its liabilities.* This is the ownership interest in a company. Literally it means if you add up what a company has (assets) and subtract what it owes on what it has (liabilities), the result is the portion of the assets that are owned free and clear by the owner or owners of the company. Equity in a company comes from two sources:

a. **Investments by owners.** This is the amount invested by the owner or owners of the company. It represents "seed money" put into the company to get it started or to finance expansion.

b. **Earned equity.** This represents the total amount a company has earned since it was first started, less any amounts that have been taken out by the owner or owners. Earned equity comes from the profitable operation of the company over time.

The present financial position of an entity can be captured in these three elements.

Organization of the Balance Sheet

A constant relationship exists among the three elements on the balance sheet (assets, liabilities, and owners' equity). Logically, what a company has (assets) will always be equal to the claims that are made on those assets. In other words, the assets of a company must be owned by someone. Either the creditors of the company have a claim to them (liabilities), or the owners own them free and clear (owners' equity). In most cases, the assets of a company are claimed, in part, by creditors and, in part, by owners. This relationship can be stated as an equation, as follows:

$$ASSETS = LIABILITIES + EQUITY$$

This is usually referred to as the **accounting equation**, but we think it would be better called the **business equation**, because it describes the reality of business. Accounting merely uses it to measure that reality. The equation could also be presented as:

$$ASSETS - LIABILITIES = EQUITY$$

meaning that if you take what a company has and subtract what it owes on what it has, you find what it really has. This presentation of the equation shows equity for what it is: the owner's residual interest in the company. To make sure we don't forget whose equity we are talking about, we usually use the phrase

143

"owners' equity," instead of the word "equity." The business (accounting) equation, then, is usually presented as:

ASSETS = LIABILITIES + OWNERS' EQUITY

You should memorize this equation because we will deal with it over and over again. A simple rote memorization, however, will not suffice. In order to understand the balance sheet, you must understand the meaning of the equation.

The term "balance sheet" comes from this equation. It is a nickname only and frankly is not very descriptive of the statement's purpose. This financial statement's formal name is the **Statement of Financial Position**, or **Statement of Financial Condition**, either of which is more descriptive than balance sheet. The informal title has been used for so long, however, that there is little chance of this statement being referred to as anything else.

One of the most common formats of a balance sheet is called the **account form**. As you can see below, the story told by the balance sheet is ASSETS = LIABILITIES + OWNERS' EQUITY:

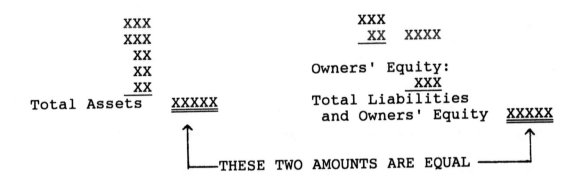

Barton Company
Balance Sheet
December 31, 1993

Assets: Liabilities:

            XXX   XXX
            XXX   XX   XXXX
            XX
            XX   Owners' Equity:
            XX   XXX
Total Assets   XXXXX   Total Liabilities
                                      and Owners' Equity   XXXXX

                    └─────THESE TWO AMOUNTS ARE EQUAL─────┘

The same information presented above can be placed on the page in a vertical format called the **report form**:

Barton Company
Balance Sheet
December 31, 1993

        Assets:
                    XXX
                    XXX
                    XX
                    XX
                    XX
        Total Assets   XXXXX ←─────┐

                                            │
        Liabilities: THESE TWO AMOUNTS ARE EQUAL

                    XXX   │
                    XX   XXXX   │

        Owners' Equity: │
                        XXX   │
        Total Liabilities   │
          and Owners' Equity XXXXX ←──────┘

145

The balance sheet is a financial "snapshot" of a company. As with any snapshot, *it only shows what existed on the day it was taken.* It is not a valid representation of the day before it is taken, nor the day after. What it says is that on the day the financial snapshot was taken, these are the assets the company possessed, and here's who had claim to those assets.

STARTING A BUSINESS — INVESTMENTS BY OWNERS

Now, let's imagine it's time to begin the operations of your new company. What needs to be done?? Starting out BIG may require lots of things — hiring a secretary and/or other employees, getting a company car, or renting office space. Even if you plan to just start a one-person operation, there are things to consider. What about having stationery and/or business cards printed? What about insurance to protect the company in case of lawsuits?

Even the smallest company will have start-up costs. In other words, your new operation will need CASH! In most cases, the first activity in which the new company is involved is obtaining the cash to get started. The most logical source for this initial funding is the owner/owners themselves. As we see the balance sheet develop, we will assume that the new company will be initially financed with cash from owners.

Recall that we have discussed three major forms of business organization: proprietorships, partnerships, and corporations. Each form requires a slightly different presentation of the initial financing of a new company.

Balance Sheet — Proprietorship

A proprietorship, with only one owner, must keep track of only that one owner's equity. If the owner of a proprietorship began a business on January 1, 1993 by investing $5,000 cash in the operation, the first balance sheet of the company would look like:

Rosita's Business
Balance Sheet
January 1, 1993

Assets:		Liabilities:	$ 0
Cash	$5,000		
		Owner's Equity:	
		Rosita, Capital	5,000
Total Assets	$5,000	Total Liabilities and Owner's Equity	$5,000

Notice that the business (accounting) equation still holds true:

$$\text{ASSETS} = \text{LIABILITIES} + \text{OWNERS' EQUITY}$$
$$\$5,000 = 0 + \$5,000$$

The owner's claim to the assets held by a sole proprietorship is represented by a capital account bearing the owner's name. In a proprietorship, there is only one owner; therefore, there will be only one capital account.

Balance Sheet — Partnership

Partnerships, you should recall, are companies similar in organizational form to proprietorships. The major distinction is that a partnership has more than one owner. Assume that the new company was being started by two partners, Rosita and Caroline. If Rosita invested $3,000 and Caroline invested $2,000 to begin operations, the partnership's first balance sheet would look like this:

Rosita and Caroline's Business
Balance Sheet
January 1, 1993

Assets:		Liabilities:	$ 0
Cash $5,000			
		Owners' Equity:	
		Rosita, Capital $3,000	
		Caroline, Capital 2,000	
		Total Owners' Equity	5,000
Total Assets	$5,000	Total Liabilities and Owners' Equity	$5,000

Compare the balance sheet for this partnership with that of the proprietorship. Notice that the total assets, $5,000 in cash, are the same. Total owners' equity ($5,000) is the same, also. The only difference is that we must keep track of each partner's claim to the assets in a separate capital account.

The example above assumes that Rosita provided 60 percent of the beginning capital ($3,000/$5,000 = 60 percent). Caroline invested only $2,000, 40 percent of the initial capital. The proportional size of a partner's initial investment is generally reflected by the proportional size of the beginning balance in the partner's capital account.

Partnership agreements may be simple or complex, but as long as the partners agree and understand clearly how their claims to the assets of the company (their capital balances) are being calculated, any rules can be adopted.

Balance Sheet — Corporation

A corporation is a legal entity. That characteristic sets it apart from proprietorships and partnerships. With very few exceptions, such as national banks (which are incorporated under federal law), United States corporations are created by obtaining a **corporate charter** from one of the 50 states. This charter is a legal contract between the state and the corporation allowing the company to conduct business.

To form a corporation, states require the **incorporators** to submit a formal application for the corporate charter and file it with the appropriate state agency. The application, called the **articles of incorporation**, generally must include: (1) basic information about the corporation and its purpose, (2) details of the types of stock to be issued, and (3) names of the individuals responsible for the corporation.

If the application is approved, a charter is issued and the corporation is legally entitled to begin operations. The incorporators then meet to formulate the corporate **bylaws**. These bylaws serve as basic rules to be used by management in conducting the business of the corporation. Next, capital is raised by issuing stock, exchanging ownership interests in the corporation for cash. Once stock is issued, there are stockholders, and they elect a permanent board of directors. The directors then meet to appoint a president and such other officers as they deem necessary to manage the company.

CORPORATE ORGANIZATIONAL STRUCTURE

In the preceding section we referred to several groups of people within the structure of the corporate form. Because these groups are critical to the successful operation of a corporation, we will now discuss each of them in greater detail.

The Stockholders

The stockholders are the owners of the corporation. They are also referred to as **shareholders** because they have provided cash or other assets to the corporation in exchange for ownership shares in the company. In most corporations, the stockholders are not involved in the daily management of the company, unless they have been elected to the board of directors or have been appointed as officers or managers.

When stockholders invest in the corporation they receive a **stock certificate**, a legal document providing evidence of ownership and containing the provisions of the stock ownership agreement. The stockholders usually meet once a year to elect members of the board of directors and conduct other business important to the corporation.

Board of Directors

The board of directors has ultimate responsibility for managing the corporation. In practice, however, most boards restrict themselves to formulating very broad corporate policy and appointing officers who conduct the daily operation of the corporation. The board serves as a link between the stockholders and the officers of the company. If the officers are not managing the corporation in the best interests of the stockholders, the board of directors, acting on behalf of the stockholders, replaces the officers.

Corporate Officers

A corporation's **chief executive officer (CEO)** is usually the president, and this person is responsible for all activities of the company. In addition to the president, most corporations have one or more vice-presidents who are responsible for specific functions of the company, such as marketing, finance, and production.

Other officer positions in many corporations include the **controller**, who is responsible for all accounting functions; the **treasurer**, who is responsible for managing the company's cash; and the **secretary**, who maintains the minutes of meetings of the board of directors and stockholders and may represent the company in legal proceedings.

4-3. In his book, <u>Short-term America</u>, Michael Jacobs reports that "nearly 80 percent of the chief executives of U.S. companies also serve as chairman of the board" (1991, p.82). In light of our discussion of the functions of corporate officers and the board of directors, express your views concerning this information. Is there cause for concern, or is this just "the way it is". Support your view with specific reasons.

4-4. As a follow-up item to the issue raised in the Discussion Question above, Michael Jacobs reports that "This practice is used by only 30 percent of British firms, 11 percent of Japanese companies, and never in Germany" (1991, p.82). Why do you think there is such a difference between the way business operates here in America and the way things are handled in other countries? Does this new information affect your response to the original question above?

CORPORATE CAPITAL STRUCTURE

As part of the formal application to create a corporation, the incorporators must include details of their plans to sell shares of stock. They request the authority to issue (sell) a certain number of shares of stock. **Authorized shares** is the maximum number of shares that can legally be issued under the corporate charter. The shares do not exist until they are issued, and ownership in the corporation is based on issued, not authorized, shares. **Issued shares** refers to the number of shares of stock already distributed to stockholders in exchange for cash or other assets. **Outstanding shares** refers to shares of stock currently being held by stockholders. In many instances, issued shares and outstanding shares will be the same. Occasionally however, a corporation may reacquire shares of stock it has previously issued. This reacquired stock is called **treasury stock** and will cause the issued shares and the outstanding shares to be different. For example, assume a corporation issued 10,000 shares of its stock and then later reacquired 2,000 of those shares. The company still has 10,000 shares issued but now has only 8,000 outstanding.

Previously, we have referred to the owners' interest in a company as owners' equity. In the corporate form of business organization, owners' equity is called **stockholders' equity**. There is no real difference between the two because in the corporate form, the equity of the owners (stockholders) is the excess of assets over

154

liabilities, just as it is with proprietorships and partnerships. There are, however, some differences in the way equity items are classified on the balance sheet.

In the corporate form, the owners' capital accounts are replaced by stock accounts. Most state corporation laws require stockholders' equity to be divided into the portion invested by the owners and the portion earned by the company and retained in the corporation. Amounts received by the corporation in exchange for shares of stock are called **contributed capital** or **paid-in capital**. A classification called **retained earnings** is used to reflect earnings reinvested in the company rather than distributed to the owners in the form of **dividends**. Total stockholders' equity is a combination of contributed capital and retained earnings.

As previously explained, the owners of a corporation are shareholders. If someone wants to have an ownership interest in a corporation, he or she must acquire shares of stock. The individual ownership interests of each shareholder are not disclosed on the face of the balance sheet. Instead, only totals of the ownership interests represented by each class of stock are shown. The two basic classes of stock are **common stock** and **preferred stock**.

Common Stock

Common stock is the voting stock of the corporation. Each share of common stock represents an equal share in the ownership of the corporation; therefore, the owners' equity portion of a corporate balance sheet will show information about common stock.

Common stock may or may not have a **par value**. Par value is an arbitrary amount placed on the stock by the incorporators at the time they make application for the corporate charter, and has nothing to do with the value of the stock. There was a time when all states required common stock to carry a par value, but all 50 states have now done away with the requirement. So why do we even discuss par value if it is no longer required? Because most of the large corporations in the United States were formed before the requirement was done away with, and their stocks carry a par value. Also, many newly formed corporations elect to issue **par value stock**.

Most corporations set the par value of their stock considerably below its actual value because most states do not allow stock to be sold for less than par value. It is not unusual to see par values as low as $1.00 per share, or even lower. Disney Corporation, for example, has a par value on its stock of 10 cents per share.

To illustrate issuing par value common stock, assume Rosita Corporation began operations on January 1, 1993 by issuing (selling) 1,000 shares of its $1 par value stock for $5 per share. The business receives a total of $5,000 cash, so assets increase by that amount. The transaction also affects the other side of the accounting equation in stockholders' equity. Most states require that only the par value of the stock multiplied by the number of shares issued can be classified as common stock. In the case of Rosita Corporation, that would be $1,000 (1,000 shares X $1 par value). The remaining $4,000 ($5,000 cash received less the $1,000 classified as common stock) is classified on the balance sheet as **additional paid-in capital** or some similarly descriptive title. A balance sheet prepared immediately after the sale of the stock would look like this:

Rosita Corporation
Balance Sheet
January 1, 1993

Assets:		Liabilities:		$ 0
Cash $5,000				
		Owners' Equity:		
		Common Stock	$1,000	
		Additional paid-in capital	4,000	
		Total Shareholders' Equity		5,000
Total Assets	$5,000	Total Liabilities and Owners' Equity		$5,000

Understand what this balance sheet *can* and *cannot* tell you. The $1,000 shown as common stock is the par value of the common stock multiplied by the number of shares issued thus far by the

157

corporation. Combining that amount with the $4,000 additional paid-in capital tells you that the corporation received a total of $5,000 in return for the shares of common stock. What is the value of those shares of common stock today? The answer to that question cannot be found on the balance sheet. Amounts shown on the corporate financial statements are intended to provide information about the results of past activities of the corporation — not the current values of stock already issued to shareholders.

Discussion Questions

4-5. If the balance sheet of a corporation does not show the current market value of the shares of stock, where do you think an investor could find this information?

No-Par Stock

Stock that does not have a par value is known as **no-par stock**. No-par stock is considered by many to have several distinct advantages over par value stock. These include:

- Accounting for stock transactions is less complicated for no-par stock than it is for par value stock.

- No-par stock prevents confusion as to the amount received from the sale of the stock. The relevant information is what shareholders were willing to pay for the stock, and an arbitrary par value may mislead some investors.

If the Rosita Corporation's common stock in the previous example had been no-par stock, the entire $5,000 proceeds from the sale of the stock would be classified as common stock, and the balance sheet immediately after the sale would look like this:

Rosita Corporation
Balance Sheet
January 1, 1993

Assets:	Liabilities:	$ 0
Cash $5,000		
	Owners' Equity:	
	Common Stock $5,000	
	Total Shareholders' Equity 5,000	
Total Assets $5,000	Total Liabilities and Owners' Equity	$5,000

Just as was the case with the previous example, this balance sheet can tell us how much was received from the sale of stock, but the information does not tell us about the current market value of the stock.

Preferred Stock

Preferred stock, also referred to as preference stock, is so named because it has certain preference features over common stock. Preferred stock is non-voting stock. Ownership of this type of

160

stock does not give these shareholders voting rights, but other features, which are outlined in the stock agreement, provide different types of benefits. Two benefits of ownership that are found in virtually all preferred stock agreements are:

- Owners of preferred stock must receive a dividend before any dividend is paid to owners of common stock. *but liabilities paid first*

- In the event of a corporation's liquidation, preferred shareholders receive a distribution of assets before any assets can be distributed to common shareholders. Liquidation refers to the process of going out of business. The corporation is shut down, all assets are sold, and all liabilities are settled.

Preferred stock is almost always par value stock. While par value has become almost meaningless for common stock, the par value on preferred stock is important because dividends are usually stated as a percentage of the par value. For example, if a corporation issued 8 percent preferred stock with a par value of $100 per share, the annual dividend would be $8.00 per share ($100 X 8 percent = $8). Most corporations must offer a reasonable dividend in order to encourage investors to buy the preferred stock. Because the dividends are stated as a percentage of par, the par value of preferred stock is normally much higher than is the par value of common stock.

To illustrate the issuing of preferred stock, assume that Rosita Corporation (from the previous discussion of common stock) also issued (sold) 50 shares of $100 par value preferred stock for $150 per share on January 1, 1993. Now the total amount the business received from the sale of stock is $12,500 (50 shares of preferred stock X $150 = $7,500 + $5,000 from the sale of the common stock). Under most states laws, only the par value of the preferred stock multiplied by the number of shares issued may be classified as preferred stock (50 shares X $100 par value = $5,000). The remaining $2,500 of the proceeds is classified as additional paid-in capital. A balance sheet prepared immediately after the sale of the two classes of stock would look like this:

Rosita Corporation
Balance Sheet
January 1, 1993

Assets:	Liabilities:	$ 0
Cash $12,500		
	Owners' Equity:	
	Preferred Stock	$5,000
	Additional paid-in capital-Preferred Stock	2,500
	Common Stock	1,000
	Additional paid-in capital-Common Stock	4,000
	Total Shareholders' Equity	12,500
Total Assets $12,500	Total Liabilities and Shareholders' Equity	$12,500

Again, the balance sheet reveals the amounts received for issuing each class of stock ($5,000 for common and $7,500 for preferred), but the current market value of the stock is not shown.

162

```
*****************************************************************
```

The information below is a portion of the December 31, 1983 balance sheet of Investors Accumulation Plan, Inc.   Look through it carefully, and then answer the questions below.

Common stock, $100 par value, Authorized 10,000 shares;
                            issued 5,000 shares $500,000
Additional paid-in capital 533,000

```
*****************************************************************
```

(a.) What total amount did the corporation receive in the sale of its stock?   *1,033,000*

(b.) What was the average selling price per share?

       $206.60

(c.) If the corporation wanted to sell all the stock possible, how many more shares could it sell?

      5000

(d.) If all the stock mentioned in question (c.) were sold, how much would the corporation receive?

      533,000

Try each question again - don't give up. Use the given information above - that's all you need...

O.K., if you are ready to check your answers, here goes:

(a.) What total amount did the corporation receive in the sale of its stock?

In total, the corporation received $1,033,000 for its stock. That is the total of the par value and the paid-in capital ($500,000 + $533,000).

(b.) What was the average selling price per share?

If the corporation received a total of $1,033,000 from the sale of its stock, the average selling price was $206.60. ($1,033,000 / 5,000 shares = $206.60 per share).

(c.) If the corporation wanted to sell all the stock possible, how many more shares could it sell?

The corporation has been authorized to sell up to 10,000 shares. If 5,000 shares have already been issued, an additional 5,000 shares could be sold.

(d.) If all the stock mentioned in question (c.) were sold, how much would the corporation receive?

Based solely on the information provided, there is no way to determine the current market value of the stock. If the stock is traded on a public stock exchange, the current selling price is common knowledge. Business periodicals such as The Wall Street

<u>Journal</u> publish stock prices daily. We will provide more
information about the trading of stock later in this chapter.

THE STOCK MARKET

In Chapter 1, we discussed the relative advantages and
disadvantages of the three forms of business organization (sole
proprietorship, partnership, corporation). One of the advantages
we listed under corporations was greater access to capital (money).
We stated that by dividing ownership into relatively low-cost
shares, corporations could attract a great number of investors. We
also mentioned that some corporations in the United States have
more than a million different stockholders (owners).

Another advantage of the corporate form that we listed in Chapter
1 was easy transferability of ownership. We stated that because
shares of ownership in corporations are relatively low-cost, they
can usually be purchased and sold by individual investors much more
easily than an ownership interest in either a proprietorship or a
partnership.

In this chapter, we used the example of Rosita Corporation to
demonstrate the sale of common (par and no-par) stock and preferred
stock and how the sale of those classes of stock would be reflected
in Rosita's balance sheet. But how did Rosita go about finding
people interested in buying her company's stock? If she desires to

raise a great deal of money by selling shares of stock in her corporation, she must find a way to contact many more people than she knows personally. Once investors have purchased stock in Rosita Corporation, how do they go about selling their shares if and when they decide they no longer desire to be stockholders?

If corporations are to have access to many potential investors, and if there is to be easy transferability of shares already owned by investors, there must be some mechanism to bring interested buyers and sellers of stock together. There is such a mechanism, and it is called the **stock market**. As with many terms in business, this one is used rather loosely. Many people think of Wall Street when they hear the words "stock market," but that thinking is too narrow. While Wall Street is a very important part of the stock market, there is much more to it than that. For one thing, there is not one single stock market. There are several in the United States, including the New York Stock Exchange (NYSE), the American Stock Exchange (AMEX), and several regional stock exchanges, such as the Midwest Stock Exchange in Chicago and the Pacific Stock Exchange in Los Angeles and San Francisco.

A **stock exchange** is an organization created to provide a place where interested buyers and sellers of shares of stock can get together. As recently as 1980, the U.S. stock market (encompassing all the national and regional exchanges) accounted for better than half the stock trading in the world. By 1990, that total was down to just over 34 percent, and the trend toward worldwide exchanges is expected to continue into the next century. Stock exchanges in Tokyo, London, and many other cities throughout the world are as important to stock trading as the ones in the United States.

Primary and Secondary Markets

When a corporation (such as Rosita Corporation) desires to raise capital (money) by selling shares of stock, it makes what is referred to as a **stock offering**. A stock offering gives investors the opportunity to purchase ownership shares in the company. The company announces the offering in such business periodicals as The Wall Street Journal. The announcement outlines the number of shares being offered and the anticipated selling price. If investors are interested in purchasing shares of the stock, the company is able to sell them and raise the money it needs.

Although a company can market its stock directly to the public, most offerings are made through **investment bankers**. Investment bankers are also called **underwriters** and their function is to act as an intermediary between the company issuing the shares of stock and the investors who ultimately purchase those shares. An investment banker purchases all the shares of stock being offered, then resells the shares to other investors (for a higher price). Examples of well-known investment banking firms are: Merrill Lynch, Salomon Brothers, and Morgan Stanley.

What we have described in the preceding two paragraphs is the **primary stock market**. Primary means first, or initial in this instance, not main or most important. Earlier in the chapter we illustrated the issuing (sale) of stock for Rosita Corporation and how the sale of that stock was reflected on the company's balance sheet. What we were demonstrating in that illustration was the primary, or initial sale of the stock.

After a company has initially sold shares of its stock, all sales of those shares take place in what is called the **secondary stock market**. The company itself receives no money from the sale of its stock in the secondary market. It needs to be notified, of course, when shares of its stock are sold from one investor to another, because it must know to whom it should send dividend payments. But the company itself is not directly involved in the trading of its stock in the secondary market.

The daily reports we hear about fluctuations in the stock market and the Dow Jones Industrial Average are referring to the trading of previously issued shares of stock in the secondary stock market. Whether you someday own a corporation, work for one, or invest your money in one, a basic understanding of corporate structure and the operation of the stock market is very valuable.

Government Influence on the Stock Market

As the secondary stock market grew in importance during the early part of the 20th century, there was little government influence in the way buying and selling of corporate stock were conducted. That all changed with the stock market crash of 1929, which led to the Great Depression.

In the aftermath of the stock market crash, the United States Congress took steps to standardize the practices on Wall Street and regulate the buying and selling of corporate securities in the secondary stock market. Congress passed two very significant pieces of legislation — the Securities Act of 1933, and the Securities Exchange Act of 1934. The second of these two laws created the **Securities And Exchange Commission (SEC)**.

One of the express purposes of the SEC is to regulate the procedures involved in the buying and selling of corporate stock on the U.S. stock markets. Any company whose shares of stock are traded on one of the recognized national or regional stock markets in the United States is required by law to file periodic reports with the SEC. The influence of this government agency on the way stock markets operate has grown significantly since it was first created in 1934.

In addition to its authority to regulate the buying and selling of corporate stock, the SEC also has the power to regulate the buying and selling of corporate bonds. Selling corporate bonds is a very sophisticated form of borrowing, and is one of the major topics addressed in the next chapter.

CHAPTER SUMMARY

The balance sheet is a financial tool that provides information about the present financial position of an entity. This financial statement shows the relationship of three accounting elements: assets, liabilities, and owners' equity. This relationship is known as the accounting equation or business equation:
ASSETS = LIABILITIES + OWNERS' EQUITY.

Basically, assets are what the company owns, liabilities are what the company owes to outsiders, and owners' equity is the residual interest that the owners can claim. Regardless of the type of business, the balance sheet shows the relationship among the company's assets, liabilities, and owners' equity.

Generally, the first activity of a new company is acquiring the cash needed to begin operations. Most often, this cash comes from the owner or owners of the company. The balance sheet for each type of business organization presents the results of this investment by owners in a slightly different way. Proprietorships will have a single capital account, representing the ownership interest of the proprietor. Partnerships generally show a separate capital account for each partner, because their levels of ownership interest may vary. Corporations are owned by their stockholders; therefore, ownership interests are shown in common stock and additional paid-in capital accounts.

Because it is a separate legal entity, a corporation is more complex in its organizational structure than either of the other two business forms. After issuing ownership interests in the form of shares of stock, the corporation has owners, called shareholders or stockholders. Corporate stockholders elect a board of directors to oversee the management of a corporation. The board, however, usually restricts itself to setting broad corporate policy; it appoints officers to conduct the daily affairs of the corporation. Corporate officers normally consist of a chief executive officer (usually the president), one or more vice-presidents, a controller, a treasurer, and a secretary.

Corporations may issue both common stock and preferred stock. Common stock is voting stock, and the owners of common shares are the real owners of the business. Common stock may have a par value, or it may be no-par stock. Preferred (preference) stock is usually non-voting stock but has certain preferences over common stock. The two primary preferences given to preferred shareholders relate to dividends (which are usually based on some percentage of the par value) and to a claim on the assets if liquidation of the corporation occurs.

Corporate capital (stockholders' equity) is classified by source: Paid-in (contributed) Capital and Retained Earnings. Paid-in capital represents the cash or other assets acquired by the company from the owners, generally through the sale of stock. Retained earnings represents the amount of earnings reinvested in the business rather than distributed to the owners in the form of dividends. For a number of reasons, a corporation might reacquire shares of stock previously issued. Reacquired stock is known as treasury stock. Treasury stock is still considered issued stock, but is no longer considered outstanding; it is shown on the balance sheet as a reduction of stockholders' equity.

The balance sheet is a representation of the financial position of the business on a particular date. As a financial statement reader, you will not be able to determine the current market value of the corporation's stock from its balance sheet. Rather, the balance sheet will provide information about how much was received by the corporation for the stock when it was originally issued.

Corporate stock is initially issued in the primary stock market, either to individuals or to an investment banker. The secondary stock market includes all subsequent trading of the shares of stock. Although the corporation does not receive money from trades in the secondary market, these trades influence the market value of the stock and are certainly important to the corporation. Activity in both the primary and secondary stock markets is regulated by the Securities and Exchange Commission (SEC).

Account form. A format of the balance sheet placing assets on the left side of the page and liabilities and owners' equity on the right side of the page.

Accounting elements. The categories under which all accounting transactions can be classified. We discussed three in this chapter (Assets, Liabilities, and Equity).

Accounting equation. Assets = Liabilities + Owners' Equity. Also called the business equation.

Additional paid-in capital. The amount in excess of the stock's par value received by the corporation when stock is issued.

Articles of incorporation. An application for a charter allowing the operation of a corporation.

Assets. An accounting element. These are probable future economic benefits controlled by an entity as a result of previous transactions or events — what a company has.

Authorized shares. The maximum number of shares of stock a corporation has been given permission to issue under its corporate charter.

Balance sheet. A financial statement providing information about an entity's present condition. Reports what a company possesses (assets) and who has claim to those possessions (liabilities and owners' equity).

Business equation. Assets = Liabilities + Owners' Equity. Also called the accounting equation.

Bylaws. The basic rules by which a corporation is operated.

Chief executive officer (CEO). The person responsible for all activities of the corporation. Usually also the president.

Common stock. A share of ownership in a corporation. Each share represents one vote in the election of the board of directors and other pertinent corporate matters.

Contributed capital. Total amount invested in a corporation by its shareholders. Also called paid-in capital.

Controller. The person in charge of all accounting functions of a corporation.

Corporate charter. A legal contract between a corporation and the state in which it is incorporated.

Dividend. A distribution of earnings from a corporation to its owners.

Earned equity. The total amount a company has earned since its beginning less any amounts distributed to the owner or owners. In a corporation, this is called retained earnings.

Equity. An accounting element. It is the residual interest in the assets of an entity that remains after deducting liabilities.

Incorporators. Individuals who make application to form a corporation.

Investment bankers. Intermediaries between the corporation issuing stock and the investors who ultimately purchase the shares. Also called underwriters.

Investments by owners. The part of owners' equity generated by the receipt of cash (or other assets) from the owners.

Issued shares. Stock that has been distributed to the owners of the corporation in exchange for cash or other assets.

Liabilities. An accounting element. These are probable future sacrifices of assets arising from present obligations of an entity as a result of past transactions or events — what a company owes.

No-par stock. Stock that has no par value assigned to it.

Outstanding shares. Shares of stock actually held by shareholders. May be different than issued stock because a corporation may reacquire its own stock (treasury stock).

Owners' equity. The owners' residual interest in the assets of a company after consideration of its liabilities.

Paid-in capital. The portion of stockholders' equity representing amounts invested by the owners of the corporation. Consists of common stock, preferred stock, and amounts received in excess of the par values of those stocks. Also called contributed capital.

Par value. An arbitrary amount assigned to each share of stock by the incorporators at the time of incorporation.

Par value stock. Stock with a par value printed on the stock certificate (see par value).

Preferred (preference) stock. Has preference over common stock as to dividends and to assets upon liquidation of the corporation. Usually non-voting stock.

Primary stock market. Business activity involved in the initial issue of stock from a corporation.

Report form. The vertical format of a balance sheet, in which assets, liabilities, and owners' equity are shown one after another down the page.

Retained earnings. Earnings reinvested in a corporation. Equal to the total profits of the corporation since it was organized less amounts distributed to the stockholders in the form of dividends.

Secondary stock market. The business activity focusing on trades of stock among investors subsequent to the initial issue.

Secretary. The person who maintains the minutes of meetings of the board of directors and stockholders of a corporation. This person may represent the corporation in legal proceedings.

Securities and Exchange Commission (SEC). The government agency empowered to regulate the buying and selling of stocks and bonds.

Shareholders. The owners of a corporation. Also called stockholders.

Statement of Financial Condition. Another name for the balance sheet.

Statement of Financial Position. Another name for the balance sheet.

Stock certificate. Document providing evidence of ownership of shares in a corporation.

Stock exchange. A place that brings together buyers and sellers of stock.

Stock market. A general term referring to the activities in the secondary stock market.

Stock offering. The process of announcing the issue of shares of stock.

Stockholders' equity. Replaces owners' equity in the corporate form. Divided into contributed capital and retained earnings.

Treasurer. The person in charge of managing the cash of a corporation.

Treasury stock. A corporation's stock which has been issued and then reacquired.

Underwriters. Intermediaries in the primary stock market. Also called investment bankers.

REVIEW THE FACTS

1. List and define the three accounting elements that are components of the balance sheet.

2. Describe the two sources from which a company builds equity.

3. State the business or accounting equation.

4. What is a more formal and descriptive name for the balance sheet?

5. List and describe the two formats of the balance sheet.

6. How do the balance sheets of a proprietorship and partnership differ?

7. In what ways are a stockholder of a corporation and a partner in a partnership different?

8. Explain the difference among authorized, issued, and outstanding shares of stock.

9. Define treasury stock.

10. Name and describe the two major components of stockholders' equity.

11. What are the two major classes of stock and how do they differ?

12. What is meant by the par value of stock and what significance does it hold?

13. Explain what a stock exchange and a stock offering are.

14. What is the role of underwriters or investment bankers?

15. Distinguish between the primary stock market and the secondary stock market.

16. What type of organization is the SEC and what is its function?

Chapter 4
APPLY WHAT YOU HAVE LEARNED

A4-1. On January 2, 1995, Marty McDermitt started a business by
investing $3,000 cash in the operation. He cleverly named
the company MARTY McDERMITT ENTERPRISES.

REQUIRED:

a.   Prepare a balance sheet as of January 2, 1995 for
Marty's business to reflect his investment, assuming
the company is a sole proprietorship.

b.   Now assume that the business organized on January 2,
1995 was a partnership started by Marty and his brother
Barton, which they have named M&B ENTERPRISES. Marty
invested $2,000 and Barton invested $1,000. Prepare a
balance sheet as of January 2, 1995 for the company to
reflect the partners' investment.

c.   Now assume that the business organized on January 2,
1995 was a corporation started by Marty and his brother
Barton, which they have named M&B ENTERPRISES, INC.
Marty invested $2,000 and received 200 shares of common
stock. Barton invested $1,000 and received 100 shares
of common stock. The common stock has a par value of
$2 per share. Prepare a balance sheet as of January 2,
1995 for the company to reflect the stockholders'
investment.

d.   Assume the same facts as in requirement c, except that
the common stock is no-par stock. Prepare a balance
sheet as of January 2, 1995 for the company to reflect
the stockholders' investment.

A4-2.   Fisher Corporation began operations in 1972 by issuing
        10,000 shares of its no-par common stock for $5 per share. = $50,000
        The following details provide information about the
        company's stock in the years since that time:

1.   In 1982, the company issued an additional 50,000 shares = 750,000
        of common stock for $15 per share.

2.   Fisher Corporation stock is traded on the New York
        Stock Exchange (NYSE). During an average year, about
        25,000 shares of its common stock are sold by one set
        of investors to another.

3.   On December 31, 1994, Fisher Corporation common stock
        was quoted on the NYSE at $38 per share.

4.   On December 31, 1995, Fisher Corporation common stock
        was quoted on the NYSE at $55 per share.

REQUIRED:

a.   Which of the stock transactions described above
        involved the primary stock market and which ones
        involved the secondary stock market?

b.   How much money has Fisher Corporation received in total
        from the sales of its common stock since it was
        incorporated in 1972?

c.   When Fisher Corporation prepares its balance sheet at
        December 31, 1995, what dollar amount will it show in
        the owners' equity section for common stock?

d.   What, if anything, can you infer about Fisher
        Corporation's performance during 1995 from the price of
        its common stock on December 31, 1994 and December 31,
        1995?

A4-3.   Presented below is a list of items relating to the
        corporate form of business, followed by definitions of those
        items in a scrambled order:

        a.   Incorporators.
        b.   Charter.
        c.   Bylaws.
        d.   Stockholders.
        e.   Stock Certificate.
        f.   Board of Directors.
        g.   Corporate Officers.
        h.   Par Value.
        i.   Additional Paid-In Capital.

1. ___   An arbitrary value placed on either common stock or
            preferred stock at the time a corporation is formed.

2. ___   The group of men and women who have the ultimate
            responsibility for managing a corporation.

3. ___   The owners of a corporation.

4. ___   Any amount received by a corporation when it issues
            stock that is greater than the par value of the stock
            issued.

5. ___   The formal document which legally allows a corporation
            to begin operations.

6. ___   The group of men and women who manage the day-to-day
            operations of a corporation.

7. ___   The person or persons who submit a formal application
            with the appropriate government agencies to form a
            corporation.

8. ___   A legal document providing evidence of ownership in a
            corporation.

9. ___   Rules established to conduct the business of a
            corporation.

REQUIRED:

Match the letter next to each item on the list with the
appropriate definition. Each letter will be used only once.

A4-4.   Atkinson Corporation began operations on July 10, 1995 by issuing 5,000 shares of $3 par value common stock and 500 shares of $100 par value preferred stock. The common stock sold for $10 per share and the preferred stock sold for $120 per share.

REQUIRED:

Prepare a balance sheet for Atkinson Corporation at July 10, 1995 immediately after the common stock and preferred stock were issued.

A4-5.   The questions below are based on this selected information from the balance sheet of E.I.duPont de Nemours and Company (DuPont):

(Dollars in millions)

| | December 31 | |
	1991	1990
Common Stock, $.60 par value; 900,000,000 shares authorized; issued at Dec.31: 1991 - 671,242,137; 1990 - 669,847,961	$ 403	$ 402
Additional paid-in capital.	4,418	4,342

REQUIRED:

a.   What was the average selling price of the stock that had been issued as of December 31, 1990?

b.   The par value of the outstanding shares of common stock as of December 31, 1991 is shown as $403 million. This is actually a rounded amount. What is the exact par value of the common stock outstanding as of that date?

c.   How many shares of common stock were issued during 1991?

d.   How many shares would DuPont be allowed to issue during 1992?

CHAPTER 5

THE BALANCE SHEET (CONTINUED):

ADDITIONAL FINANCING — BORROWING FROM OTHERS

No matter what organizational form a company takes (proprietorship, partnership, corporation), or what type of company it is (service, merchandise, manufacturing), all companies have one thing in common: they must obtain capital (money) to support operations. In the long run, a company must be financed by its profitable operations. This is known as **internal financing**. However, either when just starting out or in a time of expansion, almost all companies find it necessary to obtain capital from sources other than their profits. This is called **external financing**.

The two external sources of capital are known as **equity financing** and **debt financing**. Equity financing involves offering ownership interest in the company in exchange for the needed cash. Most businesses begin their operations using cash invested by the owners. Chapter 4 illustrated the impact of this initial financing on the balance sheets of proprietorships, partnerships, and corporations. In many cases, however, even more cash is needed to get the operation started. Almost all companies, at one time or another, need additional funds from outsiders. More ownership shares in the company can be sold or funds can be borrowed. Borrowing funds for business operations is called **debt financing**.

Neither a borrower nor a lender be!

William Shakespeare

This advice from William Shakespeare may serve you well in your personal life, however, many companies would not be able to survive if it weren't for the borrowing and lending that is an integral part of today's business world. As we will see later in this chapter, financial institutions function as primary lenders, and companies borrow funds for various reasons. The bond market also serves as a source of debt financing. Needing funds from external sources is NOT necessarily a sign of weakness in the company. Often, funds are needed for expansion because the company is growing even faster than expected.

In this chapter, we will learn about several different approaches to debt financing, and after you have completed your work on this chapter, you should be able to:

1.   Describe how banks earn profits.

2.   Explain the effects on a company's balance sheet if funds are borrowed from a bank.

3.   Distinguish among notes, mortgages, and bonds.

4.   Calculate interest payments for notes and bonds.

5. Explain the functions of underwriters in the process of issuing bonds.

6. In your own words, describe the effect of market interest rates on bond selling prices.

7. Contrast the operations of the primary and secondary bond markets.

8. Compare and contrast two investment alternatives — equity investment and debt investment.

The financing requirements of companies fall into two general categories. A company needs short-term financing to run its day-to-day operations and long-term financing to achieve its long range goals. **Short-term financing** is generally defined as any financing that must be repaid within five years. **Long-term financing**, then, can be defined as any financing in which repayment extends past five years. However, don't consider those definitions as hard and fast. Understand that different people have different interpretations of what short-term and long-term mean. In any event, several sources have developed to provide these two types of financing.

BORROWING FROM FINANCIAL INSTITUTIONS

At one time or another, almost everyone has had dealings with a
bank.   You may have had a savings account (time deposit), a
checking account (demand deposit), or a loan to finance a car, a
stereo, or some other purchase.   Individuals borrow money from
financial institutions every day, but this activity represents only
one type of borrowing.   Financial institutions must meet the needs
of both individuals and companies.   This demand leads to two
distinct types of borrowing: consumer and commercial.

Consumer borrowing refers to loans obtained to pay for such items
as the car and stereo mentioned in the previous paragraph.   While
most of the loans classified as consumer loans are relatively
small, the definition has to do with the purpose of the loan, not
its amount.   If an item is for personal use rather than for use in
business, the loan obtained to finance it is classified as consumer
borrowing.   When a company obtains a loan to finance day-to-day
operations or achieve long-term goals, that loan is referred to as
commercial borrowing.   The word "commercial" comes from the word
"commerce," which was, as you will recall, listed in the dictionary
as one of the definitions of the word "business."

Banks are not the only places to go for a loan.   Actually, there
are several distinct types of financial institutions whose major
business function is lending money.   Although their functions have

become somewhat blurred over the past several years, certain of the financial institutions discussed below were developed specifically to satisfy the need for consumer loans. Others came into being to meet the financing needs of companies.

- *Savings and Loan Associations (S&L)* and *Mutual Savings Banks (MSB)*. Savings and loan associations were created primarily to lend money for home mortgages. Over time, S&Ls began lending money for other consumer items. In the 1980s, many S&Ls ventured into other lending arrangements, such as real estate speculation, and in many instances the results were disastrous. Mutual savings banks are somewhat different from S&Ls in that they are owned by their depositors, and any profits earned are divided proportionately among those depositors. Like S&Ls, MSBs began as consumer lending institutions (particularly for home mortgages), but over time began to broaden their lending activities. And, as was the case with S&Ls, many have experienced financial difficulty in the last decade.

- *Credit Unions (CU)*. Credit unions are typically formed by a company, labor union, or professional group. They accept deposits and lend money only to their members, and to become a member of a credit union, a person must meet a specific set of qualifications. This usually means working for a particular employer or belonging to the organization that formed the credit union. Traditionally, CUs have concentrated on short-term consumer loans (financing cars and stereos, for example) and savings deposits for their members. In recent years, many credit unions have developed checking accounts for their members (called share draft accounts), but their lending activities are still mostly for consumer purchases by members, rather than for financing business activities.

- *Commercial Banks*. This is what most people think of when they think of a bank. As the name implies, commercial banks are heavily involved in commercial lending. In fact, while they have ventured into the area of consumer lending, the vast majority of lending by these institutions is to companies, for commercial purposes. There are roughly 13,000 commercial banks in the United States today. The following is a list of the ten largest American banks:

	LOCATION	ASSETS (in $billions)
Citicorp	New York	$217.4
BankAmerica	San Francisco	193.6
Chemical Bank	New York	135.4
NationsBank	Charlotte, NC	118.2
Chase Manhattan	New York	98.5
J.P. Morgan	New York	96.9
Bankers Trust	New York	58.9
Wells Fargo	San Francisco	54.4
First Interstate Bancorp	Los Angeles	50.3
Banc One	Columbus, Ohio	49.3

This book deals primarily with business and how accounting information is used in making business decisions. Therefore, whenever we make reference to "the bank," we are referring to commercial banks.

How Banks Earn Profits

Think back to our discussion of Ralph and his shoe store in Chapter 1. In order to stay in business, Ralph must be profitable. He must sell shoes for enough to recover what the shoes cost him, plus pay all other expenses associated with running the store. Whatever is left after all those costs is his profit. Well, banks are companies, too, and in order to stay in business, a bank must be profitable. As stated earlier, the majority of a bank's income is from the **interest** paid on loans by borrowers.

You can think of interest as rent paid on borrowed money. The bank rents money from its depositors and then rents it out to others. Logic dictates that the rent (interest) the bank pays must be less than the rent (interest) it receives if it is to be profitable. For example, let's say you open a savings account at the bank by depositing $100. The bank agrees to pay you 5 percent annual interest on the amount you have deposited. This means if you leave the $100 in the bank for a full year, you will earn $5 interest.

Let's say further that nine other people did exactly as you did and opened savings accounts at the bank by depositing $100 each. The bank has agreed to pay them 5 percent annual interest on their deposits, as well. The bank now has $1,000 ($100 X 10 depositors), and the interest the bank must pay on this $1,000 is $50 ($5 to each of the ten depositors).

The bank can now take the $1,000 and lend it to someone. Obviously, it must charge something greater than 5 percent interest on the loan (or loans) it makes with the $1,000 or it will lose on the exchange. So let's say the bank lends the $1,000 to someone for one year and that person agrees to pay the bank 9 percent annual interest on the loan.

At the end of the year, the person who borrowed the $1,000 repays the loan, plus $90 interest ($1,000 X 9 percent). The bank then adds $5 to the account of each of the ten depositors, and the bank has earned a gross profit of $40, calculated as:

```
Interest the bank received on the loan........$90
Less the interest paid to the ten depositors..  50
Equals gross profit on the loan..............$40
```

It's a simple enough process, right? Wrong! In fact, there are a number of possible complications in this process.   Two that immediately come to mind are:

1.   The person who borrowed the $1,000 may fail to repay the loan. Failure to repay is known as **defaulting** on the loan.

2.   One or more of the ten depositors may decide not to leave their $100 deposit in the bank for the full year.

Discussion Questions

5-1. What other factors can you think of that complicate the process of banks earning their profits by making loans?

5-2. What steps would you suggest to the bank to overcome the two complications we listed plus the ones you thought of in your response to Discussion Question 5-1?

By the way, the $40 profit we calculated for the bank on the loan does not constitute the real profit. Just as was the case with Ralph selling the pair of shoes to Marty, the profit we calculated above represents gross profit, because all other costs involved in running the bank must be deducted before the net profit can be calculated.

Notes Payable

If a company needs to borrow funds for only a short time (usually five years or less), a bank may lend them money and require them to sign a **note payable**. The amount of money lent and the term (length) of the loan will be determined by the bank's policies and the judgement of the lending officer. Borrowing funds by signing a note payable adds to the assets of the company, but at the same time creates a liability. Building upon the example introduced in the previous chapter, the effects of borrowing funds are illustrated below:

Rosita Corporation
Balance Sheet
January 1, 1993

Assets:		Liabilities:		
		Notes Payable $1,000		
Cash	$6,000	Total Liabilities		$1,000
		Owners' Equity:		
		Common Stock	$1,000	
		Additional paid-in capital	4,000	
		Total Shareholders' Equity		5,000
Total Assets	$6,000	Total Liabilities and Owners' Equity		$6,000

195

The information provided in the balance sheet indicates that the company borrowed $1,000 by signing a note payable. This transaction provided the company with $1,000 additional cash, so total assets rose to $6,000. Because the additional asset amount is claimed by someone external to the business (probably a bank), it counts as a liability. Notice that the business equation still holds true:

$$\text{ASSETS} = \text{LIABILITIES} + \text{OWNERS' EQUITY}$$
$$\$6,000 = \$1,000 + \$5,000$$

A note payable generally requires the signing of a legal "promise to repay." In addition, the lender may require the use of **collateral** to secure the loan. Collateral is something of value that is forfeited to the lender if the borrower fails to make payments as agreed. For example, if you borrow money from BankAmerica to buy a new car, the car generally serves as collateral. That is, if you fail to make the payments, the bank may repossess the car and sell it to get their money back.

By offering collateral, companies may be able to borrow more funds for a greater length of time. This type of larger, longer-term debt that identifies a specific item as collateral is called a **mortgage**. For instance, a company can mortgage a piece of property it owns by allowing it to serve as collateral for a loan. In this case, the lender (bank) has the right to seize the property if the borrower defaults (fails to repay the loan).

Calculating Interest

The cost of borrowing these funds can be determined using information about the note payable. You should become familiar with the terminology used when funds are borrowed. Here's an example:

> Boston Brothers borrowed $5,000 on January 2, 1993 by signing an 8 percent, 3-year note. The lender requires interest payments to be made each year.

First of all, the amount of interest involved is always stated in annual terms. Therefore, 8 percent refers to the amount of interest the lender expects each year. Interest is based on the amount borrowed, the **principal**. The formula to determine annual interest is:

$$PRINCIPAL \times RATE = ANNUAL\ INTEREST$$

In our example of the Boston Brothers' note, the amount of interest due each year is calculated as:

$$\$5,000 \times .08 = \$400$$

Notice that for purposes of calculations, the percentage rates can be converted to numbers. The lender would expect $400 payment of interest on January 1, 1994 and January 1, 1995. On January 1, 1996, the lender expects another $400 interest payment as well as the principal, because this was a three year note. The payment that Boston Brothers is required to make to the bank on January 1, 1996 is $5,400. This amount reflects both the interest due ($400) and the return of the principal amount ($5,000).

The term (length) of notes payable varies. If Boston Brothers needed to borrow the funds from the bank for only a short time, the note may have been described as a:

$5,000, 8 percent, 90-day note

This terminology would suggest that the $5,000 must be repaid 90 days (3 months) from the day the funds were borrowed. On that day, Boston Brothers would pay the lender the principal ($5,000) and the interest due. Recall that interest rates are stated in annual terms. 8 percent indicates the amount of interest that would be due if the funds were held for one year. If the funds are held for three months, only a portion of the year's interest would be due. Now, we can use a formula that considers the length of time that the funds are held:

PRINCIPAL X RATE X TIME = INTEREST

P X R X T = I

The calculation to determine the interest owed by the Boston Brothers is:

$$\$5,000 \text{ X } .08 \text{ X } 3/12 = \$100$$

Because the interest rate is annual, the time factor in the calculation is a proportion of the year. If the funds are borrowed for three months, time is represented by 3/12, indicating three months out of the total twelve in a year.

In calculations such as this one, the time factor may be represented by the number of days involved as a proportion of the number of days in a year. When this method is used, the number of days in a year is generally rounded to 360. Thus, the calculation above could be presented as:

$$\$5,000 \text{ X } .08 \text{ X } 90/360 = \$100$$

When the time period involved is a number of whole months, either approach will work. If the funds are borrowed for some other time period, such as 45 days, using 360 as the number of days per year is much clearer.

Interest costs are an important factor in the decision of whether or not to borrow funds. Business persons in various capacities (e.g. CEO's, regional managers, store managers) are faced with financing decisions often.

Discussion Questions

5-3. In the example above, describing the Boston Brothers' 3-month loan, what is the lender's return OF investment and return ON investment?

NOTE: The next two Discussion Questions require that you locate information from a local newspaper. Go to the business section of the paper, and look up the current interest rates.

5-4. What are the different rates a bank will pay on various certificates of deposit (CD's)? Explain why the bank offers these various rates.

5-5. What are the current rate banks charge for mortgages? What are the current credit card rates? Why are there differences between these two rates?

We began our discussion of how companies are financed by saying that companies require both short-term financing to run day-to-day operations and long-term financing to achieve long range goals. While the use of collateral may allow a company to secure financing for a longer term, the commercial banks discussed in the previous section are ideally suited to provide short-term financing. At the end of 1991, the total dollar amount of loans outstanding from banks was nearly $1.5 trillion. Most of these loans were to companies, and most of them fell under the definition we used for short-term financing (repayment within five years).

While there is no law to prevent banks from lending money to companies for very long periods of time, there are a couple of factors that make this type of lending arrangement unfeasible for most banks. First, many companies are looking for financing for as long as 40 years, and most banks are not interested in making loans of that duration. Second, and perhaps more importantly, the amount of money required for long-term financing in many large companies is more than a single bank can accomodate. Even very large banks are unwilling or unable to address the borrowing needs of these large companies. For this reason, another source of financing is available for corporations.

BONDS

A **bond** is similar to a note payable in that it is an interest-bearing debt instrument. The main differences between the two are the length of time the debt will be outstanding and the amount of money borrowed. Notes payable are usually up to five years in duration and are limited to the amount of money a single lender is willing to lend. Bonds payable can be as long as 40 years in duration and, because they are sold to many different parties, the amount of money borrowed can usually be much greater.

Corporate debt, in the form of bonds, is a major factor in our economy. In 1980, 412 billion dollars worth of corporate bonds were outstanding, and this figure has risen steadily each year. By the end of 1989, the figure had topped one trillion dollars. By the end of 1991, bonds accounted for 1.174 trillion dollars worth of corporate debt (U.S. Department of Commerce 1992, 493). This figure represents 53.5 percent of total corporate debt, indicating that bonds are a major source of funds for American business.

Bonds are issued in some set denomination, generally $1,000 for each bond. The **par value** of such bonds is then $1,000. This indicates that when the borrower pays back the debt, $1,000 will be repaid. Par value is also called **maturity value**, **face value**, or **principal**, and these terms are used interchangeably.

The **nominal interest rate** is the specified annual interest paid on a bond and is a percentage of the par value of the bond. In other words, it is the rate of interest that the issuing company (borrower) has agreed to pay. The nominal rate is also called the **contract rate**, **coupon rate**, or **stated rate**, and these terms are used interchangeably.

Information such as the par value and the nominal interest rate is included in the bond **indenture**. This legal document details the agreement between the company issuing the bonds (the borrower) and the buyers of the bonds (the lenders). Information concerning timing of the interest payments and timing of total repayment (retirement) of the bonds is also included in the indenture.

In contrast to the nominal interest rate, which is set at the time bonds are issued and remains constant, the **effective interest rate** fluctuates with market conditions. The effective interest rate is the actual interest rate that will be earned by the bondholder over the life of the bond. Unlike the nominal rate, which is determined by the issuing company, the effective rate is determined by the financial markets and may cause a bond to sell for more or less than its par value. The effective rate is also called the **yield rate**, or **market interest rate**, and the terms are used interchangeably.

The **selling price** is the amount for which a bond actually sells and is also called the **market price**. As stated above, it is determined by the effective, or market interest rate. If the effective interest rate and the nominal interest rate are the same, a bond is said to be selling at 100, meaning 100 percent of its face, or par value. Bonds may sell for less than par value. For instance, a selling price of 95 means 95 percent of the bond's par value. Bonds may even sell for more than their par value. A bond with a sale price of 106 sold for 106 percent of its par value.

Issuing Bonds Sold at Par

To illustrate the impact of issuing bonds at par value, assume Rosita Corporation issued $300,000 worth of ten-year, 8 percent bonds on January 1, 1993. Building on the previous example, Rosita Corporation has also sold $5,000 worth of common stock and borrowed $1,000 from the bank.

Rosita Corporation
Balance Sheet
January 1, 1993

Assets:	Liabilities:		
	Notes Payable	$ 1,000	
	Bonds Payable	300,000	
Cash $306,000	Total Liabilities		$301,000
	Owners' Equity:		
	Common Stock	$1,000	
	Additional		
	paid-in capital	4,000	
	Total Shareholders' Equity		5,000
Total Assets $306,000	Total Liabilities and Owners' Equity		$306,000

On January 1, 1993 (the day the bonds were sold), Rosita Corporation would record the sale of the bonds. Assets (cash) would increase by $300,000, and liabilities (bonds payable) would increase by the same amount. The business equation remains in balance:

$$\text{ASSETS} = \text{LIABILITIES} + \text{OWNERS' EQUITY}$$
$$\$306,000 = \$301,000 + \$5,000$$

As stated earlier, most bonds are issued in denominations of $1,000; Rosita sold 300 of these $1,000 bonds, agreeing to pay 8 percent of the par value per year in interest. Therefore, the nominal rate on the bonds is 8 percent. If other opportunities for investors offer 8 percent per year for using their money, the market interest rate is said to be 8 percent. When the market interest rate and the nominal interest rate are the same, investors are generally indifferent between buying the bonds and choosing other investment opportunities. This indifference results in these bonds being sold at 100, meaning 100 percent of their par value.

Interest payments on corporate bonds are generally paid semiannually (twice each year). In the case of Rosita Corporation, interest would be paid each June 30 and December 31. As we did for the examples of notes payable, we can calculate the annual interest due on the corporate bonds issued by Rosita Corporation:

$$\$300,000 \times .08 = \$24,000$$

This indicates that $24,000 is the annual interest the corporation owes to its bondholders. If interest payments are made every six months, upon each interest payment date, Rosita Corporation would send a total of $12,000 to its bondholders. The semi-annual interest payments are to be made throughout the ten-year life of the bonds. At the end of ten years, Rosita Corporation must pay back the principal amount borrowed, $300,000.

Corporate bonds were developed to address companies' long-term
financing needs. Bonds also facilitate borrowing larger sums of
money than any single lender is either willing or able to handle.
If companies are to have access to large sums of money, there must
be some mechanism to get companies wishing to issue bonds together
with those investors interested in buying them. That mechanism is
the bond market, and it is similar to the stock market.

Initial Offerings — The Primary Bond Market

As was the case with the stock market, there is both a primary bond
market and a secondary bond market. The initial sale of bonds by
the issuing corporation is the focus of the primary bond market.
Most corporations are not equipped to handle the details of the
actual sale of bonds to individual investors. For this reason,
most large bond offerings are made through an intermediary
investment banker, or a group of such bankers called a **syndicate.**
The bankers, serving as **underwriters**, buy all the bonds available
in the offering and then resell them to interested investors at a
higher price. The underwriters' basic fee is known as

> the spread, the difference between the price
> paid to the issuer and the price at which
> securities are sold to the public. . . . In
> debt issues, the price spread typically
> ranges from a low of 0.5 percent to as high
> as 2 percent, with typical spreads in the 1
> percent to 1.5 percent range.
> Logue 1994, p. A2-18

Underwriting is a primary source of income for investment banking firms. A list of the major underwriters is shown below. Many of the firms' names are probably familiar to you.

Top Global Underwriters of Debt and Equity

Source: Securities Data Company, Inc.

Manager	Amount	1992 Market Share	1991 Market Share
Merrill Lynch & Co., Inc.	$ 150.7	13.3%	13.0%
Goldman, Sachs & Co.	119.6	10.6	10.1
Shearson Lehman Brothers Inc.	106.2	9.4	8.3
The First Boston Corporation	98.7	8.7	9.0
Kidder, Peabody & Co. Incorporated	81.0	7.1	6.0
Salomon Brothers Inc.	80.3	7.1	5.8
Morgan Stanley Group Inc.	72.5	6.4	6.9
Bear, Stearns & Co. Inc.	53.4	4.7	3.9
J.P. Morgan Securities Inc.	29.2	2.6	2.0
Prudential Securities Incorporated	28.6	2.5	2.0
Top 10	$ 820.30	72.4%	67.0%
Industry total	$1,133.10	100.0%	100.0%

Note: Dollars in billions.

The underwriter assists the corporation in completing all the necessary steps for a successful bond issue. One of the most important steps in the process is preparation of the **prospectus**. This document provides important information to prospective buyers of the bonds. Information is provided about the issuing corporation, as well as the bond issue itself. The preliminary prospectus is just one of the documents that must be filed with the Securities and Exchange Commission (SEC). This preliminary version of the prospectus contains no selling price information and no offering date. While the SEC is reviewing the documents filed by the corporation, no sale of the bonds may take place. Clearly, the preliminary prospectus does not provide all the information a potential buyer should want. In fact, the actual selling price of the bonds is not determined until the very last minute.

The final selling price of the bonds is a result of negotiations between the underwriter and the corporation. A crucial meeting takes place after SEC approval has been obtained, and often just one day prior to offering the bonds for sale. At that meeting, the final coupon rate and selling price of the bonds is negotiated. Bond selling prices are stated in relation to their par value. That is, if a bond sells below its par value, it is said to be selling at a **discount**. Bonds with prices above par value are said to be selling at a **premium**. Most underwriters hope to have bonds selling for par value, or at a slight discount. Psychologically, it is easier to sell a bond that is priced at or below par value than it is to sell one at a premium. Rarely are new issues sold at a premium.

When the bonds are ready to be sold to the public, the underwriter makes a bond offering, similar to the stock offering discussed in Chapter 4. The offering is announced in business periodicals, such as The Wall Street Journal, and in major newspapers across the country. The announcement includes information about the number of bonds being offered, the denomination of each bond, the interest rate being offered, the term of the bonds (how long before the debt is repaid), and other features of the bonds. If the underwriter has negotiated well, investors will buy the bonds within a few days, and the risk originally taken by the underwriter is eliminated. At that point, the agreement is between the issuing corporation and the investors. Any subsequent trades are part of the secondary bond market.

Interest Rates and the Secondary Bond Market

Once the bonds have been issued, those who purchased them are free to sell the bonds to other investors. There is, then, a secondary bond market, just as there is a secondary stock market, and the process works the same way. After a company initially sells its bonds, it receives no money when those bonds are resold. It needs to be notified, of course, when the bonds pass from one investor to another, because it must know to whom it should send the interest payments and who should receive the repayment amount when the bonds are retired (paid off).

During the life of a bond (20, 30, 40 years), the investment may be traded many times. Remember that the coupon rate was fixed prior to the original sale of the bonds. The market rate of interest, what investors expect as a return on their investments,

fluctuates considerably. For this reason, during the life of a
bond, its price on the secondary market may fluctuate
considerably, as well.

If the investors can get more than 10% interest on their money in
other areas of investment, bonds with a coupon rate of 10% will
trade at a discount. By paying less than the face value for the
bonds, the investor can actually realize a return greater than
the coupon rate. Let's look at an example from an investor's
point of view:

If a $1,000 bond paying 10% interest is bought for par, the
investor has spent $1,000 to receive $100 ($1,000 X 10%) each
year. His annual effective interest rate is 10%. Common sense
may tell you that, but the annual effective interest rate can be
calculated by dividing the annual return on investment by the
invested amount. In this case:

$$\$100 \ / \ \$1,000 = 10\%$$

If the investor is able to buy the bond for only $980 (sale price
is 98), his effective interest rate will be greater than 10%. He
will still receive $100 each year from the corporation that
issued the bonds because the interest paid is based on the coupon
rate. To determine the investor's annual effective interest
rate, we can once again divide the annual return on his

investment by the amount invested:

$$\$100 \ / \ \$980 = 10.2\%$$

Again, it is important to understand that market pressure, and competing opportunities for investors will affect the bond price in the secondary market. Also, be sure to remember that the obligation on the part of the corporation is set by the coupon rate, and is unaffected by the current selling price of the bonds.

Discussion Questions

5-6. Think about the effects of premiums on the effective interest rate. What annual effective interest rate is an investor earning on a $1,000 bond that pays 12.5% interest if he pays 105 to buy it?

5-7. What if an investor with more funds bought $10,000 of the bonds described in the Discussion Question above? What annual effective interest rate would he earn?

The bond market does not receive as much attention from the media as the stock market. Nevertheless, it plays a significant role in the way corporations finance their long-term capital needs. From an investment point of view, the stock market and the bond market offer two distinct choices to potential investors.

EQUITY AND DEBT INVESTMENTS COMPARED

Our presentation of equity and debt financing in this and the preceding chapter was from the standpoint of the company receiving the proceeds from the sale of stocks and bonds. We will now look at the same subject from the standpoint of the investor. Consider the following:

Charlene's Aunt Tillie (whom she had met only once, at a family reunion) recently passed away and left Charlene $1,000,000. (Charlene saved Aunt Tillie's cat from Uncle Fred's pit bull at the reunion.) After all inheritance taxes were paid, Charlene had $750,000 and, upon mature reflection, decided to blow $250,000 on cars, world cruises, and other such extravagant items. She plans to invest the remaining $500,000 on January 2, 1996 and has narrowed the list of possible investments to the following two. Both alternatives involve Fotheringap Corporation, a large company with an impressive track record over the past 35 years.

- Charlene can purchase shares of Fotheringap's no-par common stock. On January 2, 1996, the stock will be selling for about $50 per share, so Charlene would be able to purchase 10,000 shares. Fotheringap has a million shares of common stock outstanding, so Charlene would own only 1 percent of the company.

212

- Charlene can purchase 500 of Fotheringap's $1,000, fiveyear, 8 percent bonds. Interest is to be paid semi-annually on June 30 and December 31. The bonds will be issued on January 2, 1996 and will mature on December 31, 2000. The first interest payment will be made on June 30, 1996.

Does it make more sense for Charlene to buy stock in Fotheringap (equity investment) or to buy the company's corporate bonds (debt investment)? Well, let's see how the two investment alternatives answer the three questions:

1.   Will I be paid?

2.   When will I be paid?

3.   How much will I be paid?

Remember that inherent in these three questions is a consideration of return on the investment and return of the investment.

Equity Investments

Question #1: *Will Charlene be paid?*

There is no way to answer this question with absolute certainty; it is dependent on how Fotheringap performs in the future. If it is a solid company with a good market for its products and/or services, the economy is (and stays) strong, and the industry is (and stays) healthy, Charlene will probably receive both a return on and a return of her investment. She should be aware, however,

213

that with only a 1 percent ownership interest, Charlene will be able to exert little influence on how the company is run.

Question #2: *When will Charlene be paid?*

There is no way to answer this question with absolute certainty, either. Payment on a stock investment is of two types. First, Charlene may receive a periodic dividend on each share of stock she owns. Remember, however, that corporations are not required to pay dividends. Fotheringap may or may not pay dividends to its stockholders. The second form of payment Charlene may receive would be from the sale of the stock she owns. This would be on the secondary stock market and is dependent on whether there are investors willing to buy Fotheringap common stock. In any event, the company itself is under no obligation whatever to return Charlene's $500,000. She has contributed that amount to the company and must find some third person if she desires to sell her shares.

Question #3: *How much will Charlene be paid?*

As with the first two questions, this one cannot be answered with absolute certainty. Before we talk too much about the answer to this question, we need to explain the two components of return on investment for an equity investment:

a.   *Dividends*. This component is pretty easy to understand. Charlene pays $50 for each of the 10,000 shares she buys. If Fotheringap pays an annual dividend of $1.50 per share, Charlene will receive $15,000 (10,000 shares X $1.50). This constitutes a part of the return on her $500,000 investment.

b.   *Stock Appreciation*. In most instances, this component represents the greater part of return on investment. If Fotheringap performs well in the future, the price of each share of its common stock will go up in the secondary stock market. This happens because as the company does well, more and more investors will desire to own its shares of stock. They will, in effect, bid up the price. For example, let's say the company is very profitable and within two years its common stock is selling for $125 per share. If Charlene sells her 10,000 shares, she will have earned a return on investment of $75 per share, a total of $750,000, calculated as follows:

214

	Per Share	Total
What Charlene sold the stock for....	$125	$1,250,000
What Charlene paid for the stock....	50	500,000
Charlene's Return on Investment.....	$ 75	$ 750,000

Something you should note from this example is that when Charlene sold the stock, she received not only a return ON her investment, but also a return OF her investment. Something else you should note is that we talked about this stock appreciation and sale as if it had already happened. As Charlene ponders whether or not to buy the shares of common stock, she has no way of knowing for sure if Fotheringap Corporation will perform well enough to drive the stock price to the level we used (or even if the company will be profitable at all).

In the final analysis, the equity investment alternative is pretty vague in its answers to the three questions. Now let's see how the debt investment alternative answers the same three questions.

Debt Investments

Question #1: *Will Charlene be paid?*

The answer to this first question is essentially the same for the debt investment alternative as it was for the equity investment alternative. That is, it is dependent on how Fotheringap performs in the future. Again, if it is a solid company with a good market for its products and/or services, the economy is (and stays) strong, and the industry is (and stays) healthy, Charlene will probably receive both a return on and a return of her investment.

As a creditor of the company, rather than as a stockholder, Charlene will have absolutely no voice in how Fotheringap conducts its business, so long as it makes the periodic interest payments on the bonds and accumulates a sufficient amount of cash to retire the bonds when they mature.

Charlene must also consider that the investors who purchase the bonds will be paid the periodic interest before any dividends are paid to the investors who purchase the shares of common stock.

Question #2: *When will Charlene be paid?*

Assuming Fotheringap performs well enough to make the interest payments on the bonds and retire them upon maturity, the answer to this question is absolutely certain. Charlene will be paid interest every June 30 and December 31 throughout the life of the bonds. On December 31, 2000, in addition to the final interest payment, Charlene will receive her initial investment back.

Question #3: *How much will Charlene be paid?*

The answer to this question, too, is absolutely certain assuming Fotheringap performs well enough to meet the financial obligations created by issuing the bonds. Over the life of the bonds, Charlene will earn a return on her investment of $200,000 ($20,000 X 10 semi-annual interest payments). On December 31, 2000, she will receive $500,000, which represents the return of her investment.

In the final analysis, if Charlene satisfies herself as to question #1, the answers to the last two questions are very certain for the debt investment alternative.

Which Is Better, Equity Investment Or Debt Investment?

Take a few minutes to ponder the way the two investment alternatives answered the three questions. If you were advising Charlene, which investment would you suggest she make? If you were the one with the $500,000 to invest, which would you choose?

On the surface, it appears to be no contest. While the answer to question #1 was essentially the same for both alternatives, the debt investment alternative is much more certain in its answers to question #2 and question #3 than is the equity investment alternative. So, why would Charlene (or anyone else for that matter) even consider the equity investment as an alternative? There is a one word answer to that question: POTENTIAL!

Although there is risk associated with any investment, equity investments are inherently riskier than debt investments. Along with the additional risk, however, comes the potential for greater reward.

Let's return for a moment to the example of Charlene's two investment alternatives in Fotheringap Corporation. Assume the company has net income each year of $10 million for the next five years. If Charlene chooses the bond alternative she will receive $20,000 interest every six months for five years and then will receive her $500,000 back. But, what if we assume Fotheringap's net income to be $100 million each year for the next five years? How about $1 billion each year? The answer is that it doesn't matter how profitable Fotheringap is, Charlene will only receive the $20,000 every six months, plus the return of her $500,000 when the bonds mature after five years.

If Charlene chooses to buy the 10,000 shares of stock, however, the return on her $500,000 investment will be very different if Fotheringap earns $1 billion profit each year than it will be if the company earns $10 million or $100 million each year. The more profitable the company is, the higher the dividends are likely to be. The market price of the stock in the stock market will almost certainly increase as the company's profits increase, thereby increasing Charlene's return. In other words, the potential associated with the equity investment alternative is theoretically unlimited.

Whether a person chooses an equity investment or a debt investment depends upon how that person feels about the trade-off between the amount of risk involved and the potential reward. The real key to evaluating any investment alternative is reducing the uncertainty surrounding the question: *Will I be paid?* In attempting to predict an alternative's future cash flow potential, economic decision makers must consider the past performance and present condition of that alternative. In Chapters 4 and 5, we have introduced you to the balance sheet, a financial tool that provides information about the present condition of a company. Chapter 6 will introduce you to two additional financial tools — the income statement and the statement of owners' equity.

CHAPTER SUMMARY

Companies often need more funds than they can get from their owners. The other major source of external financing is debt financing — borrowing. Banks earn their profits by charging borrowers interest. Therefore, at agreed upon intervals or when the loan is repaid, the company will pay interest in addition to the original amount borrowed.

If a company makes a bank loan, it incurs a liability — commonly called notes payable — and it receives cash. For short-term financing (5 years or less), loans from commercial banks usually meet the needs of companies.

A company may be required to provide collateral for its loan. If a particular asset is identified in the loan agreement, the note is generally referred to as a mortgage. Bank loans are generally only suitable for short-term financing; if a company needs long-term financing (even as long as 40 years), the alternative is to issue bonds. Bonds are similar to notes payable in that: (1) both are liabilities, and (2) both require repayment of the borrowed amount plus interest. Bonds are issued in set denominations, generally $1,000, and are sold to many different investors. Corporations can issue bonds for very large amounts ($ millions).

Regardless of the type of borrowing involved, the amount of interest being charged can be calculated using:

PRINCIPAL X RATE X TIME = INTEREST

In this calculation, principal refers to the amount owed. The rate refers to the annual interest rate, and the time factor reflects how much of the year is being considered in the situation.

Most corporations do not have the special expertise necessary to complete all the details involved in issuing bonds. Documents must be filed with regulatory agencies, and the actual transactions of issuing bonds to a large number of investors may be quite involved. For this reason, underwriters are often used. These investment bankers, for a fee, will assist the corporation in the details of preparing for the bond issue. Then, the underwriters assume the risk by actually buying the entire bond issue. They will then immediately resell the bonds to individual investors.

The face value or par value of a bond is the principal amount that must be repaid (generally in denominations of $1,000). If a bond is said to be selling at par, it is sold for $1,000. In order to entice investors, bond issuers may have to sell their bonds at a discount (below par value). This occurs when the market rate of interest is higher than the rate paid on the bond.

The buying and selling of bonds is the focus of the bond market. As is the case with the stock market, the bond market consists of activity in both a primary and secondary market. The primary bond market centers its activity around the initial issuance of corporate bonds. In the secondary bond market, the debt investments are traded. If the market rate of interest is lower than the nominal rate, investors will pay a premium (a sale price above par value) on the bonds. Conversely, if the market rate of interest (the return available to investors through other investments) is higher than the rate paid by a bond, that bond will sell below its par value (at a discount).

Activity in the bond market is very similar to that found in the stock market. These two markets represent activity of investors with regards to two different investment alternatives. Investors may purchase bonds (make a debt investment) or purchase stock (make an equity investment). Each type of investment has its own advantages and disadvantages. Debt investment and equity investment were compared in light of the three questions asked by economic decision makers:

1.   Will I be paid?

2.   When will I be paid?

3.   How much will I be paid?

KEY TERMS DEFINED

Bonds. Liabilities that allow corporations to borrow large amounts of funds for long periods of time.

Collateral. Something of value that will be forfeited if a borrower fails to repay a mortgage.

Commercial borrowing. The process that businesses go through to obtain financing.

Consumer borrowing. Loans obtained by individuals to buy homes, cars, or other personal property.

Contract rate. The nominal interest rate stated on a bond.

Coupon rate. Another name for contract rate or nominal interest rate.

Debt financing. Acquiring funds by borrowing. One type of external financing.

Defaulting. Failing to repay a loan as agreed.

Discount. If a bond's selling price is below its par value, the bond is being issued at a discount.

Effective interest rate. The rate of interest actually earned by a bondholder. This amount will be different from the nominal interest rate if the bond is bought at a discount or premium. Also called yield rate and market rate.

Equity financing. Acquiring funds by giving up ownership interest in the company. For a corporation, this means issuing capital stock. This is one type of external financing.

External financing. Aquiring funds from outside the company. Equity and debt financing are the two major types.

Face value. The amount of money borrowed. Also called principal or maturity value.

Indenture. The legal agreement made between a bond issuer and a bondholder. States repayment terms and other details.

Interest. The cost of using someone else's money. Also, what can be earned by lending someone else money.

Internal financing. Providing funds for the operation of a company through the earnings process of that company.

Long-term financing. Any financing in which repayment extends beyond five years. This type of financing supports the long range goals of the company.

Market interest rate. The rate of interest actually earned by bondholders. Also called effective interest rate and yield rate.

Market price. The selling price of a bond. Generally stated as a percentage of the bond's par value.

Maturity value. The amount that is payable upon the maturity of a liability. For bonds, also called face value or par value.

Mortgage. A document that states the agreement between a lender and a borrower who has secured the loan by offering something of value as collateral.

Nominal interest rate. The interest rate set by the issuers of bonds, stated as a percentage of the par value of the bonds. Also called the contract rate, coupon rate, and stated rate.

Note payable. An agreement between a lender and borrower that creates a liability for the borrower.

Par value. The amount that must be paid back upon maturity of a bond. Also called maturity value or face value.

Premium. The amount above the par value for which a bond is sold. Bonds sell at premiums when the nominal rate is above the market rate.

Principal. In the case of notes and mortgages, the amount of funds actually borrowed. In the case of bonds, the amount upon which interest is calculated; the par value.

Prospectus. A description of an upcoming bond issue, provided as information for potential investors.

Selling price. The amount received when bonds are issued. This amount is affected by the difference between the nominal interest rate and the market rate. Selling price is usually stated as a percentage of the bond's par value.

Short-term financing. Financing secured to support an operation's day-to-day activity. Repayment is required within five years.

Stated rate. Same as coupon, contract, and nominal interest rates.

Syndicate. A group of underwriters working together to get a large bond issue sold to the public.

Underwriters. Professionals in the field of investment banking. Most often, they buy an entire bond issue from a corporation at a reduced price, and then immediately resell the bonds to the public.

Yield rate. Same as the effective interest rate and the market rate.

REVIEW THE FACTS

1. Explain the difference between internal and external financing.

2. What are the two major sources of external financing?

3. Contrast consumer borrowing and commercial borrowing.

4. What are the three major types of financial institutions providing financing in the United States today?

5. What is interest?

6. Describe the effects of borrowing on the balance sheet of a business.

7. Explain the formula used to determine the amount of interest owed for a particular time period.

8. What is collateral? How can it help a borrower?

9. What is a mortgage, and how is it different from a note payable?

10. Why are bonds sometimes necessary to meet the borrowing needs of businesses?

11. Explain the terms par value and stated rate as they pertain to bonds.

12. How do the nominal rate and the market rate of bonds differ?

13. What is the relationship between the selling price of a bond and its face value?

14. What is the primary function of underwriters?

15. Explain what causes a bond to sell for either a premium or discount.

16. How do the primary and secondary bond markets differ?

17. Explain the calculation used to determine the annual effective interest rate earned by an investor.

18. On what basis do investors choose between equity investments and debt investments?

Chapter 5
APPLY WHAT YOU HAVE LEARNED

A5-1.   Marty and Barton McDermitt formed M&B ENTERPRISES, INC.
on January 2, 1995. Marty invested $2,000 and received
200 shares of common stock. Barton invested $1,000 and
received 100 shares of common stock. The common stock
has a par value of $2 per share. A balance sheet
prepared immediately after the corporation was formed
was as follows:

M&B ENTERPRISES, INC
Balance Sheet
January 2, 1995

Assets:		Liabilities:		$ -0-
Cash	$3,000	Owners' Equity:		
		Common Stock	$ 600	
Total Assets	$3,000	Additional Paid-in		
		Capital	2,400	
		Total Owners' Equity		3,000
		Total Liabilities		
		& Owners' Equity		$3,000

On January 3, 1995, M&B ENTERPRISES borrowed $10,000 from the
2nd National Bank by signing a one-year, 8% note. The
principal and interest on the note must be paid to the bank
on January 2, 1996. $800

REQUIRED:

a.   Prepare a balance sheet for M&B ENTERPRISES, INC. at
January 3, 1995 to reflect the $10,000 note payable.

b.   Calculate the amount of interest M&B ENTERPRISES must
pay on January 2, 1996.

c.   Think about the three questions all economic decision
makers are trying to answer (Will I?; When?; How much?).
Assuming the bank has satisfied itself as to the first
question, what are the answers to the 2nd and 3rd
questions regarding the loan to M&B?

A5-2.   Assume the same facts as Application 5-1 (above), except that the note was for three months rather than one year, so it must be repaid on April 2, 1995.

REQUIRED:

a.   Prepare a balance sheet for M&B ENTERPRISES, INC. at January 3, 1995 to reflect the $10,000 note payable.

b.   Calculate the amount of interest M&B ENTERPRISES must pay on April 2, 1995.

c.   Think about the three questions all economic decision makers are trying to answer (Will I?; When?; How much?). Assuming the bank has satisfied itself as to the first question, what are the answers to the 2nd and 3rd questions regarding the loan to M&B?

A5-3.   Marty and Barton McDermitt formed M&B ENTERPRISES, INC.
on January 2, 1995. Marty invested $2,000 and received
200 shares of common stock. Barton invested $1,000 and
received 100 shares of common stock. The common stock
has a par value of $2 per share. A balance sheet
prepared immediately after the corporation was formed
was as follows:

M&B ENTERPRISES, INC
Balance Sheet
January 2, 1995

Assets: Liabilities: $ -0-

  Cash $3,000   Owners' Equity:
                                 Common Stock $ 600
Total Assets $3,000   Additional Paid-in
                                   Capital   2,400
                                 Total Owners' Equity   3,000

                                 Total Liabilities
                                 & Owners' Equity $3,000

On January 3, 1995, M&B ENTERPRISES sold 100 of its $1,000,
five year, 10% bonds. Interest is to be paid semi-annually
on June 2 and January 2. The bonds mature (must be repaid)
on January 2, 2000.

REQUIRED:

a.   Prepare a balance sheet for M&B ENTERPRISES, INC. at
     January 3, 1995 to reflect the sale of the bonds,
     assuming they sold at their par value.

b.   Calculate the amount of interest M&B must pay each June
     2 and January 2.

c.   How much would M&B ENTERPRISES, INC. have received from
     the sale of the bonds on January 3, 1995, assuming they
     sold at 98 (a discount).

d.   How much would M&B ENTERPRISES, INC. have received from
     the sale of the bonds on January 3, 1995, assuming they
     sold at 103 (a premium)?

231

A5-4.   Presented below are some items related to notes payable and bonds payable followed by definitions of those items in a scrambled order:

a. Interest.
b. Nominal interest rate.
c. Effective interest rate.
d. Maturity value.
e. Discount.
f. Premium.
g. Principal.
h. Defaulting.
i. Note payable.
j. Bond payable.

1. ____ The amount above par value for which a bond payable is sold.

2. ____ The amount of funds actually borrowed.

3. ____ The rate of interest actually earned by a bondholder.

4. ____ Failing to repay a loan as agreed.

5. ____ Liabilities that allow corporations to borrow large amounts of money for long periods of time.

6. ____ The cost of using someone else's money.

7. ____ The amount below par value for which a bond payable is sold.

8. ____ An agreement between a lender (usually a bank) and borrower that creates a liability for the borrower.

9. ____ The interest rate set by the issuers of bonds, stated as a percentage of the par value of the bonds.

10. ____ The amount that is payable at the end of a borrowing arrangement.

REQUIRED:

Match the letter next to each item on the list with the appropriate definition. Each letter will be used only once.

A5-5. Assume a five-year, $1,000 bond paying 8% interest is bought for $970 (sale price is 97).

REQUIRED:

a. How much cash will the person buying the bond receive each year as interest?

b. Calculate the effective interest rate on the $1,000 bond.

A5-6. Assume a five-year, $1,000 bond paying 9% interest is bought for $960 (sale price is 96).

REQUIRED:

a. How much cash will the person buying the bond receive each year as interest?

b. Calculate the effective interest rate on the $1,000 bond.

c. Calculate the return on investment and the return of investment over the life of the bond.

CHAPTER 6

TOOLS OF THE TRADE PART II — INCOME STATEMENT AND
STATEMENT OF OWNERS' EQUITY

In Chapters 4 and 5, you were introduced to the first financial tool — the balance sheet. This financial statement provides information that helps economic decision makers evaluate the present condition of a company. The balance sheet tells what the company owns (assets), what the company owes (liabilities), and what claim the owners have to the remaining resources (owners' equity). This picture of the financial position of a company is an important item of information. It is *not*, however, enough information to support the decision making process.

In order for economic decision makers to make wise decisions, they must gather all the necessary information to assess the future timing and amounts of cash flows. Economic decision makers rely on several financial tools to provide all pieces of the "information puzzle". Accurate prediction of the future performance of a company depends on quality assessment of both the present condition and the past performance of the firm.

We have seen that the balance sheet provides information pertaining to a company's present condition. However, to assess the past performance of a company, decision makers rely on another financial tool — the **income statement**. The income statement provides information about the business activities of a company during a particular period.

In addition to introducing the income statement, material presented in this chapter will introduce you to one other financial tool — the **statement of owners' equity**. This third financial statement provides a bridge between the information provided by the income statement and that provided by the balance sheet.

After completing your work on this chapter, you will have explored three financial statements. Remember that these are provided as tools for economic decision makers. The importance of these statements lies in their usefulness and contribution to the decision making process. When you have completed your work on this chapter, you will be able to:

1. Describe in your own words how the income statement provides information about the past performance of a business.

2. Distinguish between single-step and multi-step income statements.

3. Explain the impact of net income or net loss on owners' equity.

4. Construct statements of capital for proprietorships and partnerships.

5. Identify the differences between statements of stockholders' equity and statements of retained earnings for corporations.

6. Compare and contrast the impact of drawings on statements of capital and the impact of dividends on statements of stockholders' equity and statements of retained earnings.

7. Explain why dividends are paid and under what circumstances they can be paid.

8. Describe in your own words the articulation of income statements, balance sheets, and statements of owners' equity.

INTRODUCTION TO THE INCOME STATEMENT

The income statement is a financial tool that provides information about a company's past performance. Recall that the balance sheet, the previous financial tool we have seen, is comprised of assets, liabilities, and owners' equity, which are accounting elements as described by the FASB in the Statements of Accounting Concepts. The income statement is also comprised of accounting elements. The italicized definitions below are those provided by the Financial Accounting Standards Board. A less formal definition of each element follows the words of the FASB.

1. **Revenues.** *Inflows of assets to an entity from delivering or producing goods, rendering services, or carrying out other activities.* Revenue represents what a company's customers pay for its goods or services. Revenues are the reward of doing business.

2. **Expenses.** *Outflows or other using up of assets from delivering or producing goods, rendering services, or carrying out other activities.* Expenses are the sacrifices required to attain revenues.

The difference between the rewards (revenues) and the sacrifices (expenses) for a given period of activity is the net reward of doing business, which we call **net income.** Accountants also call net income **earnings, net earnings,** or **profit.** If the expenses for the period are greater than the revenues for the period, the result is a **net loss.** The relationship between revenues, expenses, and either net income or net loss can be represented by the following equation:

REVENUES - EXPENSES = NET INCOME (or NET LOSS)

As was the case with the balance sheet equation, you should memorize the income statement equation, because we will deal with

237

it over and over again. Once again, however, a simple rote memorization will not suffice. You must understand the meaning of the equation in order to understand the income statement.

Discussion Question

6-1. Identify the transactions in your personal finances during the last month. Which transactions resulted in revenues and which resulted in expenses?

6-2. Use the equation above, and your responses to Discussion Question 6-1 to determine if you had a net income or net loss for the month.

Construction of the Income Statement

The basic format of an income statement is:

```
                    Rosita's Business
                    Income Statement
           For the Year Ending December 31, 1993


        Revenues:
                XXX
                 XX
                 XX
        Total Revenues:        XXXX

        Expenses:
                 XX
                 XX
                 XX
                  X
                  X
        Total Expenses:         XXX

                Net Income       XX
```

The heading for an income statement must include the name of the business, the name of the statement, and the *period* for which activity is being reported. As you will recall, the heading for the balance sheet must include the precise date for which the information is being presented. If the balance sheet is, as we said, a snapshot of a business at a particular point in time, then the income statement is something of a "home movie" of a company for a *period of time* (usually a month, quarter, or year). For that reason, the heading includes the period of time described — not just a single date. The income statement says that during this specific time period, the company earned so much revenue, incurred so much expense, and produced either a net income or net loss, depending on whether the revenues were greater than the expenses or vice versa. Income statements may be produced annually, quarterly, monthly, or at whatever interval necessary to provide useful accounting information.

The term "income statement" is only a nickname, and, as was the case with the term "balance sheet," it is not too descriptive of the statement's purpose. The statement's formal name is the **Statement of Results of Operations**, which is a far better description of its function. It is also sometimes called the **Statement of Earnings**. However, the informal title, income statement, is still more widely used than the others. The authors of Accounting Trends and Techniques report that of 600 companies surveyed, about half of them used "income" as a key word in the headings of their 1992 financial statements. However, when these statements showed a net loss, the title "Statement of Operations" was frequently chosen. When a net loss must be shown, the title "Income Statement" does seem a bit out of place.

Notice that the basic format of the income statement illustrated above suggests that a company may have more than one type of revenue. Revenues are the inflows of the company, and these inflows may come from a variety of earnings activities. A business may be a service organization, producing service revenues, often called professional fees. Law firms, lawn service companies, and accounting firms are examples of service organizations. If a business is involved in merchandising or manufacturing, its major revenue will be sales of tangible units of product.

Discussion Question

6-3. Which of the following companies would you classify as merchandisers? Which are manufacturers? Which are service organizations?

a. General Motors

b. Exxon

c. Walmart

d. Taco Bell

e. Prudential Insurance

f. B. Dalton Bookstores

In addition to the revenues produced from its major operations, a company may produce revenues through other activities. For example, it may rent out portions of the office building it owns. That activity would produce rent revenue. If the company has invested some of its cash, interest revenue may be produced.

The income statement format above also allows for several different types of expenses. Expenses are the outflows of the company, and they, too, may take many different forms. For example, if a company has employees, the income statement will show salaries or wages expense. If a company is responsible for maintaining vehicles, the income statement may show gas expense and/or maintenance expense, or if the building used by a company is not owned by them, the company may have rent expense. These are just a few examples of the numerous expenses a company might face.

Discussion Question

6-4. Some items could be in either the revenue or expense category (e.g., interest, rent). If you were in charge of keeping track of a company's revenues and expenses, describe how you would know if "rent" or "interest" were a revenue or expense.

Merchandising operations and manufacturers sell goods for their primary revenue. Costs associated with these goods are the primary expense. This expense is called **cost of goods sold**. For many companies, cost of goods sold is the major expense of doing business. This expense is **also called cost of sales** or **cost of products sold**.

Single-step Format of the Income Statement

In the basic form of the income statement, all revenues are added to provide "total revenues," and all expenses are added together to create "total expenses." This format is called the **single-step income statement** because in one step, total expenses are subtracted from total revenues to determine net income (or net loss).

We can use Rosita's Business to illustrate the single-step format of the income statement. Assume that Rosita's Business had $2690 in sales revenue and $990 in rent revenue during 1993. Also assume that the company's expenses for the period were $955 for cost of goods sold, $675 for wages, $310 for utilities, and $120 for interest payments. Based on that information, the company's 1993 income statement, prepared in a single-step format, would be:

243

```
                    Rosita's Business
               Income Statement (Single-step)
            For the Year Ending December 31, 1993

        Revenues:
            Sales                   $2690
            Rent Revenue              990
            Total Revenues:                    $3,680

        Expenses:
            Cost of goods sold  $ 955
            Wages Expense         675
            Utilities Expense     310
            Interest Expense      120
            Total Expenses:                     2,060
                    Net Income                 $1,620
```

Unlike the balance sheet, the income statement is not directly
affected by the type of business organization involved. Income
statements for proprietorships, partnerships, and corporations all
take the same general form. The only difference is in the name of
the company included in the heading of the statement. Companies
do, however, have the option of using either of the basic formats;
they may choose to present a **multi-step income statement** or one
using the single-step format.

Multi-step Format of the Income Statement

The multi-step income statement provides two items of information
not presented when a single-step format is used: (1) **gross margin
or gross profit**, and (2) **operating income or income from
operations**. Each of these items is discussed in detail below. The
"bottom line", net income, is not affected by the choice of format.
However, what information is provided within the income statement

is different. The single-step income statement format gathers all revenues together to form total revenues. All expenses are gathered together to form total expenses. No special treatment is given to any specific revenue or expense. On the other hand, the multi-step format highlights relationships among various items of accounting information.

Gross margin is one piece of information not shown on a single-step income statement. This item highlights the relationship between sales revenue and cost of goods sold. **Sales revenue** (often **referred to simply as sales**) is the revenue produced by the primary activity of the firm, which for a merchandiser or manufacturer comes from selling tangible units of product. Cost of goods sold is the cost of the tangible units of product sold and is very often the largest expense relating to sales. The difference between sales revenue and cost of goods sold is called gross margin or gross profit.

For example, sales of running shoes is the revenue produced by Nike, Inc. Cost of goods sold is the cost of the shoes. The difference between these amounts represents Nike's gross margin.

6-6. Focus on the example of Nike, Inc. What
specific costs are included in the cost of
goods sold related to the running shoes?

6-7. Identify two additional companies. Describe
the source of their sales revenues and the
components of their costs of goods sold.

A merchandiser or manufacturer cannot possibly be profitable unless it sells its product for more than what it paid for that product. Gross margin represents how much more a company received from the sale of its products than what the products cost the company. It also represents the amount available from sales to cover all other expenses the company has. For example, assume Magill Company (a merchandiser) sells its product for $20 per unit. Each unit of product costs Magill $14. If the company sold 5,000 units of product in January, it would have a gross margin of $30,000 calculated as follows:

```
Sales (5,000 X $20)                            $100,000
Less: Cost of goods sold (5,000 X $14)           70,000
Gross margin                                    $ 30,000
```

This $30,000 is what Magill has remaining from sales to cover all the other expenses of the company for the month of January. Assuming the company had no revenues other than sales, if those other expenses were less than $30,000, the company had a net income for the month; if they were greater than $30,000, the company experienced a net loss. Economic decision makers frequently use gross margin in evaluating the performance of a manufacturing or merchandising company. Examining gross margin allows financial statement readers to quickly see the relationship among revenue produced by selling product, the cost of the product, and all the other expenses the company incurs.

Discussion Question

6-8. Consider the following simplified multi-step income statement for Early Company:

```
                        $275
Sales (1,000 units)...... $275,000
Less: Cost of goods sold..(280,000)
      Gross margin........($ 5,000)
Less: Other expenses......( 42,000)
      Net income (loss)....($47,000)
```

a. What can you learn about Early Company from the gross margin?

b. How many units must the company sell in order to earn a profit?

In addition to highlighting the relationship between sales and cost of goods sold, the multi-step income statement separates income generated from the ongoing major activity of the firm from the revenues and expenses produced by other business activity. Operating income or income from operations denotes the results of the merchandising or manufacturing activity that is the company's primary business activity. This income can be expected to continue, while some of the revenues and expenses associated with secondary activities of the company may not be repeated. When economic decision makers are attempting to use the past performance of a company as presented on the income statement to predict the future, operating income may be more useful than final net income as an indicator of performance. Therefore, multi-step income statements, which show both net income and operating income, may often be more useful to users of accounting information than single-step income statements, which show only net income.

An example of Rosita's income statement for 1993, using a multi-step format is provided below:

```
                      Rosita's Business
                  Income Statement (Multi-step)
               For the Year Ending December 31, 1993

   Sales                    $2690
      Less:
   Cost of goods sold        955
        Gross Margin                  $1735
   Wages Expense          $675
   Utilities Expense       310
        Total operating expenses 985

   Operating Income                   $ 750
   Other revenues:
           Rent Revenue              990
   Other expenses:
           Interest Expense         (120)

           Net Income               $1620
```

Notice that the net income reported is the same as that shown earlier, using the single-step format. The multi-step format makes two important stops before arriving at the "bottom line". Gross margin and operating income are the steps along the way; thus, the term multi-step.

Net Income as an Increase in Owners' Equity

Net income represents an increase in the owners' interest in the business. As you'll recall from our discussion of the elements found in a balance sheet, one of the two sources of owners' equity is earned equity. Earned equity is directly affected by net income because each revenue is an asset received (increasing earned equity) and each expense is an asset sacrificed (decreasing earned equity). A net profit, therefore, increases earned equity, while a net loss decreases earned equity.

If a company's earned equity increases, it follows that its owners' equity also increases. Net income, or profit, is thus a particular period's addition to the owners' equity in the company and links the information on the income statement with the information on the balance sheet. This link is very logical when you realize that the past performance of a company is at least partially responsible for the present condition of that company.

INTRODUCTION TO THE STATEMENT OF OWNERS' EQUITY

Some companies prepare only an income statement and balance sheet. There is a third financial statement, however, which is actually a "bridge statement" showing how the income statement and balance sheet are related. It is called the statement of owners' equity. Basically, this statement shows how the owners' equity, as shown on the balance sheet, moved from its balance at the beginning of the period to its balance at the end of the period. Although the specifics of the statement vary depending on the organizational form of the company, the basic format of this financial statement is:

```
                    Rosita's Business
                 Statement of Owners' Equity
           For the Year Ending December 31, 1993

        Beginning Owners' Equity         XXX
            ADD: Net Income                X
        Ending balance in Owners' Equity        XXX
```

Proprietorships — Statement of Capital

Depending on the form of a business, earned equity can go by various names. For proprietorships and partnerships there is usually not a distinction made between the equity from owners' investment and earned equity. Because those forms of business are legally considered to be extensions of the owner or owners, the two types of equity are normally lumped together under the title owners' equity or owners' capital; the statement of owners' equity is generally called the statement of capital. The format of a statement of owners' equity prepared for a proprietorship, then, would be:

```
                    Rosita's Business
                  Statement of Capital
           For the Year Ending December 31, 1993

        Rosita, Capital  January 1, 1993   $5,000
            ADD: Net Income                 1,620
        Rosita, Capital  December 31, 1993           $6,620
```

You should notice from the heading that, like the income statement, the statement of owners' equity deals with activity during a particular time period. For this reason, the heading of a statement of owners' equity includes the designation of the time period covered rather than just a specific date. The beginning balance used in this statement would actually be the ending balance from the previous period. The net income amount would be drawn directly from the income statement, and the ending balance would be calculated as shown. This ending balance appears not only on the statement of capital, but in the owners' equity section of the balance sheet, as well. We referred to the statement of owners' equity earlier as a bridge statement because it uses the net income figure from the income statement for the period and shows the calculation of the ending owners' equity amount shown on the balance sheet.

Partnerships — Statement of Capital

A similar statement produced for a partnership would follow the same general outline. Of course, there would be a capital balance for each partner, and the net income for the period ($1,620) would be shared by the partners according to the rules stated in their partnership agreement. Using Rosita and Caroline as an example, a statement of capital for this type of business form would look like this:

```
               Rosita and Caroline's Business
                     Statement of Capital
             For the Year Ending December 31, 1993

          Rosita, Capital  January 1, 1993   $3,000
               ADD: Net Income                  972
          Rosita, Capital  December 31, 1993           $3,972

          Caroline, Capital  January 1, 1993 $2,000
               ADD: Net Income                  648
          Caroline, Capital  December 31, 1993          2,648
               Total Capital, December 31, 1993       $6,620
```

The example above assumes that the partners, Rosita and Caroline, have agreed to share the net income in the same proportion as their initial investments. Rosita's capital balance would be increased by 60 percent of the total net income for the period, and Caroline's capital balance would increase by 40 percent of the net income.

Corporations — Statement of Stockholders' Equity

Because a corporation is a legal entity separate from its owner or owners, there are legal requirements to keep the equity from owners' investment and earned equity separated. In corporations, the investment by owners is called contributed capital, and earned equity is called retained earnings. A statement providing information about a corporation would use a format similar to the following:

Rosita Corporation
Statement of Stockholders' Equity
For the Year Ending December 31, 1993

	Common Stock	Additional Paid-in Capital	Retained Earnings	Total Stockholders' Equity
Balance, January 1	$1,000	$4,000	$ 0	$5,000
Net income			1,620	1,620
Balance, December 31	$1,000	$4,000	$1,620	$6,620

Again, the beginning balances would be the previous period's ending balances, the net income figure would come from the income statement, and the ending balance would be calculated as shown. Note that the statement of stockholders' equity reflects activity in both parts of total owners' equity — contributed capital and earned equity. Common stock and additional paid-in capital are components of contributed capital; retained earnings represents the earned equity portion of stockholders' equity. The four totals at the bottom of the statement of stockholders' equity would all be shown in the stockholders' equity section of the balance sheet prepared at the end of the period.

If additional shares of stock had been issued during 1993, the activity would have been reported in the contributed capital section of Rosita's statement of stockholders' equity. The activity in retained earnings is not affected by such changes in the contributed capital sections. The amount of retained earnings is increased by net income each period and decreased by net loss.

Thus, if the beginning balance of retained earnings was 0, it can be assumed that this statement describes activity during the first year of operations for the company. In addition to the effects of net income and net loss, owners' equity is affected by the distribution of assets to the owners.

Discussion Question

6-9. How would it be possible for Rosita Corporation to have a zero balance in retained earnings on January 1, 1993 if 1993 were not the company's first year of business?

DISTRIBUTIONS TO OWNERS

As time goes by, if the operations of a company are successful, owners' equity will increase. Eventually, the owner, or owners, will expect some type of distribution of this equity. Just as net income increases owners' equity, distributions to owners decrease owners' equity.

Do not interpret distributions to owners as being some sort of salary paid to the owners. These distributions are not considered expenses of the company and are not shown on the income statement.

Rather, they are payments to owners, representing a return on the investment they have made. Distributions to owners are handled in different ways, depending on the organizational form of the company. However, in each case, these distributions reduce total owners' equity.

Drawings — Proprietorships and Partnerships

In the case of a proprietorship, there is very little to restrict the owner from taking funds out of the company. If the cash is there, the owner may take it for his or her personal use. In this case, the distributions to the owner are called **drawings** or **withdrawals**. If Rosita chose to take $500 in cash from her proprietorship, the drawing would be reflected on the statement of capital as follows:

```
                    Rosita's Business
                   Statement of Capital
            For the Year Ending December 31, 1993

        Rosita, Capital  January 1, 1993    $5,000
             ADD: Net Income                  1,620
                                             $6,620
                  LESS: Drawings                500
        Rosita, Capital  December 31, 1993   $6,120
```

Partnership agreements may state explicitly when and in what amounts partners may take drawings or withdrawals. Clearly, the partnership must have sufficient cash to support the actions of its owners. If a partner has the opportunity to make a withdrawal of

256

cash from the company, he or she must also consider the impact of the action on his or her capital account. Using the partnership of Rosita and Caroline, let's examine the impact of a withdrawal made by only one of the partners. Assume that Caroline has found herself in a bit of a cash bind in her personal finances. If there is no restriction within the partnership agreement and there is sufficient cash on hand, Caroline may make a withdrawal of $500. This action would reduce her capital account and the total amount of owners' equity, but would have no impact on Rosita's capital balance. The resulting statement of capital for the partnership would be:

```
                 Rosita and Caroline's Business
                       Statement of Capital
                For the Year Ending December 31, 1993

        Rosita, Capital  January 1, 1993   $3,000
            ADD: Net Income                    972
        Rosita, Capital  December 31, 1993            $3,972

        Caroline, Capital  January 1, 1993 $2,000
            ADD: Net Income                    648
                                           $2,648
            LESS: Drawings                     500
        Caroline, Capital  December 31, 1993            2,148
                Total Capital, December 31, 1993       $6,120
```

Distributions to Owners — Corporate Form

Distributions to owners in a corporate setting are called **dividends**. Owners of corporations (shareholders) have much less control over when and in what amount they receive a distribution than do owners of a proprietorship or partnership. This is

257

particularly true in large corporations. Although they are not legally required to, virtually all corporations pay dividends at some point in their existence.

Why do corporations pay dividends if they are not legally required to do so? The reason is that in the long run, investors (those who buy the corporation's stock) demand it. There are a number of factors causing a company's stock to either go up or go down in value, but probably the most important is whether the company is profitable. That profitability is best demonstrated by the payment of dividends. If a corporation is profitable, it may periodically (usually every three months) pay a dividend to its stockholders as a demonstration of its ability and willingness to reward the stockholders for investing in the company.

If a corporation is not profitable and cannot pay dividends, or for some reason does not pay dividends even when it is profitable, investors and potential investors become nervous or unhappy at the lack of return on their investment. The demand for shares of that company's stock then declines, and the price falls. When this happens, the corporation may find it difficult to obtain funds necessary to support operations. Opportunities for both major types of external funding — issuing stock and borrowing funds — may disappear. Eventually, if enough people lose faith in the company, it will run out of cash and cease to exist.

All decisions associated with dividends are made by the corporation's board of directors. These decisions include whether or not to pay a dividend, the type of dividend to be paid, and when the dividend will be paid. Companies can choose to distribute additonal shares of their stock as a dividend. It is, however, much more common for companies to distribute cash dividends. Of the 600 companies surveyed by <u>Accounting Trends and Techniques</u>, 75 percent issued a cash dividend in 1992.

Cash dividends on common stock

A cash dividend is what most of us think of when we hear the word "dividend." In order to be able to pay a cash dividend, a corporation must possess two things: sufficient retained earnings and sufficient cash.

1. *Sufficient Retained Earnings.* Dividends are distributions of earnings; however, corporations are not restricted to the current year's earnings to cover the distribution. While it may be desirable for a company to pay dividends out of the current year's earnings, dividends are actually paid out of retained earnings. Remember that net income is only this period's addition to retained earnings, thus it is not necessary that current net income be greater than the dividend amount. The real requirement is that there be a sufficient balance in retained earnings to cover the dividend.

Retained earnings represents the portion of a corporation's earnings that has not been distributed to the owners in the form of dividends. A more descriptive name might be reinvested earnings, because it is the portion of total corporate earnings reinvested

259

(plowed back) into the company. This portion may have gone to purchase new plant and equipment, inventory, and other items necessary for the continued operation of the company. The table below shows how retained earnings are created over time and how they are affected by net income, losses, and dividends.

	1991	1992	1993	1994	1995
Beginning Balance	$ -0-	$ 800	$1,300	$ 700	$1,150
Net Income/(Loss)	800	1,000	(100)	950	400
Dividends	-0-	(500)	(500)	(500)	(500)
Ending Balance	$ 800	$1,300	$ 700	$1,150	$1,050

There are two things you should note as you look at this table. First, the ending balance of one period (in this case, a year) becomes the beginning balance of the next period. Second, the payment of dividends is not directly related to profits in a given period. In 1993, this company paid dividends even though it experienced a net loss for the year, and in 1995 it paid out more in dividends than it earned for the year. This company appears to have adopted a policy of paying $500 per year in total dividends, regardless of the net income or loss for a particular year. This policy is perfectly acceptable, as long as the company has both sufficient retained earnings and sufficient cash each year to cover the dividend amount.

2.   *Sufficient Cash*. Retained earnings is not cash. It is simply an amount representing all the profits a corporation has not yet distributed to its owners in the form of dividends. In general, the amount of retained earnings a corporation has and the amount of cash it has at a given time will be different. A corporation must make certain it has sufficient cash to pay

260

the dividend. Some companies feel it so important to pay a regular cash dividend that they will actually borrow money if they have insufficient cash to cover their usual dividend amount.

The Rosita Corporation, from our previous example, has sufficient retained earnings and sufficient cash to pay a dividend to its shareholders. Recall that the corporation has 1000 shares of $1 par value common stock outstanding. If the corporation declared a $.50 per share dividend, the total dividend amount would be $500. In a sense, this is very similar to the $500 owner withdrawal in the proprietorship and partnership examples. However, remember that corporate owners' equity is divided between contributed capital and retained earnings. The funds received from the sale of ownership interests in the corporation are reflected in the stock and additional paid-in capital accounts. These funds are considered contributed capital and they do NOT increase retained earnings. The dividends are a reduction of retained earnings; thus the Rosita Corporation's statement of stockholders' equity after the payment of a $500 dividend is:

Rosita Corporation
Statement of Stockholders' Equity
For the Year Ending December 31, 1993

	Common Stock	Additional Paid-in Capital	Retained Earnings	Total Stockholders' Equity
Balance, January 1	$1,000	$4,000	$ 0	$5,000
Net income			1,620	1,620
Dividends			(500)	(500)
Balance, December 31	$1,000	$4,000	$1,120	$6,120

261

Notice that once again, the only section of stockholders' equity to reflect the results of activity is retained earnings. Both net income and dividends change the balance in retained earnings, but neither affects any portion of contributed capital.

Statement of retained earnings

If a corporation has not issued stock or engaged in any other activity that would affect contributed capital, it may issue a **statement of retained earnings** instead of the more comprehensive statement of stockholders' equity. A statement of retained earnings is very similar in form to the statement of capital for proprietorships and partnerships. An example of Rosita Corporation's statement of retained earnings is:

Rosita Corporation
Statement of Retained Earnings
For the Year Ending December 31, 1993

Retained Earnings January 1, 1993	$ 0
ADD: Net Income	1,620
	$1,620
LESS: Dividends	500
Retained Earnings December 31, 1993	$1,120

This simpler statement is an acceptable substitute for the statement of stockholders' equity if no changes have been made in a corporation's contributed capital. However, because most corporations are frequently involved in activities affecting their stock accounts or other parts of their contributed capital, the statement of stockholders' equity is more widely used than the statement of retained earnings. Of the 600 companies surveyed in Accounting Trends and Techniques, 80 percent used the statement of stockholders' equity in 1992. Only 13 percent of the corporations presented a statement of retained earnings. The remaining group chose not to present either form of this "bridge statement".

Dividend dates

The ownership shares of most large corporations are held by many different people, and those shares of stock trade hands constantly. Because their shares of stock are widely traded, most corporations do not know exactly who their stockholders are on a given day. For this reason, most corporations do not declare and pay a dividend on the same day. Three important dates are associated with the payment of a cash dividend:

1. **Date of Declaration.** As stated earlier, the board of directors decides if and when a cash dividend is to be paid. The day the board votes to pay a dividend is known as the date of declaration. The date of declaration marks the creation of a legal liability for the corporation.

2. **Date of Record.** Whoever owns shares of stock on this date will receive the dividend. This date may follow the date of declaration by several weeks. Every time a company's stock changes hands, the company is notified, but that notification, especially in large corporations, may take several days or even weeks.

3. **Date of Payment.** This is the date the dividend is actually paid. Payment of the dividend is made to whomever owned shares of stock on the date of record, even though some of

263

those people have sold their shares of stock between the date of record and the date of payment. When the cash dividend is paid, the liability for the dividend is removed from the records of the company.

Generally, when the board of directors declares a dividend, the date of record and the date of payment are announced.

Cash dividends on preferred stock

The procedures associated with the payment of dividends on preferred stock are exactly the same as those for common stock. The distinctions between these two classes of stock are based on the preference features of preferred stock. As discussed in an earlier chapter, one of those preferences involves dividends. If a corporation has preferred stock and elects to pay dividends, the preferred stockholders receive their dividend before the common stockholders can be paid.

6-10. As you listened to a broadcast of consumer
news on public radio, you heard an angry
consumer advocate, Ms. Nadia Ralphino, accuse
large corporations of taking advantage of the
small stockholder. As part of her angry
attack, she cited the following example:

Mega-Millions, Incorporated pays only $.62
per share dividend each year on its common
stock, even though its retained earnings
balance is now in excess of $7 billion.

She then accused Mega-Millions of hoarding
profits. How would you respond to Ms.
Ralphino's accusation if you were the
spokesperson for Mega-Millions, Incorporated?

ARTICULATION

Earlier in this chapter, we referred to the link between income and owners' equity. This link is an example of what is called **articulation** of the financial statements. The three financial statements we have discussed thus far are definitely linked. This linkage, or articulation, is an important concept for you to understand. The income statement tells the story of this period's earnings activity, and the balance sheet presents a picture of the current financial position. The third statement we introduced, the statement of owners' equity, provides a bridge between the two. Now, let's take a closer look at how the three tools we have learned about thus far fit together.

Financial Statements of a Proprietorship

For a proprietorship, the set of statements would as follows:

Rosita's Business
Income Statement
For the Year Ending December 31, 1993

Sales		$2690↓
Less:		
Cost of goods sold	955	
Gross Margin		$1735 ↓
Wages Expense	675	
Utilities Expense	310	
Total operating expenses	985	
Operating Income		$ 750 ↓
Other revenues:		
Rent Revenue	990	
Other expenses:		
Interest Expense	(120)	
Net Income		$1620 ↓

Rosita's Business
Statement of Capital
For the Year Ending December 31, 1993

Rosita, Capital January 1, 1993	$5,000
ADD: Net Income	1,620 ←
	$6,620 ↓
LESS: Drawings	500
Rosita, Capital December 31, 1993	$6,120 ↓

Rosita's Business
Balance Sheet
December 31, 1993

Assets:		Liabilities:	
		Notes Payable	$1,000
Cash $7,120↓			
		Owners' Equity:	
		Rosita, Capital	6,120 ←
Total Assets	$7,120↓	Total Liabilities and Owners' Equity	$7,120↓

$$A = L + OE$$

$$\$7,120 = \$1,000 + \$6,120$$

The statements above offer a visual representation of articulation. The arrows connecting items from the three financial statements show the relationships that should always exist. Net income is calculated on the income statement and used on the statement of capital. The ending balance shown on the statement of capital is used on the balance sheet. The illustration of the accounting equation below the statement shows that this important relationship still holds true.

This presentation includes a very simplistic form of each statement. Notice that the business has only one asset — cash. This presumes that all activity recorded in these statements involved cash. If only life really WERE so simple. Make sure you know how to use the information provided on this simple set of statements before we move on to investigate tougher and more complex sets of statements. Also, be sure you can explain in your own words how the information provided on each statement is affected by that which is shown on the others.

Discussion Question

6-11. If a clerk in Rosita's business decided to slip the cash from a sale into his pocket and not record the sale at all, how would each of the statements above be affected?

Financial Statements of a Partnership

By now it should be clear to you that the formats of the financial statements of partnerships are only slightly different than the ones presented above for a proprietorship. However, in order to provide a complete set of examples, the articulated statements of Rosita and Caroline's business are presented next:

                 Rosita and Caroline's Business
                        Income Statement
              For the Year Ending December 31, 1993

    Sales $2690
       Less:
    Cost of goods sold 955
          Gross Margin $1735
    Wages Expense   675
    Utilities Expense   310
          Total operating expenses 985

    Operating Income $ 750
    Other revenues:
          Rent Revenue   990
    Other expenses:
             Interest Expense (120)

          Net Income $1620 ─────────────┐
                                                 │
                                                 │
                  Rosita and Caroline's Business │
                        Statement of Capital   │
              For the Year Ending December 31, 1993
                                                 │
                                                 │
       Rosita, Capital January 1, 1993 $3,000 │
          ADD: Net Income   972 ←┤
       Rosita, Capital December 31, 1993   │ $3,972
                                                 │
       Caroline, Capital January 1, 1993 $2,000 │
          ADD: Net Income   648 ←┘
                                         $2,648
          LESS: Drawings   500
       Caroline, Capital December 31, 1993   2,148
             Total Capital, December 31, 1993 $6,120 ──┐
                                                            │
                                                            │
                  Rosita and Caroline's Business   │
                        Balance Sheet   │
                      December 31, 1993   │

Assets: Liabilities: │
                                  Notes Payable $1,000 │
    Cash $7,120   │
                               Owners' Equity: │
                                  Rosita, Capital $3,972   │
                                  Caroline, Capital 2,148   │
                               Total Capital   6,120 ←┘

Total Assets $7,120   Total Liabilities and
                                  Capital $7,120

                              270

The arrows again show the articulation between statements. The major difference between this set of statements and the set prepared for a proprietorship is that these provide information about the activity in each partner's capital account.

As explained in Chapter 1, not all partnerships are small organizations. The Arthur Anderson Worldwide Organization, one of the largest accounting firms in America, operates over 300 offices and has more than two thousand partners. With an organizational structure of that size, the financial statements of Arthur Anderson clearly would not offer details of each partner's holdings. Instead, figures are presented in terms of amounts "per partner."

Financial Statements of a Corporation

Financial statements providing information about corporate activities differ from those based on the activities of proprietorships or partnerships. Income statements for the three business forms generally use the same format. The differences occur in the other two financial statements. To illustrate these differences, let's examine the full set of three financial statements for Rosita Corporation:

Rosita Corporation
Income Statement
For the Year Ending December 31, 1993

Sales	$2690	
Less:		
Cost of goods sold	955	
Gross Margin		$1735
Wages Expense	675	
Utilities Expense	310	
Total operating expenses	985	
Operating Income		$ 750
Other revenues:		
Rent Revenue		990
Other expenses:		
Interest Expense		(120)
Net Income		$1620

Rosita Corporation
Statement of Stockholders' Equity
For the Year Ending December 31, 1993

	Common Stock	Additional Paid-in Capital	Retained Earnings	Total Stockholders' Equity
Balance, January 1	$1,000	$4,000	$ 0	$5,000
Net income			1,620	1,620
Dividends			(500)	(500)
Balance, December 31	$1,000	$4,000	$1,120	$6,120

Rosita Corporation
Balance Sheet
December 31, 1993

Assets:		Liabilities:	
		Notes Payable	$1,000
Cash $7,120			
		Owners' Equity:	
		Common Stock	$1,000
		Additional paid-in capital	4,000
		Total Contributed Capital	$5,000
		Retained Earnings	1,120
		Total Shareholders' Equity	6,120
Total Assets	$7,120	Total Liabilities and Owners' Equity	$7,120

Once again, the arrows show the articulation of these corporate statements. As you can see, the income statement is unchanged, because the form of business organization does not affect that statement. The information from the income statement is used on the statement of stockholders' equity. The balance sheet, although different from that of a proprietorship or partnership, still reflects the ending balance shown on the statement of stockholders' equity.

Discussion Question

6-12. The balance sheet for the corporate form of business is just a bit more detailed than that for the proprietorship. Comparing the two, what can you learn from the corporate balance sheet that you would not know from looking at the proprietorship's balance sheet?

In order to complete the illustration of articulation, the following set of financial statements shows Rosita Corporation using a statement of retained earnings instead of the statement of stockholders' equity. The same relationships among the statements hold true.

Rosita Corporation
Income Statement
For the Year Ending December 31, 1993

Sales $2690
  Less:
Cost of goods sold   955
      Gross Margin $1735
Wages Expense   675
Utilities Expense   310
      Total operating expenses 985

Operating Income $ 750
Other revenues:
      Rent Revenue   990
Other expenses:
      Interest Expense   (120)

      Net Income $1620

Rosita Corporation
Statement of Retained Earnings
For the Year Ending December 31, 1993

Retained Earnings January 1, 1993 $ 0
      ADD: Net Income   1,620
                                   $1,620
      LESS: Dividends   500
Retained Earnings December 31, 1993 $1,120

Rosita Corporation
Balance Sheet
December 31, 1993

Assets: Liabilities:
                              Notes Payable $1,000
   Cash $7,120
                           Owners' Equity:
                              Common Stock $1,000
                              Additional paid-in capital   4,000
                              Total Contributed Capital $5,000
                              Retained Earnings   1,120
                              Total Shareholders' Equity
                                                           6,120

Total Assets $7,120 Total Liabilities and
                              Owners' Equity $7,120

Now that you have been introduced to the first three major financial statements and you have seen how they fit together, you may be wondering when you will actually get to start using these tools to make lots of decisions. Do you feel you are ready to use them to predict future cash flows? We sincerely hope not, because without an understanding of the basis upon which these financial statements are prepared, it is impossible to use them effectively. At this point, then, it is premature to talk about how to use the tools. We must first discuss the way the items included in the financial statements are measured. The next chapter provides an introduction and discussion of two different measurement bases After completion of your work on that chapter, you will be better prepared to use the income statement, statement of owners' equity, and balance sheet to predict future cash flows.

CHAPTER SUMMARY

The income statement is a financial statement providing information about the past performance of a company during a particular period of time. It consists of information about the rewards of doing business (revenues) and the sacrifices of doing business (expenses). The income statement shows the result of subtracting expenses from revenues. If revenues were greater than expenses, the result is net income; if expenses were larger than revenues for the period, the result is net loss.

Income statements may be prepared following either the single-step or multi-step format. The single-step income statement format gathers all revenues together to form total revenues. Then, all expenses are listed and totalled to form total expenses. In one step, expenses are subtracted from revenues, and the resulting net income or net loss is presented. The multi-step format begins with one special revenue — sales. From that revenue, cost of goods sold is subtracted to determine gross margin. All remaining operating expenses are then subtracted to determine income from operations. Any other revenues or expenses are then presented to arrive at the final net income or loss. The bottom line (net income) of the two formats of income statements is the same, but the presentation of the revenues and expenses for the period is different.

Regardless of the income statement format chosen, net income results in an increase in owners' equity; net losses result in a decrease in owners' equity. The effect of net income or net loss on owners' equity is shown on the statement of owners' equity. This financial statement shows the beginning balance in owners' equity at a particular point in time and how the balance was affected during the period to arrive at the ending balance.

Depending on the organizational form of the company, the statement of owners' equity will take one of several forms. The owners' equity sections of proprietorships and partnerships consist of capital accounts for each owner. Therefore, statements for these business forms are called statements of capital.

Corporations prepare statements of stockholders' equity. These statements can show changes in all parts of owners' equity — stock accounts, additional paid-in capital accounts, and retained earnings. Net income or loss affects retained earnings, and if this portion of stockholders' equity is the only one having activity during the period, a corporation may simply prepare a statement of retained earnings.

In addition to net income or net loss, another item that affects the balance of owners' equity is distributions to owners. For proprietorships and partnerships, these distributions are called drawings or withdrawals. In a corporate setting, distributions to owners are called dividends, and cause a reduction of retained earnings. Both dividends and drawings reduce total owners' equity.

Dividends are paid to provide investors a return on their investment, and to indicate the corporation's financial well-being. Two criteria must be met before a corporation is able to pay a dividend: (1) there must be sufficient cash available to actually make the payment, and (2) the corporation's balance in retained earnings must be large enough to cover the dividend amount.

The income statement, statement of owners' equity, and balance sheet are all connected. The way in which these statements fit together is known as articulation. The net income (or net loss) reported on the income statement is shown as an increase (or decrease) to owners' equity on the statement of capital, statement of stockholders' equity, or statement of retained earnings. The ending balance shown on this "bridge statement" is reported on the balance sheet. Articulation exists among the financial statements of companies regardless of the form of business organization.

REVIEW THE FACTS

1. Name and define in your own words the accounting elements used to determine net income.

2. What is the primary expense associated with the products sold by merchandisers and manufacturers?

3. Name the two formats of the income statement, and describe the differences between them.

4. What item is responsible for the primary increase in the capital account?

5. What is the difference between a statement of stockholders' equity and a statement of retained earnings?

6. What is the effect of owners' drawings, and on what financial statement is this information reported?

7. Under what circumstances is a corporation able to pay a dividend?

8. How is a corporation's financial position affected by the payment of a dividend?

9. Explain the terms: date of declaration, date of record, and date of payment.

10. Describe the meaning of articulation as it is used in accounting.

KEY TERMS DEFINED

Articulation. The relationships (links) between the financial statements.

Cost of Goods Sold. The cost of the product sold as the primary business activity of a company.

Cost of Products Sold. Another name for cost of goods sold.

Cost of Sales. Another name for cost of goods sold.

Date of Declaration. The date upon which a corporation announces plans to distribute a dividend. At this point, the corporation becomes legally obligated to make the distribution. A liability is created.

Date of Payment. The date a corporate dividend is actually paid. The payment date is generally announced on the date of declaration.

Date of Record. Owners of the shares of stock on this day are the ones to receive the dividend announced on the date of declaration.

Dividends. Distributions made to the owners of corporations (stockholders). Dividends are most commonly distributed in the form of cash.

Drawings. Distributions to the owners of proprietorships and partnerships. Also called withdrawals.

Earnings. Another name for net income.

Expenses. An accounting element representing the outflow of assets resulting from an entity's ongoing major or central operations. These are the sacrifices required to attain the rewards (revenues) of doing business.

Gross Margin. An item shown on a multi-step income statement, calculated as SALES minus COST OF GOODS SOLD.

Gross Profit. Another name for gross margin.

Income from operations. Another name for operating income, shown on the multi-step income statement.

Income Statement. A financial statement providing information about an entity's past performance. Its purpose is to measure the results of an entity's operations for some specific time period. This statement provides information about revenues and expenses.

Multi-step Income Statement. An income statement format that highlights gross margin and operating income.

Net earnings.   Another term used to refer to net income.

Net Income.   The net reward of doing business for a specific time period.   It is derived by subtracting expenses for that period from the revenues of that period.

Net Loss.   The difference between revenues and expenses of a period in which expenses are greater than revenues.

Operating Income.   Income produced by the major business activity of the company.   An item shown on the multi-step income statement.

Profit.   A less formal name for net income.

Revenues.   An accounting element representing the inflows of assets as a result of an entity's ongoing major or central operations. These are the rewards of doing business.

Sales (or Sales Revenue).   The revenue generated from the sale of a tangible product as a major business activity.

Single-step Income Statement.   A format of the income statement that gathers all revenues into "total revenues" and all expenses into "total expenses."   Net income is calculated as a subtraction of total expenses from total revenues.

Statement of Earnings.   Another name for the income statement.

Statement of Owners' Equity. The financial statement that reports activity in the capital accounts of proprietorships and partnerships and in the stockholders' equity accounts of corporations. This statement serves as a bridge between the income statement and the balance sheet.

Statement of Results of Operations. The formal name of the income statement.

Statement of Retained Earnings. A corporate financial statement that shows the changes in retained earnings during a particular period.

Withdrawals. Distributions to the owners of proprietorships and partnerships. Also called drawings.

Chapter 6
APPLY WHAT YOU HAVE LEARNED

A6-1. George Adams & Company had $56,412 in sales revenue during 1995. In addition to the regular sales revenue, Adams rented out a small building it owned and received $3,600 for the year. Cost of goods sold for the year totaled $31,812. Other expenses for the year were:

```
          Rent.........$12,500
          Utilities....  2,140
          Advertising..  3,265
          Wages........ 10,619
          Interest.....    856
```

REQUIRED:

a. Prepare a 1995 income statement for George Adams & Company using a single-step format.

b. Prepare a 1995 income statement for George Adams & Company using a multi-step format.

A6-2. Cederloff Company was organized on January 3, 1995. While many companies are not profitable in their first year, Cederloff actually experienced a modest net income of $7,500 in 1995.

REQUIRED:

a. Prepare a Statement of Capital for Cederloff Company for the year ending December 31, 1995, assuming Karen Cederloff began the company as a sole proprietorship by investing $10,000.

b. Prepare a Statement of Capital for Cederloff Company for the year ending December 31, 1995, assuming Karen Cederloff, Stephen Sommers, and Barry Figgins began the company as a partnership. The three partners have agreed to share any income or loss in the same proportion as their initial investments, which were as follows:

```
              Cederloff....$ 5,000
              Sommers......  3,000
              Figgins......  2,000
              Total........$10,000
```

c. Prepare a Statement of Stockholders' Equity for Cederloff Company for the year ending December 31, 1995, assuming Karen Cederloff, Stephen Sommers, and Barry Figgins organized the company as a corporation. The corporate charter authorized 50,000 shares of $2 par-value common stock. The following shares were issued on January 3, 1995 (all at $10 per share):

```
     500 shares to Cederloff....$ 5,000
     300 shares to Sommers......  3,000
     200 shares to Figgins......  2,000
     Total....................$10,000
```

A6-3. This is a continuation of the previous problem (A6-2). It is now December 31, 1996 and it is time to prepare the Statement of Owners' Equity for Cederloff Company. Net income for the year ending December 31, 1996 was $12,000 and there were no additional owner investments during the year.

REQUIRED:

a. Prepare a statement of capital for Cederloff Company for the year ending December 31, 1996, assuming the business was a proprietorship and that Karen Cederloff took drawings totaling $8,000 during 1996.

b. Prepare a statement of capital for Cederloff Company for the year ending December 31, 1996, assuming the partnership form. Recall from the previous problem that the partners share income in the same proportion as their initial investment. Drawings by the three partners during 1996 were as follows:

```
Cederloff....$ 4,000
Sommers......  2,500
Figgins......  1,500
Total........$ 8,000
```


c. Prepare a statement of stockholders' equity for Cederloff Company for the year ending December 31, 1996, assuming the corporate form. Recall from the previous problem that 1,000 shares of common stock were issued at the time of incorporation. Dividends paid during the year were $8.00 per share.

d. Repeat the previous requirement, but this time prepare a statement of retained earnings, rather than a statement of stockholders' equity.

A6-4. Use the following set of financial statements to meet the requirements below:

Ben Hernandez Company
Income Statement
For the Year Ending December 31, 1995

Sales	$88,722	
Less: COGS	41,912	
Gross Margin		$46,810
Rent	17,500	
Wages	14,408	
Advertising	7,345	
Utilities	1,640	
Total operating expenses		40,893
Operating income		$ 5,917
Other Revenues:		
Rent revenue		2,700
Other expenses:		
Interest expense		1,166
Net Income		$ 7,451

Ben Hernandez Company
Statement of Capital
For the Year Ending December 31, 1995

Hernandez, Capital January 1, 1995	$33,806	
ADD: Net Income	7,451	
	$41,257	
LESS: Drawings	9,000	
Hernandez, Capital December 31, 1995		$32,257

Ben Hernandez Company
Balance Sheet
December 31, 1995

Assets:		Liabilities:	
Cash	$57,257	Notes Payable	$25,000
		Owners' Equity:	
		Hernandez, Capital	32,257
Total Assets	$57,257	Total Liabilities & Owners' Equity	$57,257

REQUIRED:

a. Is Hernandez a sole proprietorship, a partnership, or a corporation? Explain how you arrived at your answer.

b. Is Hernandez Company's income statement single-step or multi-step? Explain how you determined your answer.

c. Explain the term *articulation*, and describe how the financial statements of Hernandez Company articulate.

287

A6-5. Presented below is a list of items relating to the concepts presented in this chapter, followed by definitions of those items in a scrambled order:

a. Revenues.
b. Expenses.
c. Income Statement.
d. Statement of Owners' Equity.
e. Dividends.
f. Drawings.
g. Date of declaration.
h. Date of record.
i. Date of payment.
j. Articulation.

1. ___ The date distribution of earnings to owners of a corporation are actually paid.

2. ___ Inflows of assets from delivering or producing goods, rendering services, or other activities.

3. ___ Distribution of earnings to the owners of a corporation.

4. ___ The link between the income statement and the balance sheet.

5. ___ A bridge statement showing how the income statement and balance sheet are related.

6. ___ Distribution of earnings to the owners of proprietorships and partnerships.

7. ___ Outflows or other using up of assets from delivering or producing goods, rendering services, or carrying out other activities.

8. ___ The date a corporation announces it will make a distribution of earnings to its owners.

9. ___ A financial tool providing information about an entity's past performance.

10. ___ Whoever owns shares of stock on this date will receive the distribution of earnings previously declared.

REQUIRED:

Match the letter next to each item on the list with the appropriate definition. Each letter will be used only once.

CHAPTER 7

KEEPING SCORE: BASES OF ECONOMIC MEASUREMENT

Thus far we have explored the development of three financial tools — the income statement, the statement of owners' equity, and the balance sheet. Each of these statements provides accounting information designed to assist in the decision making process. Economic decision makers rely heavily on the information contained in the financial statements provided by companies.

All three of the financial statements examined thus far are comprised of measurements of economic activity. However, before decision makers use this accounting information, one basic question must be answered: *From what perspective have the measurements been made?* It is imperative that users of the financial statement information know what basis of economic measurement was in place. Otherwise, the information provided is of little value as an aid to their decision making.

There are two general bases of economic measurement; it is important that you understand the distinctions between them. In this chapter, we will consider two different approaches to measuring revenue and expense for a particular time period. When you have completed your work on this chapter, you should be able to do the following:

1.   Explain the difference between reality and the measurement of reality.

2.   Apply the criteria for revenue and expense recognition under the cash basis of accounting to determine periodic net income.

3.   Determine periodic net income, applying the rules of revenue and expense recognition required by accrual accounting.

4.   Explain the concept of matching, and describe how it relates to depreciation.

5.   Describe the difference between accruals and deferrals, and provide examples of each.

6.   Contrast the cash basis and accrual basis of economic measurement, describing the relative strengths and weaknesses of each basis.

REALITY VS. THE MEASUREMENT OF REALITY

There are two things going on in every company. First, there is reality. A company makes purchases, sells goods, provides services, pays employees, and performs a thousand other activities. These activities are the reality of being in business and doing business. Second, there is the measurement of reality. As

291

transactions and events occur in the company, their effects are recorded in an attempt to measure the reality. But remember this: *measurement of reality, whether or not it reflects reality is not reality.* In other words:

Reality is what reality is!

- Anonymous

As an example of what we're talking about, assume Rosita Company purchased some office supplies and wrote a check for $480. In recording the check in the check register, the accountant read the amount of the check incorrectly and recorded $48. After deducting the $48, the check register indicated a balance of $1127. The fact that the accountant recorded the amount of the check incorrectly in no way changes the reality of how much money was spent and how much is actually in the checking account.

Discussion Questions

7-1. Assuming no other errors in the check register, what is the actual cash balance in Rosita Company's checking account?

7-2. In what ways could this incorrect measurement of reality have an effect on reality? Explain.

The concept that errors may cause differences between reality and the measurement of reality is relatively easy to grasp. However, many people find it difficult to believe that there might be perfectly legitimate reasons for a difference between reality and its measure. This discrepency is best demonstrated in the measurement of the revenues and expenses to be reported in the income statement of a company for a particular time period.

The Problems of Periodic Measurement

Most discrepencies between reality and its measure occur when earnings activities are measured for a *specific period of time*. Regardless of the time period (month, quarter, year, etc.), it is not always readily apparent which revenues and which expenses should be included in determining the earnings (net income) of that period. In fact, the only true measure of net income for a company is a comparison between revenues and expenses over the entire life of that company.

```
┌─────────────────────────────────────────────────────────────┐
│                    Discussion Questions                       │
│                                                               │
│                                                               │
│    7-3. Checker Business Systems sells computer               │
│                                                               │
│         equipment to small businesses.  During 1994,          │
│                                                               │
│         the sales activity was as follows:                    │
│                                                               │
│         February:  Sold $6,000 of equipment on account.  The  │
│                                                               │
│         customers paid in full on March 15.                   │
│                                                               │
│         March:  Sold $4,500 of equipment on account.          │
│                                                               │
│         Customers paid in full on April 15.                   │
│                                                               │
│         Describe the impact of different periodic             │
│                                                               │
│         measurements.  That is, what activity would be        │
│                                                               │
│         included in each period if the business activity is   │
│                                                               │
│         measured:                                             │
│                                                               │
│         a.   each month?                                      │
│                                                               │
│         b.   each quarter?                                    │
│                                                               │
│         c.   each year?                                       │
│                                                               │
│                                                               │
└─────────────────────────────────────────────────────────────┘
```

In some ways, determining net income in the fifteenth century was actually easier and more precise than it is today. In the days of Christopher Columbus, if an entrepreneur planned to sail to the New World and bring back goods to sell, the net income for that particular venture could be measured. The entrepreneur began with a pile of money. With that, he bought a ship and supplies, and hired men to help with the expedition. The group would set sail, gather up treasures from the New World, return and sell the goods. Then, the workers could be paid off, the ship could be sold, and the entrepreneur would end up, once again, with a pile of money. If the pile of money at the end was greater than the pile of money he had begun with, the difference would be net income. If the ending amount of money was smaller than the amount he started with, the entrepreneur suffered a loss on the venture.

In today's world, it is unrealistic to expect companies to stop operations, sell off all their assets, and determine their "true" net income. Although lifetime net income would be a more precise measurement of an operation's success or failure, users of accounting information demand current information every year, or quarter, or month. It is this need to artificially break the company's operations into various time periods that requires us to make decisions about when revenues and expenses should be reported.

Revenue and Expense Recognition

In accounting, the word **recognition** has a very specific meaning. It refers to the process of

1. recording in the books

    and

2. reporting in the financial statements.

The problem of when to recognize something applies to all of the accounting elements we have discussed so far (and to the ones we have yet to discuss). The greatest difficulties of recognition, however, concern revenues and expenses.

When should a revenue be recognized? When should an expense be recognized? These are two *very* difficult questions, for which there are no "right" answers. A set of criteria must be established to determine when accounting elements, particularly revenues and expenses, are recognized. Over time, several different systems have been developed, each attempting to find some rational basis for the measurement of revenue and expense in a particular time period.

Those of you who have ever had another accounting class may have been taught a particular set of criteria for revenue and expense recognition. We are *not* asking you to forget what you learned. What we *are* asking you to do is slide those criteria to the back of your mind. What you may have learned in that other accounting class is *a* set of criteria, not *the* set of criteria.

```
+------------------------------------------------------------+
|                  Discussion Questions                      |
|                                                            |
|                                                            |
|   7-4. If a revenue is defined as the reward of doing      |
|        business, at what point do you think it should      |
|        be recognized?  Explain.                            |
|                                                            |
|                                                            |
|   7-5. If an expense is defined as the sacrifice           |
|        necessary to obtain a revenue, at what point do     |
|        you think it should be recognized?  Explain.        |
|                                                            |
+------------------------------------------------------------+
```

Bases of Economic Measurement

There are two basic approaches to recording economic activity. As they are discussed, you will see that each has certain advantages over the other. Neither of them is "correct" in the sense of being in accordance with some natural law of finance and accounting. They are simply different approaches to the measurement of revenues, expenses, assets, liabilities, and owners' equity.

We will use a single set of data to illustrate the two bases of measurement. Consider the following information concerning Wooster Company (a proprietorship) for January, 1993:

1. Bertie Wooster started the company on January 2, by investing $200,000.

2. Wooster Company borrowed $100,000 from the Friendly Bank on January 2, by signing a one-year, 12 percent note payable. Although the $100,000 does not have to be repaid until January 2, 1994, the interest charge must be paid each month, beginning on February 2, 1993.

3. The company purchased a vehicle on January 2 for $14,000 cash. Bertie's best guess is that the vehicle will fill the company's needs for four years, after which he estimates the vehicle can be sold for $2,000.

4. The company paid cash for $75,000 of merchandise inventory on January 8.

5. On January 15, the company sold $42,000 of the merchandise inventory for a total selling price of $78,000 and collected the cash the same day.

6. On January 22, the company sold $15,000 of the merchandise inventory for a total selling price of $32,000 on account (a credit sale). The terms of the sale were 30 days, meaning Wooster can expect to receive payment by February 22.

7. Cash payments for operating expenses in January totaled $22,500.

8. Besides the bank loan, the only amounts owed by the company at the end of the month were:

   a. $2,000 to employees of the company for work performed in January. They will be paid on February 3.

   b. A $700 utility bill which was received on January 31, and will be paid on February 15.

The above information is the reality of what happened in the Wooster Company during the month of January, 1993. But what of the measurement of that reality? It will be different depending on the basis of accounting used to recognize the transactions. Remember, both treatments are based on exactly the same reality. *They are simply different methods of measuring reality.*

CASH BASIS OF ECONOMIC MEASUREMENT

The first approach to measuring economic activity is **cash basis accounting**. This is the simpler of the two bases. Everyone understands what cash is and can therefore readily grasp the measurement criterion of this method. Its greatest strength, however, lies in the fact that it keeps the user's eye on the ball. As its name implies, the cash basis has only one measurement criterion: CASH!

Under cash basis accounting, economic activity is recognized only when the associated cash is received or paid. Thus, a revenue is recognized as such only when the associated cash is received by the company. Also understand that only cash received as a result of the earnings process would be considered to be revenue. Cash received from the owners of the company, for example, is considered an investment by those owners rather than revenue. Also, cash received when a company borrows money is considered a liability rather than revenue.

Similarly, not all cash paid out is considered an expense under the cash basis. If a company paid a dividend to its owners, for example, the cash paid out is not an expense to the company. Such a payment is considered to be a distribution of profits or a return on the owners' original investment. Transactions such as these, which involve cash but are not considered revenues or expenses, will be reported on the statement of owners' equity and/or the balance sheet, but not the income statement.

There are two keys to revenue and expense recognition under the cash basis. First, cash must be involved in the transaction. Second, the receipt or disbursement must relate to *delivering or producing goods, rendering services, or other activities*. If a transaction meets *both* of these requirements, it is a revenue or expense transaction (depending on whether the cash is received or paid), and will be reported on the income statement.

Cash Basis Financial Statements

In preparing the income statement, statement of capital, and balance sheet using the cash basis, you must first isolate the events and transactions involving cash. For our example of the Wooster Company, only the following meet that requirement:

1. Bertie Wooster started the company on January 2, by investing $200,000.

2. Wooster Company borrowed $100,000 from the Friendly Bank on January 2, by signing a one-year, 12 percent note payable. Although the $100,000 does not have to be repaid until January 2, 1994, the interest charge must be paid each month, beginning on February 2, 1993.

3. The company purchased a vehicle on January 2 for $14,000 cash. Bertie's best guess is that the vehicle will fill the company's needs for four years, after which he estimates the vehicle can be sold for $2,000.

4. The company paid cash for $75,000 of merchandise inventory on January 8.

300

5. On January 15, the company sold $42,000 of the merchandise inventory for a total selling price of $78,000 and collected the cash the same day.

7. Cash payments for operating expenses in January totaled $22,500.

These transactions, then, will be recorded in Wooster's books and reported on one or more of the financial statements: the income statement, statement of owners' equity, or balance sheet. In order to determine which of the transactions should be reported on the income statement, we must determine which are directly related to Wooster's major or central operation (which appears to be the buying and selling of some product). Transactions 3, 4, 5, and 7 meet that criterion. Using the cash basis of accounting, the income statement for the month of January, 1993, based on those transactions looks like this:

WOOSTER COMPANY
Income Statement
For The Month Ended January 31, 1993
Cash Basis

Sales Revenue......................	$ 78,000	
Cost of Goods Sold..................	75,000	
Gross Margin.................................		$ 3,000
Expenses:		
Cost of Vehicle.........................$ 14,000		
Cash Operating Expenses................ 22,500		
Total Operating Expenses...................		(36,500)
Net Loss.......................................		$(33,500)

•   *Sales Revenue.* Because only $78,000 in cash was received from sales in the month of January, that is the amount shown as revenue.

301

- *Cost of Goods Sold.* Wooster paid $75,000 in cash for merchandise inventory during January. Thus, this is the amount recognized as COGS.

- *Expenses.* The cash expenses of $22,500 plus the entire $14,000 for the vehicle purchased were recognized as expenses in January. Other expenses will be recognized as the cash is paid by the company.

Transaction #1 reflects an inflow of cash, so the cash basis of measurement requires that it be recognized. This transaction represents an investment by the owner, Bertie Wooster. This investment by owner would be an increase in the capital account, while the net loss determined above would be a decrease. The statement of owners' equity prepared using the cash basis of measurement would be:

WOOSTER COMPANY
Statement of Owner's Equity
For The Month Ended January 31, 1993
Cash Basis

B. Wooster, Capital, January 1, 1993.............. $ 0
Investment by owner............................... 200,000
Net Loss.. (33,500)
B. Wooster, Capital, January 31, 1993............. $166,500

The remaining cash transaction of the Wooster Company during January 1993 is Transaction #2, the $100,000 bank loan. Borrowing money creates a liability that would appear on the balance sheet. Under cash basis accounting, Wooster Company's balance sheet at January 31, 1993, would be:

```
                     WOOSTER COMPANY
                     Balance Sheet
                   January 31, 1993
                       Cash Basis

ASSETS:
Cash...................$266,500      LIABILITIES:
Total Assets..........$266,500       Note Payable........$100,000
                                     OWNER'S EQUITY:
                                     B. Wooster, Capital. 166,500
                                     Total Liabilities
                                     and Owner's Equity..$266,500
```

Notice the articulation of the financial statements for the Wooster

Company.   The net loss from the income statement is shown on the

statement of owners' equity, and the ending balance in the capital

account from the statement of owners' equity is used on the balance

sheet.   The cash amount showing on the balance sheet is simply the

$200,000 the owner invested in the company plus the $100,000

borrowed from the bank less the $33,500 net loss for the month of

January.

asset side

Discussion Questions

7-6. Assume for a moment that you are Wooster's loan officer at the bank. How would you evaluate the income statement and balance sheet presented above in terms of the primary qualitative characteristic of relevance, including predictive value and feedback value? (Hint: See Chapter 3.)

7-7. If your response to the question above led you to the conclusion that there is a problem in terms of predictive value and feedback value, what item or items do you feel caused the problem? How do you think the company could account for the item or items to better relate costs to the revenues they generate?

Strengths and Weaknesses of Cash Basis Accounting

Besides its relative simplicity, the greatest strength of the cash basis is objectivity. Because cash is the only measurement criterion, less subjective judgment is required than with the other measurement basis we will discuss. This is not to say the cash basis is totally objective. For example, a company can manipulate the expenses reported in a particular income statement period by simply delaying the payment of amounts owed. The greatest weakness of the cash basis is that it makes no attempt to recognize expenses in the same period as the revenues they helped generate. This makes the cash basis income statement very difficult to use in either predicting future profitability or assessing past performance if cash is not immediately received when earned or paid when owed.

Discussion Questions

7-8. Provide two examples of situations in which your checkbook balance did not provide relevant information.

ACCRUAL BASIS OF ECONOMIC MEASUREMENT

The second basis of economic measurement we will discuss is **accrual basis accounting**. This system does not rely on the receipt or payment of cash to determine when revenues and expenses should be recognized. The key to understanding accrual-based accounting is to understand the word **accrue**. To accrue means:

305

To come into being as a legally enforceable claim.

Essentially, in accrual based accounting, sales, purchases, and all other business transactions are recognized whenever a legally enforceable claim to the associated cash is established. The main focus of accrual accounting is determining when a legally enforceable claim to cash has been established between the parties involved in the transaction.

Revenue Recognition

Revenue is recognized under accrual accounting when it is deemed to be earned. In other words, revenue is recognized when the company has a legally enforceable claim to the cash associated with that revenue. Under accrual accounting, the recognition of revenue is completely unrelated to when the cash is received. There are three possibilities as to when cash is received in relation to when revenue is considered earned:

1. Cash is received *at the time* the revenue is earned. An example of this is when you pay cash for a pair of jeans at Gap. Cash is received by Gap at the same time as the store recognize revenue from the sale.

2. Cash is received *after* the revenue has been earned. An example of this is a sale of merchandise on account (a

credit sale). Napa Auto Parts records revenue for sales made to their regular customers in January, but the cash is not collected until February.

3. Cash is received *before* the revenue has been earned. An example of this is the payment received from a customer for a year's subscription to Time Magazine.

Remember that under accrual accounting, the trigger mechanism for determining when revenue should be recognized is the earning process, *not* when the cash is received. In Examples #1 and #2, the revenue is recorded in the books and shown on the financial statements at the time the sale is made. The fact that in Example #2 the company did not receive cash at that time does not affect recognition of the revenue. In Example #3, the receipt of cash does not cause revenue to be recognized. Under accrual accounting, the revenue is not recognized until it is earned (when the magazines have been sent to the customer).

Identifying the point in time when a revenue is earned is not always a simple matter. There are three questions accountants try to answer in determining when revenue has been earned and should therefore be recognized. Please note that these are in no way related to the three examples above:

a. *Has **title** (legal ownership) to whatever was sold transferred to the customer?* If the answer to this question is yes, the revenue should definitely be recognized. This question can be applied more easily to the sale of tangible products than it can be to the sale of services.

b. *Has an exchange taken place?* Exchange refers to the customer taking receipt of whatever he or she purchased. If the answer to this question is yes, the revenue will likely be recognized. This question, too, is more applicable to the sale of tangible products than it is to the sale of services.

c. *Is the earnings process virtually complete?* This is the toughest of the three questions to answer and applies better to the sale of services than it does to the sale of tangible products. Let's say, for example, that you have contracted with Joe Dokes to have your kitchen remodeled. It's a two week job, and midway through the second week Joe decides he doesn't want to be a remodeler anymore. Are you obligated to pay him for removing your old cabinets, stripping the wallpaper, and making a hole in the wall for the new window? Probably not. He cannot recognize revenue until the job is "virtually" complete.

It is not necessary for all three questions to be answered "yes" for revenue to be recognized. In most cases, a positive answer to any one of them is persuasive evidence that revenue has been earned and should be recognized.

Discussion Questions

7-9. On Saturday morning, you finally decide which model of IBM computer to buy. The salesperson has agreed to have all the software you need installed and have the machine delivered to you by Tuesday afternoon. Because your last computer was purchased at Carl's Computer Shop, the store has agreed to extend credit to you. You have thirty days to pay for your new computer. As of Monday,

1. Has title passed?

2. Has an exchange taken place?

3. Is the earnings process complete?

7-10. When should Carl's Computer Shop recognize revenue:

a. under the cash basis?

b. under the accrual basis?

Expense Recognition

Under accrual accounting, expenses are recognized when the benefit from the expense is received. As was the case with revenue recognition, the recognition of expense under accrual accounting is completely unrelated to the movement of cash. Again, there are three possible relationships between the timing of the cash movement and the recognition of the transaction.

1. Cash is paid *at the time* the expense is incurred. An example of this is a cash purchase of the food served at the company Christmas party held that same day.

2. Cash is paid *after* the expense has been incurred. An example of this is Napa Auto Part's payment of a utility bill in February which was really for electricity used in January.

3. Cash is paid *before* the expense has been incurred. An example of this is insurance. Time Magazine buys insurance covering a full year and pays the entire premium when the policy is purchased.

The key to expense recognition under accrual accounting is revenue recognition. That's right — *revenue recognition*. Remember that to be useful in predicting future profitability and cash flow, an

310

income statement should measure revenues for a specific period of time, as well as the expenses required to obtain those revenues. Thus, accrual accounting attempts to establish a relationship between revenues and expenses. This relationship is referred to as **matching**.

The Concept Of Matching

The first step in the accrual matching process is to determine in which income statement period to recognize a particular revenue. Step two then, is to determine which expenses helped to generate that revenue. Those expenses are then recognized in that same financial statement period. This approach makes the income statement for that time period more reflective of true earnings results, and therefore more relevant in predicting future potential. It is important to note that it can be very difficult to determine which expenses are responsible for generating which revenue, so a significant amount of judgement is required in expense recognition under the accrual basis of accounting.

There are two possible relationships between revenues and expenses, which determine when expenses are recognized:

1. *Direct cause and effect.* This is the most desirable situation, because a direct link can be found between an expense and the revenue it helped generate. An example is

311

sales commissions. If Prudential Insurance Company pays a 10% sales commission to its salespersons, and a salesman makes a sale of $1,000, the company incurs a $100 expense. Once it is determined in which income statement period the $1,000 revenue should be recognized, the $100 expense is recognized in that same period. Unfortunately, relatively few expenses can be linked directly to the revenues they help generate.

2. *No direct cause and effect.* This is a more common situation. In this case, there are two possible treatments:

a. *Immediate recognition.* There are two situations in which recording the expense immediately is the most appropriate action. If a purchased item has no discernable future benefit, the cost of the item is recognized as an expense immediately. A good example of an expense requiring immediate recognition is Ford Motors' television advertising intended to increase the sales of the Taurus. The future benefit of this type of advertising is not discernable. Television ads purchased and presented to the public in one period almost certainly benefit future periods, but how many periods and how much in each of those periods cannot be reasonably estimated. Thus, the cost of television advertising is usually recognized as an expense in the periods when the ads are presented to consumers.

The second situation requiring the immediate recognition of an expense is when allocation of the cost of a purchased item provides no additional useful information. An example of this situation is the purchase of a $10 item such as a stapler. Even if the stapler will be used in the office for five years, allocation of the $10 cost over the five year period serves no useful purpose. Remember, the purpose of accounting is to provide information useful to decision makers. Will allocating this minor cost over a five-year period provide useful accounting information? Since most decision makers would be unaffected by the treatment of a $10 item, the answer is no. The recordkeeping cost of recording the stapler as an asset on the balance sheet and then allocating $2 per year as an expense on the income statement for five years far outweighs the benefit of doing so. Recognizing the $10 cost as an immediate expense makes more sense.

b. *Allocation to the periods benefited.* If a purchased item has discernable benefit to future income statement periods and the periods can be reasonably estimated, the item is recorded as an asset when purchased. The cost of that item is then systematically converted to expense in the periods benefited. An example of this is insurance. If a premium for two years of insurance coverage is paid, there is no question that a benefit to future periods exists. Further, the estimate of those periods is clear — benefits will be derived for two years. As time passes, during the two years, the cost of the insurance coverage is allocated to expense.

The concept of "allocation to the periods benefited" has a more widely used application than the one described above. When assets that will benefit the company for several periods (often many years) are acquired, the cost is recorded as an asset amount on the balance sheet. As time passes, the cost is transferred to expense on the income statement. This form of "allocation to the periods benefited" is a process known as depreciation.

What Depreciation Is (And What It Is Not)

Depreciation is defined as *a systematic (methodical) and rational (reasoned) allocation of the cost of a long-lived item from asset to expense.* You should recall that under cash basis accounting, Wooster Company's purchase of a $14,000 vehicle resulted in a $14,000 expense because that amount of cash was spent. The real question is whether this asset has been "used up" (has the company received the benefit from the vehicle?) or does the asset still have a future benefit? The answer to the question is clearly that the asset (vehicle) has neither been used up, nor has the company received all the benefit from it. The accrual basis of measurement

314

takes the position that this cash payment of $14,000 should not be considered an expense at the time the cash is paid. Rather than recognize the cost of the vehicle as an expense immediately, under the accrual basis it is recorded as an asset because it has probable future benefit. Over time, the cost of the vehicle will be converted from asset to expense as the benefit is derived from the use of the vehicle. The resulting expense is called **depreciation expense.**

There is probably nothing in all of accounting as misunderstood as the concept of depreciation. The confusion is caused by the use of the word depreciation itself. In virtually every context except accounting, depreciation means the lowering of value. In accounting it simply means the allocation of cost to the periods benefited. This allocation requires two highly subjective estimates: (1) the useful life of the asset, and (2) the residual value of the asset.

The useful life of an asset is simply the length of time that asset will be of use to the company, not the length of time an asset will exist. Notice that in the case of the Wooster Company, Bertie Wooster feels the vehicle will fill the company's needs for four years. This is not the same thing as saying the vehicle will last four years. There is an important distinction.

If the estimated useful life of an asset is less than the physical life of that asset, it follows that the asset will probably be sold at the end of its useful life. The estimated amount for which the asset can be sold at the end of its useful life is known as its **residual value**. It is also sometimes referred to as **salvage value** or **scrap value**.

In calculating depreciation, any estimated residual value is subtracted from the cost of an asset to arrive at what is called the **depreciable amount**, or **depreciable base**. In the case of the Wooster Company, the cost of the vehicle was $14,000, but the company estimated that at the end of its useful life, the vehicle could be sold for $2,000. The depreciable amount, therefore, is $12,000 ($14,000 - $2,000). In one sense, the true cost of the vehicle to Wooster is $12,000, because $2,000 of the purchase price is expected to be recouped when the vehicle is sold.

Once the useful life and residual value of the asset have been estimated, a method of depreciation must be selected, and there have been several developed over the years. The simplest is **straight-line depreciation** and we will use it to demonstrate how depreciation expense is calculated.

The straight-line approach allocates an equal amount of depreciation expense to each period of the asset's estimated useful life. The amount of expense is calculated by dividing the estimated useful life of the asset into the depreciable amount of the asset. In the case of Wooster's vehicle, which cost $14,000 and has a 4-year estimated useful life and a $2,000 residual value, the amount of expense works out to $3,000 per year ($12,000/4). Each year of the 4-year estimated useful life, Wooster will transfer $3,000 of the asset "vehicle" on the balance sheet into the expense "depreciation" on the income statement. At the end of the four years all the cost of the vehicle (except the $2,000 residual value) will have been recognized as expense.

Depreciation is an important process that is based upon accrual accounting's attempt to recognize expenses in the periods in which they help to generate revenue. Even though all $14,000 in cash was spent during January for the Wooster Company's vehicle, the entire benefit expected from the asset has not been received. Because the company expects the asset to help generate revenues in future periods, part of the cost will be allocated to depreciation expense in those periods. The depreciation process is just one result of accrual accounting's attempt to match expenses and revenues. Additional examples are the other adjustments explored next.

```
┌─────────────────────────────────────────────────────────────┐
│                                                               │
│               Discussion Questions                            │
│                                                               │
│                                                               │
│     7-11. Recall the scenario involving your purchase of      │
│                                                               │
│          a computer from Carl's Computer Shop,                │
│                                                               │
│          introduced in a previous Discussion Question.        │
│                                                               │
│          If the computer is to be used in the business        │
│                                                               │
│          you operate from your home, how should the           │
│                                                               │
│          purchase be treated:                                 │
│                                                               │
│          a.    under the cash basis?                          │
│                                                               │
│          b.    under the accrual basis?                       │
│                                                               │
└─────────────────────────────────────────────────────────────┘
```

Accruals and Deferrals

Because accrual accounting attempts to recognize revenues in the
income statement period they are earned, and attempts to match the
expenses that generated the revenue to the same income statement
period, **adjustments** must be made each period to ensure that these
guidelines have been followed. The adjustment process takes place
at the end of the financial statement period, but before the
financial statements are prepared. This process involves reviewing
the financial records to be sure that all items that should be
recognized in the current period have been recorded. In addition,
during the adjustment process, it is ascertained that no items that
should be recognized in future periods appear in the current

period's records. The two basic types of adjustments that are necessary are accruals and deferrals.

1. **Accruals.** These adjustments are made to recognize items that should be included in the income statement period, but have not yet been recorded. Accrual adjustments recognize revenue or expense *before* the associated cash is received or paid. In other words, this type of adjustment comes before the cash flow takes place. There are two types of accruals:

   (a.) **Accrued revenues.** These are revenues considered earned during the financial statement period because they met the criteria (answered the questions), but which have not yet been recognized. As an example, consider Warner Management Consulting Services, Inc. For the clients that use the services on an ongoing basis, the company sends bills on the 2nd of each month for the work done during the previous month. Warner has a legal claim at the end of December to what was earned in that month. Revenues recognized (recorded) should reflect the amount earned in December, even though the clients will not be billed until January 2nd of the next year.

   (b.) **Accrued expenses.** These are expenses deemed to have been incurred during the financial statement period, but which have not yet been recognized. An example of this is accrued wages for employees. Assume Pellum Company pays its employees every two weeks for work performed in the previous two weeks. If part of the two week pay period is in 1991 and part is in 1992, Pellum must make an adjustment at the end of 1991 to recognize the portion of wages expense incurred during that period. Even though the company will not spend any money until payday in January of 1992, part of that pay period's wages are 1991 expenses.

2. **Deferrals**. These are adjustments made after the cash has been received or paid. Deferrals are adjustments of revenues for which the cash has been collected but not yet earned, and of expenses for which cash has been paid but no benefit has yet been received.

(a.) **Deferred revenues**. These are created when cash is received before it is earned. For example, Larry's Lawn Service provides lawn care to many wealthy Miami families. On June 1, the Weatherby family sends Larry's Lawn Service $450 for the cost of 3 months' lawn service. As of June 1, Larry's Lawn Service has not earned any revenue, even though it has received cash. In fact, at that point, a liability has been created. The company *owes* the Weatherby family either 3 months of lawn service or their money back. The key here is who has legal claim to the cash. Because Larry's Lawn Service has no legal claim to the cash, it cannot rightly account for it as earned. By the time financial statements are prepared at the end of June, however, one month's worth of lawn service was performed, and $150 should be recognized as revenue. The remaining $300, representing two months of service is a deferred revenue. This amount represents a liability for Larry's Lawn Service, and will remain so until the company either performs the services required to attain a legal claim to the cash or returns the cash to the Weatherby family.

(b.) **Deferred expenses.** These are created when cash is paid before an expense has been incurred. On January 2, 1992, Crockett Cookie Company purchased a three year insurance policy for $2175. By December 31, 1992, 1/3 of the insurance coverage has expired (1/3 of the benefit has been received). Financial statements prepared for 1992 should reflect the fact that 1/3 of the cost of the policy ($725) is an expense for that year. The remaining portion of the policy, two years worth of coverage, is an asset providing future benefits to the company. Even though the entire $2175 was spent in 1992, 2/3 of the cost is a deferred expense, an asset which will be recognized as an expense in future periods.

Accruals and deferrals are adjustments made to be sure that the financial statements reflect the guidelines of accrual accounting. Accruals occur in situations where the cash flow has not yet taken place, but the revenue or expense should be recognized. Deferrals are necessary in cases when the cash flow has already taken place,

321

but the correct amount of revenue or expense for a particular period has not been recognized. You should understand too, that the original transaction (the receipt or payment of cash) is not an adjustment, but rather creates a situation where an adjustment (deferral) will be necessary later.

Whether they reflect expenses or revenues, accruals and deferrals will always possess the following three characteristics:

1. *A revenue item or an expense item will always be affected.* This is logical because the whole purpose of the adjustment process is to make certain that revenues and expenses associated with a given financial statement period are recognized in that period. Clearly, adjustments will always affect the income statement.

2. *An asset item or a liability item will always be affected.* This means the balance sheet will also be affected by the adjustment process.

3. *Cash is never affected by accruals or deferrals.* Remember, adjustments are made to properly recognize accounting elements. It is assumed that inflows and outflows of cash were properly recorded at the time they occurred.

Accrual Basis Financial Statements

Let us once again turn to the transactions of the Wooster Company for the month of January, 1993. For your convenience, the descriptions of the company's transactions are presented again:

1. Bertie Wooster started the company on January 2, by investing $200,000.

2. Wooster Company borrowed $100,000 from the Friendly Bank on January 2, by signing a one-year, 12 percent note payable. Although the $100,000 does not have to be repaid until January 2, 1994, the interest charge must be paid each month, beginning on February 2, 1993.

3. The company purchased a vehicle on January 2 for $14,000 cash. Bertie's best guess is that the vehicle will fill the company's needs for four years, after which he estimates the vehicle can be sold for $2,000.

4. The company paid cash for $75,000 of merchandise inventory on January 8.

5. On January 15, the company sold $42,000 of the merchandise inventory for a total selling price of $78,000 and collected the cash the same day.

6. On January 22, the company sold $15,000 of the merchandise inventory for a total selling price of $32,000 on account (a credit sale). The terms of the sale were 30 days, meaning Wooster can expect to receive payment by February 22.

7. Cash payments for operating expenses in January totaled $22,500.

8. Besides the bank loan, the only amounts owed by the company at the end of the month were:

    a. $2,000 to employees of the company for work performed in January. They will be paid on February 3.

    b. A $700 utility bill which was received on January 31, and will be paid on February 15.

323

All eight transactions will affect the income statement and/or the balance sheet and statement of owners' equity under the accrual basis of accounting. The income statement for January, 1993 looks like this:

WOOSTER COMPANY
Income Statement
For The Month Ended January 31, 1993
Accrual Basis

```
Sales Revenue.............................$ 110,000
Cost of Goods Sold........................    57,000
     Gross Margin.................................. $ 53,000
Expenses:
Cash Operating Expenses...................$22,500
Wages Expense............................. 2,000
Utilities.................................   700
Interest Expense.......................... 1,000
Depreciation Expense......................   250
     Total Operating Expenses....................  (26,450)
Net Income.......................................  $ 26,550
```

Most of the items on this income statement differ from those on the income statement prepared under the cash basis. Let's discuss each item:

- *Sales Revenue*. Under the accrual basis, revenue is recognized when it is earned, regardless of when the associated cash is received. Transaction #6 says the company made a $32,000 sale on January 22. The fact that the cash is not expected to be received until February 22 is irrelevant. Therefore, total sales revenue for the month using accrual accounting is $110,000 ($78,000 cash sale + $32,000 credit sale).

- *Cost of Goods Sold*. Under accrual accounting, there is an attempt to match all expenses to the same income statement period as the revenues they help generate. In the case of merchandise inventory, it is relatively easy to establish a direct cause and effect between the revenue (sale of the inventory) and the expense (cost of the inventory sold). Transaction #5 says $42,000 of merchandise inventory was sold

324

on January 15, and transaction #6 says $15,000 of merchandise inventory was sold on January 22. The total cost of this merchandise is $57,000, thus this is the amount shown on the accrual basis income statement as cost of goods sold. This means, of course, that there is $18,000 of merchandise inventory not yet accounted for ($75,000 purchased - $57,000 sold). We will discuss this remaining inventory when we talk about the balance sheet.

- *Cash Operating Expenses.* This is the clearest and most understandable expense figure on the Wooster Company's income statement. Under both cash basis and accrual basis measurement, expenses paid in cash this period to support operations this period are expenses this period.

- *Wages Expense* of $2,000. Because these wages were earned by employees during January, Wooster has a legal liability at January 31 for this amount. Further, since the benefit derived from the employees' work was in January, the expense should be recognized in January regardless of when the employees will actually be paid.

- *Utilities* of $700. Since the bill was received in January, it can be assumed that it was for utilities purchased during January. Therefore, the expense should be recognized in January.

- *Interest Expense* of $1,000. The cost of the $100,000 loan is the interest Wooster must pay. Because the company had the $100,000 throughout the month of January, the interest cost for the month should be recognized as an expense even though it will not be paid until February 2. The amount is calculated using the formula explained in Chapter 5:

$$\begin{array}{cccccc} P & x & R & x & T \\ \$100,000 & x & 12\% & x & 1/12 \end{array}$$

- *Depreciation Expense* of $250. Under cash accounting, the cost of the vehicle was considered an expense the day it was paid for. Instead, as explained earlier, under accrual accounting, only a portion of the cost is recognized as expense each period. Using straight-line depreciation, the amount of depreciation is calculated as: ($14,000 - $2,000)/4 = $3,000. This $3,000 represents the amount of depreciation expense that should be recognized during each year of the assets's useful life. Because the financial statements we are using in the Wooster Company example are only for the month of January, 1993, the amount of depreciation expense would be only $250 ($3,000/12) for the month.

Now that we have discussed the effect of accrual accounting on the income statement, we can see the effects of this system on the statement of owners' equity. The $200,000 investment by the owner is treated just as it was under the cash basis. However, the results presented on the income statement under accrual accounting will be different than they were under the cash basis, so the statement of owners' equity will be different under the accrual basis of measurement.

WOOSTER COMPANY
Statement of Owner's Equity
For The Month Ended January 31, 1993
Accrual Basis

B. Wooster, Capital, January 1, 1993.............. $ 0
Investment by owner............................... 200,000
Net Income.. 26,550
B. Wooster, Capital, January 31, 1993............. $226,550

The balance sheet for Wooster Company at January 31, 1993 using the

accrual basis of accounting is presented below. You will note that

the items we discussed for the income statement have had an effect

on the balance sheet as well.

WOOSTER COMPANY
Balance Sheet
January 31, 1993
Accrual Basis

ASSETS
Current Assets:
Cash...................$266,500
Accounts Receivable... 32,000
Inventory............. 18,000
Total Current Assets.. 316,500
Long-Term Assets:
Vehicle........ $14,000
Less: Accum. Dep. (250)
Net Long-Term Assets.. 13,750
Total Assets.........$330,250

LIABILITIES & OWNER'S EQUITY
Current Liabilities:
Accounts Payable....$ 700
Wages Payable.......   2,000
Interest Payable....   1,000
Total Current Liabs.   3,700
Long-Term Liabs:
Note Payable.......$100,000
Total Liabilities... 103,700
B. Wooster, Capital. 226,550
Total Liabilities
and Owner's Equity..$330,250

Again, many items on this balance sheet differ from those on the

balance sheet prepared under the cash basis. Each item on the

statement is discussed in turn:

- *Cash* of $266,500. The amount of cash is counted and reported. The basis of economic measurement in place cannot change the amount of cash on hand. Note, however, that under the accrual basis, net income is affected by several items not directly related to cash. Therefore, net income is not equal to the increase in cash.

- *Accounts Receivable* of $32,000. This asset was created by transaction #6. Wooster recognized the sale because an exchange had taken place and title to the merchandise inventory had passed to the customer. When that transaction occurred, Wooster had a legal claim to the $32,000. This is certainly an item that has probable future benefit to the business and is therefore shown as an asset. It will remain classified as an asset until such time as the customer pays Wooster the cash.

- *Inventory* of $18,000. This is the remaining amount of merchandise inventory not recognized as cost of goods sold on the income statement. It is classified on the balance sheet as an asset because Wooster has not sacrificed it yet to generate revenue (it has probable future benefit). It will remain classified as an asset until such time as it is sold.

- *Vehicle* of $14,000. The original cost of the vehicle still shows on the balance sheet.

- *Accumulated Depreciation* of $250. To show that a portion of the original cost of the vehicle has been converted to expense, an amount called **accumulated depreciation** has been deducted to arrive at what is called Net Long-Term Assets. This figure, $13,750 is also called the **book value** of the vehicle. In future periods, as more depreciation expense is recorded, the total amount recorded since the asset was acquired is shown as accumulated depreciation. Therefore, as time passes, accumulated depreciation increases, and the book value of the asset decreases. This method of presentation tells decision makers what the assets originally cost and the amount not yet converted to expense (depreciated).

- *Accounts Payable* of $700. This is for the utilities; the liability was created in the adjustment process. Wooster has recognized the utilities expense, but the bill has not yet been paid. It is properly classified as a liability because it is an amount owed by the company and will require the sacrifice of assets (in this case, cash) in the future. It will remain classified as a liability until such time as Wooster pays the bill.

- *Wages Payable* of $2,000. This is the amount Wooster owes its employees at the balance sheet date; the liability was created in the adjustment process.

- *Interest Payable* of $1,000. This is the amount of interest Wooster owes the bank at the balance sheet date. Again, this liability was created in the adjustment process.

- *Note Payable* of $100,000. This is a liability representing the amount Wooster Company owes to Friendly Bank.

- *Capital* of $226,550. This is the ending balance shown on the accrual basis statement of capital. This amount is different than the capital balance shown on the cash basis balance sheet because of the difference in net income.

The accrual basis balance sheet differs from that of the cash basis not only in the specific items shown, but in the basic presentation of these items, as well. The accrual-based balance sheet groups the assets and liabilities into categories to provide additional information. **Current assets** are those that are either cash or expected to become cash within the next year. As you can see, accounts receivable and inventory are examples of current assets. **Long-term assets** are those that are expected to last longer than a year. Depreciable assets such as buildings, equipment, and vehicles are all examples of long-term assets. The **current liabilities** are those debts that are expected to require payment within one year. Certainly, the wages, interest, and accounts payable shown on the accrual-based balance sheet will need to be paid within a year. The note payable is due in one year, and thus, qualifies as a **long-term liability**. Classifying assets and liabilities into current and long-term provides additional information to financial statement readers.

Strengths and Weaknesses of Accrual Basis Accounting

The strength of the accrual basis is that it attempts to establish a relationship between revenues and the expenses incurred in generating the revenue. This is helpful to economic decision makers as they assess the past performance of a company and as they attempt to predict a company's future profitability.

Accrual accounting's most glaring weakness is that it takes the user's eye off cash. Decision makers are provided no information about inflows or outflows of cash when looking at the income statement. Because revenue and expense recognition under the accrual basis are *totally* unrelated to the receipt or payment of cash, net income does not represent an increase in cash for the period covered by the income statement. Neither does a net loss represent a decrease in cash.

7-14. What complications can you see if a revenue is recognized in December of 1991, but the cash is not collected until January of 1992?

7-15. What complications might arise if a company decides to depreciate an asset over a five-year period, but the asset lasts only three years? What if it lasts eight years?

COMPARING THE TWO BASES OF ECONOMIC MEASUREMENT

On the following pages, you will find two sets of financial statements prepared for the Wooster Company. The first set used the cash basis of economic measurement, and the second set used the accrual basis.

Each set illustrates the articulation of the financial statements. The net loss presented on the cash basis income statement results in a reduction of the owner's capital account. The accrual-based income statement shows a net income of $22,800, which increases the owner's capital account. In both sets of statements, the ending balance in the capital account, shown on the statement of owner's equity, is used on the balance sheet.

Remember that both sets of statements were prepared using exactly the same transactions and events. The differences are caused, not by the reality of what happened in Wooster Company during January, 1993, but by the different measurement criteria used by the cash and accrual bases of accounting.

WOOSTER COMPANY
Income Statement
For The Month Ended January 31, 1993
Cash Basis

Sales Revenue.......................... $ 78,000
Cost of Goods Sold....................   75,000
    Gross Margin.................................... $ 3,000
Expenses:
Cost of Vehicle.......................$ 14,000
Cash Operating Expenses...............   22,500
    Total Operating Expenses................... (36,500)
Net Loss...$(33,500)

WOOSTER COMPANY
Statement of Owner's Equity
For The Month Ended January 31, 1993
Cash Basis

B. Wooster, Capital, January 1, 1993.............. $ 0
Investment by owner...............................   200,000
Net Loss.. (33,500)
B. Wooster, Capital, January 31, 1993............. $166,500

WOOSTER COMPANY
Balance Sheet
January 31, 1993
Cash Basis

ASSETS:
Cash..................$266,500   LIABILITIES:
Total Assets.........$266,500   Note Payable.......$100,000
                                        OWNER'S EQUITY:
                                        B. Wooster, Capital. 166,500
                                        Total Liabilities
                                        and Owner's Equity..$266,500

```
                     WOOSTER COMPANY
                    Income Statement
           For The Month Ended January 31, 1993
                      Accrual Basis


Sales Revenue...........................$ 110,000
Cost of Goods Sold......................    57,000
    Gross Margin................................ $ 53,000
Expenses:
Cash Operating Expenses.................$22,500
Accrued Wages...........................  2,000
Utilities...............................    700
Interest Expense........................  1,000
Depreciation Expense....................    250
    Total Operating Expenses................... (26,450)
Net Income..................................... $ 26,550
```

```
                     WOOSTER COMPANY
                Statement of Owner's Equity
           For The Month Ended January 31, 1993
                      Accrual Basis


B. Wooster, Capital, January 1, 1993.............. $    0
Investment by owner...............................  200,000
Net Income........................................   26,550
B. Wooster, Capital, January 31, 1993............. $226,550
```

```
                     WOOSTER COMPANY
                     Balance Sheet
                    January 31, 1993
                     Accrual Basis


ASSETS                          LIABILITIES & OWNER'S EQUITY
Current Assets:                 Current Liabilities:
Cash.................$266,500    Accounts Payable....$    700
Accounts Receivable...  32,000  Wages Payable.......   2,000
Inventory.............  18,000  Interest Payable....   1,000
Total Current Assets.. 316,500  Total Current Liabs.   3,700
Long-Term Assets:               Long-Term Liabs:
Vehicle......... $14,000        Note Payable........$100,000
Less: Accum. Dep. (  250)       Total Liabilities...  103,700
Net Long-Term Assets..  13,750  B. Wooster, Capital.  226,550
Total Assets.........$330,250   Total Liabilities
                                and Owner's Equity..$330,250
```

334

Discussion Questions

7-16. Which of the two sets of financial statements do you think more closely relates the measurement of reality to reality? In other words, which set do you think is the better presentation of what actually happened during January, 1993? Explain.

7-17. Which of the two sets of financial statements do you think better reflects Wooster Company's future profit potential? Explain.

7-18. Are you coming to the conclusion that accounting lacks the exactness you once thought it possessed? Explain.

So, which of the bases is better? Neither. They each have strengths and weaknesses in relation to the other, and each of them is appropriate for certain entities in certain situations. However, the major purpose of financial statements is to provide information useful to economic decision makers. Often, decision makers are evaluating choices among various companies. If one company uses cash basis accounting and another uses accrual accounting, what are decision makers to do?

We have seen what different outcomes result when the two different measurement bases are used to measure the same reality. Imagine how difficult it would be to evaluate two sets of financial statements if they were developed using different measurement bases *and* they were based on different business activities! Even if the companies being compared both use accrual basis measurement, there are a number of factors that complicate the comparison. Chapters 8 and 9 explore areas in which flexibility in the recognition of revenues and expenses is allowed. These variations reduce the comparability of financial statement information between companies. However, in order to make the best use of accounting information, you should be aware of the variations.

CHAPTER SUMMARY

There are two things going on in business. First, there is the reality of business transactions and events. Second, there is an attempt to measure the reality in the accounting records and reports. For a number of reasons, the measurement of reality may not precisely reflect reality. Some of the differences between reality and the measurement of reality are a result of the basis selected to recognize revenues and expenses in a particular time period. This chapter presented two distinct bases: the cash basis and the accrual basis.

The cash basis of accounting is fairly simple and straightforward. Under this basis, revenue is recognized when the cash associated with it is received, and expense is recognized when the cash associated with it is paid. Periodic net income (or loss) under the cash basis is simply the difference between revenues and expenses.

Under accrual accounting, periodic net income (or loss) is determined as it is under the cash basis — as a difference between revenues and expenses. However, the two bases differ as to the criteria necessary to record revenues and expenses. Under accrual accounting, revenue is recognized when it is earned (when the company has a legal claim to the associated cash). Expenses are recognized when their benefit is deemed to have been received

337

regardless of when the associated cash is paid. Further, accrual accounting attempts to recognize expenses in the same income statement period as the revenues they helped generate.

Accrual accounting's attempt to match expenses to the same income statement period as the revenues they helped to generate is the key to a concept called matching. This concept provides the foundation for accrual accounting's treatment of long-lived assets whose benefit to the company extends beyond a single income statement period. The cost of these items is recorded as an asset because the benefit lies in the future. Then, the cost is systematically and rationally converted from asset to expense in the income statement periods benefited. This conversion process is known as depreciation.

In addition to depreciation, other adjustments to the accounting records are required to assure that accrual accounting's revenue and expense recognition guidelines have been met before financial statements are prepared. The two basic types of adjustments are accruals and deferrals. Accruals are adjustments made prior to any cash flow taking place. These adjustments record revenues for which the cash has not yet been received, and expenses for which the cash has not yet been spent. Deferrals, on the other hand, are adjustments made for situations in which the cash flow has already occurred. Revenues which have not yet been earned, but for which cash has already been received, require a deferral adjustment.

Accrual
adjustment
made before
cash
flow

adj → cash

Deferral
cash flash,
then
adjustment

cash → adj

Cases in which cash has already been spent, but the related expense has not yet been incurred result in deferral adjustments, also.

The greatest strength of accrual accounting is its attempt to show the relationship between expenses and the revenues they help generate. Doing so makes the income statement and balance sheet more useful as predictive and feedback tools than financial statements prepared under the cash basis. The cash basis does a poor job of relating expenses to the revenues they generate in a given income statement period. For this reason, financial statements prepared using the cash basis of accounting make the prediction of future profitability (and therefore cash flow) very difficult. The cash basis' greatest strength (besides its simplicity) is that it keeps the financial statement user's eye on cash. Accrual accounting's greatest weakness is that it takes the financial statement user's eye off cash because recognition of revenue and expense is not related to cash flow. Neither accrual accounting or cash basis accounting is "right" or "correct". They are simply different methods of recognizing revenues and expenses.

KEY TERMS DEFINED

Accrual basis accounting. A method of accounting in which revenues are recognized when they are earned, irregardless of when the associated cash is collected. The expenses incurred in generating the revenue are recognized when the benefit is derived rather than when the associated cash is paid.

Accruals. Adjustments made to record items that should be included on the income statement, but have not yet been recorded.

Accrue. As used in accounting, this means to come into being as a legally enforceable claim.

Accrued expenses. Expenses appropriately recognized under accrual accounting in one income statement period although the associated cash will be paid in a later income statement period.

Accrued revenue. Revenue appropriately recognized under accrual accounting in one income statement period although the associated cash will be received in a later income statement period.

Accumulated depreciation. The total amount of cost that has been systematically converted to expense since a long-lived asset was first purchased.

Adjustments. Changes made in recorded amounts of revenues and expenses in order to follow the guidelines of accrual accounting.

Book value. The original cost of a long-lived asset less its accumulated depreciation. This item is shown on the balance sheet.

Cash basis accounting. A basis of accounting in which cash is the sole criterion in measuring revenue and expense for a given income statement period. Revenue is recognized when the associated cash is received, and expense is recognized when the associated cash is paid.

Current Assets. Assets that are either cash or will become cash within one year.

Current Liabilities. Liabilities that must be paid within one year.

Deferrals. Adjustments of items for which the income statement effect is delayed until some later period. Deferred revenues are recorded as liabilities, and deferred expenses are recorded as assets.

Deferred expenses. Expenses in which cash is paid before any benefit is received. Because the benefit to be derived is in the future, the item is recorded as an asset. Later, when the benefit is received from the item, it will be recognized as an expense.

Deferred revenues. Results of the situation in which cash is received before the revenue is earned. Because the cash received has not yet been earned, an obligation is created and a liability is recorded. Later, when the cash is deemed to have been earned, it will be recognized as a revenue.

Depreciable Amount. Another name for depreciable base.

Depreciable Base. The total amount of depreciation expense that is allowed to be claimed on an asset during its useful life. The depreciable base is the cost of the asset less its salvage value.

Depreciation. The systematic and rational conversion of a long-lived asset's cost from asset to expense in the income statement periods benefited.

Depreciation expense. The amount of cost associated with a long-lived asset converted to expense in a given income statement period.

Long-term Assets. Assets that are expected to benefit the company for longer than one year.

Long-term Liabilities. Amounts that are not due for repayment until at least one year from now.

Matching. Relating the expenses to the revenues of a particular income statement period. Once it is determined in which period a revenue should be recognized, the expenses that helped to generate the revenue are matched to that same period.

Recognition. The process of recording an event in your records and reporting it on your financial statements.

Residual Value. The estimated value of an asset when it has reached the end of its useful life. Also called salvage or scrap value.

Salvage Value. Another name for residual value.

Scrap Value. Also called salvage or residual value.

Straight-line depreciation. One of several acceptable methods of calculating periodic depreciation. The depreciable base of an asset is divided by its estimated useful life. The result is the amount of depreciation expense to be recognized in each year of the item's estimated useful life.

(Cost - residual value)/N = annual depreciation expense

Title. Proof of legal ownership of an item.

REVIEW THE FACTS

1. Explain the difference between reality and the measurement of reality, and provide an example of each.

2. How does periodic measurement create complications?

3. In accounting, what does it mean to be "recognized"?

4. Under the cash basis of measurement, when does revenue recognition occur?

5. Under the cash basis, when are expenses recognized?

6. What is the greatest strength of the cash basis?

7. What is the greatest weakness of the cash basis?

8. Under the accrual basis of measurement, when does revenue recognition occur?

9. Under the accrual basis, when are expenses recognized?

10. Explain the concept of matching.

11. What is depreciation, and why is it necessary in accrual accounting?

12. Compare and contrast accruals and deferrals.

13. What is the greatest strength of the accrual basis?

14. What is the greatest weakness of the accrual basis?

Chapter 7
APPLY WHAT YOU HAVE LEARNED

A7-1.   Vicki Wright Company began operation on January 2, 1996.
During its first month of operation, the company had the
following transactions:

•   Purchased $35,000 of merchandise inventory on January
2. The amount due is payable on February 2.

•   Paid January office rent of $3,000 on January 3.

•   Purchased $10,000 of merchandise inventory on January
5. Paid cash at the time of purchase.

•   Sold $18,000 of merchandise inventory for $30,000 to a
customer on January 10 and received the cash on that
date.

•   Sold $5,000 of merchandise inventory for $9,000 to a
customer on January 20. The sale was on account and
the customer has until February 20 to pay.

•   Paid cash expenses during January of $7,500.

•   Received bills for utilities, advertising, and phone
service totaling $1,500. All these bills were for
services received in January. They will all be paid
the first week in February.

REQUIRED:

a.   Prepare a January, 1996 multi-step income statement for
Vicki Wright Company using the cash basis of
accounting.

b.   Do you think the income statement you prepared for the
previous requirement provides a good measure of the
reality of the company's performance during January?
Explain your reasoning.

A7-2. Vicki Wright Company began operation on January 2, 1996. During its first month of operation, the company had the following transactions:

P. 324, 334

- Purchased $35,000 of merchandise inventory on January 2. The amount due is payable on February 2.

- Paid January office rent of $3,000 on January 3.

- Purchased $10,000 of merchandise inventory on January 5. Paid cash at the time of purchase.

- Sold $18,000 of merchandise inventory for $30,000 to a customer on January 10 and received the cash on that date.

- Sold $5,000 of merchandise inventory for $9,000 to a customer on January 20. The sale was on account and the customer has until February 20 to pay.

- Paid cash expenses during January of $7,500.

- Received bills for utilities, advertising, and phone service totaling $1,500. All these bills were for services received in January. They will all be paid the first week in February.

REQUIRED:

a. Prepare a January, 1996 multi-step income statement for Vicki Wright Company using the accrual basis of accounting.

b. Do you think the income statement you prepared for the previous requirement provides a good measure of the reality of the company's performance during January? Explain your reasoning.

347

A7-3.   Phil Galor & Company began operation on January 2, 1996. During its first month of operation, the company had the following transactions:

• Paid January office rent of $2,000 on January 2.

• Purchased $25,000 of merchandise inventory on January 5. The amount due is payable on February 5.

• Purchased $15,000 of merchandise inventory on January 8. Paid cash at the time of purchase.

• Sold $12,000 of merchandise inventory for $18,000 to a customer on January 16 and received the cash on that date.

• Sold $9,000 of merchandise inventory for $13,500 to a customer on January 26. The sale was on account and the customer has until February 26 to pay.

• Paid February office rent of $2,000 on January 31.

REQUIRED:

a. Prepare a January, 1996 multi-step income statement for Phil Galor & Company using the cash basis of accounting.

b. Prepare a January, 1996 multi-step income statement for Phil Galor & Company using the accrual basis of accounting.

c. Explain in your own words what caused the differences between the income statement prepared under the cash basis and the one prepared under the accrual basis.

d. Which of the two income statement presentations do you think:

1) provides better information as to cash flow for the month of January?

2) provides better information as to what Galor earned during the month of January?

3) better reflects Galor's ability to generate future earnings and cash flow?

A7-4. This is a continuation of the Phil Galor & Company problem begun in A7-3. During the month of February, 1996, the company had the following transactions:

- Sold all the merchandise inventory it had on hand at the beginning of February for $28,500 on February 2.

- On February 5, the company paid the $25,000 it owed for the merchandise inventory it purchased on January 5.

- Purchased $20,000 of merchandise inventory on February 11. Paid cash at the time of purchase.

- Sold the $20,000 of merchandise inventory it had purchased on February 11 for $30,000 to a customer on February 21 and received the cash on that date.

- On February 26, Galor collected the $13,500 from the sale of January 26.

REQUIRED:

a. Prepare a February, 1996 multi-step income statement for Phil Galor & Company using the cash basis of accounting.

b. Prepare a February, 1996 multi-step income statement for Phil Galor & Company using the accrual basis of accounting.

c. Explain in your own words what caused the differences between the income statement prepared under the cash basis and the one prepared under the accrual basis.

d. Which of the two income statement presentations do you think:

   1) provides better information as to cash flow for the month of February?

   2) provides better information as to what Galor earned during the month of February?

   3) better reflects Galor's ability to generate future earnings and cash flow?

A7-5. This is a continuation of the Phil Galor & Company problem begun in A7-3 and A7-4. During the months of January and February, 1996, the company (which began operations on January 2, 1996) had the following transactions:

- Paid January office rent of $2,000 on January 2.

- Purchased $25,000 of merchandise inventory on January 5. The amount due is payable on February 5.

- Purchased $15,000 of merchandise inventory on January 8. Paid cash at the time of purchase.

- Sold $12,000 of merchandise inventory for $18,000 to a customer on January 16 and received the cash on that date.

- Sold $9,000 of merchandise inventory for $13,500 to a customer on January 26. The sale was on account and the customer has until February 26 to pay.

- Paid February office rent of $2,000 on January 31.

- Sold all the merchandise inventory it had on hand at the beginning of February for $28,500 on February 2.

- On February 5, the company paid the $25,000 it owed for the merchandise inventory it purchased on January 5.

- Purchased $20,000 of merchandise inventory on February 11. Paid cash at the time of purchase.

- Sold the $20,000 of merchandise inventory it had purchased on February 11 for $30,000 to a customer on February 21 and received the cash on that date.

- On February 26, Galor collected the $13,500 from the sale of January 26.

REQUIRED:

a. Prepare a multi-step income statement for Phil Galor & Company using the cash basis of accounting for the two month period ending February 28, 1996.

b. Prepare a multi-step income statement for Phil Galor & Company using the accrual basis of accounting for the two month period ending February 28, 1996.

c. Explain in your own words what caused the differences between the income statement prepared under the cash basis and the one prepared under the accrual basis.

A7-6. Presented below is a list of items relating to the concepts presented in this chapter, followed by definitions of those items in a scrambled order:

a. Cash basis revenues.
b. Accrual basis expenses.
c. Immediate recognition.
d. Matching concept.
e. Title passes to customer.
f. Depreciation.
g. No direct cause and effect between costs and revenues.
h. Cash basis expenses.
i. Residual value.
j. Accrual basis revenues.

i 1. ___ The amount of the cost of a long-lived asset which is not allocated to the periods supposed benefited.

a 2. ___ Recognized when cash associated with a sale is received.

g 3. ___ The situation which causes costs to be either recognized immediately as an expense or allocated to the income statement periods supposed benefited.

e 4. ___ One of the three evidences that revenue has been earned under accrual accounting.

h 5. ___ Recognized when the cash associated with a cost is paid.

j 6. ___ Recognized when there is a legal claim to the cash associated with a sale.

d 7. ___ An attempt to recognize expenses in the same income statement period as the revenues they generate.

b 8. ___ Recognized when the benefit is received rather than when the cash is paid.

f 9. ___ The process of converting the cost of a long-lived item from asset to expense.

c 10. ___ The treatment for costs where no future benefit can be determined, or allocation to future periods serves no useful purpose.

REQUIRED:

Match the letter next to each item on the list with the appropriate definition. Each letter will be used only once.

CHAPTER 8

CHALLENGING ISSUES UNDER ACCRUAL ACCOUNTING:
LONG-LIVED DEPRECIABLE ASSETS — A CLOSER LOOK

As we saw in Chapter 7, accrual accounting has the disadvantage of being less objective than the cash basis of accounting. Because it recognizes revenues in the periods in which they were earned, and it tries to record expenses in the same periods as the revenues which they helped earn, accrual accounting requires more judgement and estimation than cash accounting does. One of the best examples of the effects of estimates in accrual accounting is the depreciation of long-lived assets.

In this chapter we will extend our discussion of depreciation by considering several issues that further complicate the depreciation process. First, we will consider the impacts of the estimates made by management. You should recall from the discussion in Chapter 7 that management's estimates of an asset's useful life and its salvage value are integral components of the depreciation process.

Secondly, we will examine the issue of depreciation method choice. Various methods of calculating depreciation are used by different companies. We will explore the effects of these different methods and the effects of management's choice to use one instead of another.

The third major topic of discussion in this chapter focuses on the effects of asset disposal. Generally, when a company gets rid of an asset, the transaction results in the recognition of a gain or loss. As we will see, the estimates made and the depreciation method chosen will have effects on the determination of gains and losses. Our discussion of this topic will help you learn to properly interpret the meanings of gains and losses.

The coverage in this chapter is not intended as an exhaustive treatment of the complex measurement issues surrounding the depreciation process. Instead, it is designed to help you understand the nature of these complexities and how they influence the financial statements prepared using the accrual basis of accounting. When you have completed your work on this chapter, you will be able to:

1. Explain the process of depreciating long-lived assets as it pertains to accrual accounting.

2. Determine depreciation expense amounts using both straight-line and double-declining-balance depreciation methods.

   Describe in your own words the effects on the income statement and balance sheet if different depreciation methods are used.

4. Compare and contrast gains and losses with revenues and expenses.

5. Calculate a gain or loss on the disposal of a long-lived depreciable asset.

6. Explain the effects on the financial statements when a company disposes of a depreciable asset.

7. Draw appropriate conclusions when presented with gains or losses on an income statement.

DEPRECIATION

As you recall from our discussion in Chapter 7, depreciation is defined as a systematic (methodical) and rational (reasoned) allocation of the cost of a long-lived asset. Over time, the cost of the item is transferred from asset on the balance sheet to expense on the income statement. The purpose of this process is to more closely match the expenses with the revenues they help produce.

If, when an item is purchased, it is determined that the item will be used to produce revenues in more than one income statement period, the item is not recognized as an expense in the period in which it is purchased. Instead, it is recorded as an asset on the balance sheet. Then, in each year of the asset's *useful* life — useful because the asset is producing revenues — some portion of the cost of the item is recognized as an expense on the income statement for that year. Just how much is recognized as expense in a given year depends on several factors, including the estimates made and the depreciation method used.

The Effect Of Estimates

Estimates of the length of the asset's useful life and the amount of its residual value directly affect the amount of depreciation expense recognized each year. For example, assume Marconi-Bozeman, a law firm, purchases an a new copy machine for $20,000. If management estimates that the copier has a residual value of $4,000, the asset has a depreciable base of $16,000 (cost less residual value). The amount of depreciation expense recognized each year will be different if the useful life is estimated to be four years than it would be if the useful life is estimated to be three years or five years. By the same token, the depreciable base will be different if the residual value is estimated to be $3,000 rather than $4,000. As you can see in the chart below, if the depreciable base is different, the amount of depreciation expense recognized each year of the useful life will be changed accordingly.

MARCONI-BOZEMAN'S NEW $20,000 COPIER

OPTION	DETAILS	DEP. BASE	ANNUAL EXPENSE
Decision 1	Residual Value: $4,000	$16,000	$4,000
	Useful Life: 4 years		
Decision 2	Residual Value: $4,000	$16,000	$3,200
	Useful Life: 5 years		
Decision 3	Residual Value: $3,000	$17,000	$4,250
	Useful Life: 4 years		
Decision 4	Residual Value: $3,000	$17,000	$3,400
	Useful Life: 5 years		

Discussion Questions

8-1. What factors do you think a company should consider in determining the estimated useful life of a long-lived asset?

8-2. How do you think a company would go about determining the estimated residual value of a long-lived asset?

8-3. Consider a long-lived asset with a cost of $30,000. How would net income be affected by using an estimated useful life of four years and an estimated residual value of $5,000 rather than a five year estimated useful life and a residual value of $5,000? Explain.

8-4. How does the definition of "a systematic and rational allocation of cost" fit your explanation of the outcomes resulting from the two different estimates described in Discussion Question 8-3?

The Effect Of Different Depreciation Methods

Several different depreciation methods are available to companies. Most companies have more than one depreciable asset; they are free to choose one method for one type of asset and a totally different method for another. This situation results in many companies using more than one depreciation method. As users of the financial accounting information provided by these companies, it is important that you understand the impact of depreciation method choice on financial statements. To illustrate these effects, we will explore in detail the two most commonly used depreciation methods.

The first depreciation method we will explore is straight-line depreciation. Not only is this method the simplest one, it is the method most widely used by companies in the United States. Of the 600 companies surveyed by the authors of Accounting Trends and Techniques, 94 percent used the straight-line method to calculate depreciation expense reported in their financial statements for the year 1992.

Even though the straight-line method is used by the vast majority of companies in calculating depreciation expense, other methods are also used, and it is important for you to see how an alternative method works. Several depreciation methods record a larger amount of depreciation expense in the early years of an asset's life than in the later years. These methods are known as a accelerated

depreciation methods. During 1992, 17 percent of the companies surveyed by the authors of Accounting Trends and Techniques used some type of accelerated depreciation.

How do companies make the choice between using straight-line depreciation and using an accelerated depreciation method? Recall that a basic premise of accrual accounting is that expenses should be matched to the revenues they help produce. With that in mind, straight-line depreciation should be used for assets that produce the same amount of revenue in each period of their useful lives. Conversely, accelerated depreciation methods should be chosen for assets that produce more revenue in the early years, and a lesser amount as time goes by. Theoretically, this is the case. Practically speaking, however, depreciation method choice is more likely to be made based on less theoretical grounds. Often, a depreciation method is chosen for its ease of implementation. This explains the widespread use of the straight-line method. The other reason for management's choice of a depreciation method is likely to be the anticipated effect on the financial statements during the asset's useful life. As we explore the consequences of depreciation method choice, you will become aware of the significant impact this decision can have on the accounting information offered to economic decision makers.

To illustrate the impact of depreciation method choice on a company's financial statements, we will contrast the results of straight-line depreciation with those of an accelerated depreciation method. Our example will explore the **double-declining-balance method,** the most widely used of the accelerated methods. We will explore the application of this method not simply so you can learn the mechanics of how to use it, but more importantly to demonstrate the impact the choice of depreciation method can have on depreciation expense (and therefore reported net income).

Straight-line depreciation

In Chapter 7, we introduced the concept of depreciation with an example of the straight-line method. To review how straight-line depreciation is calculated, assume Barlow Corporation purchased an asphalt paving machine on January 2, 1995 for a total price of $300,000. Barlow's management estimates the useful life of this machine to be five years, at the end of which the machine will be sold for an estimated $25,000. For this example, assume this machine is the only long-lived asset Barlow owns.

Using the straight-line method, Barlow's yearly depreciation expense is $55,000. This amount was calculated by determining the depreciable base of $275,000 ($300,000 cost less the $25,000 estimated residual value) and dividing that base by the five-year estimated useful life ($275,000/5 years = $55,000 per year).

In each of the 5 years of the asset's useful life, $55,000 of the original cost of the asset will be removed from the asset total on the balance sheet and shown as depreciation expense on the income statement. To illustrate this point, Barlow Corporation's income statements and balance sheets for the years 1995 through 1999 follow. For ease of interpretation, we have held constant most of the items not affected by the depreciation process applied to the machine.

BARLOW CORPORATION'S FINANCIAL STATEMENTS USING STRAIGHT-LINE DEPRECIATION

INCOME STATEMENTS

	1995	1996	1997	1998	1999
Sales.............	$755,000	$755,000	$755,000	$755,000	$755,000
Cost of Goods Sold.	422,000	422,000	422,000	422,000	422,000
Gross Margin.......	$333,000	$333,000	$333,000	$333,000	$333,000
Operating Expenses other than depreciation......	(236,000)	(236,000)	(236,000)	(236,000)	(236,000)
Depreciation Exp...	(55,000)	(55,000)	(55,000)	(55,000)	(55,000)
Net Income........	$ 42,000	$42,000	$ 42,000	$ 42,000	$ 42,000

BALANCE SHEETS

	1995	1996	1997	1998	1999
ASSETS:					
Cash..............	$ 50,000	$ 96,000	$157,000	$213,000	$289,000
Accounts Receivable	206,000	257,000	293,000	334,000	355,000
Inventory.........	77,000	77,000	77,000	77,000	77,000
Machine...........	300,000	300,000	300,000	300,000	300,000
Less: Accumulated Depreciation......	(55,000)	(110,000)	(165,000)	(220,000)	(275,000)
Total Assets.......	$578,000	$620,000	$662,000	$704,000	$746,000
LIABILITIES & STOCKHOLDERS' EQUITY:					
Accounts Payable...	$206,000	$206,000	$206,000	$206,000	$206,000
Notes Payable......	170,000	170,000	170,000	170,000	170,000
Common Stock.......	100,000	100,000	100,000	100,000	100,000
Additional Paid-In Capital...	10,000	10,000	10,000	10,000	10,000
Retained Earnings..	92,000	134,000	176,000	218,000	260,000
Total Liabilities & Stockholders' Equity	$578,000	$620,000	$662,000	$704,000	$746,000

Note that regardless of what else happened in Barlow's operations for the years 1995 through 1999, the amount of depreciation expense each year did not change. This constant depreciation expense is one of the main characteristics of straight-line depreciation. You should also note that there is a direct correlation between the yearly depreciation expense shown on the income statements and the book value of the machine on the balance sheets. You will recall from Chapter 7 that book value is the cost of a long-lived asset less all the depreciation expense recognized since the asset was placed in service. The total depreciation expense recognized since the asset was put in service is reflected in the balance of accumulated depreciation. Therefore,

$$\text{COST} - \text{ACCUMULATED DEPRECIATION} = \text{BOOK VALUE}$$

Each year, as $55,000 of depreciation expense is recognized, the balance in accumulated depreciation increases by that amount, reducing the book value of the machine by that same $55,000. This example illustrates that *straight-line depreciation causes the book value of assets to decline by the same amount each year.* The book value at the end of 1999 is $25,000 ($300,000 - $275,000), which is equal to the estimated residual value. A total of $275,000 depreciation expense has been recorded. That is the amount of the depreciable base and is therefore the maximum amount of allowable depreciation expense. At this point, the asset is considered to be fully depreciated.

8-5. Refer back to the chart illustrating Marconi-Bozeman's four possible sets of estimates relating to its new copy machine. For each decision setting, determine the book value of the asset after three years' of depreciation had been recorded.

Obviously, a different estimated useful life or a different estimated residual value would change the amount of yearly depreciation expense. So, too, would the selection of a different method of calculating yearly depreciation expense. To demonstrate how the choice of depreciation method can affect depreciation expense, we will now explore the most widely used accelerated depreciation method.

Double-declining-balance depreciation

The double-declining-balance method got its name because it calculates depreciation expense at twice the straight-line rate. Rather than using the depreciable base to calculate yearly depreciation expense, as the straight-line method does, double-declining-balance calculates depreciation expense for a given year by applying the percentage rate to the book value of the asset. As a result, the double-declining-balance method ignores the estimated residual value in the depreciation calculation. There are three simple steps to calculating depreciation using the double-declining-balance method:

(1.) Figure the straight-line rate in percentages.
(100% / N, where N=number of years in the asset's useful life)

(2.) Double the straight-line percentage.

(3.) Apply that percentage to the book value of the asset.

As an example, let's apply this method to Barlow's asphalt paving machine. Each step below follows the directions above:

(1.) 100% / 5 = <u>20%</u> (per year)
(2.) 20% X 2 = <u>40%</u> (per year)
(3.) 40% X $300,000 = <u>$120,000</u> (for the first year)

For 1995, Barlow Corporation would record $120,000 depreciation expense. Step 3 of this process uses the book value of the asset. Note that in the first year of the asset's useful life, before any depreciation has been recorded, the book value of the asset equals the cost of the asset.

The following information shows how yearly depreciation expense would be calculated on Barlow's $300,000 machine using double-declining-balance depreciation and a five-year estimated useful life:

Year	Book Value At The Beginning Of The Year		Depreciation Percentage		Yearly Depreciation Expense
1995	$300,000	X	40%	=	$120,000
1996	$180,000	X	40%	=	$ 72,000
1997	$108,000	X	40%	=	$ 43,200
1998	$ 64,800	X	40%	=	$ 25,920
1999	$ 38,880				$ 13,880
Total Depreciation.................					$275,000

As you examine the preceding calculations, there are several points you should note. First, the book value of the machine declines each year by the amount of depreciation expense recognized that year. For example, the book value at the beginning of 1995 is the full $300,000 cost of the machine. At the beginning of 1996, the book value has dropped to $180,000 ($300,000 cost less $120,000 depreciation for 1995). The book value continues to drop until at the beginning of 1999 the book value of the machine is $38,880.

The second point you should note is that depreciation expense for 1999 ($13,880) is not 40 percent of the book value at the beginning of the year. The amount of depreciation expense in 1999 has been limited to $13,880 because companies are not allowed to depreciate assets beyond the point at which the book value of the asset is equal to its estimated residual value. In other words, the book value of an asset may never be lower than its residual value. This limitation is the same as stating that depreciation expense over the life of the asset cannot exceed the depreciable base (cost - residual value).

As the book value declines toward the residual value and the accumulated depreciation rises toward the maximum allowed, we must be careful not to exceed the limits. In 1999, the depreciation expense recorded is not the amount provided by the calculation using the double-declining-balance method; rather, it is the amount required to reduce the book value of the asset to its estimated residual value. This is the maximum depreciation expense allowed in that period. At that point, the asset is fully depreciated.

Since the double-declining-balance method does not take into consideration the residual value as depreciation expense is calculated, this method does not automatically depreciate exactly the allowable amount of depreciation over the life of the asset. For this reason, companies using this method must be careful not to depreciate an asset beyond its residual value.

The third point you should note about the calculations based on the double-declining-balance method is that during an asset's useful life, depreciation expenses start out high but quickly decrease. This rapid decrease is characteristic of all accelerated depreciation methods and has a profound effect on the financial statements of companies using accelerated depreciation methods. Barlow Corporation's income statements for the years 1995 through 1999 and its balance sheets at the end of each of those years using the double-declining balance method of calculating depreciation are shown to illustrate this point. Again, many items not affected by the company's choice of depreciation method have been held constant from year to year.

BARLOW CORPORATION'S FINANCIAL STATEMENTS USING
DOUBLE-DECLINING-BALANCE DEPRECIATION

INCOME STATEMENTS

	1995	1996	1997	1998	1999
Sales..............	$755,000	$755,000	$755,000	$755,000	$755,000
Cost of Goods Sold.	422,000	422,000	422,000	422,000	422,000
Gross Margin.......	$333,000	$333,000	$333,000	$333,000	$333,000
Operating Expenses other than depreciation......	(236,000)	(236,000)	(236,000)	(236,000)	(236,000)
Depreciation Exp...	(120,000)	(72,000)	(43,200)	(25,920)	(13,880)
Net Income (Loss)..	($ 23,000)	$25,000	$ 53,800	$ 71,080	$ 83,120

97000

BALANCE SHEETS

	1995	1996	1997	1998	1999
ASSETS:					
Cash..............	$ 50,000	$ 96,000	$157,000	$213,000	$289,000
Accounts Receivable	206,000	257,000	293,000	334,000	355,000
Inventory..........	77,000	77,000	77,000	77,000	77,000
Machine............	300,000	300,000	300,000	300,000	300,000
Less: Accumulated Depreciation......	(120,000)	(192,000)	(235,200)	(261,120)	(275,000)
Total Assets.......	$513,000	$538,000	$591,800	$662,880	$746,000

393000

	1995	1996	1997	1998	1999
LIABILITIES & STOCKHOLDERS' EQUITY:					
Accounts Payable...	$206,000	$206,000	$206,000	$206,000	$206,000
Notes Payable......	170,000	170,000	170,000	170,000	170,000
Common Stock.......	100,000	100,000	100,000	100,000	100,000
Additional Paid-In Capital...	10,000	10,000	10,000	10,000	10,000
Retained Earnings..	27,000	52,000	105,800	176,880	260,000
Total Liabilities & Stockholders' Equity	$513,000	$538,000	$591,800	$662,880	$746,000

Understanding the impact of depreciation method choice

Compare Barlow Corporation's income statements and balance sheets prepared using straight-line depreciation with those same statements prepared using double-declining-balance depreciation. You should notice several differences and similarities:

• There are significant differences in the reported depreciation expense in each of the five years.

• There are significant differences in the reported net income in each of the five years.

- *Total* depreciation expense and *total* net income over the five-year period are exactly the same regardless of which depreciation method is used. The differences occur in the individual years, not over the total five-year period.

- There are significant differences in the amounts of accumulated depreciation on the balance sheets for years 1995 through 1998. The 1999 balance sheet, however, shows exactly the same amount of accumulated depreciation in both presentations. In fact, the 1999 balance sheets in the two presentations are identical.

Neither the straight-line method nor the double-declining-balance method is better than the other. Our purpose in presenting a comparison between them is simply to make the point that the choice of depreciation method can have a substantial effect on reported net income and on portions of the balance sheet.

8-8. Explain why the 1999 balance sheets for Barlow Corporation, using the two different depreciation methods, are identical while all five income statements and the first four years' balance sheets are different.

8-9. Compare the amount of cash shown on the Barlow Corporation balance sheets using straight-line depreciation and double-declining-balance depreciation for each given year. Explain your findings.

We have now seen how Barlow's machine would be depreciated using both the straight-line method and the double-declining-balance method. To summarize the results, the information below presents a comparison of the depreciation expense, net income, and book value of the machine resulting from use of the two different methods.

	Straight-Line			Double-Declining-Balance		
Year	Deprec. Expense	Net Income	Book Value of Machine	Deprec. Expense	Net Income	Book Value of Machine
1995	$ 55,000	$ 42,000	$245,000	$120,000	($ 23,000)	$180,000
1996	$ 55,000	($ 11,000)	$190,000	$ 72,000	($ 28,000)	$108,000
1997	$ 55,000	$ 18,000	$135,000	$ 43,200	$ 29,800	$ 64,800
1998	$ 55,000	$ 34,000	$ 80,000	$ 25,920	$ 63,080	$ 38,880
1999	$ 55,000	$ 24,000	$ 25,000	$ 13,880	$ 65,120	$ 25,000
Total	$275,000	$107,000		$275,000	$107,000	

Discussion Questions

8-10. If the chart above depicted information from
two different companies, how would you make a
decision based on the given information?
Assume you were making an investment decision
in 1996, when only the 1995 accounting
information above were available.

DISPOSAL OF DEPRECIABLE ASSETS

In an ideal situation, a long-lived asset would be used for exactly
the time originally estimated, after which it would be sold for
exactly the residual value originally estimated. In reality, such
an ideal situation rarely, if ever, exists. The actual useful life
of an asset may differ greatly from the estimated useful life. In
fact, a company may dispose of an asset at any time. There is no
law that forces a company to keep an asset, regardless of any

373

estimates made at the time the asset was acquired. Conversely, there is nothing that requires a company to dispose of an asset at the end of its depreciable life. There is also no guarantee that a company will receive the estimated residual amount when it does sell the asset. The decision to keep or dispose of an asset should be based on the needs of the business, not on accounting considerations.

As a general rule, disposing of a depreciable asset does not constitute a company's ongoing major or central operations. Rather, this type of transaction is incidental or peripheral to the day-to-day operation of the business. For this reason, any increase in equity from the disposal of depreciable assets is not normally considered revenue. Nor is any decrease in equity associated with this type of transaction normally considered expense. They are considered accounting elements, however, and are reported on the income statement as **gains** (inflows) and **losses** (outflows).

Gains and Losses — Important Accounting Elements

In <u>Statement of Concepts #6</u>, the FASB defined these two elements as:

1. *Gains. Increases in equity from peripheral or incidental transactions of an entity and from all other transactions and other events and circumstances affecting the entity except those that result from revenues or investments by owners.* The

374

characteristics of gains are very similar to those of revenues. Both of these elements represent inflows of assets. The distinction between these two elements results from the source of the inflows. Revenues are generated from the major business activity of the company. Gains result from other types of activity.

2. *Losses. Decreases in equity from peripheral or incidental transactions of an entity and from all other transactions and other events and circumstances affecting the entity except those that result from expenses or distributions to owners.* Losses are very similar to expenses; both are outflows of assets. As was the case with gains and revenues, losses and expenses differ by source. Expenses are the results of the company's major business activity, whereas losses are incurred as a result of other activities.

Remember that the purpose of the income statement is to provide information about the past performance of a company so that decision makers can better predict the company's future success. Because gains and losses are incidental to a company's central operations and are usually one-time events, they should not be depended upon to predict the future success of a company's operations. In order to allow decision makers to evaluate the inflows of assets generated by the major or central operations of a business (revenues) differently than the inflows of assets generated by incidental activities (gains), the two are reported separately on the income statement. The same holds true for the outflow of assets. The outflows required for the major or central operations of a business (expenses) are reported separately from outflows associated with incidental activities (losses) on the income statement.

Although they are reported separately on the income statement, gains affect reported net income in exactly the same way that revenues do, and the effect of losses is exactly the same as that of expenses. The income statement equation introduced in Chapter 6 can be expanded, then, as follows:

$$REVENUES + GAINS - EXPENSES - LOSSES = NET\ INCOME$$

Calculating Gains and Losses

Calculating gains and losses that result from the disposal of long-lived depreciable assets is straightforward. When a company records this activity, the difference between what the company receives (most often cash) and the book value of the asset sold will be the amount of gain or loss on the sale. Let's return once again to the Barlow Corporation and its $300,000 asphalt paving machine. Assume Barlow depreciated this machine using the straight-line method over a five-year estimated useful life with a $25,000 estimated residual value (the first example in the chapter).

It is now January 2, 2000, and Barlow has decided to sell the machine because it is of no further use to the operation of the company. The machine has a $25,000 book value at the end of 1999 ($300,000 cost - $275,000 accumulated depreciation). How much will Barlow be able to sell it for, do you think? If your answer is

$25,000, you should reconsider. $25,000 is the book value — not the market value. The book value is based on an estimate made way back in 1995. In truth, most potential buyers won't know the book value as reflected in Barlow's records, nor would they care if they did. A buyer will pay what she or he thinks the item is worth. This amount will depend on a number of factors, such as the condition of the machine, the state of technology, what comparable used machines are selling for, and other similar concerns. It's highly unlikely that Barlow will receive exactly $25,000, but it's hard to say whether it will receive more or less.

Gain on disposal

Assume Barlow is able to sell the machine for a cash price of $32,000. Because the company received more than the book value of the machine, there is a gain, which can be calculated as $32,000 cash received - $25,000 book value = a $7,000 gain. The $7,000 will be reported as a gain on the income statement for the year 2000. Shown below are Barlow's income statements for the years 1999 and 2000 and its balance sheets at the end of each of those years, reflecting a $7,000 gain on the disposal of its machine.

Barlow Corporation
INCOME STATEMENTS

	1999	2000
Sales............................	$755,000	$941,000
Cost of Goods Sold...............	422,000	525,000
Gross Margin.....................	$333,000	$416,000
Operating Expenses		
other than depreciation.........	(236,000)	(319,000)
Depreciation.....................	(55,000)	-0-
Operating Income.................	$ 42,000	$ 97,000
Gain on Sale of Machine..........	-0-	7,000
Net Income.......................	$ 42,000	$104,000

Barlow Corporation
BALANCE SHEETS

	1999	2000
ASSETS:		
Cash.............................	$289,000	$225,000
Accounts Receivable.............	355,000	313,000
Inventory.......................	77,000	172,000
Machine.........................	300,000	-0-
Less: Accumulated Depreciation...	(275,000)	-0-
Total Assets....................	$746,000	$710,000
LIABILITIES &		
STOCKHOLDERS' EQUITY:		
Accounts Payable.................	$206,000	$216,000
Notes Payable...................	170,000	20,000
Common Stock....................	100,000	100,000
Additional Paid-In Capital.......	10,000	10,000
Retained Earnings...............	260,000	$364,000
Total Liabilities &		
Stockholders' Equity............	$746,000	$710,000

As you examine these financial statements, there are several points you should note:

- On the income statement for the year 2000, the $7,000 gain is shown in a different place than revenues from Barlow's ongoing major operations.

- The $7,000 gain has exactly the same effect on net income as the revenues from Barlow's ongoing major operations on the income statement for the year 2000.

- Both the cost of the machine ($300,000) and the accumulated depreciation ($275,000) have been removed from the balance sheet at the end of the year 2000.

Discussion Questions

8-11. Note that Barlow Corporation's income statements are presented in a multi-step format. What specific items on the income statements are unique to this format and would not appear on a single-step statement?

Loss on disposal

Now assume Barlow is able to sell the machine for a cash price of only $19,000. Because the company received less than the book value of the machine, there is a loss, which can be calculated as $19,000 cash received - $25,000 book value = a $6,000 loss. The $6,000 will be reported as a loss on the income statement for the year 2000. Barlow's income statements for the years 1999 and 2000 and its balance sheets at the end of each of those years, reflecting a $6,000 loss on the disposal of its machine, follow.

Barlow Corporation
INCOME STATEMENTS

	1999	2000
Sales...........................	$755,000	$941,000
Cost of Goods Sold..............	422,000	525,000
Gross Margin....................	$333,000	$416,000
Operating Expenses		
other than depreciation.........	(236,000)	(319,000)
Depreciation....................	(55,000)	-0-
Operating Income................	$ 42,000	$ 97,000
Loss on Sale of Machine.........	-0-	(6,000) 25,000
Net Income.....................	$ 42,000	$ 91,000

Barlow Corporation
BALANCE SHEETS

	1999	2000
ASSETS:		
Cash............................	$289,000	$212,000
Accounts Receivable.............	355,000	313,000
Inventory.......................	77,000	172,000
Machine.........................	300,000	-0-
Less: Accumulated Depreciation...	(275,000)	-0-
Total Assets...................	$746,000	$697,000
LIABILITIES &		
STOCKHOLDERS' EQUITY:		
Accounts Payable................	$206,000	$216,000
Notes Payable...................	170,000	20,000
Common Stock....................	100,000	100,000
Additional Paid-In Capital.......	10,000	10,000
Retained Earnings...............	260,000	$351,000
Total Liabilities &		
Stockholders' Equity............	$746,000	$697,000

As you study these financial statements, there are several points you should note:

- On the income statement for the year 2000, the $6,000 loss is shown in a different place than expenses required to support Barlow's ongoing major operations.

- The $6,000 loss has exactly the same effect on net income as the expenses required to support Barlow's ongoing major operations on the income statement for the year 2000.

- Both the cost of the machine ($300,000) and the accumulated depreciation ($275,000) have been removed from the balance sheet at the end of the year 2000.

In our examples of both a gain and a loss, we have assumed that Barlow was able to sell its machine for some amount of cash. However, there are times when an asset has no market value and must simply be abandoned. If this were the case with the Barlow machine, it would result in a loss of $25,000 ($0 cash received − $25,000 book value = a $25,000 loss).

Disposal with no gain or loss

Now let's assume Barlow is able to sell the machine for a cash price of $25,000. Because the company received exactly the book value of the machine, there is neither a gain nor a loss. ($25,000 cash received - $25,000 book value = $0 gain or loss). As the following statements show, sale of the machine will not directly affect the income statement for the year 2000, but the balance sheet will be affected.

Barlow Corporation
INCOME STATEMENTS

	1999	2000
Sales..............................	$755,000	$941,000
Cost of Goods Sold...............	422,000	525,000
Gross Margin......................	$333,000	$416,000
Operating Expenses		
other than depreciation.........	(236,000)	(319,000)
Depreciation......................	(55,000)	-0-
Operating Income.................	$ 42,000	$ 97,000
Gain (Loss) on Sale of Machine...	-0-	-0-
Net Income.......................	$ 42,000	$ 97,000

Barlow Corporation
BALANCE SHEETS

	1999	2000
ASSETS:		
Cash..............................	$289,000	$218,000
Accounts Receivable..............	355,000	313,000
Inventory.........................	77,000	172,000
Machine...........................	300,000	-0-
Less: Accumulated Depreciation...	(275,000)	-0-
Total Assets.....................	$746,000	$703,000
LIABILITIES &		
STOCKHOLDERS' EQUITY:		
Accounts Payable.................	$206,000	$216,000
Notes Payable....................	170,000	20,000
Common Stock.....................	100,000	100,000
Additional Paid-In Capital.......	10,000	10,000
Retained Earnings................	260,000	357,000
Total Liabilities &		
Stockholders' Equity............	$746,000	$703,000

As you examine these statements, there are two points you should note:

- There is no gain or loss from the disposal of the machine on the income statement for the year 2000.

- Both the cost of the machine ($300,000) and the accumulated depreciation ($275,000) have been removed from the balance sheet at the end of the year 2000.

Thus far you have seen how to calculate gains and losses, as well as how these elements impact the financial statements. It is now time for you to learn how to properly interpret gains and losses when they are a part of the accounting information made available during the decision making process.

UNDERSTANDING THE TRUE MEANING OF GAINS AND LOSSES

Let's assume there are two companies whose business activities are identical in almost all respects. The companies have the exact same sales for the year, and all their operating expenses (except depreciation) are the same.

We'll call the two companies in this example Marvella Corporation and Clarissa Corporation. Both companies purchased a fleet of trucks for $228,000 on January 2, 1994. In addition, both companies estimated a useful life of four years and a residual value of $92,000 for the trucks. Because Marvella Corporation uses straight-line depreciation and Clarissa Corporation uses the double-declining-balance method, we expect differences in their financial statements. The 1994 income statement and balance sheet for each company follow:

Income Statements
For the Year Ending December 31, 1994

	Marvella Corporation		Clarissa Corporation	
Sales		$769,000		$769,000
Less:				
Cost of goods sold	295,500		295,500	
Gross Margin		$473,500		$473,500
Wages Expense	$ 67,500		$ 67,500	
Utilities Expense	31,000		31,000	
Depreciation Expense	34,000		114,000	
Total operating expenses		132,500		212,500
Operating Income		$341,000		$261,000
Other revenues and expenses:				
Interest Expense		(120,000)		(120,000)
Net Income		$221,000		$141,000

Balance Sheets
December 31, 1994

	Marvella Corporation		Clarissa Corporation	
Assets:				
Cash		$226,000		$226,000
Accounts Rec.		198,000		198,000
Inventory		223,000		223,000
Trucks	$228,000		$228,000	
Acc.Dep.	(34,000)		(114,000)	
Trucks, net		194,000		114,000
TOTAL ASSETS		$841,000		$761,000
Liabilities:				
Accounts Payable	$ 22,000		$ 22,000	
Notes Payable	61,000		61,000	
Total Liabilities		$ 83,000		$ 83,000
Owners' Equity:				
Common Stock	$200,000		$200,000	
Add. Paid-in Capital	194,000		194,000	
Contributed Capital	$394,000		$394,000	
Retained Earnings	364,000		284,000	
Total Shareholders' Equity		758,000		678,000
TOTAL LIABILITIES AND OWNERS' EQUITY		$841,000		$761,000

straight
228000   4 yrs   residual 92000
136000 / 4 = 34000 per year

double declining
228000   4 yrs   92000
100% / 4 = 25% ×2 = 50%
228000 × 50% = 114,000
114000 × 50% = 57000

Discussion Questions

Refer to the 1994 financial statements of Marvella Corporation and Clarissa Corporation to answer the following Discussion Questions:

8-13. The amount of depreciation expense recorded by each company is given. Provide computations to explain how these amounts were determined.

8-14. The financial statements indicate four items on the income statements that differ between the companies. There are six items on the balance sheets that differ between the companies. Identify each item and explain the cause of the difference.

8-15. Assuming that no dividends were paid by either company, what was the balance in retained earnings on January 1, 1994, for each company?

8-16. What is the depreciation expense and accumulated depreciation for each company? Are these two items always the same?

8-17. What is the accumulated depeciation and book value of the trucks for each company? Why are Clarissa Corporations figures the same, while Marvella's figures differ?

The impact of the choice of depreciation method becomes even more evident over time. Let's examine the income statements and balance sheets of Marvella Corporation and Clarissa Corporation at the end of 1995. Again, we have held constant the items that are not affected by the use of different depreciation methods.

Income Statements
For the Year Ending December 31, 1995

	Marvella Corporation		Clarissa Corporation	
Sales	$769,000		$769,000	
Less:				
Cost of goods sold	295,500		295,500	
Gross Margin		$473,500		$473,500
Wages Expense	$ 67,500		$ 67,500	
Utilities Expense	31,000		31,000	
Depreciation Expense	34,000		57,000	
Total operating expenses		132,500		155,500
Operating Income		$341,000		$318,000
Other revenues and expenses:				
Interest Expense		(120,000)		(120,000)
Net Income		$221,000		$198,000

Balance Sheets
December 31, 1995

	Marvella Corporation		Clarissa Corporation	
Assets:				
Cash	$426,000		$426,000	
Accounts Rec.	253,000		253,000	
Inventory	223,000		223,000	
Trucks $228,000			$228,000	
Acc.Dep. (68,000)			(171,000)	
Trucks, net	160,000		57,000	
TOTAL ASSETS		$1,026,000		$959,000
Liabilities:				
Accounts Payable	$ 22,000		$ 22,000	
Notes Payable	61,000		61,000	
Total Liabilities		$ 83,000		$ 83,000
Owners' Equity:				
Common Stock	$200,000		$200,000	
Add. Paid-in Capital	194,000		194,000	
Contributed Capital	$394,000		$394,000	
Retained Earnings	585,000		482,000	
Total Shareholders' Equity		979,000		876,000
TOTAL LIABILITIES AND OWNERS' EQUITY		$1,026,000		$959,000

In addition to the differences occurring on the financial statements as the companies record depreciation, a more profound effect of depreciation method differences can be shown. Suppose that Marvella Corporation and Clarissa Corporation both decide to sell their trucks on December 31, 1995. The assets being sold are identical in age, condition, and market value. Each company receives $150,000 cash in exchange for its trucks. The $150,000 is the market value of the trucks on the day of the sale. This transaction would still require the companies to record depreciation for the year, just as it was reflected in the previous statements.

Discussion Question

8-18. Were the companies wise to sell the assets? Did they get "a good deal"? What information would you want before deciding whether it was a good deal?

Even though the actual business activity performed by Marvella Corporation and Clarissa Corporation is identical, the presentation of the results on their financial statements is quite different. The financial statements that follow show the impact of the sale on the financial statements of Marvella Corporation and Clarissa Corporation.

Income Statements
For the Year Ending December 31, 1995

	Marvella Corporation		Clarissa Corporation	
Sales	$769,000		$769,000	
Less:				
Cost of goods sold	295,500		295,500	
Gross Margin		$473,500		$473,500
Wages Expense	$ 67,500		$ 67,500	
Utilities Expense	31,000		31,000	
Depreciation Expense	34,000		57,000	
Total operating expenses		132,500		155,500
Operating Income		$341,000		$318,000
Other revenues and expenses:				
Gain on Sale of Trucks				93,000
Loss on Sale of Trucks	(10,000)			
Interest Expense	(120,000)		(120,000)	
Net Income		$211,000		$291,000

(handwritten annotations near the Gain/Loss lines, partly illegible: "book value (228000 −68 000)", "180000 book value −150,000", "book value 150000 ← −57000", "228000 −171,000")

Balance Sheets
December 31, 1995

	Marvella Corporation		Clarissa Corporation	
Assets:				
Cash	$576,000		$576,000	
Accounts Rec.	253,000		253,000	
Inventory	223,000		223,000	
TOTAL ASSETS		$1,052,000		$1,052,000
Liabilities:				
Accounts Payable	$ 22,000		$ 22,000	
Notes Payable	61,000		61,000	
Total Liabilities		$ 83,000		$ 83,000
Owners' Equity:				
Common Stock	$200,000		$200,000	
Add. Paid-in Capital	194,000		194,000	
Contributed Capital	$394,000		$394,000	
Retained Earnings	575,000		575,000	
Total Shareholders' Equity		969,000		969,000
TOTAL LIABILITIES AND OWNERS' EQUITY		$1,052,000		$1,052,000

The most obvious impact of depreciation method choice shown on the income statements and balance sheets above is the result of the sale. Note that Marvella Corporation recorded a $10,000 loss, but the same activity resulted in a $93,000 gain for Clarissa Corporation. The moral of the story? As smart financial statement users, do not be overly impressed by gains or overly alarmed by losses. Remember, these elements are merely a result of the difference between the book value and market value of assets sold. Don't assume that if a gain is shown, the sale was "good for business" or that if a loss is shown on the income statement, somehow management made a bad move. In the preceding example, there is not enough information available to determine if the sale of the trucks for $150,000 was a wise business decision or not. Clearly, though, the sale was no wiser for one company than for the other.

Also note that the retained earnings balance shown by Marvella Corporation and Clarissa Corporation is the same — $575,000. As you know, over the time that a long-lived asset is owned, its cost is transferred from asset on the balance sheet to expense on the income statement through the process of depreciation. By claiming a large amount of depreciation in the early years of the asset's life, as happens when using an accelerated method of calculating depreciation, a company lowers its net income for those years. In this way, the company also lowers the asset's book value, which then may be much lower than the asset's market value. In our example, the book value of Clarissa Corporation's trucks was so low that the company registered quite a large gain on their sale. Conversely, if a company claims a smaller amount of depreciation, as is the case with the straight-line method, the asset's book value will be higher. In our example, the book value of Marvella's trucks was so high at the time of sale that the company incurred a loss.

The following chart illustrates the impacts of the method of depreciation on net income in our example. Note that in a specific period, the two companies experience differences, but over the entire period of ownership for the trucks the method of depreciation has no effect on net income.

	Marvella Corp.	Clarissa Corp.
1994 Depreciation expense; (Reduction of net income)	($ 34,000)	($114,000)
1995 Depreciation expense; (Reduction of net income)	(34,000)	(57,000)
1995 Result of sale (gain or loss)	(10,000)	93,000
TOTAL IMPACT OF ASSET OWNERSHIP	($ 78,000)	($ 78,000)

The preceding chart illustrates why it isn't wise for decision makers to focus solely on the impact of gains and losses. Clearly, the result of the sale of an asset is only one component of the overall impact that ownership of that asset has had on the company over time.

As you can see by our discussion of the items presented in this chapter, the depreciation and disposal of long-lived depreciable assets can have a significant impact on a company's reported net income for a given year during the useful life of an asset. The issues surrounding depreciation can be very complex, and informed users of financial statements must have some understanding of them if they hope to be able to use the financial statements for predicting the future or assessing past performance.

In addition to depreciation, there are many other issues that have similar complicating effects under the accrual basis of accounting. We will continue our discussion of these complications in Chapter 9 as we consider issues surrounding the sale of merchandise inventory.

CHAPTER SUMMARY

Depreciation is the process of allocating the cost of long-lived assets to the periods in which they help to earn revenues. When an asset is purchased, its cost is recorded on the balance sheet. As time passes, the cost is transferred from an asset on the balance sheet to an expense on the income statement. The recording of depreciation expense accomplishes this transfer. The amount of accumulated depreciation for an asset represents all the depreciation expense related to that asset that has been recognized thus far. Accumulated depreciation is reported on the balance sheet as a reduction of the asset cost.

There are several acceptable depreciation methods. Calculating depreciation expense is easiest using the straight-line method. This method allocates depreciation expense evenly over the useful life of the asset. Accelerated depreciation methods recognize a greater amount of depreciation expense in the early years of an asset's life and a smaller amount in the later years. One such method is double-declining-balance.

The choice of depreciation methods affects companies' financial statements. In total, over the useful life of an asset, straight-line and double-declining-balance depreciation methods record the same amount of depreciation expense. However, in any particular period, different depreciation methods may result in different amounts of depreciation expense. This would cause a difference in reported net income. Because the amount of depreciation expense affects accumulated depreciation, the balance sheets of companies using different depreciation methods will also be different.

From time to time, companies sell some of their depreciable assets. Often, these transactions result in gains or losses. Gains and losses affect net income in a manner similar to that of revenues and expenses, but they are shown as separate items on the income statement. Gains and losses result from activities peripheral to the major activity of the company; revenues and expenses are direct results of the company's primary business activity.

An asset's book value is its cost less the amount of its accumulated depreciation. If an asset is sold for more than its book value, the transaction results in a gain. Conversely, selling an asset for less than its book value results in a loss.

If the disposal of an asset results in a gain or loss, that outcome is reported on the income statement. If, however, an asset is sold for exactly its book value, the transaction results in no gain or loss. In any case, when a company disposes of an asset, both the asset and its corresponding accumulated depreciation account are removed from the balance sheet.

Remember: If the sale of an asset results in a gain, it cannot be assumed that this was a "wise move" or that management received a good price for the asset. A gain simply indicates that the asset was sold for more than its book value. Conversely, disposing of an asset at a loss is not necessarily an indication of poor performance. Losses result when less than the book value is received for the asset. Book values of assets are affected by depreciation method choice and estimates of the useful life and residual value. Selling price is determined by what the buyer is willing to pay. Gains and losses are merely an indication of the relationship between book value and selling price, and should not be interpreted as anything more than that.

KEY TERMS DEFINED

Accelerated Depreciation Methods. Those methods that record more depreciation expense in the early years of an asset's life and less in the later years.

Double-Declining-Balance Method. An accelerated depreciation method. Depreciation expense is twice the straight-line percentage multiplied by the book value of the asset.

Gains. Net inflows resulting from peripheral activities of a company. An example is the sale of an asset for more than its book value.

Losses. Net outflows resulting from peripheral activities of a company. An example is the sale of an asset for less than its book value.

REVIEW THE FACTS

1. Provide three examples of long-lived depreciable assets.

2. In your own words, describe the depreciation process.

3. What are the two estimates made by management that will affect the amount of depreciation recorded each period?

4. What is the depreciable base of an asset?

5. Explain what is meant by an accelerated depreciation method.

6. Theoretically, in what situation is an accelerated depreciation method the appropriate choice?

7. Explain how the amount of depreciation expense is calculated using straight-line depreciation.

8. What is meant by an asset's book value?

9. What does the amount of accumulated depreciation represent?

10. In your own words, describe the process of determining depreciation expense using the double-declining balance method.

11. Compared to straight-line depreciation, what is the effect of an accelerated depreciation method on the balance sheet? On the income statement?

12. Regardless of what depreciation method is used, at what point is an asset considered "fully depreciated"?

13. On what financial statement do gains and losses appear?

14. What is the difference between a revenue and a gain? A loss and an expense?

15. How is a gain or loss calculated?

16. What effect does the disposal of an asset, resulting in no gain or loss have on the income statement? On the balance sheet?

A8-1.   Pat Garcia & Company has just purchased a lathe for use
in its manufacturing operation. The machine cost $50,000,
has a five-year estimated useful life, and will be
depreciated using the straight-line method. The only thing
remaining to be determined before yearly depreciation
expense can be calculated is the estimated residual value.
The alternatives are:

1) $5,000 estimated residual value.

2) $10,000 estimated residual value.

3) $15,000 estimated residual value.

REQUIRED:

a.   Calculate the yearly depreciation expense for the new
     lathe under each of the alternatives given.

b.   Which of the three alternatives will result in the
     highest net income?

c.   How long will the new lathe be useful to Garcia &
     Company?

A8-2.   Brent Bird Publishing Company purchased a new printing press for a total installed cost of $350,000. The printing press will be depreciated straight-line, in accordance with corporate policy. Roberta Swensen, the corporate controller, is trying to decide on an estimated useful life and an estimated residual value for the asset. The alternatives are:

1)   A six-year estimated useful life with a $20,000 estimated residual value.

2)   A five-year estimated useful life with a $50,000 estimated residual value.

3)   A four-year estimated useful life with a $70,000 estimated residual value.

REQUIRED:

a.   Calculate the yearly depreciation expense for the new printing press under each of the alternatives given.

b.   Which of the three alternatives will result in the lowest yearly net income?

c.   What should be the deciding factor in which of the three alternatives is selected?

A8-3.   Anatole Company purchased a high-tech assembler on January 2, 1995 for a total cost of $600,000. The assembler has an estimated useful life to the company of five years. Anatole thinks it will be able to sell the used assembler for $50,000 residual. The company has decided to depreciate the new assembler using the double-declining-balance method.

REQUIRED:

a.   Prepare a schedule showing the amount of depreciation expense for each of the five years of the estimated useful life.

b.   What will be the book value of the assembler at the end of the five-year estimated useful life?

c.   What does book value represent?

401

A8-4.   Wanda Company purchased a very sophisticated stamping machine on January 2, 1996 for $480,000. The estimated useful life of the stamping machine is five years. The machine has an estimated residual value at the end of its useful life of $40,000.

REQUIRED:

a.   Calculate the yearly depreciation expense for the stamping machine assuming the company uses the straight-line depreciation method.

b.   Prepare a schedule showing the amount of depreciation expense for each of the five years of the estimated useful life assuming the company uses the double-declining-balance depreciation method.

A8-5.   Bandicoot, Inc. purchased a fleet of delivery trucks on January 2, 1996 for $350,000. The estimated useful life of the vehicles is four years, after which Bandicoot thinks it will be able to sell the entire fleet for $25,000.

REQUIRED:

a.   Calculate the yearly depreciation expense for the fleet of vehicles assuming the company uses the straight-line depreciation method.

b.   Prepare a schedule showing the amount of depreciation expense for each of the four years of the estimated useful life assuming the company uses the double-declining-balance depreciation method.

c.   Address the following questions:

1)   Double-declining-balance calculates depreciation at twice the straight-line rate. Why is the amount of depreciation expense in 1996 under double-declining-balance not exactly twice the amount under straight-line for 1996?

2)   Over the four-year estimated useful life of the vehicles, how much depreciation expense will be charged against income using the straight-line method? How much will be charged against net income using the double-declining-balance method?

A8-6. Shubert Company purchased a machine in January of 1993 and paid $200,000 for it. When originally purchased, the machine had an estimated useful life of five years and an estimated residual value of $25,000. The company uses straight-line depreciation. It is now January 2, 1996, and the company has decided to dispose of the machine.

REQUIRED:

a. Calculate the book value of the machine as of December 31, 1995.

b. Calculate the gain or loss on the sale of the machine assuming Shubert sold it for $102,000.

c. Calculate the gain or loss on the sale of the machine assuming Shubert sold it for $25,000.

A8-7. Lydia and Lynette are twin sisters. Each of them has her own company. Three years ago, on the same day, they each purchased copy machines for use by their companies. The machines were identical in every way and cost exactly the same amount ($28,000). The copiers had the same estimated useful life (five years) and the same estimated residual value ($3,000). The only difference was the depreciation method chosen. Lydia chose to depreciate her copier straight-line, and Lynette selected an accelerated depreciation method.

Due to rapid technological developments in copiers, Lydia decided at the end of two years to sell her old copier and buy a new one. Lynette decided to do the same thing. In fact, they each received exactly the same amount when they sold their machines ($16,500). Later, while they were having lunch together, Lynette mentioned that she had sold her copier and had a gain of more than $6,000 on the sale. Lydia didn't say anything, but she thought something was fishy because she knew she had sold her copier for exactly the same amount Lynette had, yet the sale of her copier had resulted in a loss of $1,500.

REQUIRED:

Explain how Lydia could have had a loss of $1,500 on the sale of her copier, while Lynette had a sizeable gain.

Lydia
dep. $5000 per year
exp.
    × 2
  10,000 acc. dep.

book value 28000
      −10,000
       18000
      −16500
       1500 loss

Lynette
28000 × 40% = 11,200
16800 × 40% = 6720
17920 acc. dep.

$\frac{100}{5} = 20 \% (×2) = 40\%$

book value 28000
      −17920
       10080
      −16500
       6420 gain

403

A8-8. Presented below is a list of items relating to the concepts presented in this chapter, followed by definitions of those items in a scrambled order:

a. Accelerated depreciation.

b. Book value.

c. Gain on sale of asset.

d. Losses.

e. Estimated useful life.

f. Straight-line depreciation.

g. Gains.

h. Loss on sale of asset.

i. Depreciable base.

e 1.____ One of the factors determining how much of an asset's cost will be allocated to the periods supposed benefited.

d 2.____ Net outflows resulting from peripheral activities.

a 3.____ More of the cost of a long-lived asset is converted to expense in the early years of its life than in later years.

i 4.____ The cost of a long-lived asset less the estimated residual value.

c 5.____ Results when a depreciable asset is sold for more than its book value.

f 6.____ An equal amount of a long-lived asset's cost is converted to expense in each year of its useful life.

g 7.____ Net inflows resulting from peripheral activities.

b 8.____ The cost of a long-lived depreciable asset less its accumulated depreciation.

h 9.____ Results when a depreciable asset is sold for less than its book value.

REQUIRED:
Match the letter next to each item on the list with the appropriate definition. Each letter will be used only once.

404

A8-9. Return to the financial statements of Barlow Corporation based on the company's use of double-declining balance depreciation. Use the income statements and balance sheets presented as a basis to complete the requirements below:

p. 309

REQUIRED:

a. Prepare statements of retained earnings for Barlow Corporation as of the end of 1996, 1997, 1998, and 1999.

b. What can you conclude about the dividend policy of Barlow Corporation from the information provided and your response to requirement a. above?

c. If no depreciation had been recorded, how would the statements of retained earnings been different?

CHAPTER 9

CHALLENGING ISSUES UNDER ACCRUAL ACCOUNTING:
MERCHANDISE INVENTORY AND COST OF GOODS SOLD

In Chapter 8 we explored one source of variation across companies' financial statements — depreciation method choice. Recall that this issue results from accrual accounting's attempt to recognize revenue in the period earned and match the expenses to the revenue they helped to generate. This characteristic of accrual accounting results in other differences among the financial statements of various companies as well. One such instance of variation occurs as companies keep track of the movement of the products they buy and sell.

Cash basis accounting recognizes revenue from sales only when cash is received. On the other hand, accrual accounting requires that sales revenue be recognized when earned, regardless of whether or not cash is received. Cash basis accounting recognizes the expenses related to the products as the cash is spent. Under cash basis accounting, the fact that the products may not yet have been sold is irrelevant. Accrual accounting focuses on matching the expenses, in this case the cost of the product, with the revenue generated by the sale. A method must be developed to determine the amount of expense to recognize in a given period. Actually, several methods are available, and companies may use whichever method they prefer. This situation results in another example of ways in which the financial statements of several companies using accrual accounting can vary.

The way merchandise inventory purchases and sales are accounted for can have a direct and significant impact on a company's reported net income. When you have completed your work on this chapter, you should be able to:

1. Name the components of goods available for sale (GAFS) and explain what GAFS is.

2. Describe in your own words the relationship between ending inventory and cost of goods sold.

3. Differentiate between the physical flow of merchandise and the cost flow of merchandise.

4. Explain the differences between periodic and perpetual inventory systems.

5. List three different inventory cost flow assumptions and contrast how the use of each affects reported net income on the income statement.

6. Calculate cost of goods sold and ending inventory using FIFO, LIFO, and average cost inventory cost flow assumptions.

TRACKING INVENTORY COSTS

Recall that in Chapter 1 you were introduced to the three major types of business activity — manufacturing, merchandising, and service. Manufacturers make products to sell, merchandisers buy products to sell, and service companies sell services rather than tangible products. The tangible products that manufacturers and merchandisers sell are referred to as **merchandise inventory**, or simply **inventory**. For example, Walmart Corporation has inventory comprised of tubes of toothpaste, lawnmowers, clothing, and thousands of other products. Henredon Furniture Company's inventory includes beds, dressers, tables, desks and chairs. General Motors owns desks and chairs, too. But these desks and chairs are *not* inventory. These items would be assets of General Motors, probably referred to simply as "furniture". Inventory items are those held by a company for resale. The inventory of General Motors includes cars, trucks, vans and a wide variety of auto parts.

Unfortunately, the terms "merchandise inventory" and "inventory" are often used to describe the *cost* of the items as well as the items themselves. Therefore, when you see the term *merchandise inventory*, you must analyze the context in which the term is used to determine whether it is describing the actual physical units of inventory or the cost of that inventory.

The amount of merchandise inventory on hand at the beginning of the period is usually called **beginning inventory**, and the amount of merchandise inventory purchased during the period is usually called **purchases**. Both of these terms can be used to refer to the units themselves or the cost of the units. The total amount of merchandise inventory a company *could* sell in a given income statement period is the amount they started with (beginning inventory) plus the amount they bought (purchases). This total is referred to as **goods available for sale**. Again, "goods available for sale" is used to describe either the physical amount of merchandise inventory available for sale or the cost of that inventory. Whether referring to the physical amount of inventory or its cost, the following relationship between beginning inventory (BI), purchases (Purch), and goods available for sale (GAFS) holds true:

$$BI + Purch = GAFS$$

Under the accrual basis of accounting, merchandise inventory is reported as an asset when it is purchased because it has probable future benefit (it should generate future revenues). As the merchandise is sold and revenues are generated, the cost of the merchandise is converted from an asset on the balance sheet to an expense on the income statement. This expense is known as **cost of goods sold**, or **cost of sales**, and was discussed briefly in Chapter 6. The cost of goods sold (COGS) can be determined by subtracting the amount of inventory on hand at the end of the period, **ending**

inventory, from goods available to sell. In other words, the total amount that we *could* have sold (GAFS) minus the amount we still had at the end of the period (EI) equals the amount we must have sold (COGS):

$$GAFS - EI = COGS$$

Conversely, if we know cost of goods sold, we can determine a company's ending merchandise inventory for a given period. The total amount we *could* have sold (GAFS) less the amount we *did* sell (COGS) is the amount we have left at the end of the period (EI).

$$GAFS - COGS = EI$$

These relationships hold true whether we are considering the amount of inventory (physical units) or the cost of that inventory. The following illustration shows examples of these relationships in terms of both units and dollar amounts.

	Units	Cost	
Beginning Inventory.......	20	$200	BI
+ Purchases...............	70	700	+ Purch
= Goods Available For Sale..	90	$900	GAFS
- Ending Inventory.........	15	150	- EI
= Cost of Goods Sold........	75	$750	COGS

OR

	Units	Cost	
Beginning Inventory.......	20	$200	BI
+ Purchases...............	70	700	+ Purch
= Goods Available For Sale..	90	$900	GAFS
- Cost of Goods Sold........	75	750	- COGS
= Ending Inventory.........	15	$150	EI

410

In the first presentation above, ending inventory is used to calculate cost of goods sold and in the second one, cost of goods sold is used to calculate ending inventory. It is important to learn from the two preceding calculations that *the total of ending inventory and cost of goods sold will always equal goods available for sale (in units and in dollars)*.

Think of your local Tower Record Store. All of the records and CD's in the store on the first of the month (BI) plus any new records or CD's the store receives during the month (Purch) are the total of what the store could sell (GAFS). The products (GAFS) are either gone or still in the store at the end of the month. If items are gone, we presume they were sold (and consider them part of cost of goods sold). NOTE: Some of the items could have been broken or stolen. What's still in the store at the end of the period is the store's ending inventory.

REMEMBER: All GAFS become either COGS or EI.

```
┌─────────────────────────────────────────────────────┐
│                 Discussion Question                    │
│  ┌───────────────────────────────────────────────┐   │
│  │                                                │   │
│  │ 9-1. You decide to throw a weekend party, so you │ │
│  │                                                │   │
│  │      begin to plan.  After checking-out what's in │ │
│  │                                                │   │
│  │      the house, you find you have some hot dogs, │ │
│  │                                                │   │
│  │      buns, and pretzels.  That stuff's a good start, │ │
│  │                                                │   │
│  │      but you dash to the store and buy beer, soda, │ │
│  │                                                │   │
│  │      chips, dip, peanuts, and ice cream.  The party │ │
│  │                                                │   │
│  │      was a GREAT HIT.  Your guests devoured all the │ │
│  │                                                │   │
│  │      food and drinks, except for the ice cream — it │ │
│  │                                                │   │
│  │      was never touched!                        │   │
│  │      As you relax and enjoy the memories of the │   │
│  │                                                │   │
│  │      party's finest moments, you decide to figure │ │
│  │                                                │   │
│  │      out what the event cost you.  What was your: │ │
│  │      A.  Beginning inventory?                  │   │
│  │                                                │   │
│  │      B.  Purchases?                            │   │
│  │                                                │   │
│  │      C.  Goods available?                      │   │
│  │                                                │   │
│  │      D.  Ending inventory?                     │   │
│  │                                                │   │
│  │      E.  "Cost" of the party?                  │   │
│  │                                                │   │
│  └───────────────────────────────────────────────┘   │
└─────────────────────────────────────────────────────┘
```

Now, let's look closer at the process of tracking a company's inventory and its cost as items are bought and sold.

The Physical Movement of Inventory (Reality)

```
+------------------------------------------------------------------+
|                   picture of computer here                       |
+------------------------------------------------------------------+
```

The picture above shows a computer. It was purchased by Computer Exchange, Inc., a retail merchandiser, from a wholesaler on January 17, 1995, for $800. Then, the computer was moved to Computer Exchange's warehouse. The computer was purchased for the purpose of resale and was, in fact, sold and delivered to a customer on February 6, 1995, for $1,500.

Because the computer was purchased for the purpose of resale, it was considered merchandise inventory by Computer Exchange. Had the company purchased the computer for its own use, the item would not have been considered inventory. Rather, it would be a long-lived asset and would be depreciated.

The following diagram illustrates the physical movement of the computer from the time it was purchased from the wholesaler until it was sold and delivered to the customer.

```
+------------------------------------------------------------------+
|         Purchase                              Sale               |
|         1/17/95                               2/6/95             |
|  Wholesaler              Warehouse                  Customer      |
|  ----------------------------->  -------------------------->      |
|                                                                  |
+------------------------------------------------------------------+
```

The Flow of Inventory Cost (Measurement of Reality)

Under accrual accounting, Computer Exchange would attempt to match expenses to the same income statement period as the revenues they help generate. For this reason, the company would not recognize the cost of the computer as an expense when it was purchased. Instead, the computer (and its $800 cost) would be considered an asset. As of January 31, 1995, the computer had not been sold and was in the company's warehouse. Therefore, its cost would be shown on the balance sheet prepared at the end of January as merchandise inventory (an asset). Nothing related to the computer would be reported on the income statement. We can calculate the cost of goods sold and ending inventory for Computer Exchange, Inc. as of January 31, 1995, as:

	Units	Cost	
Beginning Inventory (1/1).	0	$-0-	BI
+ Purchases..................	1	800	+ Purch
= Goods Available For Sale..	1	$800	GAFS
- Cost of Goods Sold........	0	-0-	- COGS
= Ending Inventory (1/31)...	1	$800	EI

Assuming Computer Exchange had no business transactions during January except those related to the computer and the payment of warehouse rent, the company's income statement for the month of January, 1995, and its balance sheet at January 31, 1995, would be:

414

```
              Computer Exchange, Inc.
                  Income Statement
         For The Month Ended January 31, 1995

         Sales......................$ -0-
         Less Cost of Goods Sold.....   -0-
         Gross Margin...............$ -0-
         Operating Expenses:
         Warehouse Rent..............$(  200)
         Net Income (Loss)...........$(  200)

              Computer Exchange, Inc.
                  Balance Sheet
              At January 31, 1995

         ASSETS:
         Cash.......................$22,000
         Merchandise Inventory.......    800
         Total Assets...............$22,800

         LIABILITIES &
         STOCKHOLDERS' EQUITY:
         Common Stock...............$15,000
         Additional Paid-In Capital..  8,000
         Retained Earnings...........(   200)
         Total Liabilities &
         Stockholders' Equity.......$22,800
```

Discussion Question

9-2. Can you tell how long Computer Exchange, Inc. has been in business by looking at the income statement and balance sheet above?   Explain.

As you recall, Computer Exchange sold the computer on February 6, 1995, and delivered it to the customer on that day.   We can calculate the cost of goods sold that should be reported on

February's income statement and the amount of ending inventory to be shown on the February 28 balance sheet as follows:

	Units	Cost	
Beginning Inventory (2/1).	1	$800	BI
+ Purchases..............	0	-0-	+ Purch
= Goods Available For Sale..	1	$800	GAFS
- Cost of Goods Sold.......	1	800	- COGS
= Ending Inventory (2/28)...	0	$-0-	EI

Assuming Computer Exchange had no business transactions during February except those related to the computer and the payment of rent, the company's income statement for the month of February, 1995, and its balance sheets at January 31, 1995, and February 28, 1995, would be:

Computer Exchange, Inc.
Income Statement
For The Month Ended February 28, 1995

Sales......................	$ 1,500
Less Cost of Goods Sold.....	800
Gross Margin................	$ 700
Operating Expenses:	
Warehouse Rent.............	$(200)
Net Income (Loss)..........	$ 500

Computer Exchange, Inc.
Balance Sheets
At January 31, 1995 & February 28, 1995

ASSETS:	January	February
Cash........................	$22,000	$21,800
Accounts Receivable........	-0-	1,500
Merchandise Inventory.......	800	-0-
Total Assets...............	$22,800	$23,300
LIABILITIES &		
STOCKHOLDERS' EQUITY:		
Common Stock................	$15,000	$15,000
Additional Paid-In Capital..	8,000	8,000
Retained Earnings..........	(200)	300
Total Liabilities &		
Stockholders' Equity.......	$22,800	$23,300

We have included both the January 31 balance sheet and the February 28 balance sheet to demonstrate how the $800 cost of the computer flowed through the financial statements. This flow can be seen by following the arrows in the presentation above. The $800 was reported as an asset (merchandise inventory) on the January 31 balance sheet. Because the computer was sold during February, no merchandise inventory is listed on the February 28 balance sheet. Instead, the $800 cost has been converted to an expense and is reported on the February income statement as cost of goods sold. Cost of goods sold then affects the gross margin and thus the net income, as well. The $500 net income is reflected in the February 28 balance sheet as an increase both in the total assets and in total liabilities & stockholders' equity. Total assets increase by $500 because while the company sacrificed $1,000 of assets during February ($800 cost of goods sold and $200 rent on the warehouse), those sacrifices generated a $1,500 asset (accounts receivable). As the arrow shows, stockholders' equity increases by $500 as a result of the net income figure being combined with the previous retained earnings balance to arrive at the updated retained earnings balance of $300.

Earlier, we illustrated the physical movement of the computer from the time it was purchased by Computer Exchange to the time it was sold to the customer. The diagram below presents the physical flow of the computer again and also shows the flow of the cost associated with the computer.

```
┌─────────────────────────────────────────────────────────────┐
│                                                               │
│                   Purchase                          Sale      │
│                   1/17/95                          2/6/95     │
│  Physical Path:                                               │
│                                                               │
│                   Wholesaler      Warehouse       Customer    │
│                                                               │
│                   ─────────────────────>  ──────────────────>│
│  Cost Flow:                                                   │
│                                                               │
│                   Balance Sheet              Income Statement │
│                   $800 Asset                  $800 COGS       │
│                                                               │
│                   ──────────────────────────────────────────>│
│                                                               │
└─────────────────────────────────────────────────────────────┘
```

Computer Exchange purchased a computer, which was delivered to the company's warehouse. This is reality. Computer Exchange sold the computer and delivered it to its customer. This too, is reality. The $800 cost of the computer was initially reported on the balance sheet as an asset; when the computer was sold, the $800 was transferred to an expense (COGS) on the income statement. This is the measurement of reality. As shown above, in this simple example involving only one unit of inventory, the physical flow of the merchandise inventory and the flow of the cost associated with the merchandise inventory coincide. Actually, however, when a company has many units of inventory, the physical flow of merchandise (reality) and the cost flow of that merchandise (measurement of reality) are not always the same. This situation is another source of variation among companies' accounting information. To some degree, the differences are influenced by the type of inventory system a company chooses to use.

INVENTORY SYSTEMS

In our previous example, Computer Exchange transferred the $800 cost of the computer from an asset to an expense when the item was sold on February 6, 1995. This conversion, however, is not always immediate. The timing of the conversion of this cost depends on what kind of inventory system a company employs. An **inventory system** is a set of procedures adopted by a company to account for both the physical flow of merchandise and the flow of the cost of the merchandise. Over time, two major inventory systems have been developed. They are the *periodic inventory system* and the *perpetual inventory system*.

Periodic Inventory Systems

Under a **periodic inventory system**, all inventory and cost of goods sold calculations are done at the end of the income statement period. Detailed inventory records are not updated during the period; companies using this system do not know which merchandise inventory has been sold until the end of period, when the company prepares its financial statements. The cost of the inventory sold can then be reported as cost of goods sold on the income statement for the period and the cost of the inventory still on hand can be reported as an asset on the balance sheet at the end of the period.

The strength of the periodic inventory system is that it involves relatively litte record keeping. Its greatest weakness is that it provides no day-to-day information to the company about the status of its inventory.

Prior to the computer age, virtually all companies with even a moderate volume of inventory employed periodic inventory systems. Keeping detailed inventory records manually was too time-consuming. Now, however, rapid advances in computer technology have made the task of keeping daily records of inventory transactions a reasonably efficient process. For this reason, perpetual inventory systems have grown in popularity. Therefore, all of the examples we will use in the remainder of this chapter will be based on the perpetual inventory system.

Perpetual Inventory Systems

Under a **perpetual inventory system,** both the physical count of inventory units and the cost classification (asset or expense) are updated whenever there is a transaction involving inventory. To illustrate, let's return to our original example of Computer Exchange and its $800 computer. Under a perpetual system, Computer Exchange would have an inventory control report similar to the following:

Date	Explanation	Purchases Units	Unit Cost	Total Cost	Cost of Goods Sold Units	Unit Cost	Total Cost	Merchandise Inventory Balance Units	Unit Cost	Total Cost
1/17	Purchase	1	$800	$800				1	$800	$800
2/06	Sale				1	$800	$800	0		$-0-

As you can see, the report shows the purchase of the computer on January 17, 1995, and the sale of the computer on February 6, 1995. At the end of the income statement period (February in this case), the total cost column in the cost of goods sold section would be added up to determine the amount of cost for this inventory item to report as COGS on the income statement. The last amount showing in the total cost column of the merchandise inventory balance section at the end of February would be the amount of merchandise inventory to appear on the balance sheet.

Since a running balance of merchandise inventory on hand is kept (the far right side of the report), the company can tell at any time the number of physical units it has on hand. This report can also be used to determine the dollar amount which has been transferred from asset (merchandise inventory) on the balance sheet to expense (cost of goods sold) on the income statement.

If Computer Exchange employed a manual (non-computerized) accounting system, this inventory control report would normally be in the form of a card kept in a file box. Whenever the company had a transaction involving inventory, the card would have been removed from the file and updated.

Computer Exchange uses a computerized accounting system to generate its inventory control reports automatically. Purchases and sales of inventory are registered either by keyboard entries or, more commonly, by a scanning device. Retailers use scanners to read bar codes - formally known as a Universal Product Codes, or UPC's - printed on their inventory. The computer can be programmed to assign a given price to a given piece or type of inventory, and the computer can thus perform the necessary calculations to update inventory records.

Chances are, when you purchased this book, the clerk in the bookstore either ran a stylus over the UPC on the back of the book or ran the back of the book over a little window on the check-out counter.

Besides ringing up the sales price of the book, the use of the UPC also updated the bookstore's inventory records. The number of physical units on hand was changed, and the transfer of the cost of the book from merchandise inventory to cost of goods sold was recorded. By utilizing this technology, the bookstore employees can determine the number of books sold and the number of books remaining on the shelf without going out and physically counting them. Whenever they want, the employees can review an inventory control report similar to the one presented earlier. This report can help managers, or other employees, decide when to reorder which inventory.

Discussion Questions

9-4. How might the use of UPC technology differ between an auto parts store and a grocery store?

9-5. Assume the inventory control report on this textbook shows 25 books remaining on the shelf. Just to make sure, the bookstore manager goes out to the shelf, counts the remaining books and finds there are only 22. What might explain the discrepancy?

The Necessity of a Physical Inventory Count

The amount of ending inventory (units and dollars) generated by a perpetual inventory system is called **book inventory** and may or may not reflect the reality of the merchandise inventory actually on hand at the end of the period. Errors in entering transactions into the inventory control report and theft of inventory are two potential causes for book inventory to differ from actual inventory on hand. Sometimes, inventory is damaged and discarded, or if the inventory is perishable, it may even spoil as time passes. Because of these sources of discrepancies between the inventory records of a perpetual inventory system and the reality of the inventory on hand, physical inventory counts must be made from time to time.

Results of the physical inventory count take precedence over the book inventory generated by the inventory records. Cost of goods sold for the period is adjusted for any differences between the physical count and the book count. To illustrate, let's return to the cost of goods sold and ending inventory calculation used earlier.

		Units	Cost	
	Beginning Inventory.......	20	$200	BI
+	Purchases................	70	700	+ Purch
=	Goods Available For Sale..	90	$900	GAFS
-	Cost of Goods Sold.......	75	750	- COGS
=	Ending Inventory.........	15	$150	EI

The figures in this calculation came from the company's inventory control report. The ending inventory of 15 units and $150 is the book inventory. However, a physical count reveals that there are only 13 units on hand. The calculation would be extended as follows:

		Units	Cost
	Beginning Inventory.......	20	$200
+	Purchases................	70	700
=	Goods Available For Sale..	90	$900
-	Cost of Goods Sold (Book).	75	750
=	Ending Inventory (Book)...	15	$150
-	Actual Ending Inventory....	13	$130
=	Additional COGS...........	2	$ 20

The cost of goods sold reported as an expense on the income statement for the period would be $770 ($750 from the records + $20 from the inventory adjustment = $770). The ending merchandise inventory reported as an asset on the balance sheet would be $130, which reflects the reality of the number of units actually on hand at the end of the period.

COST FLOW ASSUMPTIONS

It is quite logical to assume merchandise inventory costs flow through the system the same way the physical units of merchandise inventory flow through the system. Unfortunately, these flows are not always the same. This is another example of the difference between reality and the measurement of reality, leading to some complexities in accrual accounting.

To illustrate these complexities, let's return once again to the example of Computer Exchange, Inc. You will recall the company had no units of merchandise inventory as of February 28, 1995. The presentation below shows the five identical computers purchased by Computer Exchange during March, 1995. Under the picture of each computer is the date of purchase and the amount paid for each. As you can see, the purchase price of this model of computer increased significantly during the month, even though the five computers are identical in every way.

426

[Pictures of 5 computers will be added to this illustration.]

	#1	#2	#3	#4	#5
Purchased:	3/3/95	3/11/95	3/17/95	3/26/95	3/29/95
Cost:	$800	$1,000	$1,200	$1,300	$1,400

Computer Exchange sold a computer on March 22 and another on March 30. Due to competition from nearby computer stores, Computer Exchange was not able to increase the amount it charges its customers for these computers, so the selling price remained $1,500 per computer.

Considering what you know about when the five computers were purchased and the dates of the two sales, which computer would you say was sold on March 22 and which do you think was sold on March 30? You may have said the one purchased on March 3 (computer #1) was sold on March 22 and the one purchased on March 11 (computer #2) was sold on March 30.

It's logical to think that the first computers purchased would be the first ones sold. Actually, however, the ones sold were probably the ones most conveniently located in the warehouse (the ones closest to the door). Remember, these are identical computers. One is no more special than another, so it doesn't matter to the customer which one he or she receives. About the only thing you can determine is that the computer sold on March 22 was either #1, #2, or #3, and the one sold on March 30 was one of the four still in the warehouse on that day.

Discussion Questions

9-6. Why must the computer sold on March 22 have been #1, #2, or #3?

9-7. In what type of business would it be important for the first units of merchandise inventory purchased to be the first ones sold? Explain.

9-8. In what type of business would it be impossible to identify individual units of inventory, as we did with the computers?

Because the prices of the five computers varied, it is impossible for us to determine the cost of goods sold if we don't know which computers were sold. What we need is a method of determining cost flow that will allow us to calcultate COGS regardless of which computers were sold.

Over time, several inventory cost flow methods have been developed. We will discuss three of them in the sections that follow. Before we do, however, please understand two points:

1. None of the three methods we will discuss has anything whatever to do with the physical movement of the actual units of merchandise inventory.

2. Our discussions of the three methods are not intended to be exhaustive. Instead, we want you to understand the basics of these methods because the choice of a particular inventory cost flow assumption can have a significant effect on a company's financial statements.

First-In, First-Out Method (FIFO)

The **first-in, first-out method (FIFO)** is so named because it assumes that the first units purchased are the first units sold. The following illustration shows an inventory control report for the transactions of Computer Exchange, Inc. during March using the FIFO method.

		Purchases			Cost of Goods Sold			Merchandise Inventory Balance		
Date	Explanation	Units	Unit Cost	Total Cost	Units	Unit Cost	Total Cost	Units	Unit Cost	Total Cost
3/01	Beg. inv.							0		$ -0-
3/03	Purchase	1	$ 800	$800				1	$ 800	$ 800
3/11	Purchase	1	$1,000	$1,000				1	$ 800	
								1	$1,000	$1,800
3/17	Purchase	1	$1,200	$1,200				1	$ 800	
								1	$1,000	
								1	$1,200	$3,000
3/22	Sale				1	$ 800	$ 800	1	$1,000	
								1	$1,200	$2,200
3/26	Purchase	1	$1,300	$1,300				1	$1,000	
								1	$1,200	
								1	$1,300	$3,500
3/29	Purchase	1	$1,400	$1,400				1	$1,000	
								1	$1,200	
								1	$1,300	
								1	$1,400	$4,900
3/30	Sale				1	$1,000	$1,000	1	$1,200	
								1	$1,300	
								1	$1,400	$3,900

You can see by following the arrows on the preceding inventory control report that each time a computer was sold, the first one available was the one assumed to have been sold. Using the information from the report we can now calculate the cost of goods sold that should be reported on March's income statement and the amount of ending inventory to be shown on the March 31 balance sheet.

```
                                   Units    Cost
     Beginning Inventory (3/1).  0      $ -0-
   + Purchases................  5       5,700*
   = Goods Available For Sale..  5     $5,700
   - Cost of Goods Sold........  2       1,800**
   = Ending Inventory (3/31)...  3     $3,900***
```

```
*     ($800 + $1,000 + $1,200 + $1,300 + $1,400 = $5,700)
**    ($800 + $1,000 = $1,800)
***   ($1,200 + $1,300 + $1,400 = $3,900)
```

Assuming the company had no business transactions during March except those related to the five computers and the payment of rent, and the company's income statement for the month of March, 1995, and its balance sheets at February 28, 1995, and March 31, 1995, based on the FIFO cost flow method would be as follows:

Computer Exchange, Inc.
Income Statement
For The Month Ended March 31, 1995

```
     Sales.......................$ 3,000    (1500 x 2)
     Less Cost of Goods Sold.....  1,800
     Gross Margin................$ 1,200
     Operating Expenses:
     Warehouse Rent..............$(  200)
     Net Income..................$ 1,000
```

Computer Exchange, Inc.
Balance Sheets
At February 28, 1995 & March 31, 1995

```
ASSETS:                           February        March
Cash.........................$21,800         $23,100
Accounts Receivable.........  1,500           3,000
Merchandise Inventory.......   -0-            3,900
Total Assets................$23,300          $30,000

LIABILITIES &
STOCKHOLDERS' EQUITY:
Accounts Payable............$ -0-           $ 5,700
Common Stock................ 15,000          15,000
Additional Paid-In Capital..  8,000           8,000
Retained Earnings...........    300           1,300
Total Liabilities &
Stockholders' Equity........$23,300          $30,000
```

We have included both the February 28 balance sheet and the March 31 balance sheet to demonstrate how the cost of the computers flows through the financial statements. Computer Exchange, Inc. had no merchandise inventory on February 28, as reflected on the balance sheet. The $5700 cost of the five computers purchased in March can be seen in the merchandise inventory on the March balance sheet and the cost of goods sold on the March income statement. The $3900 worth of merchandise inventory listed on the March balance sheet represents the three unsold computers, while the $1800 cost of goods sold represents the two computers that were sold in March. The cost of goods sold then affects the gross margin and thus the net income, as well. The $1,000 net income has been combined with the previous retained earnings balance ($300) to arrive at the updated retained earnings balance of $1,300.

Discussion Question

9-9. Can you tell by looking at the financial
    statements of Computer Exchange, Inc. whether
    the company has paid for the five computers it
    purchased by the end of March, 1995? Explain.

Last-In, First-Out Method (LIFO)

The last-in, first-out method (LIFO) is so named because it assumes that the last units purchased are the first ones sold. The following inventory control report reflects the transactions of Computer Exchange in March using the LIFO method.

Date	Explanation	Purchases Units	Unit Cost	Total Cost	Cost of Goods Sold Units	Unit Cost	Total Cost	Merchandise Inventory Balance Units	Unit Cost	Total Cost
								0		$ -0-
3/01	Beg. inv.							1	$ 800	$ 800
3/03	Purchase	1	$ 800	$800				1	$ 800	
3/11	Purchase	1	$1,000	$1,000				1	$1,000	$1,800
3/17	Purchase	1	$1,200	$1,200				1	$ 800	
								1	$1,000	
								1	$1,200	$3,000
3/22	Sale				1	$1,200	$1,200	1	$ 800	
								1	$1,000	$1,800
3/26	Purchase	1	$1,300	$1,300				1	$ 800	
								1	$1,000	
								1	$1,300	$3,100
3/29	Purchase	1	$1,400	$1,400				1	$ 800	
								1	$1,000	
								1	$1,300	
								1	$1,400	$4,500
3/30	Sale				1	$1,400	$1,400	1	$ 800	
								1	$1,000	
								1	$1,300	$3,100

You can see by following the arrows on the preceding inventory control report that each time a computer was sold, the last one available was the one assumed to have been sold. Using the information from the report we can now calculate the cost of goods sold that should be reported on March's income statement and the amount of ending inventory to be shown on the March 31 balance sheet.

```
                                  Units       Cost
      Beginning Inventory (3/1).   0      $  -0-
    + Purchases.................   5         5,700*
    = Goods Available For Sale..   5       $5,700
    - Cost of Goods Sold........   2         2,600**
    = Ending Inventory (3/31)...   3       $3,100***
```

*   ($800 + $1,000 + $1,200 + $1,300 + $1,400 = $5,700)
**   ($1,200 + $1,400 = $2,600)
***   ($800 + $1,000 + $1,300 = $3,100)

Assuming the company had no business transactions during March except those related to the five computers and the payment of rent, the company's income statement for the month of March, 1995, and its balance sheets at February 28, 1995, and March 31, 1995, based on the LIFO cost flow method of determining cost of goods sold and ending merchandise inventory would be as follows:

Computer Exchange, Inc.
Income Statement
For The Month Ended March 31, 1995

```
    Sales......................$ 3,000
    Less Cost of Goods Sold.....  2,600
    Gross Margin................$   400
    Operating Expenses:
    Warehouse Rent..............$(  200)
    Net Income..................$   200
```

Computer Exchange, Inc.
Balance Sheets
At February 28, 1995 & March 31, 1995

ASSETS:	February	March
Cash.........................	$21,800	$23,100
Accounts Receivable.........	1,500	3,000
Merchandise Inventory.......	-0-	3,100
Total Assets................	$23,300	$29,200
LIABILITIES & STOCKHOLDERS' EQUITY:		
Accounts Payable............	$ -0-	$ 5,700
Common Stock................	15,000	15,000
Additional Paid-In Capital..	8,000	8,000
Retained Earnings...........	300	500
Total Liabilities & Stockholders' Equity........	$23,300	$29,200

Once again, we have included both the February 28 balance sheet and the March 31 balance sheet to demonstrate how the cost of the computers flows through the financial statements. There was no merchandise inventory reported on the February 28 balance sheet. The $5,700 cost of the five computers purchased during March can be seen in the merchandise inventory on the balance sheet and the cost of goods sold on the income statement. The $3100 worth of merchandise inventory listed on the March balance sheet represents the three unsold computers, while the $2600 cost of goods sold represents the two computers that were sold in March. The cost of goods sold then affects the gross margin and net income. The $200 net income has been combined with the previous retained earnings balance ($300) to arrive at the updated retained earnings balance of $500.

Compare the financial statements prepared for Computer Exchange using FIFO with those prepared using LIFO. Remember, these two sets of financial statements are based on exactly the same facts. Yet, applying the FIFO inventory method, the company shows net income of $1,000. Under the LIFO inventory method, the company reports net income of $200. Moreover, using FIFO results in total assets on the March 31 balance sheet of $30,000. Using LIFO results in total assets on the March 31 balance sheet of $29,200.

9-10. The financial statements prepared using FIFO show Computer Exchange, Inc. to be more profitable than do the financial statements prepared using LIFO. Is the company more profitable if it uses the FIFO method rather than the LIFO method? Explain.

9-11. How would you explain the differences between these two sets of financial statements to someone who did not know the facts behind them?

9-12. In a time of rising prices, which method (LIFO or FIFO) would inventory a higher cost? Which would expense a higher cost?

Average Cost Method

The **average cost method** is so named because it simply averages the cost of all individual units of current inventory. The following inventory control report was prepared to show the transactions of Computer Exchange in March using the average cost method.

		Purchases			Cost of Goods Sold			Merchandise Inventory Balance		
									Average	
Date	Explanation	Units	Unit Cost	Total Cost	Units	Unit Cost	Total Cost	Units	Unit Cost	Total Cost
3/01	Beg. inv.							0	$	$ -0-
3/03	Purchase	1	$ 800	$800				1 @	$ 800	$ 800
3/11	Purchase	1	$1,000	$1,000				2 @	$ 900	$1,800
3/17	Purchase	1	$1,200	$1,200				3 @	$1,000	$3,000
3/22	Sale				1	$1,000	$1,000	2 @	$1,000	$2,000
3/26	Purchase	1	$1,300	$1,300				3 @	$1,100	$3,300
3/29	Purchase	1	$1,400	$1,400				4 @	$1,175	$4,700
3/30	Sale				1	$1,175	$1,175	3 @	$1,175	$3,525

You can see by looking at the preceding inventory control report that each time a computer was sold, the average cost of the inventory units in stock on that date was used as the cost of the computer sold. Using the information from the report, we can now calculate the cost of goods sold that should be reported on March's income statement and the amount of ending inventory to be shown on the March 31 balance sheet.

```
                                      Units      Cost
        Beginning Inventory (3/1).  0        $ -0-
      + Purchases................  5          5,700*
      = Goods Available For Sale..  5        $5,700
      - Cost of Goods Sold........  2          2,175**
      = Ending Inventory (3/31)...  3        $3,525***
```

```
*     ($800 + $1,000 + $1,200 + $1,300 + $1,400 = $5,700)
**    ($1,000 + $1,175 = $2,175)
***   (Three computers @ $1,175 each = $3,525)
```

Again assuming the company had no business transactions during
March except those related to the five computers and the payment of
rent, the company's income statement for the month of March, 1995,
and its balance sheets at February 28, 1995, and March 31, 1995,
based on the average cost method of determining cost of goods sold
and ending merchandise inventory would be as follows:

Computer Exchange, Inc.
Income Statement
For The Month Ended March 31, 1995

```
        Sales......................$ 3,000
        Less Cost of Goods Sold.....  2,175
        Gross Margin................$   825
        Operating Expenses:
        Warehouse Rent.............$(  200)
        Net Income.................$   625
```

Computer Exchange, Inc.
Balance Sheets
At February 28, 1995 & March 31, 1995

```
ASSETS:                          February        March
Cash.........................$21,800          $23,100
Accounts Receivable.........   1,500            3,000
Merchandise Inventory.......    -0-             3,525
Total Assets................$23,300          $29,625

LIABILITIES &
STOCKHOLDERS' EQUITY:
Accounts Payable............$ -0-            $ 5,700
Common Stock................ 15,000           15,000
Additional Paid-In Capital..  8,000            8,000
Retained Earnings...........    300              925
Total Liabilities &
Stockholders' Equity........$23,300          $29,625
```

438

Once again, we have included the February 28 and March 31 balance sheets to demonstrate how the cost of the computers flows through the financial statements. No merchandise inventory was reported on the February 28 balance sheet. The $5,700 cost of the five computers purchased during March can be seen in the merchandise inventory in the balance sheet and the cost of goods sold on the income statement. The $3525 worth of merchandise inventory listed on the March balance sheet represents the three unsold computers, while the $2175 cost of goods sold represents the two computers that were sold in March. The cost of goods sold then affects the gross margin and the net income. The $625 net income has been combined with the previous retained earnings balance ($300) to arrive at the updated retained earnings balance of $925.

Discussion Questions

9-13. Using the Computer Exchange balance sheets for
February and March, and the income statement
for the month of March, explain the increase in
cash from $21,800 to $23,100.

439

The Effects of Inventory Cost Flow Method Choice

The financial statements prepared using the average cost method are based on exactly the same set of facts as the financial statements prepared using FIFO and LIFO. Yet, the results are in some ways very different than the results in either of those two presentations. The differences are summarized below.

	FIFO	LIFO	Average Cost
Goods Available for Sale.............	$5,700	$5,700	$5,700
Cost of Goods Sold (Income Statement).	$1,800	$2,600	$2,175
Net Income (Income Statement).........	$1,000	$ 200	$ 625
Ending Inventory (Balance Sheet)......	$3,900	$3,100	$3,525
Retained Earnings (Balance Sheet).....	$1,300	$ 500	$ 925

It appears that Computer Exchange is most profitable if it employs the FIFO method and least profitable if it uses the LIFO method. The average cost method produces results somewhere between FIFO and LIFO. Actually, Computer Exchange is no "better off" by selecting one cost flow method over another. To illustrate, let's extend our example to April.

Computer Exchange purchased no computers in April but did sell the three it had remaining at the end of March, each for $1,500. Once again assuming the company had no business transactions in April except those related to the computers and the payment of rent, the cost of goods sold and ending inventory under the three cost flow methods would be calculated as follows:

	Units	Cost Flow Method		
		FIFO	LIFO	Avg. Cost
Beginning Inventory (4/1).	3	$3,900*	$3,100**	$3,525***
+ Purchases.................	0	-0-	-0-	-0-
= Goods Available For Sale..	3	$3,900	$3,100	$3,525
- Cost of Goods Sold........	3	3,900	3,100	3,525
= Ending Inventory (4/30)...	0	$ -0-	$ -0-	$ -0-

```
*      ($1,200 + $1,300 + $1,400 = $3,900)
**     ($800 + $1,000 + $1,300 = $3,100)
***    (Three computers @ $1,175 each = $3,525)
```

Using the cost of goods sold and ending inventory calculations above, we can develop the company's income statement for the month of April, 1995, and its balance sheet at April 30 under each of the three methods.

Computer Exchange, Inc.
Income Statement
For The Month Ended April 30, 1995

	Cost Flow Method		
	FIFO	LIFO	Avg. Cost
Sales............................	$4,500	$4,500	$4,500
Less Cost of Goods Sold........	3,900	3,100	3,525
Gross Margin....................	$ 600	$1,400	$ 975
Operating Expenses:	*vs 1,200*	*vs 400*	*vs 925*
Warehouse Rent.................	$(200)	$(200)	$(200)
Net Income.....................	$ 400	$1,200	$ 775
	vs 1000	*vs 200*	*vs 625*

Computer Exchange, Inc.
Balance Sheets
At April 30, 1995

	Cost Flow Method		
	FIFO	LIFO	Avg. Cost
ASSETS:			
Cash........................	$20,200	$20,200	$20,200
Accounts Receivable.........	4,500	4,500	4,500
Merchandise Inventory.......	-0-	-0-	-0-
Total Assets................	$24,700	$24,700	$24,700
	vs 23,300	*vs 29,200*	*vs 29,625*
LIABILITIES & STOCKHOLDERS' EQUITY:			
Accounts Payable............	$ -0-	$ -0-	$ -0-
Common Stock................	15,000	15,000	15,000
Additional Paid-In Capital..	8,000	8,000	8,000
Retained Earnings...........	1,700*	1,700**	1,700***
Total Liabilities & Stockholders' Equity........	$24,700	$24,700	$24,700

* ($1,300 balance at 4/1 + $400 April net income = $1,700)
** ($500 balance at 4/1 + $1,200 April net income = $1,700)
*** ($925 balance at 4/1 + $775 April net income = $1,700)

While the income statements for April are different under the three inventory cost flow methods (as they were for March), the balance sheet at April 30 is identical under the three methods.

442

```
┌──────────────────────────────────────────────────────────────┐
│                                                                │
│                     Discussion Question                        │
│                                                                │
│   9-14.       Because the balance sheet is affected by         │
│                                                                │
│               the income statement, how can the balance        │
│                                                                │
│               sheet at the end of April be identical           │
│                                                                │
│               under the three inventory cost flow              │
│                                                                │
│               methods when the income statements for           │
│                                                                │
│               April were different?                            │
│                                                                │
└──────────────────────────────────────────────────────────────┘
```

No one method of determining cost flow is better than another
because, in the long run, they all produce the same results. Any
differences, such as those we saw on the financial statements of
Computer Exchange, Inc., are caused by attempting to measure
earnings activities (revenues and expenses) for relatively short
periods of time (one month, three months, one year).

When the authors of <u>Accounting Trends and Techniques</u> surveyed 600
companies to determine which inventory cost flow method they used
for the year 1992, this was the response:

FIFO:	415
LIFO:	358
Average Cost:	193
Other:	45
Total:	1011

As you can see, the total of 1011 exceeds the 600 companies surveyed. This is because many companies use one method for one type of merchandise inventory and another method for a different type of merchandise. Computer Exchange, for example, might use the average cost method on its computers, but FIFO on the computer software it sells. Clearly, FIFO, LIFO, and average cost are the most widely used methods. As financial statement readers, you are most likely to see these three methods.

As was the case with accounting for depreciation of long-lived assets, discussed in Chapter 8, accounting for the cost of merchandise inventory has a significant impact on a company's reported net income for a given income statement period. The amounts reported as inventory on the balance sheet are also greatly affected. Informed users of financial statements must have an understanding of the impact of inventory cost flow method choice if they hope to be able to use the accounting information to the fullest extent possible.

What is needed, then, is another tool. That tool is called the statement of cash flows. Its purpose is to bring the focus back to cash, and it is the subject of the next chapter.

CHAPTER SUMMARY

Merchandise inventory, or just inventory, is the term for the physical units of goods that a company plans to sell. The actual amount of inventory a company has on hand in its warehouse or storeroom is known as goods available for sale. For a given income statement period, goods available for sale can be divided into the inventory on hand at the beginning of the period, or beginning inventory, and purchases made during the period. Any inventory left unsold at the end of the period is known as ending inventory.

When inventory is purchased or made, its cost is considered an asset to the company and is listed as such on the balance sheet. As inventory is sold, its cost is converted from an asset to an expense, which is listed on the income statement as cost of goods sold. For any income statement period, cost of goods sold combined with ending inventory will always equal the original amount of goods available for sale during that period.

Two types of systems have been developed to trace both the flow of inventory as well as the cost of inventory. The periodic system counts inventory and traces costs only at the end of each income statement period, while the perpetual system updates inventory counts and costs each time a sale or purchase is made. Perpetual inventory systems tend to make use of computer technology and are

445

commonly linked to scanners that read UPC codes. Physical inventory counts are still necessary under a perpetual inventory system.

Tracing inventory cost flows, especially cost of goods sold, can become very difficult as purchase prices vary. Several methods have been developed to alleviate this problem. The first-in, first-out method assumes that the first units of inventory purchased are the first ones sold. Conversely, the last-in, first-out method (LIFO) assumes that the last units of inventory purchased are the first sold. The average cost method simply averages the prices of all similar units of inventory.

KEY TERMS DEFINED

Average Cost Method. The inventory cost flow method that averages the costs of all units in inventory to establish the cost of goods sold.

Beginning Inventory. The amount of merchandise inventory (units or dollars) on hand at the beginning of the income statement period.

Book Inventory. The amount of ending inventory (units and dollars) generated by a perpetual inventory system.

Cost of Goods Sold. The cost of the merchandise inventory no longer on hand, and assumed sold during the period.

Cost of Sales. Another term for cost of goods sold.

Ending Inventory. The amount of inventory (in units or dollars) that is still on hand at the end of an accounting period.

First-In, First-Out Method (FIFO). The inventory cost flow method based on the assumption that the first units of inventory purchased are the first ones sold.

Goods Available for Sale. The total amount of merchandise inventory a company has available to sell in a given income statement period.

Inventory. Another term for merchandise inventory.

Inventory System. A set of procedures adopted by a company to account for both the physical flow of merchandise and the flow of the cost of merchandise.

Last-In, First-Out Mehtod (LIFO). The inventory cost flow method based on the assumption that the last units of inventory purchased are the first ones sold.

Merchandise Inventory. The physical units (goods) a company buys (or makes) to resell as part of its business operation.

Periodic Inventory System. An inventory system in which all inventory and cost of goods sold calculations are done only at the end of the income statement period.

Perpetual Inventory System. An inventory system in which both the physical count of inventory units and the cost classification (asset or expense) are updated whenever there is a transaction involving inventory.

Purchases. The amount of merchandise inventory bought during the income statement period.

REVIEW THE FACTS

1. Define the terms "inventory" and "merchandise inventory".

2. What two amounts are added to determine goods available for sale (GAFS)?

3. GAFS is allocated to two places. Name them.

4. Under accrual accounting, the cost of items that are still on hand at the end of the period are shown on which financial statement?

5. Under accrual accounting, the cost of items that are no longer on hand at the end of the period are shown on which financial statement?

6. Define the difference between the physical flow of merchandise and the cost flow of merchandise.

7. What are the two types of inventory systems? Explain the differences between them.

8. List three causes of differences between book inventory and the results of a physical inventory count.

9. What characteristic makes specific identification different from all the other inventory methods discussed in this chapter?

10. Why are FIFO, LIFO, and average cost referred to as "assumptions"?

11. Describe in your own words the differences among FIFO, LIFO, and average cost.

Chapter 9
APPLY WHAT YOU HAVE LEARNED

A9-1.   Nathlee Flandro Company began the month of March, 1996 with 152 units of product on hand at a total cost of $1,824. During the month, the company purchased an additional 409 units at $15 per unit.   Sales for March were 366 units at total cost of $5,034.

REQUIRED:

From the information provided, complete the following schedule:

	Units	Cost
Beginning Inventory.......	152	1824
+ Purchases.................	409	6135
= Goods Available For Sale..	561	7959
- Cost of Goods Sold........	366	5034
= Ending Inventory..........	195	2925

A9-2.   Robert Randolph Company began the month of April, 1996 with 226 units of product on hand at a cost $27 per unit. During the month, the company purchased an additional 750 units at a total cost of $20,250. At the end of April, there were 308 units still on hand.

REQUIRED:

From the information provided, complete the following schedule:

	Units	Cost
Beginning Inventory.......	226	6102
+ Purchases.................	750	20250
= Goods Available For Sale..	976	26352
- Ending Inventory..........	308 x27 8316	
= Cost of Goods Sold........	668	18036

451

A9-3.   Paul Jackson & Company began the month of February, 1996 with 325 units of product on hand at a total cost of $5,525. During the month, the company purchased an additional 942 units at $18 per unit. Sales for February were 867 units at $32 per unit. The total cost of the units sold was $15,406 and operating expenses totaled $9,450.

REQUIRED:

a.   From the information provided, complete the following schedule:

	Units	Cost
Beginning Inventory.......	325	5525
+ Purchases.................	942×18 16956	
= Goods Available For Sale..	1267	22481
- Cost of Goods Sold........	867×32 15466	
= Ending Inventory..........	400	7075

b.   Prepare Jackson & Company's income statement for the month ended February 28, 1996.

A9-4.   Connie Borg TV Sales & Service began the month of March with 2 identical TV sets in inventory. During the month, six additional TV sets (identical to the two in beginning inventory) were purchased as follows:

        2 on March 1
        2 on March 9
        1 on March 13
        3 on March 24

The company sold two of the TV sets on March 12, another one on March 17 and two more on March 28.

REQUIRED:

a.   If the company uses a perpetual inventory system and the First-In, First-Out cost flow method, which two computers were sold on March 12?

b.   If the company uses a perpetual inventory system and the Last-In, First-Out cost flow method, the cost of which three computers will be included in inventory at the end of March?

A9-5. Edmunds Company buys and then resells a single product as its primary business activity. This product is called the Do-Daw and is subject to rather severe cost fluctuations. Following is information concerning Edmunds' inventory activity for the Do-Daw product during the month of July, 1996:

July 1: 431 units on hand, $3,017.

July 2: Sold 220 units.

July 9: Purchased 500 units @ $11 per unit.

July 12: Purchased 200 units @ $9 per unit.

July 16: Sold 300 units.

July 21: Purchased 150 units @ $6 per unit.

July 24: Purchased 50 units @ $8 per unit.

July 29: Sold 500 units.

REQUIRED:

Assuming Edmunds employs a perpetual inventory system, calculate Cost of Goods Sold (units and cost) for the month of July, 1996 and Ending Inventory (units and cost) at July 31, 1996 using the following:

a. First-In, First-Out method.

b. Last-In, First-Out method.

c. Average Cost method (Round all unit cost calculations to the nearest dollar).

d. Which of the three methods resulted in the highest cost of goods sold for July?

e. How would the differences in cost of goods sold under the three methods affect the income statement and balance sheet for the month?

A9-6. Presented below is a list of items relating to the concepts presented in this chapter, followed by definitions of those items in a scrambled order:

a. Periodic Inventory System.

b. Perpetual Inventory System.

c. Goods Available For Sale.

d. Cost of Goods Sold.

e. Merchandise Inventory.

f. First-In, First-Out method.

g. Last-in, First-Out method.

h. Average Cost method.

c ___ The total amount of merchandise inventory a company can sell during a particular income statement period.

a ___ All inventory and cost of goods sold calculations are done at the end of the period.

f ___ Cost of goods sold is determined based on the assumption that the first units acquired are the first ones sold.

b ___ Updates both the physical count of inventory units and the cost classification of those units whenever there is a transaction involving inventory.

e ___ The physical units of product a company buys and then resells as part of its business operation.

g ___ Cost of goods sold is determined based on the assumption that the last units acquired are the first ones sold.

h ___ Cost of goods sold is determined based on the total cost of inventory units divided by the number of units.

d ___ The cost of merchandise inventory that has been converted from an asset on the balance sheet to an expense on the income statement.

REQUIRED:

Match the letter next to each item on the list with the appropriate definition. Each letter will be used only once.

CHAPTER 10

TOOLS OF THE TRADE PART III — THE STATEMENT OF CASH FLOWS: BRINGING THE FOCUS BACK TO CASH

Net income is an opinion; cash is a fact.

- Anonymous

In a very real sense, the statement above about net income is absolutely true, particularly when the accrual basis of accounting is used to measure periodic earnings. Recall that accrual accounting is affected by a number of items which we have discussed:

- The difficulties in determining when revenue should be recognized under accrual accounting.

- The difficulties in matching expenses to the same income statement period as the revenues they helped generate.

- The estimates of useful life and residual value required for depreciation.

- Choices of inventory cost flow assumption (e.g., FIFO, LIFO) and depreciation method (e.g., straight-line, double-declining-balance).

These are just a few of the items that cause net income under accrual accounting to be different from the change in cash. And while accrual accounting has much to recommend it, it does have the weakness of taking the focus off cash. To address this problem and bring the financial statement user's focus back to cash, a fourth financial statement tool has been developed: the **statement of cash flows**. The main purpose of the statement of cash flows is to provide information about a company's cash receipts and cash payments during a specific period. It should also help investors, creditors, and other external parties to:

a.   Assess a company's ability to generate positive future net cash flows.

b.   Assess a company's need for external financing, and its ability to pay its debts and pay dividends.

c.   Reconcile the differences between net income and the change in cash.

When this additional information is combined with the information from the other three financial statements, a more complete picture of a company's financial health is available for decision makers.

```
+-------------------------------------------------------------+
|                   Discussion Question                        |
|                                                             |
|     10-1. How do revenue recognition and expense            |
|           recognition criteria under accrual accounting     |
|           take the focus off cash?                          |
|                                                             |
+-------------------------------------------------------------+
```

After completing your work on this chapter, you should be able to do the following:

1.   Explain the purpose of the statement of cash flows.

2.   Describe the three types of activities that can either generate or use cash in any business.

3.   Reconcile accrual net income to the change in cash.

4.   Explain where a company obtains its financing by examining its statement of cash flows.

INTRODUCTION TO THE STATEMENT OF CASH FLOWS

In its present format, the statement of cash flows has been in existence only since 1988. Other forms of the statement, however, have been used for a very long time. These previous forms were known by such names as the "Where-Got and Where-Gone Statement", "The Funds Statement", the "Statement of Source and Application of Funds" and the "Statement of Changes in Financial Position".

All of these earlier statements had the same objectives as the statement of cash flows; however, most included items other than cash in their analyses. For this reason, while they were useful to financial statement users in helping to interpret the impact of accrual accounting procedures, they were not successful in bringing the user's focus directly back to cash.

The statement of changes in financial position (SCFP) is the form of the statement which immediately preceded the currently used statement of cash flows. At the time the SCFP was first introduced in 1971, the vast majority of companies prepared their statements of changes in financial position using the working capital format.

This format was based on the assumption that **working capital**, which is defined as current assets less current liabilities, is a good approximation of cash. The working capital format was sufficient to meet the information needs of users during the 1970's.

In the early 1980s, the financial environment changed significantly. Many companies became concerned about their cash flows as they began taking on increasing amounts of debt. As the financial community became more interested in obtaining information about cash flows, it became dissatisfied with the working capital format of the SCFP. Beginning in 1981, there was growing pressure from users of the financial statements, for companies to provide more detailed information about the sources and uses of their cash. In 1988, the new statement of cash flows was introduced.

Direct Method vs. Indirect Method

There are two methods for preparation of the statement of cash flows. They are known as the **direct method** and the **indirect method**; both arrive at the same "bottom line". The direct method may be somewhat easier to follow conceptually; however, it does not tie as directly to the accrual method of economic measurement. It involves a series of calculations to determine the amount of cash inflow (from customers, interest earned on loans and dividends) and cash outflow (to suppliers, employees, creditors, etc.). This detail as to the individual sources and uses of cash associated with the operating activities of a company may be useful, but very few companies use the direct method. Accounting Trends and Techniques reports that of the 600 companies surveyed, only 15 used the direct method for preparation of the statement of cash flows.

The indirect method is more closely tied to accrual accounting than is the direct method. Unlike the direct method, it does not attempt to provide any detail as to the individual sources and uses of cash associated with the operating activities of a company.

460

When the indirect method is used, the statement of cash flows begins with the accrual net income for the period. Then, adjustments are made for all items included in the calculation of net income that did not either generate or use cash. Since the vast majority of firms use the indirect method, this is the method we will concentrate on in this chapter.

BASIC CONSTRUCTION OF THE STATEMENT OF CASH FLOWS

We have established the purpose of the statement of cash flows and how it came to be in its present form, but how does the statement go about fulfilling that purpose? Well, the process begins by comparing the cash balance at the beginning of the period to the cash balance at the end of the period. The statement of cash flows discloses exactly what caused the change in the cash balance from the beginning of the period to the end of the period. The illustration below shows the basic format of a statement of cash flows. As you can see, the bottom line of the statement is the increase or decrease in cash during the period.

```
                      SANGUINE COMPANY
                  STATEMENT OF CASH FLOWS
             FOR THE YEAR ENDED DECEMBER 31, 1996

Cash Flows From Operating Activities:
 Net Income                                              $ XXXX
 Adjustments to reconcile net income to net
  cash provided by operating activities:
                                                  XXX
                                                   XX
                                               _____
Net Cash Provided (Used) By Operating Activities           ?

Cash Flows From Investing Activities:
                                                   XX
                                                   XX
                                               _____
Net Cash Provided (Used) By Investing Activities           ?

Cash Flows From Financing Activities:
                                                  XXXX
                                                   XX
                                               _____
Net Cash Provided (Used) By Financing Activities         ___?___

Net Increase (Decrease) In Cash During 1996              $ XXX
```

The statement of cash flows is organized around the three major
types of business activities which can either generate or use cash:
operating, investing and financing. The total effect of the three
categories of activities results in the net increase or decrease in
cash.

10-2. If you owned a small bookstore, what do you

think would be your:

a.   Operating activities?

b.   Investing activities?

c.   Financing activities?

Explain your reasons for the classifications

you made.

One of the most important tasks in developing a statement of cash
flows is identifying the business activities that took place during
the period, and categorizing them as operating, investing
or financing activities. Each type of activity is described below.

Operating Activities

Operating activities are those centered around the actual day-to-day business transactions of the company. A variety of transactions either generate or use cash. Cash is received (inflow) from the sale of goods or services. For example, McDonald's receives cash when its customers buy hamburgers. Cash is also received when a company earns interest on loans it has made to others, or when it receives dividends on investments it owns in other companies. Cash is paid (outflow) to suppliers for inventory, to employees for wages, to the government for taxes, to lenders for interest on loans, and to other parties for the expenses of running the company.

If you think about the items listed in the previous paragraph, you will see they are all items which are reported on the income statement. Therefore, when attempting to determine the cash inflow and cash outflow from operating activities, the place to start is the income statement for the period. If Bart's Beanery uses the cash basis of accounting, net income for the period will equal the net cash inflow (or outflow) for the period from operating activities. If, however, Bart's uses the accrual basis of accounting, the net income figure must be adjusted for any revenue item that did not provide cash during this income statement period and any expense item that was not paid during this income statement period. If this is not totally clear to you at this point, don't fret; we will show you how it is done a little later in the chapter.

Discussion Question

10-3. Think back to the situation in which you owned a small bookstore. If one of your customers purchased a large book order on account and had thirty days after she received the books to pay for them, how would this credit sale be reported for your company:

a. on a cash basis?
b. on an accrual basis?

10-4. Continuing the scenario above, for your company's statement of cash flows, how would you determine the net cash flow from operations on an accrual basis?

10-5. Where would you look for the information to determine net cash flow from operations if your business used the cash basis of accounting?

Investing Activities

Investing activities are those centered around support of the operations. This support may focus on investment in assets necessary to the operation or investments outside the company to wisely use any available funds. Campbell's Soup Company can use cash (outflow) to invest in machinery to can its soup. It can later obtain cash (inflow) if it sells this machinery. Major assets used in a company's operations are often reported on the balance sheet in a category called property, plant and equipment. This classification includes the buildings, vehicles, furniture, equipment, etc. that a business needs to run its operations. Companies normally sell these types of assets from time to time if they are no longer needed. However, clearly, the company had better not sell off assets it needs to run its operations. Otherwise, it would not be long before the cash generated through operating activities would be adversely affected. An airline, for example, could generate cash by selling its airplanes, but if it did, it would no longer be able to transport passengers. In short, the airline would be out of business. Instead of selling its property, plant and equipment to generate cash, a growing and healthy company will likely use cash to acquire additional assets used in its operations. For this reason, the net cash flow from investing activities may very well be negative (net outflow) for companies that are experiencing healthy growth.

Besides investing in property, plant, and equipment, a company can purchase the stock of other companies or loan other companies money (both outflows). Cash is generated (inflow) when a company sells equity or debt investments (stocks or bonds of other companies). These are all examples of investing activities. (Logically, the interest earned on loans to others, and dividends received from investments in the stock of other companies should be classified under investing activities. However, because the amounts are reported on the income statement of the period, cash received from interest and dividends are generally reported as results of operating activities.)

If you think about the examples of investing activities discussed in the previous two paragraphs, you will see they all involve items which are reported in the long-term asset section of the balance sheet. Therefore, when attempting to determine the cash inflow and cash outflow from investing activities, the long-term asset section of the balance sheets at the start of the period and the end of the period must be analyzed. Once again, do not be concerned if this is not totally clear to you at this point. We will demonstrate the process a little later in the chapter.

467

Financing Activities

Because internal financing is accomplished through operating activities, **financing activities** really deal with only external financing. Companies can obtain cash (inflow) from two external sources. First, they can sell shares of stock (common or preferred). This subject was discussed in Chapter 4. Second, they can borrow, either by obtaining loans from banks, or through issuing corporate bonds. This subject was presented in Chapter 5. Under the financing activity category, companies report uses (outflows) of cash resulting from repaying loans and bonds, paying dividends to shareholders, and reacquiring shares of capital stock from their stockholders. (Logically, the interest paid on borrowings should be classified under financing activities. However, because interest expense is reported on the income statement of the period, cash paid for interest is also most often reported as an operating activity.)

If you think about the examples of financing activities discussed in the preceding paragraph, you will see they all involve items which are reported in the long-term liability or owners' equity section of the balance sheet. Therefore, when attempting to determine the cash inflow and cash outflow from financing activities, those sections of the balance sheets at the start of the period and the end of the period must be analyzed. As with the previous two activity categories, do not be concerned if this is not totally clear to you at this point. We will demonstrate the process a little later in the chapter.

The chart below summarizes what we have discussed so far about the three types of activities as they are organized in the statement of cash flows. You should refer to this illustration often as we continue to discuss the uses of the statement.

Operating Activities (Income Statement Items)
 Cash inflows:
  From customers as a result of the sale of goods or services.
  From interest earned on loans to others.
  From dividends received from investment in the stock of
      other companies.
 Cash outflows:
  To suppliers for the purchase of inventory.
  To employees for salaries and wages.
  To governments for taxes.
  To creditors for interest on loans.
  To others for operating expenses.

Investing Activities (Long-Term Asset Items)
 Cash Inflows:
  From the sale of property, plant, and equipment.
  From the sale of investments in debt or equity securities of
      other companies.
 Cash Outflows:
  To purchase property, plant, and equipment.
  To purchase debt and equity investments in other companies.

**Financing Activities (Long-Term Liability and Owners' Equity
                                                        Items)**
 Cash Inflows:
  From selling shares of common stock or preferred stock.
  From bank loans or the sale of corporate bonds.
 Cash Outflows:
  To pay dividends to stockholders.
  To reacquire shares of capital stock from stockholders.
  To repay loans or redeem corporate bonds.

Companies can have some fairly exotic variations on what is listed in the chart above, but every inflow and outflow of cash can be classified as a result of either operating, investing or financing activities.

PREPARATION OF THE STATEMENT OF CASH FLOWS

We are now going to demonstrate how the statement of cash flows is prepared. Basically, we will be using an analysis of the changes in various other accounts to explain the overall change in cash. The necessary information can be found by examining balance sheets prepared in two consecutive periods. Financial statements presented with two or more consecutive periods shown at once are called **comparative financial statements**. As an example, we will use the information provided by the comparative balance sheets of Sanguine Company for 1995 and 1996, presented below. Be sure to understand that the balances in the asset, liability and owners' equity accounts at the end of one period become the beginning balances in the next period. Thus, this presentation provides beginning and ending balances for all of Sanguine Company's balance sheet accounts for the year 1996 — necessary information for the preparation of the company's statement of cash flows for 1996.

SANGUINE COMPANY
BALANCE SHEETS
AT DECEMBER 31, 1996 AND DECEMBER 31, 1995
(in thousands)

ASSETS:		1996		1995
Current Assets:				
Cash		$ 2,800		$ 2,420
Accounts Receivable		2,925		3,112
Merchandise Inventory		970		866
Prepaid Expenses		250		200
Total Current Assets		$ 6,945		$ 6,598
Plant & Equipment:				
Buildings	$9,654		$8,029	
Less Accumulated Dep.	4,597		4,417	
Buildings, Net		$ 5,057		$ 3,612
Equipment	$3,359		$2,984	
Less Accumulated Dep.	1,955		1,904	
Equipment, Net		$ 1,404		$ 1,080
Total Plant & Equipment		$ 6,461		$ 4,692
Total Assets		$13,406		$11,290
LIABILITIES:				
Current Liabilities:				
Accounts Payable		$ 2,020		$ 1,816
Notes Payable		3,400		2,700
Total Current Liabilities		$ 5,420		$ 4,516
Long-Term Liabilities		2,500		2,000
Total Liabilities		$ 7,920		$ 6,516
STOCKHOLDERS' EQUITY:				
Common Stock, no par value		$ 3,400		$ 3,000
Retained Earnings		2,086		1,774
Total Stockholders' Equity		$ 5,486		$ 4,774
Total Liabilities				
and Stockholders' Equity		$13,406		$11,290

471

```
┌─────────────────────────────────────────────────────────────┐
│ ╔═════════════════════════════════════════════════════════╗ │
│ ║                                                           ║ │
│ ║                  Discussion Question                      ║ │
│ ║                                                           ║ │
│ ║                                                           ║ │
│ ║     Refer to the Sanguine Company's comparative           ║ │
│ ║     balance sheets as you answer the following            ║ │
│ ║     questions:                                            ║ │
│ ║                                                           ║ │
│ ║                                                           ║ │
│ ║  10-6. What was Sanguine Company's balance in             ║ │
│ ║                                                           ║ │
│ ║        accounts receivable on January 1, 1996?  Did       ║ │
│ ║                                                           ║ │
│ ║        accounts receivable increase or decrease during    ║ │
│ ║                                                           ║ │
│ ║        1996?                                              ║ │
│ ║                                                           ║ │
│ ║                                                           ║ │
│ ║  10-7. What was Sanguine Company's balance in             ║ │
│ ║                                                           ║ │
│ ║        retained earnings on January 1, 1996?  What do     ║ │
│ ║                                                           ║ │
│ ║        you think caused the increase from the             ║ │
│ ║                                                           ║ │
│ ║        beginning of 1996 to the end of the year?          ║ │
│ ║                                                           ║ │
│ ╚═══════════════════════════════════════════════════════════╝ │
└─────────────────────────────────────────────────────────────┘
```

In addition to information gathered from balance sheets, preparation of a statement of cash flows also requires information from the company's income statement for the period. Remember, the starting point in figuring net inflows or outflows from operating activities is the net income of the period. Sanguine Company's income statement for the year ended December 31, 1996 is provided below.

```
                     SANGUINE COMPANY
                     INCOME STATEMENT
          FOR THE YEAR ENDED DECEMBER 31, 1996
                     (in Thousands)


Net Sales                                  $15,158
Less Cost of Goods Sold                     11,151
Gross Margin                               $ 4,007
Less Operating Expenses:
  Depreciation - Buildings                 $    180
  Depreciation - Equipment                       51
  Other Selling & Administrative             3,047
    Total Expenses                         $ 3,278
Operating Income                           $   729
Less Interest Expense                          160
Income Before Taxes                        $   569
  Income Taxes                                 120
Net Income                                 $   449
```

Before we actually get started in preparing the statement of cash flows, take a few minutes to review Sanguine's balance sheets and income statement. There are a couple of things you should note about the financial statements prepared for Sanguine Company. First, look at the cash balances on the two balance sheets. You will see that cash increased from the start of 1996 to the end of 1996 ($2,800 - $2,420 = $380). Note that the Sanguine Company's financial statements are presented "in thousands". This implies that the $380 increase in cash is really $380,000. But what caused the increase?

Look at the net income figure on the income statement. As you can see, net income for the year ended December 31, 1996 was $449,000.

Presuming Sanguine Company uses accrual accounting, you know that net income is certainly not the same as the change in cash. Even if Sanguine used the cash basis of accounting, net income would not necessarily tell the whole story, because even in a cash basis system, some cash flows are not reflected in net income. The statement of cash flows, if properly prepared and analyzed, will disclose exactly what caused cash to change by the amount it did, and will reconcile the net income figure with that change in cash.

Discussion Question

10-8. Back to the scenario in which you own a small bookstore... What cash flows could you receive or pay out in your book business that would not show up in cash basis net income?

Besides the financial statements themselves, there are a few other bits of information that will be helpful as we create the statement:

- During 1996, Sanguine purchased a building for a total cost of $1,625,000 and equipment for a total cost of $375,000. These purchases were paid in cash.

- During 1996, Sanguine paid cash dividends to its stockholders of $137,000.

Now that we have the necessary information, we can begin preparation of the Sanguine Company's statement of cash flows. This detailed explanation of the construction of this statement is not intended to make you an expert *preparer*, but rather to help you become a wiser *user* of the information. Knowing how the amounts on a statement of cash flows were determined will help you to assess their usefulness and impact on your decision making process. Now, let's start by creating a format for Sanguine's statement of cash flows.

SANGUINE COMPANY
STATEMENT OF CASH FLOWS
FOR THE YEAR ENDED DECEMBER 31, 1996
(in Thousands)

Cash Flows From Operating Activities:	
Net Income	$ 449
Adjustments to reconcile net income to net cash provided by operating activities:	
Net Cash Provided (Used) By Operating Activities	?
Cash Flows From Investing Activities:	
Net Cash Provided (Used) By Investing Activities	?
Cash Flows From Financing Activities:	
Net Cash Provided (Used) By Financing Activities	?
Net Increase (Decrease) In Cash During 1996	$ 380

There are two things you should note about the format above. First, it is divided into the three broad types of activities that can either generate or use cash (operating, investing, & financing). Second, we have already put two amounts into the statement ($449,000 net income and the $380,000 increase in cash from the end of 1995 to the end of 1996). One of the really nifty things about this statement is that we know the answer before we begin. In the case of Sanguine Company, we determined the change in cash by looking at the comparative balance sheets. *Remember, the purpose of the statement of cash flows is not only to disclose what the change in cash was, but more importantly to disclose what caused the change.*

Determining Cash Flow From Operating Activities

We begin with net income in determining cash flow from operating activities because most items involved in net income are either already cash, or should eventually become cash. Even if some components of net income do not involve cash *this* period, most will eventually. Revenues will eventually become cash inflows, and most expenses will eventually become cash outflows. Over time, net income will be the same as the change in cash. Because of the way accrual accounting recognizes revenues and expenses, however, net income for a particular income statement period does not equate to the change in cash for that same period. For that reason, *we must adjust the net income figure for any revenues that did not generate*

476

cash (during this period) and any expenses that did not use cash (during this period). That's a crucial concept, so read it again if you need to, and make sure you understand it before you proceed.

```
┌──────────────────────────────────────────────────────────┐
│ ┌──────────────────────────────────────────────────────┐ │
│ │                                                        │ │
│ │                  Discussion Question                   │ │
│ │                                                        │ │
│ │                                                        │ │
│ │   10-9. Why is retained earnings not equal to cash?    │ │
│ │                                                        │ │
│ │                                                        │ │
│ └──────────────────────────────────────────────────────┘ │
└──────────────────────────────────────────────────────────┘
```

The first adjustment we will make to Sanguine's net income figure is for depreciation expense because depreciation is a non-cash expense. To fully grasp why, you must understand what depreciation is. It is an accrual accounting process of converting the cost of long-lived items (buildings and equipment in Sanguine's case) from asset to expense. Remember, it is totally unrelated to when the buildings and equipment were paid for (cash outflow). Therefore, if we are to determine the cash flow from Sanguine's operating activities, one of the things we must do is add the depreciation expense for the period to net income. We do this because depreciation is an expense that did not use cash, but which was included in the net income figure. If you look at the income statement, you will see Sanguine had depreciation expense for the year of $231,000 ($180,000 on buildings & $51,000 on equipment).

The adjustment for depreciation expense on Sanguine's statement of cash flows is reported like this:

SANGUINE COMPANY
STATEMENT OF CASH FLOWS
FOR THE YEAR ENDED DECEMBER 31, 1996
(in Thousands)

Cash Flows From Operating Activities:
  Net Income $ 449
  Adjustments to reconcile net income to net
    cash provided by operating activities:
      Depreciation Expense $231
                                                              _____
Net Cash Provided (Used) By Operating Activities   ?

Any other adjustments to the net income figure will come from analyzing the current asset and current liability sections of the balance sheets.   Current assets and current liabilities are associated with the day-to-day operation of the company; they are therefore related to the revenues and expenses that make up the income statement. The current asset and current liability sections from Sanguine Company's comparative balance sheets are shown below. We have added a column that calculates how each item changed from the end of 1995 to the end of 1996:

478

SANGUINE COMPANY
PARTIAL BALANCE SHEETS
AT DECEMBER 31, 1996 AND DECEMBER 31, 1995
Current Assets & Current Liabilities Only
(in thousands)

	1996	1995	Increase/ (Decrease)
Current Assets:			
Cash	$ 2,800	$ 2,420	$ 380
Accounts Receivable	2,925	3,112	(187)
Merchandise Inventory	970	866	104
Prepaid Expenses	250	200	50
Total Current Assets	$ 6,945	$ 6,598	$ 347
Current Liabilities:			
Accounts Payable	$ 2,020	$ 1,816	$ 204
Notes Payable	3,400	2,700	700
Total Current Liabilities	$ 5,420	$ 4,516	$ 904

The only one of these items we will not consider as an adjustment on the statement of cash flows is cash. After all, the change in cash is the object of the entire statement of cash flows. A change in any of the other items listed will require an adjustment to net income in determining the net cash provided by operating activities. The adjustments, however, will be exactly opposite of what you probably think they should be. *An increase in any current asset item (except cash) is considered a use of cash, and a decrease in any current asset item (except cash) is considered a source of cash. An increase in any current liability item is considered a source of cash, and a decrease in any current liability item is considered a use of cash.*

While this adjustment process may seem illogical, it really makes sense if you ponder it. Consider accounts receivable, for example.

479

Where do accounts receivable come from? From selling to customers on a credit basis (they pay sometime after they purchase whatever they purchase). Now answer this question: What doesn't a company have when it sells on credit that it would have had if it sold for cash instead? The answer, of course, is CASH! Credit sales are considered revenue under accrual accounting and are therefore used in the calculation of net income. Remember, we are trying to determine the amount of cash generated by operating activities. Any increase in accounts receivable must be deducted from net income because it represents the credit sales that have not been collected as of the end of the year. Accounts receivable decrease when customers pay the cash they owe, so a decrease in accounts receivable is a source of cash.

Think about accounts payable for a minute. Where do they come from? They are created when a company buys merchandise inventory on a credit basis (it pays sometime after the purchase). Now answer this question: What does a company have when it buys on credit that it would not have if it paid cash? The answer, of course, is CASH! Therefore, an increase in accounts payable is considered a source of cash. Accounts payable decrease as the company pays the cash it owes, so a decrease in accounts payable is a use of cash.

After including the adjustments for the changes in the current

asset and current liability items, the operating activities section

of Sanguine's statement of cash flows looks like this:

SANGUINE COMPANY
STATEMENT OF CASH FLOWS
FOR THE YEAR ENDED DECEMBER 31, 1996
(in Thousands)

Cash Flows From Operating Activities:
 Net Income $ 449

Net Income		$ 449
Adjustments to reconcile net income to net cash provided by operating activities:		
Depreciation Expense	$231	
Decrease in Accounts Receivable	187	
Increase in Merchandise Inventory	(104)	
Increase in Prepaid Expense	(50)	
Increase in Accounts Payable	204	
Increase in Notes Payable	700	1,168
Net Cash Provided By Operating Activities		$1,617

We have now determined that Sanguine Company generated positive

cash flow of $1,617,000 through its operating activities during

1996. Since cash increased during 1996 by only $380,000 there must

have been cash flow in one or both of the other types of activities

(investing & financing). We will look first at investing

activities.

Determining Cash Flow From Investing Activities

Determining cash flow from investing activities is done by

analyzing the long-term asset section of the balance sheet.

Sanguine Company calls this section Plant & Equipment. We have

duplicated that section from the company's comparative balance

481

sheets below, and we have added a column that indicates how much each item changed from the end of 1995 to the end of 1996:

SANGUINE COMPANY
PARTIAL BALANCE SHEETS
AT DECEMBER 31, 1996 AND DECEMBER 31, 1995
Plant & Equipment Only
(in thousands)

	1996	1995	Increase/ (Decrease)
Plant & Equipment:			
Buildings	$9,654	$8,029	$1,625
Less Accumulated Dep.	4,597	4,417	180
Buildings, Net	$ 5,057	$ 3,612	$1,445
Equipment	$3,359	$2,984	$ 375
Less Accumulated Dep.	1,955	1,904	51
Equipment, Net	$ 1,404	$ 1,080	$ 324
Total Plant & Equipment	$ 6,461	$ 4,692	$1,769

We already know from the additional information provided about the company's activities, that Sanguine purchased a building for $1,625,000 and equipment for $375,000 during 1996. Even if these details had not been disclosed, the amounts could be determined by the increase in each asset account. We also know how much depreciation expense was recognized for 1996 from the company's income statement ($180,000 on buildings + $51,000 on equipment).

We also know Sanguine paid cash for the full $2,000,000 plant and equipment purchase and this certainly qualifies as a cash outflow under the investing activities section of the statement of cash flows. Since there are no other items listed in the Long-Term

482

Asset (Plant & Equipment) section of Sanguine's balance sheets, we know the purchase of the building and equipment is the only item that will be in this section of the statement. After including the investing activities section, Sanguine Company's statement of cash flows looks like this:

SANGUINE COMPANY
STATEMENT OF CASH FLOWS
FOR THE YEAR ENDED DECEMBER 31, 1996
(in Thousands)

Cash Flows From Operating Activities:		
Net Income		$ 449
Adjustments to reconcile net income to net cash provided by operating activities:		
Depreciation Expense	$231	
Decrease in Accounts Receivable	187	
Increase in Merchandise Inventory	(104)	
Increase in Prepaid Expense	(50)	
Increase in Accounts Payable	204	
Increase in Notes Payable	700	1,168
Net Cash Provided By Operating Activities		$ 1,617
Cash Flows From Investing Activities:		
Purchase of Building	$1,625	
Purchase of Equipment	375	
Net Cash Used By Investing Activities		$(2,000)

If we combine the cash provided by operating activities and the cash used by investing activities we arrive at a net cash outflow for 1996 of $383,000 ($1,617,000 inflow - $2,000,000 outflow). This means there must have been cash inflow from the third broad activity (financing) because we know that overall cash increased by $380,000 during 1996.

Determining Cash Flow From Financing Activities

Determining cash flow from financing activities is done by analyzing the long-term liabilities and stockholders' equity sections of the balance sheet. We have duplicated those sections from Sanguine Company's comparative balance sheets below, and we have provided a column that shows how much each item changed from the end of 1995 to the end of 1996.

SANGUINE COMPANY
PARTIAL BALANCE SHEETS
AT DECEMBER 31, 1996 AND DECEMBER 31, 1995
Long-Term Liabilities & Stockholders' Equity Only
(in thousands)

	1996	1995	Increase/ Decrease
Long-Term Liabilities	$ 2,500	$ 2,000	$ 500
STOCKHOLDERS' EQUITY:			
Common Stock, no par value	3,400	3,000	$ 400
Retained Earnings	2,086	1,774	$ 312

The $900,000 cash inflow ($500,000 in long-term debt + $400,000 from the sale of additional shares of common stock) is fairly straight-forward and can be determined simply by looking at the change in those two items on the comparative balance sheets. In addition, there was a cash outflow in the form of cash dividends during 1996 of $137,000. We already know the amount because it was the other bit of additional information provided with this example. However, the amount of dividends can be determined by considering what we know and backing into what we don't know.

484

We know the balance in retained earnings at the end of 1996 after the dividends have been paid ($2,086,000). We also know the retained earnings balance at the end of 1995 ($1,774,000), and the net income for 1996 from the income statement ($449,000). Since net income is this period's addition to retained earnings, and dividends are reductions of retained earnings, we can calculate the amount of the dividend by combining all we know. Based on the relationship that we learned in the statement of retained earnings, the following holds true:

```
Retained Earnings at 12/31/95.......................  $ 1,774,000
Plus 1996 Net Income................................      449,000
Less dividends paid during 1996.....................            ?
Equals Retained Earnings at 12/31/96 ...............  $ 2,086,000
```

The unknown amount of dividends must be $137,000. This calculation is based on the relationships we already know from the statement of retained earnings:

RE (beginning) + Net Income - Dividends = RE (ending)

With this piece of information in hand, we are now prepared to complete the final section of Sanguine Company's statement of cash flows for the year ended December 31, 1996. If we have considered everything we should have, the cash provided by operating activities combined with the cash used by investing activities and the cash provided by financing activities should be equal to the change in cash from the end of 1995 to the end of 1996.   The

completed statement is shown below:

SANGUINE COMPANY
STATEMENT OF CASH FLOWS
FOR THE YEAR ENDED DECEMBER 31, 1996
(in Thousands)

Cash Flows From Operating Activities:
Net Income $ 449
Adjustments to reconcile net income to net
 cash provided by operating activities:
   Depreciation Expense $231
   Decrease in Accounts Receivable   187
   Increase in Merchandise Inventory   (104)
   Increase in Prepaid Expense   (50)
   Increase in Accounts Payable   204
   Increase in Notes Payable   700   1,168
Net Cash Provided By Operating Activities $ 1,617

Cash Flows From Investing Activities:
Purchase of Building $1,625
Purchase of Equipment   375
Net Cash Used By Investing Activities $(2,000)

Cash Flows From Financing Activities:
Proceeds From Long-Term Loan $ 500
Proceeds from Sale of Common Stock   400
Payment of Cash Dividends   (137)
Net Cash Provided By Financing Activities $ 763
Net Increase In Cash During 1996 $ 380

Sanguine Company's statement of cash flows was a fairly simple one

to create because there were relatively few things to consider in

its construction.   As we said earlier, actual statements of cash

flows for actual companies can contain some rather exotic items.

But whether simple or complex, all statements of cash flows look

pretty much like the one we did for Sanguine Company.

HOW TO USE THE STATEMENT OF CASH FLOWS

The purpose of the statement of cash flows is to disclose where a company got cash during a specific time period, and what it used cash for. One of the most important things the statement shows is what a company invested in during the period, and how that investment was financed. We are talking here about a company's investment in long-lived productive assets that will be used to produce revenues, and eventually cash. *The things* the company invested in during the period is presented in the middle section of the statement (investing activities). *How* that investment was financed is presented in the top section of the statement (operating activities), and the bottom section of the statement (financing activities).

To demonstrate this concept, we have extracted the cash flow totals for the three types of activities from Sanguine's statement of cash flows, as follows:

    Net Cash Provided By Operating Activities.... $ 1,617,000
    Net Cash Used By Investing Activities....... $(2,000,000)
    Net Cash Provided By Financing Activities.... $ 763,000

Sanguine invested $2,000,000 in a building and equipment during 1996. The investment was made to somehow enhance the way the company conducts its business. It may have been intended to upgrade manufacturing facilities, allow entry into new markets, or develop new products. The point is, there had to be a reason to make this investment. We can't assess whether this investment was good or bad because we have no additional information about the company. However, we can determine where the cash to finance this investment came from.

There are only two sources of cash available to Sanguine (or any other company, for that matter). Cash is either generated internally (from profitable operations) or it is obtained from external sources (borrowing or selling stock). You can see by looking at the presentation above that Sanguine generated about 80% of the cash required for the investment internally (operating activities). The rest came from outside sources (financing activities).

With that in mind, focus on this important concept: *In the long run, all investment (middle section) must be financed through operations (top section).* The statement of cash flows is an economic decision maker's most valuable tool in determining how a company is financing its investments.

Careful examination of the statement of cash flows can offer insights into many aspects of a company's operations. This statement, combined with those introduced earlier (income statement, statement of owners' equity, and balance sheet) provides important information upon which economic decision makers rely. However, in order for this information to be truly useful, decision makers must be assured that the statements were prepared under a consistently applied set of guidelines. The set of guidelines and the assurance process are the topics discussed in the next chapter.

CHAPTER SUMMARY

One of the disadvantages of accrual basis accounting is that it takes the financial statement reader's eye off of cash. Over the past several decades, interest in the cash flows of companies has risen. A financial statement, the statement of cash flows, was developed to help provide information about the cash flows of companies during a particular period.

The most widely used approach to preparation of the statement of cash flows is the indirect method. The statement of cash flows provides information about cash flows used by and provided by three major types of business activities — operating, investing and financing. Information necessary for the development of a statement of cash flows can be found on comparative balance sheets and the income statement of the period.

Calculation of the cash flows provided by operating activities begins with net income. Adjustments to this figure are made for any revenue items not producing cash this period and expense items not using cash this period. Results of investing activities can be found in the long-term asset section of the balance sheet. Typical transactions which are classified as investing activities are the purchase and sale of property, plant and equipment. The financing activities section of the statement of cash flows shows what types of external financing the company used to provide funds.

Information showing the results of financing activities can be found in the long-term liability section and the owners' equity section of the balance sheet.

The statement of cash flows provides valuable information about the cash inflows and outflows of a business during a particular period. It provides an explanation of the changes in cash from the beginning to the end of a period. In this way, the statement of cash flows can be considered a financial statement analysis tool as well as a financial statement.

KEY TERMS DEFINED

Comparative Financial Statements. Financial statements providing information from two or more consecutive periods at once.

Direct Method. The format of a statement of cash flows that provides detail as to the individual sources and uses of cash associated with operating activities.

Financing Activities. Business activities such as the issuance of debt or equity, and the payment of dividends. These activities focus on the external financing of the company.

Indirect Method. The most widely used format of the statement of cash flows. This approach provides a reconciliation of accrual net income to the cash provided by or used by operating activities.

Investing Activities. Business activities related to long-term assets. Examples include the purchase and sale of property, plant and equipment.

Operating Activities. Activities that result in cash inflows and outflows generated from the normal course of business.

Statement of Cash Flows. A financial statement that provides information about the causes of a change in a company's cash balance from the beginning to the end of a specific period.

Working Capital. This value is calculated by subtracting current liabilities from current assets.

REVIEW THE FACTS

1. In its present format, when did the statement of cash flows come into existence?

2. What is the main purpose of the statement of cash flows?

3. Name the two methods for preparation of the statement of cash flows. Which method is more commonly used by publicly traded companies?

4. What are the three major classifications of activities presented on the statement of cash flows?

5. In what category are the cash flows related to interest and dividends received and interest paid usually reported?

6. Provide examples of an inflow of cash and an outflow of cash for each of the three categories of business activity shown on the statement of cash flows.

7. Where are the items included in operating activities reported in the financial statements?

8. Where are the items included in investing activities reported in the financial statements?

9. Where are the items included in financing activities reported in the financial statements?

10. Which section(s) of the statement of cash flows tell the user how much cash the company used to acquire depreciable assets?

11. Which section(s) of the statement of cash flows tell the user how investments made by the company were financed?

12. What are comparative financial statements?

13. What is the starting point for calculation of cash flows from operating activities?

Chapter 10
APPLY WHAT YOU HAVE LEARNED

A10-1. Presented below is a list of items relating to the concepts presented in this chapter, followed by definitions of those items in a scrambled order:

a. Operating activities.
b. Indirect method.
c. Depreciation expense.
d. Comparative financial statements.
e. Financing activities.
f. Working capital.
g. Direct method.
h. Investing activities.

1. _b_ Provides a reconciliation of accrual net income to the cash provided by or used by operating activities.

2. _d_ Accounting reports providing information from two or more consecutive periods at once.

3. _a_ Activities centered around the actual day-to-day business transactions of a company.

4. _f_ Current assets less current liabilities.

5. _h_ Business activities related to long-term assets.

6. _g_ Provides detail as to the individual sources and uses of cash associated with operating activities.

7. _c_ An item that reduces reported net income, but does not require the use of cash.

8. _e_ Activities such as the issuance of debt or equity and the payment of dividends.

REQUIRED:

Match the letter next to each item on the list with the appropriate definition. Each letter will be used only once.

A10-2. Listed below are the three broad types of activities which can either generate or use cash in any business, followed by examples of transactions and events.

a. Operating activities. *current assets + liabs, income statement*

b. Investing activities. *long term assets*

c. Financing activities. *long term liabs + OE*

1. __c__ Payment of dividends.

2. __a__ Adjustment for depreciation.

3. __a__ Purchase of merchandise inventory.

4. __b__ Purchase of vehicles.

5. __c__ Repayment of loans.

6. __c__ Issuing capital stock.

7. __a__ Payment of wages to employees.

8. __a__ Payment of taxes.

9. __b__ Sale of property and equipment.

10. __b__ Loans to other companies.

11. __a__ Adjustments for changes in current asset and current liability items.

12. __b__ Selling investments in other companies.

REQUIRED:

Classify each of the items listed above by placing the letter of the appropriate activity category in the space provided.

496

A10-3. Presented below are partial comparative balance sheets of Reggie Company at December 31, 1996 and 1995:

REGGIE COMPANY
PARTIAL BALANCE SHEETS
AT DECEMBER 31, 1996 AND DECEMBER 31, 1995
Current Assets & Current Liabilities Only
(in thousands)

	1996	1995	Increase/ (Decrease)
Current Assets:			
Cash	$ 3,400	$ 2,920	$ 480
Accounts Receivable	1,825	2,212	(387)
Merchandise Inventory	1,170	966	204
Prepaid Expenses	240	270	(30)
Total Current Assets	$ 6,635	$ 6,368	$ 267
	=======	=======	=======
Current Liabilities:			
Accounts Payable	$ 2,321	$ 1,740	$ 581
Notes Payable	3,100	3,300	(200)
Total Current Liabilities	$ 5,421	$ 5,040	$ 381
	=======	=======	=======

Net income for 1996 was $406,000. Included in the operating expenses for the year was depreciation expense of $175,000.

REQUIRED:

Prepare the operating activities section of Reggie Company's statement of cash flows for 1996.

A10-4. Presented below are partial comparative balance sheets of Halifax Company at December 31, 1996 and 1995:

HALIFAX COMPANY
PARTIAL BALANCE SHEETS
AT DECEMBER 31, 1996 AND DECEMBER 31, 1995
Current Assets & Current Liabilities Only
(in thousands)

	1996	1995	Increase/ (Decrease)
Current Assets:			
Cash	$ 2,110	$ 2,650	$ (540)
Accounts Receivable	1,254	977	277
Merchandise Inventory	730	856	(126)
Prepaid Expenses	127	114	13
Total Current Assets	$ 4,221	$ 4,597	$ (376)
	=======	=======	=======
Current Liabilities:			
Accounts Payable	$ 1,054	$ 1,330	$ (276)
Notes Payable	2,100	1,750	350
Total Current Liabilities	$ 3,154	$ 3,080	$ 74
	=======	=======	=======

Net income for 1996 was $86,900. Included in the operating expenses for the year was depreciation expense of $102,000.

REQUIRED:

Prepare the operating activities section of Halifax Company's statement of cash flows for 1996.

A10-5. Presented below is Montrose Company's statement of cash flows for the year ended December 31, 1995:

MONTROSE COMPANY
STATEMENT OF CASH FLOWS
FOR THE YEAR ENDED DECEMBER 31, 1995
(in Thousands)

Cash Flows From Operating Activities:		
Net Income		$ 389
Adjustments to reconcile net income to net		
cash provided by operating activities:		
Depreciation Expense	$131	
Increase in Accounts Receivable	(287)	
Increase in Merchandise Inventory	(104)	
Increase in Prepaid Expense	(70)	
Decrease in Accounts Payable	(304)	
Increase in Notes Payable	300	(334)
Net Cash Provided By Operating Activities		$ 55
Cash Flows From Investing Activities:		
Purchase of Building	($1,255)	
Purchase of Equipment	(304)	
Net Cash Used By Investing Activities		$(1,559)
Cash Flows From Financing Activities:		
Proceeds From Long-Term Loan	$ 800	
Proceeds from Sale of Common Stock	300	
Payment of Cash Dividends	(100)	
Net Cash Provided By Financing Activities		$ 1,000
Net Decrease In Cash During 1996		$(504)

REQUIRED:

Respond to the following questions:

a. For which of the three broad types of activities did Montrose use the majority of its cash during ~~1996?~~ *1995*

b. What does your answer to the previous question tell you about Montrose Company?

c. From which of the three broad types of activities did Montrose obtain the majority of its cash during ~~1996?~~ *1995*

d. Is the activity you identified in the previous requirement an appropriate source of cash in the long run? Explain your reasoning.

499

A10-6. Presented below is Hendrick Company's statement of cash flows for the year ended December 31, 1996:

HENDRICK COMPANY
STATEMENT OF CASH FLOWS
FOR THE YEAR ENDED DECEMBER 31, 1996
(in Thousands)

Cash Flows From Operating Activities:
Net Income $ 1,608
Adjustments to reconcile net income to net
  cash provided by operating activities:
    Depreciation Expense $218
    Increase in Accounts Receivable   (341)
    Decrease in Merchandise Inventory   81
    Increase in Prepaid Expense   (50)
    Increase in Accounts Payable   104
    Increase in Notes Payable   50   12
Net Cash Provided By Operating Activities $ 1,620

Cash Flows From Investing Activities:
Purchase of Building   ($1,000)
Purchase of Equipment   (200)
Net Cash Used By Investing Activities $(1,200)

Cash Flows From Financing Activities:
Repayment of Long-Term Loan $ 350
Proceeds from Sale of Common Stock   350
Payment of Cash Dividends   (100)
Net Cash Used By Financing Activities $(100)
Net Increase In Cash During 1996 $ 320

REQUIRED:

Respond to the following questions:

a.   For which of the three types of activities did Montrose use the majority of its cash during 1996?

b.   What does your answer to the previous question tell you about Montrose Company?

c.   From which of the three types of activities did Montrose obtain the majority of its cash during 1996?

d.   Is the activity you identified in the previous requirement an appropriate source of cash in the long run? Explain your reasoning.

A10-7. Use the balance sheets and income statement below and the additional information on the following page to complete this work.

[handwritten: Purchases of buildings 1,526,000   eq.   289,000]

HOGLE COMPANY
BALANCE SHEETS
AT DECEMBER 31, 1996 AND DECEMBER 31, 1995
(in thousands)

ASSETS:	1996	1995	
Current Assets:			
Cash	$ 1,618	$ 1,220	
Accounts Receivable	1,925	2,112	*(187)*
Merchandise Inventory	1,070	966	*104*
Prepaid Expenses	188	149	*39*
Total Current Assets	$ 4,801	$ 4,447	*354*
Plant & Equipment:			
Buildings, Net	$ 4,457	$ 2,992	
Equipment, Net	$ 1,293	1,045	
Total Plant & Equipment	$ 5,750	$ 4,037	
Total Assets	$10,551	$ 8,484	
LIABILITIES:			
Current Liabilities:			
Accounts Payable	$ 1,818	$ 1,686	*132*
Notes Payable	900	1,100	*(200)*
Total Current Liabilities	$ 2,718	$ 2,786	
Long-Term Liabilities	2,500	2,000	*500*
Total Liabilities	$ 5,218	$ 4,786	
STOCKHOLDERS' EQUITY:			
Common Stock, no par value	$ 3,390	$ 2,041	*1349*
Retained Earnings	1,943	1,657	
Total Stockholders' Equity	$ 5,333	$ 3,698	
Total Liabilities			
and Stockholders' Equity	$10,551	$ 8,484	

HOGLE COMPANY
INCOME STATEMENT
YEAR ENDING DECEMBER 31, 1996
(in thousands)

Net Sales	$11,228
Less Cost of Goods Sold	7,751
Gross Profit on Sales	$ 3,477
Less Operating Expenses:	
Depreciation - Buildings & Equip.	$ 102
Other Selling & Administrative	2,667
Total Expenses	$ 2,769
Operating Income	$ 708
Less Interest Expense	168
Income Before Taxes	$ 540
Income Taxes	114
Net Income	$ 426

Additional Information for A10-7:

There were no sales of plant & equipment during the year and the company paid dividends to stockholders during the year of $140,000.

REQUIRED:

a. Prepare Hogle Company's statement of cash flows for the year ended December 31, 1996.

b. In which of the three categories of activities did Hogle use the majority of its cash during 1996?

c. What does your answer to the previous question tell you about Hogle Company?

d. From which of the three types of activities did Hogle obtain the majority of its cash during 1996?

e. Is the activity you identified in the previous requirement an appropriate source of cash in the long run? Explain your reasoning.

A10-8. Presented below are the totals from the main three sections of Arlene Job & Company's most recent statement of cash flows:

   Net Cash Provided By Operating Activities.... $ 1,812,000

   Net Cash Used By Investing Activities....... $(1,280,000)

   Net Cash Used By Financing Activities....... $(153,000)

Required:

a. What do these totals tell you about Job & Company?

b. What additional information would you want to see before you analyze Job & Company's ability to generate positive cash flow in the future?

CHAPTER 11

GENERALLY ACCEPTED ACCOUNTING PRINCIPLES &

FORMS OF OUTSIDE ASSURANCE ON FINANCIAL STATEMENTS

In Chapter 7, we discussed two very different approaches to revenue
and expense recognition (cash basis and accrual basis). We
stressed that each of them has advantages and disadvantages in
relation to the other. Further, we stated that neither of them is
"correct" in the sense of being in accordance with some natural law
of accounting and finance. However, the need for comparability was
evident: The use of different measurement bases makes valid
comparisons across companies impossible.

In your study of Chapter 10, you learned about the statement of
cash flows, a financial statement designed to bring the focus of
accrual accounting back to cash. The statement of cash flows is
actually a form of financial statement analysis, a subject we will
cover in more depth in Chapter 12. The whole purpose of financial
statement analysis is for economic decision makers to draw
conclusions based on comparisons. These comparisons may be based
on accounting information of a single company over multiple years,
or the decision maker may compare companies to one another or to
industry averages.

A necessary premise of valid financial statement analysis is
comparability of the accounting information. Most large companies

use the accrual basis of measurement for external reporting purposes, so everything is fine, right? WRONG! Even within the boundaries of accrual accounting, there is much room for variations in measurement and valuation — to the rescue comes the accounting profession, armed with rules and standards to be followed.

In this chapter we will explore how the accounting profession has responded to the needs of financial statement users for consistent and comparable information. When you have finished your work on this chapter, you should be able to:

1. Explain what Generally Accepted Accounting Principles are and why they are important to economic decision makers.

2. Describe the development of Generally Accepted Accounting Principles (GAAP) since the early 1900's.

3. Describe the process used by the Financial Accounting Standards Board to create accounting standards.

4. Explain the five basic assumptions under which GAAP operate.

5. List and define the four basic principles of GAAP.

6. Describe in your own words the three modifying conventions under which it is allowable to modify GAAP.

7. Explain what an audit is and what it is not.

8. Describe the five different types of audit opinion.

9. Compare and contrast reviews and compilations.

GENERALLY ACCEPTED ACCOUNTING PRINCIPLES

In Chapter 3, entitled <u>ECONOMIC DECISION MAKING & USEFUL ACCOUNTING INFORMATION</u>, the qualitative characteristics of useful accounting information were discussed. One of those characteristics was comparability. We stated that economic decision making involves the evaluation of alternatives. In order to be useful in that evaluation, the accounting information for one alternative must be comparable to the accounting information for the other alternative(s). If the alternatives use totally different accounting methods, any comparison between or among them becomes extremely difficult. Without some assurance that the measurement criteria used by the companies were the same, any comparison among them is useless.

In its *Statement of Financial Accounting Concepts #1*, the Financial Accounting Standards Board stated that a particular problem exists for those decision makers who

lack the authority to prescribe the financial
information they want from an enterprise and
therefore must use the information that
management communicates to them. (p. 41)

The decision makers referred to by the FASB are the external
financial statement users we have discussed throughout this book.
They are not involved in the day-to-day operation of a company and
do not know what accounting methods and assumptions were used in
the preparation of the financial statements they receive. If they
are to have confidence in those financial statements, they must
have assurance that the statements were prepared in accordance with
some well-defined set of rules and guidelines.

The need for comparability between and among financial statements,
coupled with the problems faced by the external financial statement
users, led to the development of what has come to be known as
Generally Accepted Accounting Principles (GAAP).

Generally Accepted Accounting Principles can be broadly defined as
a set of standards (rules) adopted by the accounting profession to
be used in preparing accounting information for external decision
makers. Generally accepted, by the way, does not mean universally
accepted, and many of the standards we will discuss have provoked
debate and criticism.

Who is Bound by GAAP?

We have stated several times that economic decision makers can be broadly classified as either external or internal to an entity. External decision makers make decisions *about* the company, and the information at their disposal is limited to what the enterprise provides to them. Internal decision makers, on the other hand, make decisions *for* the company, and have access to a greater amount of accounting and financial information pertaining to the enterprise.

Generally accepted accounting principles were developed over time to provide assurance to the external users that the information they were using to compare alternatives in a decision situation is comparable. For this reason, GAAP apply to the information prepared for use by external parties (financial accounting information), but NOT to the information prepared for use by internal parties (managerial accounting information). This is an important distinction, so make certain you grasp it. At various times throughout your lifetime, you will make economic decisions as both an internal party and an external party (maybe even in a single decision situation). You must be aware which information is prepared under the guidelines of GAAP and which is not.

It may surprise you to learn that not all companies must adhere to GAAP in their financial accounting either. There are no GAAP police waiting to put people in jail for violating the rules. In fact, the only companies required by law to follow GAAP are those companies regulated by the Securities and Exchange Commission. Those include all companies whose stock is traded on one of the national or regional stock exchanges, or those who have bonds listed on one of the major bond exchanges. Other companies may use whatever accounting procedures they desire unless, of course, the external users demand that GAAP be followed.

Banks and other lending institutions are accustomed to seeing financial results prepared under GAAP rules and often require all companies to adhere to those rules. Once again, the logic is fairly easy to follow. A bank is deciding whether to loan money to Company A or Company B. Company A is required to follow GAAP, but Company B is not. How can the loan committee at the bank compare the two alternative investment options if the two use different accounting bases? The answer is obvious: they can't. Therefore, Company B is, for all practical purposes, forced to adopt GAAP procedures even though it is not legally required to do so.

Another factor that causes companies to adopt GAAP even when not required by law to do so is the audit. Virtually all companies that are audited end up following GAAP. The reasons for this will become clear to you later in this chapter when we discuss forms of outside assurance on financial statements.

```
┌─────────────────────────────────────────────────────────────────┐
│                                                                   │
│                     Discussion Questions                          │
│                                                                   │
│                                                                   │
│      11-1. Why do you think a company would be opposed to         │
│                                                                   │
│            adopting GAAP?                                         │
│                                                                   │
│                                                                   │
└─────────────────────────────────────────────────────────────────┘
```

The History of GAAP

Prior to 1900, the economy of the United States was relatively
unsophisticated, and accounting for that economy was equally
unsophisticated. Most businesses were family owned and operated
and the accounting reports generated were mostly for internal use.
Banks and other lending institutions dictated the only external
reports, and there was little uniformity in what they required. By
the turn of the century, however, the U.S. economy was undergoing
significant change. The emergence of large corporations with
absentee ownership created a demand for greater disclosure and more
uniformity in accounting reports. In 1903, United States Steel
became the first company in the United States to publish annual
financial statements for its stockholders and other external
parties (Searfoss p. 45-2). Clearly, the time had come for the
establishment of a generally accepted set of accounting rules and
guidelines. The result has been the development of GAAP.

The first development in the establishment of GAAP was a recommendation in 1917 by the Federal Trade Commission (FTC) that the accounting profession be regulated by the federal government and that accounting rules be established by the government. Quite naturally, the accounting profession was alarmed by this prospect and took immediate steps to demonstrate its ability to regulate itself. The American Institute of Accountants (AIA) was a relatively young (formed in 1887) and loosely organized professional association of accountants. The threat of regulation by the federal government, however, forced the AIA to get serious about setting standards for the practice of accounting. It appointed a committee to study the situation and develop accounting standards for AIA members to follow. The committee took its work seriously and convinced government officials that the accounting profession was capable of governing itself. The threat of government establishing a uniform code of accounting was averted, at least for the time being.

The second major event affecting the development of GAAP was the Great Depression. The origins of modern GAAP can really be traced to this period. After the stock market crash of 1929, pressure began to mount again for federal regulation of the profession. In 1934 Congress created the Securities and Exchange Commission (SEC) and gave it the authority to prescribe:

> ...the methods to be followed in the
> preparation of reports, in the appraisal or
> valuation of assets and liabilities, in the
> determination of depreciation and depletion,
> in the differentiation of investment and
> operating accounts, and in the
> preparation...of balance sheets or income
> accounts. (subparagraph 13(b))

With the creation of the SEC, many thought the debate over how accounting rules and standards should be developed was over. Not so. In 1938, the SEC voted (by a vote of 3 to 2) to allow the accounting profession itself to establish standards of accounting, so long as there was "substantial authoritative support" for those standards (ASR 4, subparagraph 101). This was a profoundly important decision by the SEC, because without it, today's accounting standards would very likely be a set of rules established by the federal government. Instead, accounting standards have been the product of a series of committees and boards, beginning with the **Committee on Accounting Procedure (CAP)**.

```
+------------------------------------------------------------------+
|                    Discussion Questions                          |
|                                                                  |
|                                                                  |
|    11-2. What are the pros and cons of having                    |
|          accounting rules established by the government?         |
|                                                                  |
|                                                                  |
|    11-3. What are the pros and cons of having                    |
|          accounting rules established by the accounting          |
|          profession?                                             |
|                                                                  |
+------------------------------------------------------------------+
```

The Committee on Accounting Procedure (CAP)

Formed in 1930, this committee was revitalized and enlarged in 1938
with the decision by the SEC to leave standard setting to the
accounting profession. The CAP issued pronouncements called
Accounting Research Bulletins (ARBs). This committee restricted
itself to responding to very specific accounting topics and was
criticized for failing to establish any kind of conceptual
framework for its bulletins. Fifty-one ARBs were issued by the
committee between 1938 and 1959, when the CAP was disbanded. While
the bulletins were often ambiguous and the committee lacked any
authority to enforce its recommendations, they did achieve a
measure of general acceptance among members of the AIA.

The Accounting Principles Board (APB)

In 1959, the American Institute of Certified Public Accountants (AICPA), which had evolved from the AIA dissolved the Committee on Accounting Procedure and replaced it with the **Accounting Principles Board (APB)**. The major reason for the creation of the APB was the feeling that the CAP was too concerned with practice issues and lacked the structure to conduct research into a conceptual framework. The charter of the APB provided for a research division and the hope was that finally work in this important area would begin. Unfortunately, the research never materialized. As was the case with the CAP, the APB was criticized for not establishing a conceptual framwork of accounting from which to approach the standard setting process. Essentially, critics of the Board held that its opinions addressed only what accounting practice *was* and not what accounting practice *should be*. During its existence, the APB issued 31 opinions. By the late 1960s, the AICPA had begun studying ways to improve the standard setting process. The conclusion of the study, oddly enough, was that the AICPA could best improve its role in setting standards by relinquishing its control of the process. Both the CAP and the APB were committees of the Institute. What was needed was an independent standard setting body. The result was the creation of the **Financial Accounting Standards Board (FASB)** in 1973.

Financial Accounting Standards Board (FASB)

The express mission of the FASB is:

> ...to establish and improve standards of
> financial accounting and reporting for the
> guidance and education of the public,
> including issuers, auditors, and users of
> financial information.
>
> FASB, 1987b (Searfoss p.46-8)

There are several key differences between the FASB and the two earlier standard setting groups (CAP and APB). These differences have allowed the FASB to attain a much higher degree of acceptance in both the accounting profession and the business community in general:

- The FASB is an independent body and its members work full-time. Both the CAP and APB were organizations of the AICPA and their members were volunteers who continued in their primary occupations while serving as members. Upon appointment to the FASB, the members are required to resign from their present employment and work full-time. Members serve five-year terms and are eligible for reappointment for one consecutive term.

- It is smaller in size. The CAP was composed of 22 members and the APB had 21 members. In both instances, the size of the organization, coupled with the volunteer status of the

514

members, made even holding meetings extremely difficult. When
meetings were held, it was almost impossible to obtain
agreement on issues because of the number of people involved.
The FASB, on the other hand, is composed of seven members, all
of whom work full time during their time on the Board. While
agreement among members is still not easy, it is certainly
less difficult than it was with either the CAP or the APB.

- The FASB's members are not all accountants. Both the CAP and
  APB were composed of practicing accountants and represented a
  rather narrow perspective. Members of the FASB come from
  diverse employment backgrounds, but are required to have
  knowledge of accounting, finance, and business in general.
  This diversity allows the FASB to have a broader perspective
  in its concern for the public interest in matters of financial
  accounting and reporting.

- Early on, the FASB established a conceptual framework of
  accounting from which to approach the process of standard
  setting. We have referred to this conceptual framework
  several times throughout this text. While not everyone agrees
  with the concepts established by the FASB, most agree that the
  framework has changed the emphasis in setting standards from
  one of *what is* to one of *what should be*.

• From its inception, the FASB has employed a due-process approach to standard setting. The CAP, and to a lesser extent, the APB, established accounting standards without much input from those who would be bound by those standards. This approach, while efficient, breeds discontent and resentment. FASB takes a different approach. From the time an issue that may require a new (or revised) standard is identified to the time a standard is set, there is ample opportunity for any interested party to make his or her feelings on the matter known.

11-4. Why do you think it is significant that the FASB is independent of the AICPA?

11-5. If FASB members are not required to be accountants, from what other professional backgrounds are members likely to be drawn?

11-6. How do you think a conceptual framework shifts the standard setting process from *what is* to *what should be*?

11-7. In what ways does a due-process approach to standard setting lessen discontent and resentment?

The Standard Setting Process Today

Under the structure of the FASB, standard setting is a ten-step process emphasizing the due-process feature discussed in the previous section. The ten steps are listed below. We will discuss each of them.

1. Identification of Issues
2. Agenda Setting
3. Appointing Task Forces
4. Discussion Memoranda
5. Public Hearings on Financial Accounting Standards
6. Comment Letters
7. Deliberations
8. Exposure Drafts
9. Statements of Financial Accounting Standards
10. Postenactment Review

Step #1 - Identification of Issues

Accounting issues and problems are identified either by the FASB itself or from any other interested party. Issues considered over the years have been raised by public accounting firms, the AICPA, business organizations, the U.S. Congress, and many others.

Some of the issues brought to the Board's attention are fairly simple and some are very complex. While there are no set rules for determining whether an identified issue requires attention by the FASB, there is an attempt to treat them all seriously.

Step #2 - Agenda Setting

Choosing agenda items is a critical step in the process. Obviously, not all issues raised make it to this step. The FASB must consider its own resources in considering the issue, the perceived urgency of the matter, and any interrelationship with other projects under consideration.

Step #3 - Appointing Task Forces

Once an item is placed on the agenda, a task force is appointed to see the project through to its conclusion. Projects may result in a new standard, or the project may be dropped after some investigation of the issues. Task forces are usually composed of outside experts in the area or areas involved in the project on the agenda. When appointing members to these task forces, there is an attempt to achieve a diversity of views surrounding the issues. The object is to obtain as many different perspectives on the issues as possible.

Step #4 - Discussion Memoranda

The task force appointed in Step #3 prepares a discussion memorandum, which defines the problem and the scope of the project. This document also includes several alternative solutions, but offers no recommendations. All interested parties are invited to respond to memoranda issued during this process.

Step #5 - Public Hearings on Financial Accounting Standards

While not mandatory, open public hearings on major projects being considered by the Board have always been held. These hearings are announced in the financial press, and anyone interested may attend and make an oral presentation of his views.

Step #6 - Comment Letters

Those not able to attend the public hearings to discuss the issues involved in a particular project are invited to write comment letters. Every letter is considered by the Board.

Step #7 - Deliberations

Once all interested parties have had an opportunity to express their views, either through public hearings or comment letters, the Board deliberates on whether or not to move to Step #8. Also considered in the deliberation process are recommendations from the Board's technical staff and the task force appointed in Step #3.

Step #8 - Exposure Drafts

Any project reaching this step is very likely going to result in a new standard under GAAP. In fact, an exposure draft is intended to be as close to a final pronouncement as possible. Generally, a proposed standard is exposed to public comment for at least 60 days. Often, these proposed standards undergo significant modification as a result of comments received during the exposure draft stage.

Step #9 - Statements of Financial Accounting Standards

Once a proposed standard has gone through the first eight steps of the process, the FASB approves a final **Statement of Financial Accounting Standard (SFAS)** by majority vote of the seven members and there is a new GAAP standard.

Step #10 - Postenactment Review

This is the step that actually makes GAAP standard setting a circular process. The FASB has recognized that the rules of financial accounting and reporting must be constantly reconsidered and either refined or amended. To this end, standards passed by the Board become eligible for consideration as an issue or problem and the process begins again with step #1.

Beginning with the Committee on Accounting Procedure, continuing with the Accounting Principles Board, and finally with the Financial Accounting Standards Board, there have been well over 200 official pronouncements establishing standards that constitute generally accepted accounting principles. Most of these standards focus on very narrow applications issues dealing with how specific items should be treated. Woven throughout these pronouncements, however, are several underlying assumptions, principles, and modifying conventions which provide a context for the specific applications. An understanding of these concepts is essential to anyone attempting to use financial statements prepared under the various provisions of GAAP.

BASIC ASSUMPTIONS OF GAAP

There are five basic assumptions under which GAAP operate. This means that any time economic decision makers look at financial reports prepared under GAAP, they can be assured the reports were prepared based on these assumptions:

Separate Entity

The **separate entity assumption** is that economic activity can be identified with a particular economic entity. This means the revenues and expenses reported in the income statement of General Motors, for example, are the revenues and expenses of General Motors and no other economic entity (including its owners). The same holds true with the assets, liabilities and equities reported in General Motors' balance sheet.

Going Concern

The **going concern assumption** is that unless there is persuasive evidence to the contrary, it is assumed that businesses will continue to operate indefinitely. The implications of this assumption are ENORMOUS. It is this assumption that makes accrual accounting possible. For example, revenue is recognized under accrual accounting when it is earned, not when the cash associated with the revenue is received. Unless it can be assumed the company owing the money will be around long enough to pay it, recognition before the cash is received would be inappropriate.

What is true for revenue recognition is also true for expense recognition. In fact, the going concern assumption is what allows financial statement users to rely on a balance sheet that reports accounts receivable and accounts payable.

Monetary Unit

The **monetary unit assumption** holds that all economic transactions and events can be measured using some monetary unit. It is assumed that quantitative data expressed in some monetary unit are the most useful way of measuring and communicating economic information. In the United States, we use the dollar, in England they use the pound, in Japan they use the yen, etc. It is also assumed all economic events and transactions can be reasonably measured using the chosen monetary unit.

A significant problem associated with the monetary unit assumption is caused by the dual nature of "money". The dollar, for example, is used in the United States as both a valuation instrument and as a medium of exchange. Measuring things in dollars, however, does not make them dollars. Many people mistake items in the financial statements for dollars, simply because they are measured in dollars. Here's a hint so you won't fall into that trap: In all of business, there is one item representing cash, and we have cleverly called it CASH! Anything called anything else is something measured in dollars (but it's not dollars).

Stable Dollar

The **stable dollar assumption** is that the value of the dollar does not change over time. This assumption allows inflation and

524

deflation to be ignored in financial reports prepared under GAAP. Under the stable dollar assumption, 1963 dollars and 1993 dollars are lumped together without any adjustment for changing prices during that 30 year period.

Time Period

The **time period assumption** is that the economic activities of an entity can be traced to some specific time period. The actual results of a business in total will not be known until it ceases to do business. With the going concern assumption in place, that can be a very long time. Periodically, then, companies issue reports that show how profitable they have been for some arbitrary time period (income statement), and their financial position at the end of that time period (balance sheet). The time period assumption holds that with some degree of reliability, the economic events and transactions of that time period can be measured.

BASIC PRINCIPLES OF ACCOUNTING UNDER GAAP

There are four basic principles pertaining to how transactions and events are to be measured under GAAP. Obviously, how these things are measured dictates how they are reported in financial statements. Anytime economic decision makers look at financial reports prepared under GAAP, they can be assured that the reports were prepared based on these principles:

Historical Cost

The **historical cost principle** requires that assets be reported at their cost. Contrary to popular belief, accounting does not deal with value or worth. Rather, accounting deals with cost. A balance sheet, for example, discloses the cost of assets, not what they are worth.

Many people, when they learn about the historical cost principle, are highly critical of it. They feel a balance sheet should show how much the assets are worth, not how much they cost. We agree it would be desirable to show the current value of the items on the balance sheet; this information would be very relevant in a variety of decision making settings. However, the current value of an asset is not a reliable item of information. Particularly with regards to the aspect of verifiability, current cost is not reliable. For example, if we turned to appraisers for the current value of a building, there would be some variation in the amounts. The historical cost of assets may not be as relevant as current value, but it is a reliable information item. It is verifiable, neutral, and representationally faithful.

The accounting profession has experimented with ways to make the balance sheet items more reflective of their current values, but every time it does, the subjective nature of the valuation process has caused a return to historical cost accounting. The profession is simply not comfortable with the degree of uncertainty (not to mention the lack of comparability) associated with the attempts at current value accounting.

The implications of the historical cost principle are profound and far reaching. You should, therefore, make certain you grasp its significance to financial statement users. Explore in your own mind what it means in the preparations of the income statement and the balance sheet.

Discussion Questions

11-8. What criteria would you establish to determine the current value of items presented in a company's balance sheet?

11-9. In what ways do you think a departure from the historical cost principle reduces the verifiability and, therefore, reliability of a company's financial statements?

Revenue Recognition & Expense Recognition

The **revenue recognition principle** is that revenue is recognized when it is earned, rather than when the cash associated with the revenue is collected. The **expense recognition principle** is that expenses are matched to the same income statement period as the revenues they helped generate, rather than when the cash associated with the expenses is paid.

These two principles are discussed together because besides the fact they are closely related, we have already discussed them in-depth in Chapter 7 when we presented accrual basis accounting. This means that the accounting profession has adopted accrual accounting as GAAP. Accrual accounting is not without its weaknesses. In spite of those weaknesses, the accounting profession has decided that the accrual method of revenue and expense recognition is superior to any alternative recognition basis. Make certain to keep in mind, however, that being generally accepted does not make it "correct". It simply means it has been accepted as the method the accounting profession feels is the best way to measure reality.

Full Disclosure

The **full disclosure principle** is that the financial statements prepared by a company must provide users with the information they need to make economic decisions. This should probably be called the adequate disclosure principle, because it would then more accurately describe what it means. Whenever accounting reports are prepared, accountants are faced with the dilemma of providing sufficient information for the users' needs without including so much detail that the statements become too cumbersome.

Besides the main body of the financial statements, other forms of disclosure are required. These include the notes to the financial statements, and supplementary schedules which support items included in the main body of the financial statements.

The key to what information should be included is deciding whether the inclusion or exclusion of an item will make a difference to the user. This is very difficult, because the needs of different users are different, and often conflicting. Overall, the intent is to present enough information to ensure that the reasonably prudent user will not be misled.

MODIFYING CONVENTIONS TO GAAP

The standards established as GAAP would be unworkable unless they could be modified under certain circumstances. There are three such situations, and when any of them exist, the applicable standard or standards under GAAP may be modified.

Materiality

The **materiality** convention allows for GAAP to be modified if the treatment of the item is not significant enough to matter. An item is material if its inclusion or exclusion would influence the judgment of a reasonable person. If an item is deemed to be immaterial, it need not be treated according to GAAP. As an example, assume a company purchased a wastebasket for $10 and estimated its useful life to be ten years. Accrual accounting takes the position that the wastebasket should be recorded as an asset and depreciated using some systematic and rational allocation method over its ten year life. The cost of recordkeeping, however, far outweighs any benefit derived from doing so. No reasonable person is going to be misled by expensing the wastebasket (recording the entire $10 as an expense at the time of purchase).

Materiality is a relative concept. What is material for one company may not be for another. For example, General Motors has sales revenue of well over $100 billion per year. Including a $10,000 sale in the wrong income statement period would not be material. For Harry Hardtop's Used Car Sales, which averages about $100,000 is sales each year, including a $10,000 sale in the wrong income statement period would be a material error. There are no hard and fast rules about what is material, so evaluating materiality requires a tremendous amount of judgment.

Industry Peculiarities

An **industry peculiarity** is a circumstance in which the characteristics of activity in a particular industry makes adherance to a particular GAAP rule result in misleading information. Certain industries have, over time, developed treatments of these peculiar circumstances which do not follow GAAP. When this is the case, businesses throughout the entire industry use accounting methods other than those prescribed by GAAP. Because all companies in that industry treat the item in the same manner, to do otherwise would result in financial statements that could not be compared to other companies in the industry. Some examples of industries where alternative accounting methods have been developed are food service, long-term construction, and farming.

For example, GAAP requires that long-lived assets be capitalized and then depreciated over their estimated useful life. In the food service industry, however, when a restaurant purchases its first set of tableware (plates, bowls, glasses, silverware, etc.), these items are capitalized (recorded as assets on the balance sheet), but they are not depreciated. Instead, when new tableware items are purchased as replacements, their cost is recognized as an expense on the income statement.

531

Conservatism

Conservatism means that when in doubt as to the accounting treatment of an item, the treatment least likely to overstate assets or income, or understate liabilities is selected. The purpose of conservatism is to provide a guideline in difficult valuation situations. If more than one choice of presentation or valuation method appears to meet GAAP guidelines, conservatism suggests that the alternative least likely to overstate financial position or earnings should be selected. However, conservatism in no way justifies the intentional understating of a company's assets or income.

Discussion Questions

11-10. Describe a situation in which management of a company would wish to understate the assets or income of the business.

FORMS OF OUTSIDE ASSURANCE ON FINANCIAL STATEMENTS

The purpose of Generally Accepted Accounting Principles is to give assurance to external users that the financial statements they look at were prepared according to a consistently applied set of standards. Logic dictates that these external parties cannot be expected to rely solely on the integrity of the company preparing the financial statements. Since it is in the best interest of the company issuing the statements to present them as favorably as possible (except to the government in the case of income tax reporting), there is a need for some assurance from outside the company as to the fairness of the financial statement presentation. This part of the chapter explores the ways this assurance is obtained.

History of the Audit

The word audit comes from the word auditory, meaning "to hear". While that definition does not seem to apply to our usage of the word, the reason it is used can be found in the historical development of auditing. Auditing, as we know it, goes back at least to thirteenth century England. A.C. Littleton, in the book Accounting Evolution to 1900 describes early auditing:

> Since the issue was usually one of honest
> discharge of fiscal responsibility, the
> purpose of these audits would be to test the
> proper administration of that responsibility.
> To accomplish this purpose, the facts in the
> case would need to be laid before persons who
> would recognize error or omission when
> present. In the early days this usually
> involved "hearing the accounts" for few men
> could read and very few could write; the word
> "audit" itself means to hear. (p. 262)

In the United States, the profession of auditing didn't really begin until after 1900. The emergence of large corporations with absentee ownership created a need for an independent review of a company's financial statements. To meet that need, the profession of auditing developed.

Earlier in the chapter, we mentioned that the first company to publish financial statements for its stockholders and other external parties was United States Steel in 1903. This was also the first set of financial statements to be accompanied by a statement from an independent auditor. The accounting firm performing the audit on U.S. Steel was Price Waterhouse & Co. and this was the statement they issued:

We have examined the books of the U.S. Steel
Corporation and its Subsidiary Companies for
the year ending December 31, 1902, and
certify that the Balance Sheet at that date
and the Relative Income Account are correctly
prepared therefrom.

We have satisfied ourselves that during the
year only actual additions and extensions
have been charged to Property Account; that
ample provision has been made for
Depreciation and Extinguishment, and that the
item of "Deferred Charges" represents
expenditures reasonably and properly carried
forward to operations of subsequent years.

We are satisfied that the valuation of the
inventories of stocks on hand as certified by
the responsible officials have been carefully
and accurately made at approximate cost; also
that the cost of material and labor on
contracts in progress has been carefully
ascertained, and that the profit taken on
these contracts is fair and reasonable.

Full provision has been made for bad and
doubtful accounts receivable and for all
ascertainable liabilities.

We have verified cash and securities by
actual inspection or by certificates from the
Depositories, and are of opinion that the
Stocks and Bonds are fully worth the value at
which they are stated in the Balance Sheet.

And we certify that in our opinion the
Balance Sheet is properly drawn up so as to
show the true financial position of the
Corporation and its Subsidiary Companies, and
that the Relative Income Account is a fair
and correct statement of the net earnings for
the fiscal year ending at that date.
(Carey p. 1:28-29)

The words *Relative Income Account* refer to the income statement,

which had not yet acheived a position of great importance as a

financial statement in 1903.   The audit opinion reproduced here

is much more strongly worded than Price Waterhouse & Co. would

535

have issued had this audit been for the year 1992 instead of
1902. The reasons for this are discussed in the next section.

What Exactly is an Audit?

Perhaps the best way to approach this subject is to talk about
what an audit is *not!* An audit is not the preparation of the
financial statements. The company itself prepares the
statements. In fact, the auditor has no authority to change
anything in the statements. An audit is also not an examination
of all the records to make sure the financial statements are
accurate. Read that sentence again. Does it surprise you? It
does many people, because they think that is exactly what an
audit is.

An audit consists of examining enough of the company's records to
determine whether the financial statements have been prepared in
accordance with GAAP standards. To examine everything would be
incredibly expensive. So expensive, in fact, that companies
could not afford an audit of all their records.

Auditors make no claim as to the accuracy of the financial
statements they are auditing. What they look for is *reasonable
assurance* that there are no *material misstatements* in the
financial statements. Reasonable assurance means what a rational
person would consider sufficient. Material misstatement goes

back to our discussion of materiality earlier in the chapter. The adjective material refers to something significant enough to influence the judgment of a reasonable person.

If you reread the audit opinion issued by Price Waterhouse, you will see that the auditors gave the impression of certifying the accuracy of U.S. Steel's financial statements for 1902. Over the years, the standard independent auditor opinion has evolved into something quite different than the one Price Waterhouse issued in 1903.

Who Performs Audits?

Those individuals approved to perform independent audits of American businesses are Certified Public Accountants (CPAs), but not all CPAs are auditors. Auditing is a highly specialized function and is governed by a set of standards called **Generally Accepted Auditing Standards (GAAS)**. Do not confuse GAAS with GAAP, although the auditing standards are established in much the same way as GAAP standards are.

Auditors occupy a unique position in our society. Lawyers have only one responsibility and that is to represent their clients (who pay them to fulfill that responsibility). Doctors have only one responsibility and that is to their patients (who pay them to fulfill that responsibility). Auditors, on the other hand, have a dual responsibility. They are responsible to their clients (who pay them), but they also have a responsibility to all who use the audited financial statements. They are expected to remain independent of the entity they are auditing and impartial in their assessment of the presentation in the financial statements. It is a difficult balancing act, and one that is currently subject to a tremendous amount of criticism.

The Audit Opinion

At the conclusion of an audit, the auditor issues an **opinion** as to the fairness of the financial statement presentation. There are several different opinions which can be rendered under GAAS, depending on the findings of the audit:

> **Unqualified Opinion.** This is what all companies being audited hope to receive, and in most instances do. It is also called (unofficially) a "clean" opinion. An unqualified opinion will always contain three paragraphs and in most instances will be stated word for word like the example below. The only thing changed will be the name of the company being audited, the name of the auditor, and the dates.

We have audited the accompanying balance sheets of
Rosita Company as of December 31, 1996 and 1995 and
the related statements of income, retained earnings,
and cash flows for the years then ended. These
financial statements are the responsibility of the
Company's management. Our responsibility is to
express an opinion on these financial statements
based on our audits.

We conducted our audits in accordance with generally
accepted auditing standards. Those standards
require that we plan and perform the audit to obtain
reasonable assurance about whether the financial
statements are free of material misstatement. An
audit includes examining, on a test basis, evidence
supporting the amounts and disclosures in the
financial statements. An audit also includes
assessing the accounting principles used and
significant estimates made by management, as well as
evaluating the overall financial statement
presentation. We believe that our audits provide a
reasonable basis for our opinion.

In our opinion, the financial statements referred to
above present fairly, in all material respects, the
financial position of Rosita Company as of December
31, 1996 and 1995, and the results of its operations
and its cash flows for the years then ended in
conformity with generally accepted accounting
principles.

February 12, 1997

In addition to the unqualified or clean opinion, there are four
types of modified opinion. We are not going to present the actual
opinions because their wording is different under different
circumstances. However, a key for you is that a modified opinion
will contain at least four paragraphs, as opposed to the three
paragraphs found in the unqualified opinion. The modified opinions
are:

- **Qualified Opinion.** Not long ago this form of modification was fairly common, but recent changes in GAAS have greatly reduced the number of instances where this modification is appropriate. It is issued when there is a nonpervasive departure from GAAP (meaning the effect is on no more than one of the financial statements).

- **Disclaimer.** When a material uncertainty exists that the auditor does not feel can be adequately communicated in an explanatory paragraph, a disclaimer is issued stating that the auditor is unable to render an opinion on the financial statements. A disclaimer is also issued if there is a significant restriction placed on the auditor as to what records may be examined.

- **Adverse Opinion.** This is the "kiss of death" opinion. This modification is used when there are departures from GAAP so pervasive that in the opinion of the auditor a reasonable person cannot rely on the financial statements.

- **Modification Not Affecting Opinion.** The auditor may comment on any other matter she or he feels is important to the understanding of the financial statements. There are various circumstances that might lead to this type of modification. The important point is that the auditor is still issuing a "clean" opinion when this type of modification is used.

Many feel the audit opinion should be the first thing examined by an external financial statement user. If understood as to what it is and what it is not, the audit and the resulting audit opinion can be of great benefit to the external user.

The Review

As stated in the previous section, the cost of an audit can be extremely prohibitive. Under certain circumstances, external users are willing to accept a level of assurance somewhat lower than that provided by audited financial statements. They may still desire some assurance that the financial statements are reliable. In response to this situation, the accounting profession has developed the review of financial statements. Unfortunately, many people do not understand the difference between reviewed financial statements and audited financial statements.

Perhaps the best way to distinguish between the review and the audit is to look at the standard review statement issued by an accountant. An example is provided below. Read it carefully.

We have reviewed the accompanying balance sheet of
Havershott Company as of December 31, 1996 and the
related statement of income for the year then ended,
in accordance with standards established by the
American Institute of Certified Public Accountants.
All information included in these financial
statements is the representation of the management
of Havershott Company.

A review consists principally of inquiries of
company personnel and analytical procedures applied
to financial data. It is substantially less in
scope than an examination in accordance with
generally accepted auditing standards, the objective
of which is the expression of an opinion regarding
the financial statements taken as a whole.
Accordingly, we do not express such an opinion.

Based on our review, we are not aware of any
material modifications that should be made to the
accompanying financial statements in order for them
to be in conformity with generally accepted
accounting principles.

February 18, 1997

Compare the review statement to the audit opinion presented
earlier. A careful comparison should be very illuminating.

While a review offers substantially less assurance to external
users than does an audit, it does at least provide what is known as
negative assurance. This means simply that the user can take some
comfort because the accountant is at least *not aware* of any serious
GAAP problems. It may not sound like much, but it is something,
and costs a great deal less than a complete audit.

The Compilation

Before we end this chapter, there is one other type of report we need to discuss — the **compilation**. Compiled financial statements are not intended to provide any assurance whatsoever.

We chose to discuss the subject of compilations because it is one that is greatly misunderstood and often confused with either the audit or the review. It is neither. Perhaps the best way to contrast compiled financial statements with audited and reviewed financial statements is to present the standard compilation report. You will find an example of one presented below.

We have compiled the accompanying balance sheet of
Wooster Company as of December 31, 1996, and the
related statements of income and retained earnings
for the year then ended, in accordance with
standards established by the American Institute of
Certified Public Accountants.

A compilation is limited to presenting in the form
of financial statements information that is the
representation of management. We have not audited
or reviewed the accompanying financial statements
and, accordingly, do not express an opinion or any
other form of assurance on them.

Management has elected to omit substantially all of
the disclosures required by generally accepted
accounting principles. If the omitted disclosures
were included in the financial statements, they
might influence the user's conclusions about the
company's financial position, results of operations,
and cash flows. Accordingly, these financial
statements are not designed for those who are not
informed about such matters.

February 19, 1997

As with the previously presented audit report and review report,
you should make certain you understand all the items included in
the compilation report. Take the time to compare the report to the
both the audit report and the review report.

An accountant will compile financial statements for a client
because the client lacks the necessary skills to prepare the
financial statements. The accountant is not an employee of the
company and is therefore considered independent. In preparing the
statements, the independent accountant does absolutely nothing to
verify that anything in those statements is accurate, reasonable,

or anything else. He or she is simply providing a service (known as write-up work) for the client. As strange as it may sound, the accountant is prohibited under rules established by the AICPA to do any verification of the amounts and items included in the financial statements.

Unfortunately, many people believe that because there is an independent accountant involved, there can be some assurance attached to what is presented in the financials. It is important for you to understand that this is not so. The compilation report actually states that the accountant preparing the report does "not express an opinion or any other form of assurance" as to the reliability of the financial statements.

Another thing to note is that the compilation report does not even refer to generally accepted accounting principles. The review report at least states that the accountant is not aware of any major violations of GAAP.

Of the forms of outside assurance discussed in the chapter, only the unqualified audit opinion states that the financial statements being audited are (in the opinion of the auditor) "in conformity with generally accepted accounting principles".

Generally accepted accounting principles have been developed to establish comparability between the financial statements of different companies. These principles are also intended to maintain consistency in the way companies account for events and transactions from year to year. The audit, and to a lesser extent the review, were developed as mechanisms to provide assurance to external parties that the financial statements they use to make economic decisions are prepared in accordance with the standards established over time.

Now that we have discussed generally accepted accounting principles and the forms of outside assurance, we can look a little deeper into what external and internal decision makers do with the financial statements produced by companies. Of particular interest to us at this point is the analysis of financial ratios, which is the subject of the next chapter.

In order to be useful in the economic decision making process, financial statements of different companies must be comparable. The accounting methods and procedures used by a company must also be consistent from period to period if performance over time is to be reasonably monitored. In response to the need for comparable and consistent financial information, generally accepted accounting principles (GAAP) have been developed over time. GAAP are a set of standards addressing both very broad issues and very specific applications.

The organization principally responsible for establishing GAAP in the United States is the Financial Accounting Standards Board (FASB) which was created in 1973. Prior to that time, accounting standards were established by the Accounting Principles Board (APB) and before that the Committee on Accounting Procedure (CAP). The standards set by these bodies have come about in response to needs expressed by various interested parties and the FASB emphasizes a "due-process" approach, where all parties affected by the standards have an opportunity to express their opinions on proposed standards.

The primary beneficiaries of generally accepted accounting principles are parties external to the company producing the financial statements being used. Therefore, even with GAAP established, there is a need for some form of outside assurance that the financial statements have been prepared according to the standards.

The most reliable form of outside assurance on financial statements produced by a company is the audit. An audit consists of an independent party examining enough of the company's records to determine whether the company's financial statements have been prepared in accordance with GAAP. At the conclusion of the audit, the auditor issues a statement as to the company's compliance with GAAP. This is called the audit opinion.

A less expensive alternative to the audit is the review. A review is much narrower in scope than an audit and the independent party conducting the review does not express an opinion as to whether the financial statements being reviewed were prepared according to GAAP. He or she does make a statement that nothing came to light that would indicate a major violation of GAAP. This is known as negative assurance.

A third form of involvement by a party independent of a company producing financial statements is called a compilation. This procedure consists of an outside party actually preparing a company's financial statements from records provided by the company. The fact that the financial statements were prepared by the external party provides absolutely no assurance whatever that the company complies with GAAP.

KEY TERMS DEFINED

Accounting Principles Board (APB). This organization was the immediate predecessor of the Financial Accounting Standards Board.

Adverse opinion. This opinion is given when the financial statements contain pervasive departures from GAAP.

Committee on Accounting Procedure (CAP). In operation from 1930 to 1959, this committee issued pronouncements called Accounting Research Bulletins (ARBs).

Conservatism. In a given situation, if two approaches to valuation or measurement are allowed under GAAP, the treatment least likely to overstate assets or income, or understate liabilities is to be selected.

Disclaimer. An audit opinion stating that the auditor is unable to render an opinion on the financial statements; issued when a material uncertainly exists that the auditor does not feel can be adequately communicated in an explanatory paragraph, or when the auditor's access to information has been restricted.

Expense recognition principle. Requires that expenses be matched to the same income statement period as the revenues they helped generate.

Financial Accounting Standards Board (FASB). The current accounting standards-setting body.

Full disclosure principle. The financial statements prepared by a company must provide users with the information they need to make economic decisions.

Generally Accepted Accounting Principles (GAAP). Guidelines for presentation of accounting information to meet the need for comparability between and among financial statements of different companies.

Generally Accepted Auditing Standards (GAAS). A set of standards governing the behavior of auditors.

Going concern assumption. Unless there is persuasive evidence to the contrary, it is assumed that businesses will continue to operate indefinitely.

Historical cost principle. Assets are presented on the balance sheet at their cost, not their value.

Industry peculiarity. A circumstance in which a characteristic of an industry causes adherence to a particular GAAP rule to result in misleading information.

Materiality. The modifying convention that allows departure from GAAP if the treatment of an item is not significant enough to influence the judgement of a reasonable person.

Modification not affecting opinion. A comment made by the auditor on any matter she/he feels is important to the understanding of the financial statements.

Monetary unit assumption. Holds that all economic transactions and events can be measured using monetary units.

Opinion. An auditor's judgment as to the fairness of the financial statement presentation.

Qualified opinion. The opinion issued when there is a nonpervasive departure from GAAP (meaning no more than one of the financial statements has been affected).

Revenue recognition principle. Revenue is recognized when it is earned, rather than when the cash associated with revenue is collected.

Separate entity assumption. The assumption that economic activity can be identified with a particular economic entity, and the results of activities for each entity will be recorded separately.

Stable dollar assumption. Allows financial statements to ignore the fact that the value of the dollar changes over time.

Statement of Financial Accounting Standards (SFAS). The official name of any GAAP standard.

Time period assumption. The economic activities of an entity can be traced to some specific time period, and results of the activity can be reported for any arbitrary time period chosen.

Unqualified opinion. Also called a "clean" opinion; this opinion states that the auditors find the financial statements to be fairly presented in accordance with GAAP.

REVIEW THE FACTS

1. Explain how the characteristic of comparability affects economic decision making.

2. Broadly define GAAP.

3. Which companies must adhere to GAAP?

4. Explain why companies may adopt GAAP even if they are not required to do so.

5. What two major events affected the development of GAAP?

6. What is the name and abbreviation for the current accounting standards-setting group?

7. List five differences between the FASB and its predecessors.

8. Describe the 10-step process used by FASB to set standards.

9. Explain the five basic assumptions under which GAAP operate.

10. Define the four basic principles pertaining to how transactions and events are to be measured under GAAP.

11. Describe three situations in which it is allowable to modify GAAP.

12. Name two things an audit is NOT.

13. Explain "reasonable assurance" and "material misstatements".

14. Who can perform independent audits?

15. By what standards are auditors governed?

16. Describe an auditor's dual responsibility.

17. Name and describe the five types of audit opinions that can be given.

18. What type of assurance is offered by a review?

19. Describe a compilation.

Chapter 11
APPLY WHAT YOU HAVE LEARNED

A11-1. Presented below are some items related to outside assurance discussed in this chapter followed by the definitions of those items in a scrambled order.

    a.   Audit
    b.   Review.
    c.   Compilation.
    d.   Unqualified Opinion.
    e.   Qualified Opinion.
    f.   Disclaimer.
    g.   Adverse Opinion.
    h.   Modification Not Affecting Opinion.

1. ____ Caused by a material uncertainty the auditor does not feel can be adequately communicated or if a significant restriction is placed on the auditor as to what records may be examined.

2. ____ The process of examining a company's records to determine whether the financial statements have been prepared in accordance with GAAP standards.

3. ____ Rendered when there are departures from GAAP so pervasive that a reasonable person cannot rely on the financial statements.

4. ____ Provides what is known as negative assurance.

5. ____ A comment made by an auditor in her or his report deemed to be important to the understanding of the financial statements. The opinion rendered, however, is still unqualified.

6. ____ Unofficially referred to as a "clean" opinion.

7. ____ A service provided by an independent accountant where no procedures are performed to verify the accuracy of the financial statements being prepared.

8. ____ Issued when there is a nonpervasive departure from GAAP.

REQUIRED:

Match the letter next to each item with the appropriate definition. Each letter will be used only once.

A11-2. Presented below is a list of the assumptions, principles, and modifying conventions of GAAP as discussed in this chapter followed by the definitions of those items in a scrambled order.

a. Separate entity.
b. Going concern.
c. Monetary unit.
d. Stable dollar.
e. Time period.
f. Historical cost.

g. Revenue Recognition.
h. Expense Recognition.
i. Full disclosure.
j. Materiality.
k. Industry Peculiarities.
l. Conservatism.

1. _f_ Only purchased items are shown on the balance sheet and there is no attempt to show their value.

2. _c_ Economic transactions and events can be expressed using some valuation of money.

3. _g_ Amounts earned are recorded and reported when there is a legal claim to the cash associated with the earnings.

4. _d_ Inflation and deflation are ignored in financial reports.

5. _l_ When in doubt, choose the accounting alternative least likely to overstate assets or income.

6. _a_ Economic activity can be identified with a particular economic entity.

7. _i_ Financial statements must provide users the information the need to make economic decisions.

8. _b_ Unless there is persuasive evidence otherwise, business are assumed to operate indefinitely.

9. _j_ Significant enough to influence the judgment of a reasonable person.

10. _e_ Economic activities can be traced to a specific income statement period.

11. _k_ Circumstances where adherence to GAAP would be misleading because virtually all similar companies apply alternative treatments.

12. _h_ Economic sacrifices are recognized in the same income statement period as the revenues they generate.

REQUIRED:

Match the letter next to each item on the list with the appropriate definition. Each letter will be used only once.

A11-3. Consider each of the following independent situations:

1) Monolith, Inc. is applying for a loan at the Stevens Bank & Trust and must provide the bank with current financial statements. Since the corporation has only $44,000 of assets, the accountant has decided to list the $200,000 house owned by the president of the company as an asset on Monolith's balance sheet.

2) Upper management of Mike Burbidge & Company has a problem. They have been analyzing the financial statements prepared by the corporate controller for the year ended December 31, 1995. The income statement shows a net income of $375,000 for the year; the problem is management had predicted net income of only about $50,000 for 1995. Now it looks like 1996 will be the bad year and management would like to "smooth" earnings somewhat by showing some of 1995's net income in 1996. To do this, they have decided to count all the December, 1995 sales as January, 1996 sales. This will lower the 1995 net income to $172,000. That way, the company can still show much better than expected net income for 1995, and have a head start on 1996.

3) Jan Ruttenburr, Inc. purchased a building in December, 1995 for a cash price of $250,000. Management has decided to count the entire cost of the building as an expense in 1995 because it was a bad year anyway (a $1,800,000 loss) and another $250,000 expense won't make that much difference.

4) A product liability lawsuit was filed against Betty Jo Clardy Company just as 1996 was drawing to a close. The company has decided not to make any mention of the litigation in its annual report to the stockholders. Although the outcome of the suit looks bleak, it is not absolutely certain the company will lose and management feels it would only make the stockholders nervous if they knew about it.

5) Lehi Mills & Company has owned a building for 25 years. The building originally cost $75,000 to construct and has an estimated useful life of 30 years with no residual value. The straight-line depreciation method has been used, so the building now has a book value of only $12,500. Last month, Pam Bowden Company offered Mills $450,000 for the building, so Mr. Mills (owner and president of Mills & Company) has decided to list the building on this year's balance sheet at $450,000.

A11-3 continues on the next page

6) DeLoy Fillerup is really proud of himself. He has straightened out the fixed asset accounting procedures at Aunt Alice's Restaurants, Inc. Before he became the accountant of the corporation, the procedures violated GAAP. Whenever the company opened a new restaurant, it capitalized the tableware necessary to run the operation, but never depreciated these items. Instead, it simply left them on the balance sheet as long-lived assets at their original cost and then counted replacement items as expenses as they were purchased. Under DeLoy's new policy, tableware (new & replacement) is depreciated over an estimated useful life of five years.

7) Ratliff Textiles, Inc. has purchased a new stitching machine and is trying to determine the estimated useful life for depreciation purposes. Mr. Ratliff is uneasy with using the five-year life the company normally uses for machines of this type. His business instinct tells him that new technology is just around the corner (probably within the next three years), so he thinks a three-year life might be more realistic. His general manager is trying to convince him to use the five-year life anyway, because it will result in lower depreciation expense and higher net income each year.

REQUIRED:

For each of the situations in the problem, identify the GAAP assumptions, principles, and/or modifying conventions violated. Explain your reasoning.

separate entity
going concern
monetary unit
Stable dollar
time period

historical cost
revenue recognition
expense M
full disclosure

materiality
industry peculiarity
conservatism

A11-4.   There are ten steps in the standard setting process used
by the Financial Accounting Standards Board. They are:

1) Identification of issue.
2) Agenda setting.
3) Appointing a task force.
4) Discussion memoranda.
5) Public hearings.
6) Comment letters.
7) Deliberation by the Board.
8) Exposure draft.
9) Statement of Financial Accounting Standard.
10) Postenactment review.

REQUIRED:

a. Explain in your own words what happens in each of the ten
steps of the standard setting process.

b. What is meant by a "due-process approach" to setting
accounting standards and why has this approach made the
FASB more successful than previous standard setting
bodies?

A11-5.   The Committee on Accounting Procedure (CAP) and the
Accounting Principles Board (APB) were the two bodies
responsible for setting accounting standards prior to the
creation of the FASB in 1973. The chapter identified five key
differences between the FASB and the two earlier standard
setting groups:

1) The FASB is independent and its members work full
time.

2) The FASB is smaller.

3) The FASB includes non-accountants as members.

4) The FASB established a conceptual framework of
accounting.

5) The FASB emphasizes a due-process approach.

REQUIRED:

Explain in your own words what each of the five differences
means and why they have made the FASB more successful than
either the CAP or the APB.

A11-6.   Generally accepted accounting principles have been developed over time to aid in comparability between the financial statements of different companies. They are also intended to maintain consistency in the way a firm accounts for transactions and events from period to period.

An audit is intended to provide external parties some assurance that the financial statements they examine are reasonably presented.

REQUIRED:

a.   What determines whether a company in the United States is required to prepare its financial statements according to GAAP?

b.   Why are some companies forced to adhere to GAAP even though they are not required to do so?

c.   Compare and contrast the audit, the review, and the compilation by discussing the following:

1)   The procedures involved in each.

2)   The degree of assurance each provides to external financial statement users.

CHAPTER 12

FINANCIAL STATEMENT ANALYSIS: RATIOS

Predicting the future of anything is extremely difficult because there is always some degree of uncertainty associated with the future. In attempting to predict a company's ability to generate positive cash flow in the future, economic decision makers must consider the company's present condition and past performance. Financial statements are tools that have been developed over time to provide information about a company's present condition and past performance.

For the last eight chapters we have been discussing and using various financial statements. In this chapter, we will present a specific technique you can use to analyze and interpret financial statements. This technique is known as ratio analysis. In a very real sense, we are continuing what we started in Chapter 10 because, while we presented it as a financial statement, the statement of cash flows is a form of financial statement analysis. It is a full-blown financial statement devoted to analyzing what caused the change in cash from one period to the next.

Information from the same two financial statements used to develop the statement of cash flows, the income statement and the balance sheet, provide the basis for the ratios presented in this chapter. These ratios are valuable to both internal and external financial

561

statement users. Ratio analysis is used by management (internal decision makers) as a monitoring device to assess the company's ongoing performance. External decision makers also depend on an analysis of ratios both in evaluating investment alternatives and for feedback on investments already made.

When you have finished your work on this chapter, you should be able to:

1.   Describe the purpose of ratio analysis.

2.   Calculate and interpret financial ratios analyzing the profitability of businesses.

3.   Use ratios to evaluate the liquidity of a business.

4.   Calculate and interpret ratios to analyze the solvency of businesses.

5.   State in your own words the limitations of ratio analysis.

RATIO ANALYSIS

Ratio analysis provides a means to analyze the relationship between two items from a company's financial statements for a given period. Ratios are computed by dividing the dollar amount of one item from the financial statements by the dollar amount of another item.

Important relationships may exist between two items on the same financial statement, or on different financial statements. For that reason, some ratios use items from the same financial statement (two items from the income statement or two items from the balance sheet), while some use one item from each statement.

A great many ratios have been developed by financial statement users. It is not important that you be able to recite the composition of many ratios. It is, however, important that you understand the basic relationships shown in the ratios and that you feel comfortable with ratio analysis in general, so that you will be a wise user of the accounting information available to you.

Not all ratios are appropriate for every need, and an analyst must carefully consider which ones will provide the best information in a given situation. Additionally, the ratios mean very little in and of themselves. They become meaningful only when compared to other information, such as the same ratios in other years, ratios for similar, competitive companies, or industry averages.

563

The ratios presented in this chapter utilize information from both the balance sheet and the income statement. We will use information drawn from the following comparative statements of Flores, Inc. as a basis for the examples of each ratio covered.

FLORES INC.
INCOME STATEMENTS
FOR THE YEARS ENDED DECEMBER 31, 1996 AND 1995
(in thousands)

	1996	1995
Net Sales	$14,745	$12,908
Less Cost of Goods Sold	10,213	8,761
Gross Profit on Sales	$ 4,532	$ 4,147
Less Operating Expenses:		
Advertising & Sales Commissions	$ 1,022	$ 546
General & Administrative	2,721	2,451
Total Expenses	$ 3,743	$ 2,997
Operating Income	$ 789	$ 1,150
Less Interest Expense	172	137
Income Before Taxes	$ 617	$ 1,013
Less Income Taxes	123	355
Net Income	$ 494	$ 658

FLORES, INC.
BALANCE SHEETS
AT DECEMBER 31, 1996 AND DECEMBER 31, 1995
(in thousands)

ASSETS:		1996		1995
Current Assets:				
Cash		$ 2,240		$ 1,936
Accounts Receivable		2,340		2,490
Merchandise Inventory		776		693
Prepaid Expenses		200		160
Total Current Assets		$ 5,556		$ 5,279
Plant & Equipment:				
Buildings	$7,723		$6,423	
Less Accumulated Dep.	3,677		3,534	
Buildings, Net		$ 4,046		$ 2,889
Equipment	$2,687		$2,387	
Less Accumulated Dep.	1,564		1,523	
Equipment, Net		$ 1,123		864
Total Plant & Equipment		$ 5,169		$ 3,753
Total Assets		$10,725		$ 9,032
LIABILITIES:				
Current Liabilities:				
Accounts Payable		$ 1,616		$ 1,080
Notes Payable		2,720		2,920
Total Current Liabilities		$ 4,336		$ 4,000
Long-Term Liabilities		2,000		1,600
Total Liabilities		$ 6,336		$ 5,600
STOCKHOLDERS' EQUITY:				
Common Stock, no par value		$ 3,000		$ 2,400
Retained Earnings		1,389		1,032
Total Stockholders' Equity		$ 4,389		$ 3,432
Total Liabilities				
and Stockholders' Equity		$10,725		$ 9,032

There are three major characteristics that can be evaluated using ratio analysis: profitability, liquidity, and solvency. Ratios can be broadly classified as profitability ratios, liquidity ratios, and solvency ratios. We will present representative ratios from each of these categories. For each ratio, you can learn what the ratios mean and why they are considered important. When the calculation of each ratio is presented, you will find a notation in both the numerator and the denominator indicating from which financial statement the item is drawn.

Measuring Profitability

Profitability, the ease with which companies generate income, is an important factor for economic decision makers to consider. **Profitability ratios** are of interest to present and potential stockholders, as well as long-term creditors and the company's management. In the long run, a company must maintain an acceptable level of profitability if it is to service its long-term debt and pay dividends to its stockholders. Profitability ratios are used to help predict a firm's ability to generate sufficient profits (and ultimately cash) to fulfill its obligations.

Profitability ratios, while important to external parties in assessing investment alternatives, can be extremely dangerous if used unwisely. In most cases, external decision makers are making long-term decisions. And yet, as we shall see shortly, the profitability ratios are calculated using relatively short-term results (usually one year). What this does is put enormous pressure on the management of companies to attain the highest possible profit it can for any given period. Well now, what could be wrong with that? Just this:

A PREOCCUPATION WITH SHORT-TERM PROFITS

IS DETRIMENTAL TO THE LONG-TERM VALUE OF A BUSINESS!

As you look at the profitability ratios that follow, focus not only on what they are supposed to reveal about a company, but also their potential to encourage short-sighted behavior on the part of management. It is quite common for management's decisions to be based on an attempt to make the ratios "look better."

Discussion Question

12-1. Provide an example of a management decision that would be made differently depending on whether the short-term or long-term well-being of the company is being considered. Explain the impact of the two different perspectives.

Return on total assets

The **return on total assets** ratio is a measure of return on investment. It is an attempt to measure how efficiently a company's assets are being used to produce profits. The whole purpose of investing in assets is to produce revenue and ultimately profit (net income).

567

This ratio can be calculated a number of different ways. For our purposes we will use the following formula:

$$\text{Return on Total Assets} = \frac{\text{Net Income + Interest Expense (income statement)}}{\text{Average Total Assets (balance sheet)}}$$

Interest expense is added back to net income in this formula so the numerator becomes net income before interest expense. Interest expense represents amounts paid to creditors on funds borrowed and then used to acquire assets. The purpose of this ratio is to measure how well assets are being employed, regardless of the way they were financed (by creditors or by the owners). Therefore, we must add interest expense back to net income to arrive at the total return earned on assets employed. This process eliminates the effects of financing costs on the income generated using the assets.

Another important fact to note about the formula used for the calculation of this ratio is that the denominator uses *average* total assets employed for the period rather than simply the balance at the end of the period. This makes sense if you keep in mind that the numerator in the calculation represents revenues earned and expenses incurred throughout a particular period (usually a year). Using the average assets employed for the period in the denominator gives a more reliable picture of the assets used to earn net income during the period. For our purposes, we will calculate the average total assets as follows:

$$\frac{\text{Total asset balance at the beginning of the period} + \text{Total asset balance at the end of the period}}{2} = \text{Average Total Assets}$$

On the balance sheet, the balance at the end of one year becomes the balance at the beginning of the next year. Since Flores, Inc.'s 1994 balance sheet was not provided with the comparative balance sheets, assume total assets at the end of 1994 were $8,871,000. This becomes the balance of total assets at the beginning of 1995. Average total assets for 1996 and 1995 are calculated as follows:

1996	1995
$\dfrac{\$9{,}032{,}000 + \$10{,}725{,}000}{2} = \$9{,}878{,}500$	$\dfrac{\$8{,}871{,}000 + \$9{,}032{,}000}{2} = \$8{,}951{,}500$

Flores' return on total assets ratios for 1996 and 1995 can now be calculated as follows:

1996	1995
$\dfrac{\$494{,}000 + \$172{,}000}{\$9{,}878{,}500} = 6.7\%$	$\dfrac{\$658{,}000 + \$137{,}000}{\$8{,}951{,}500} = 8.9\%$

569

Let's talk about what this ratio really means. In Chapter 10, when we presented the statement of cash flows, we determined there are three sources that companies can use to obtain the cash needed to invest in assets. A company can:

1.   Borrow cash (debt financing).

2.   Issue (sell) stock (equity financing).

3.   Earn the cash (internal financing, which is actually another form of equity financing).

There is a cost associated with each of these sources of cash. When a company invests in assets, it does so with the expectation that in the long run it will earn more on the invested cash than the cost of obtaining the cash. The cost of obtaining the cash required to invest in assets is known as the **cost of capital or hurdle rate**. If a company does not earn at least what it costs to obtain the cash, it makes no sense to make the investment.

Once the return on total assets ratio is calculated, it can be compared to the cost of capital. If the return on total assets ratio is less than the cost of capital, the company is not earning enough to pay for its investment. On the other hand, if the return on total assets is greater than the cost of capital, the company is earning more than the cost of its investment in the assets.

Before we could assess Flores' return on total assets ratios for 1995 and 1996, we would need to know its cost of capital. If the company's cost of capital is 14% these ratios would mean something very different than if the cost of capital is 3%.

Another thing to keep in mind is the concept of "the long run." A significant amount of Flores' investment in assets is in long-term assets (plant & equipment). To make a judgment of Flores' return on total assets based on such short-term results (two years) can be very misleading.

How would a company determine the cause of a low return on assets, and how would it go about improving the situation? As the following illustration suggests, the return on total assets ratio can be broken down into two components.

$$\text{Return on Total Assets} = \text{Profit Margin Percentage} \times \text{Total Asset Turnover}$$

$$\frac{\text{Net Income} + \text{Interest Expense}}{\text{Average Total Assets}} = \frac{\text{Net Income} + \text{Interest Expense}}{\text{Revenue}} \times \frac{\text{Revenue}}{\text{Average Total Assets}}$$

Each component of the return on total assets can be analyzed separately; a company can then zero in on areas in need of improvement. The two components of return on assets are the next two profitability ratios to be discussed.

Profit margin percentage

As previously indicated, the **profit margin percentage** has the same numerator as the return on asset ratio. By comparing the net income plus interest expense to the revenue figure, this calculation provides an indication of the amount of income produced by a given level of revenue. Think about that — revenues are the inflows, and net income is the remainder after consideration of expenses.

$$\text{Profit Margin Percentage} = \frac{\text{Net Income + Interest Expense (income statement)}}{\text{Revenue (income statement)}}$$

Discussion Question

12-2. What situations result in companies having a low profit margin percentage?

As Logue suggests in his Handbook of Modern Finance,

> The profit margin percentage measures a
> firm's ability to (1) obtain higher prices
> for its products relative to competitors and
> (2) control the level of operating costs, or
> expenses, relative to revenues generated. By
> holding down costs, a firm increases the
> profits from a given amount of revenue and
> thereby improves its profit margin
> percentage.

Based on the example of the Flores company financial statements, the profit margin percentages for 1995 and 1996 are as follows:

1996	1995
$\dfrac{\$494,000 + \$172,000}{\$14,745,000} = 4.5\%$	$\dfrac{\$658,000 + \$137,000}{\$12,908,000} = 6.2\%$

From the calculations above, it is clear that Flores' profit margin percentage dropped from 1995 to 1996. However, the profit margin percentage is just one component of the return on total assets ratio. The second component is equally important.

Total asset turnover

Total asset turnover indicates the amount of revenues produced for a given level of assets used. Be certain that you understand the distinction between the information provided by the asset turnover ratio (which deals with the level of revenues produced) and that provided by the return on assets (which focuses on the level of net income).

$$\text{Total Asset Turnover} = \frac{\text{Revenue (income statement)}}{\text{Average Total Assets (balance sheet)}}$$

From the financial statements of Flores, Inc., the total asset turnover ratios for 1995 and 1996 can be calculated.

1996	1995
$\dfrac{\$14,745,000}{\$9,878,500} = 1.49$	$\dfrac{\$12,908,000}{\$8,951,500} = 1.44$

Discussion Questions

12-3. Offer two separate suggestions as to how a company can make its total asset turnover ratio higher.

12-4. A company wishing to make its return on assets ratio higher, could focus its efforts on either component (profit margin percentage or asset turnover ratio). Which component do you feel would be easier for a company to improve? Explain how you came to your conclusion.

12-5. The Flores company's return on total assets fell from 1995 to 1996. What specific factors caused the decline? Offer a suggestion to Flores that could be implemented during 1997 to boost the company's return on total assets.

Earnings per share

The final measure of profitability we will discuss is earnings per share. **Earnings per share (EPS)** is perhaps the most widely used (and least understood) measure of a company's earnings performance. It is popular because it converts the total earnings of a company to the amount attributable to each share of common stock. The earnings per share ratio is calculated as follows:

$$\text{Earnings Per Share} = \frac{\text{Net Income (income statement)}}{\text{Average Shares of Common Stock Outstanding (balance sheet)}}$$

Note that the denominator of the calculation above is the average *number* of shares of common stock outstanding — not the dollar amount associated with those shares. Recall from Chapter 5 that if common stock is issued with an assigned par value, that only the par value for the shares is reported as common stock on the balance sheet. Any amount received for the stock that is in excess of the par value is shown as additional paid-in capital on the balance sheet. When the par value is shown as a separate item, the number of shares can be determined by dividing the total amount in the common stock account by the par value per share.

In our example, Flores' stock is no-par value stock. In this situation, the amount on the balance sheet cannot be used to determine the number of shares outstanding. For our purposes, assume Flores had 240,000 shares of stock outstanding throughout all of 1995. Further, assume the company issued (sold) an additional 10,000 shares of stock for $60.00 per share on January 2, 1996, so there were 250,000 shares of stock outstanding throughout all of 1996.

Flores' EPS ratios for 1996 and 1995 are calculated as follows:

1996	1995
$\dfrac{\$494,000}{250,000 \text{ Shares}} = \$1.98$	$\dfrac{\$658,000}{240,000 \text{ Shares}} = \$2.74$

EPS is usually presented at the very bottom of the income statement. The computation can be much more complex than shown here if the company has either preferred stock or bonds payable that could be converted into common stock. These complexities often result in the reporting of several EPS figures, which further reduces many financial statement users' understanding of the item.

The biggest limitation of the EPS calculation is that the per share figure tends to divert attention from the company's overall performance. EPS can be increased simply by reducing the number of shares outstanding; a company can go into the secondary stock market and buy back shares of its stock previously issued. Also, since EPS is dependent on the number of shares outstanding, comparisons among companies with differing amounts of outstanding stock are not reliable as measures of how the companies actually performed relative to one another.

In spite of its limitations, EPS can provide information, particularly when considered in conjunction with other measures of profitability. Rather than relying on any single measure of profitability, wise financial statement users turn to several different ratios. Four measures of profitability were introduced: (1) Return on total assets, (2) Profit margin percentage, (3) Total asset turnover, and (4) Earnings per share. In order to get a true picture of the profitability of a company, evaluate the figures for several of these ratios.

Measuring Liquidity

Liquidity is generally used to refer to how easily assets can be converted to cash at the discretion of management. The liquidity of a firm refers to the company's ability to generate sufficient cash to meet its short-term obligations. Although virtually all financial statement users are interested in ratios indicating a firm's liquidity, these ratios are of particular interest to short-term creditors and company's management. Clearly, it is important to consider a firm's ability to meet its short-term obligations. After all, if a company cannot meet its current obligations, it may not be around long enough to be profitable in the long run.

As we will see, the two **liquidity ratios** introduced here are closely related.

Current ratio

The **current ratio** is probably the most widely used measure of a company's liquidity. A current asset is an asset that is already cash, or is expected to become cash within one year. A current liability is any liability which must be paid within one year. The relationship between them is of great importance because current liabilities are expected to be retired using current assets. The ratio is calculated as follows:

$$\text{Current Ratio} = \frac{\text{Current Assets (balance sheet)}}{\text{Current Liabilities (balance sheet)}}$$

Flores' current ratios for 1996 and 1995 are calculated as follows:

1996	1995
$\dfrac{\$5,556,000}{\$4,336,000} = 1.28$	$\dfrac{\$5,279,000}{\$4,000,000} = 1.32$

Flores has $1.28 of current assets for every $1.00 of current liabilities at the end of 1996 and $1.32 of current assets for every $1.00 of current liabilities at the end of 1995. Many people

feel a ratio of $2.00 current assets to every $1.00 current
liabilities should be maintained, due to the uncertain nature of
some of the current assets. For example, accounts receivable may
not be collected and inventory may or may not be saleable. As you
can see, Flores does not have a current ratio of 2:1 in either of
the two years presented. This may be cause for concern on the part
of financial statement users, because Flores may have to borrow
money to pay current liabilities.

Discussion Questions

12-6. If Flores must borrow money to retire current
liabilities, it will have to pay interest on
the borrowed funds. What effect (if any) will
the additional interest expense have on the
following ratios:

a. Profit margin percentage?
b. Return on total assets?
c. Earnings per share?
d. Total asset turnover?

Quick ratio

The **quick ratio**, which is sometimes called the **acid test ratio**, is similar to the current ratio. It is a more stringent test of liquidity, however, because only current assets considered to be highly liquid (quickly convertible into cash) are included in the calculation. Some variation exists as to what assets are included in the quick ratio. For our purposes, the calculation will be:

$$\text{Quick Ratio} = \frac{\text{Cash + Marketable Securities + Accounts Receivable (balance sheet)}}{\text{Current Liabilities (balance sheet)}}$$

Examine the numerator of the ratio above. Clearly, cash is liquid — it *is* cash. Marketable securities are generally stocks and bonds that are widely traded on major exchanges. These assets can be converted into cash with a single phone call to a broker. In this form of the quick ratio, accounts receivable are also considered to be highly liquid. If additional information is available leading you to believe that the receivables are not likely to be collectible soon, this item should be omitted from the numerator.

```
+-------------------------------------------------------------+
|                   Discussion Question                       |
|                                                             |
|    12-7. If only the three assets above are considered       |
|          in the quick ratio, what current assets are not    |
|          included?                                          |
|                                                             |
+-------------------------------------------------------------+
```

In Flores' case, only cash and accounts receivable qualify as quick assets because the company has no marketable securities. The denominator of the quick ratio is identical to the one used for the current ratio. Flores' quick ratios for 1996 and 1995 are calculated as follows:

1996	1995
$\dfrac{\$2,240,000 + \$2,340,000}{\$4,336,000} = 1.06$	$\dfrac{\$1,936,000 + \$2,490,000}{\$4,000,000} = 1.11$

With many of the less liquid current assets removed from the calculation, many people feel a quick ratio of $1.00 of current assets to every $1.00 of current liabilities is a reasonable relationship. As you can see from the calculations, Flores' quick ratio seems reasonable for both 1995 and 1996. It is important to note that there are no set rules in calculating or evaluating this ratio.

```
┌─────────────────────────────────────────────────────────┐
│                                                           │
│                   Discussion Questions                    │
│                                                           │
│                                                           │
│     12-8. How would holding an excessive amount of        │
│                                                           │
│           inventory affect the following ratios:          │
│                                                           │
│                                                           │
│         a.    Profit margin percentage?                   │
│                                                           │
│         b.    Return on total assets?                     │
│                                                           │
│         c.    Earnings per share?                         │
│                                                           │
│         d.    Current ratio?                              │
│                                                           │
│         e.    Quick ratio?                                │
│                                                           │
│         f.    Total asset turnover?                       │
│                                                           │
│                                                           │
└─────────────────────────────────────────────────────────┘
```

Measuring Solvency

Solvency can be described as a company's ability to meet the obligations created by its long-term debt. If a firm cannot make periodic interest payments and ultimately retire the debt itself, the company may face bankruptcy. Solvency ratios, then, focus on interest payments and the overall debt load a company carries. Like the profitability ratios, solvency ratios are of most interest to stockholders, long-term creditors, and of course, company management. While there are several solvency ratios, we will look at only two.

Debt-to-equity ratio

The **debt-to-equity ratio** measures what proportion of a company's assets are financed by debt. By inference, it compares the relative claims of creditors and owners. Remember that the assets a company controls will always be equal to the claims to them. This can be demonstrated by looking once again at the accounting (business) equation:

ASSETS   =   LIABILITIES   +   OWNERS' EQUITY

100%   =   Some %   +   Some %

As the accounting equation above shows, all assets are financed by either liabilities or owners' equity (debt or equity). Calculation of the debt-to-equity ratio illustrates the percentage of assets that are supported by debt financing.

$$\text{Debt-to-Equity Ratio} = \frac{\text{Total Liabilities (balance sheet)}}{\text{Total Assets (balance sheet)}}$$

The format of this ratio may vary somewhat. Some analysts include total liabilities, some include only long-term liabilities, and some include long-term liabilities plus short-term interest bearing notes. For our purposes, the numerator will simply include *all* liabilities.

583

Based on the example of Flores, Inc., the debt-to-equity ratios for 1996 and 1995 are calculated as follows:

1996	1995
$\dfrac{\$ 6,336,000}{\$10,725,000} = 59.1\%$	$\dfrac{\$5,600,000}{\$9,032,000} = 62.0\%$

There is no hard and fast rule as to what amount of a company's assets should be financed through debt or what amount should be supported by equity. The value of a company's debt-to-equity ratio must be evaluated in light of the industry in which a company operates, where a company is in its life (new businesses tend to have more debt relative to equity), and the philosophy management has toward the balance between debt financing and equity financing.

Creditors and stockholders watch the debt-to-equity ratio from their individual perspectives and tend to get nervous if they perceive it to be out of balance.

Times interest earned

The **times interest earned ratio** provides an indication of a company's ability to make its periodic interest payments. It compares the amount of income available for interest payments to the interest requirements. Creditors use this ratio to assess the risk associated with lending money to a business. Bondholders, or potential investors in corporate debt, can also use this measurement to assess the likelihood of both the return on their investment and the return of their investment. The formula used to calculate this ratio is:

$$\text{Times Interest Earned} = \frac{\text{Earnings before Interest Expense and Income Taxes (income statement)}}{\text{Interest Expense (income statement)}}$$

Because the ratio is a measure of the amount of earnings available for periodic interest payments, the numerator in the formula is the amount of earnings before interest expense and tax expense. The times interest earned calculations for Flores, Inc. in 1996 and 1995 are:

1996	1995
$\dfrac{\$789,000}{\$172,000} = 4.59$	$\dfrac{\$1,150,000}{\$137,000} = 8.39$

Many analysts feel a times interest earned ratio of a least 4:1 provides an appropriate degree of safety for creditors. This means a company's earnings before interest and taxes should be at least four times as great as its interest expense. As you can see, Flores has a ratio of more than 4:1 in both 1995 and 1996.

```
┌──────────────────────────────────────────────────────────────┐
│ ┌────────────────────────────────────────────────────────────┐ │
│ │                    Discussion Question                     │ │
│ │                                                            │ │
│ │                                                            │ │
│ │    12-9. What has caused the drop in the Flores           │ │
│ │                                                            │ │
│ │         Company's times interest earned ratio from 1995   │ │
│ │                                                            │ │
│ │         to 1996?  As a bondholder, would you find this    │ │
│ │                                                            │ │
│ │         to be alarming?                                    │ │
│ │                                                            │ │
│ │                                                            │ │
│ └────────────────────────────────────────────────────────────┘ │
└──────────────────────────────────────────────────────────────┘
```

In order to get a valid assessment of a company's solvency,
financial statement users should evaluate both the debt-to-equity
and the times interest earned ratios.

In fact, when evaluating any of the three attributes discussed in
this chapter, more than one approach should be considered. The
following tables are provided as a means of summarizing the
calculations and usefulness of the ratios discussed in this
chapter.

Summary of Key Ratios

Profitability Ratios	Calculation	Purpose of Ratio
1. Return on Total Assets	$$\frac{\text{Net Income} + \text{Interest Expense}}{\text{Average Total Assets}}$$	Measures the return earned on investment in assets.
2. Profit Margin Percentage	$$\frac{\text{Net Income} + \text{Interest Expense}}{\text{Total Revenues}}$$	Measures the earnings produced from a given level of revenues.
3. Total Assets Turnover	$$\frac{\text{Total Revenues}}{\text{Average Total Assets}}$$	Measures the firm's ability to generate revenues from a given level of assets.
4. Earnings Per Share	$$\frac{\text{Net Income}}{\begin{array}{c}\text{Average Shares of}\\\text{Common Stock}\\\text{Outstanding}\end{array}}$$	Shows the amount of earnings attributable to each share of common stock.

Liquidity Ratios	Calculation	Purpose of Ratio
1. Current Ratio	$$\frac{\text{Current Assets}}{\text{Current Liabilities}}$$ 2:1	Measures a company's ability to meet short-term obligations.
2. Quick Ratio (Acid-Test Ratio)	$$\frac{\text{Cash} + \text{Marketable Securities} + \text{Accounts Receivable}}{\text{Current Liabilities}}$$ 1:1	Measures short-term liquidity more stringently than the current ratio.

Solvency Ratios	Calculation	Purpose of Ratio
1. Debt-to-Equity Ratio	$$\frac{\text{Total Liabilities}}{\text{Total Assets}}$$? differs	Indicates the proportion of assets financed by debt.
2. Times Interest Earned	$$\frac{\text{Earnings before Interest and Taxes}}{\text{Interest Expense}}$$ 4:1	Measures a company's ability to make its periodic interest payments.

588

```
                    Discussion Question


    12-10.      Martino Company uses straight-line

                depreciation; Patco Corporation uses an

                accelerated depreciation method.  If this

                is the only difference in the business

                activity of the two companies, how do

                their financial ratios compare at the end

                of their first year of operations?

                Explain the effect of the difference in

                depreciation methods on each of the eight

                ratios described in this chapter.
```

LIMITATIONS OF RATIO ANALYSIS

There are several factors that limit the usefulness of ratio analysis:

1. Attempting to predict the future using past results is problematic at best. Changes in the general economy, changes in the economy of the particular industry being studied, and changes in management are just some of the things that can cause past results to be an unreliable predictor of the future.

2. The financial statements used as the basis of the ratios are based on historical cost. In a time of changing prices, comparison between years is difficult.

3. Since most businesses have their fiscal year-end when business is slow, the balances in such accounts as receivables, payables, and inventory at year-end may not be representative of the rest of the year. In almost all instances, the numbers used in the calculation of the ratios are year-end numbers. Even when averages are used, the averages are calculated using year-end numbers from two consecutive years.

4. Comparing the ratios of a company in one industry with those of a company in another industry is difficult, because industry peculiarities will cause the ratios to differ. Comparison within an industry may not even be possible because of different accounting methods employed by different companies (depreciation methods, for example).

5. There are no hard and fast rules as to what numbers are used to calculate the ratios. We discussed this when we presented the quick ratio and the debt-to-equity ratio. The lack of uniformity in what is or is not included in the calculation of ratios makes comparison extremely difficult.

The greatest single limitation of ratio analysis, however, may be that too much reliance is placed on the ratios themselves. These cannot and should not be viewed as some sort of magical checklist in the evaluation process. They represent only a small part of what decision makers should consider when making credit, investment, and similar types of decisions.

CHAPTER SUMMARY

Predicting a company's ability to generate positive cash flow in the future is difficult because there is always uncertainty involved. In response to the need to lessen the amount of uncertainty in the decision making process, several analytical techniques have been developed over time to assist economic decision makers as they assess financial statements. The statement of cash flows presented in Chapter 10 is an example of financial statement analysis.

Another very important aspect of financial statement analysis is ratio analysis. Ratios provide a means to analyze the relationship between two items from a company's financial statements for a given period. This is done by dividing the dollar amount of one item from the financial statements by the dollar amount of another.

A great many ratios have been developed over time and not all ratios are relevant in a given decision situation. Care must be taken to select appropriate ratios to be analyzed. Additionally, it must be understood that ratios, in and of themselves, have very little meaning. They only become meaningful when compared to other relevant information, such as the same ratios from other years, ratios for similar, competitive companies, or industry averages.

Business ratios can be broadly classified as profitability ratios, liquidity ratios, and solvency ratios. Profitability ratios attempt to measure the ease with which companies generate income. Liquidity ratios are designed to measure a company's ability to generate positive cash flow in the short-run. Solvency ratios are intended to measure a company's ability to meet the obligations created by its long-term debt.

Each of the profitability, liquidity, and solvency ratios is capable of providing valuable information for both internal decision makers and external decision makers. Ratio analysis is not, however, without its limitations. Too much reliance on the financial statements and the ratios derived from them is dangerous and potentially disastrous to decision makers. Ratio analysis is a tool. As with the other tools we have discussed throughout this book, it must be used wisely, and in its proper context.

KEY TERMS DEFINED

Acid test ratio. Another name for the quick ratio.

Cost of capital. The cost of obtaining cash needed to invest in assets.

Current ratio. A liquidity ratio that measures a company's ability to meet short-term obligations by comparing current assets to current liabilities.

Debt-to-equity ratio. A solvency ratio that indicates what proportion of a company's assets is financed by debt.

Earnings per share (EPS). A measure of profitability that shows the amount of earnings attributable to each share of common stock outstanding.

Hurdle rate. Another name for cost of capital.

Liquidity. The ease with which an item, such as an asset, can be converted to cash. The liquidity of a firm refers to the company's ability to generate sufficient cash to meet its short-term obligations.

Profit margin percentage. A profitability ratio that measures the earnings produced from a given level of revenues by comparing net income plus interest expense to the revenue figure.

Profitability. The ease with which companies generate income.

Profitability ratios. Ratios used to help predict a firm's ability to generate sufficient profits (and ultimately cash) to fulfill its obligations.

Quick ratio. Similar to the current ratio, but a more stringent test of liquidity, because only current assets considered to be highly liquid (quickly converted to cash) are included in the calculation.

Ratio analysis. Provides a means to analyze the relationship between two items from a company's financial statements for a given period.

Return on total assets. A profitability ratio that measures the return earned on investment in assets.

Solvency. A company's ability to meet the obligations created by its long-term debt.

Times interest earned ratio. A solvency ratio that provides an indication of a company's ability to make its periodic interest payments.

Total assets turnover. A profitability ratio that indicates the amount of revenues produced for a given level of assets used.

REVIEW THE FACTS

1. From which financial statements are components of the ratios discussed in the chapter drawn?

2. What is profitability?

3. What three groups of decision makers are particularly interested in assessing a company's profitability?

4. List the four profitability ratios discussed in the chapter. For each one, describe the calculation used and the purpose of the ratio.

5. Describe how to calculate average total assets and explain why this amount is used instead of using simply the ending balance in assets.

6. Define the cost of capital and explain its importance in the evaluation of a company's return on total assets.

7. What are the two ratios comprising the return on total assets?

8. Explain the limitations of EPS.

9. What is meant by the liquidity of a company?

10. What is the difference between the current ratio and the quick ratio? What is the purpose in examining both?

11. What is solvency?

12. What can be learned from the debt-to-equity ratio?

13. What information can be gathered from calculating a company's times interest earned ratio?

14. Describe the six limitations of ratio analysis discussed in the chapter.

Chapter 12
APPLY WHAT YOU HAVE LEARNED

A12-1.   Presented below are some items relating to the concepts presented in this chapter, followed by definitions of those items in a scrambled order:

a.   Ratio analysis.
b.   Profitability ratios.
c.   Liquidity ratios.
d.   Solvency ratios.
e.   Cost of capital.

1.   _e_   Sometimes referred to as the hurdle rate.

2.   _c_   Designed to measure a firm's ability to generate sufficient cash to meet its short-term obligations.

3.   _a_   A means to analyze the relationship between two items from a company's financial statements for a given period.

4.   _b_   Designed to measure the ease with which a company generates income.

5.   _d_   Focus on interest payments and the overall debt load a company carries.

REQUIRED:

Match the letter next to each item on the list with the appropriate definition. Each letter will be used only once.

A12-2. Listed below are all the ratios discussed in this chapter, followed by explanations of what the ratios are designed to measure in a scrambled order.

a. Return on total assets.
b. Profit margin percentage.
c. Total asset turnover.
d. Earnings per share.
e. Current ratio.
f. Quick ratio.
g. Acid-test ratio.
h. Debt-to-equity.
i. Times interest earned.

1. _e_ Most common ratio used to measure a company's ability to meet short-term obligations.

2. _i_ Measures a company's ability to make periodic interest payments.

3. _a_ Measures the return earned on investment in assets.

4. _f_ A more stringent test of short-term liquidity than the current ratio.

5. _b_ Measures the earnings produced from a given level of revenues.

6. _d_ Shows the amount of earnings attributable to each share of common stock.

7. _g_ Also known as the quick ratio.

8. _h_ Indicates the proportion of assets financed by debt.

9. _c_ Measures a company's ability to generate revenues from a given level of assets.

REQUIRED:

Match the letter next to each item on the list with the appropriate explanation. Each letter will be used only once.

A12-3. Presented below are partial comparative balance sheets of
        Reggie Company at December 31, 1996 and 1995:

REGGIE COMPANY
PARTIAL BALANCE SHEETS
AT DECEMBER 31, 1996 AND DECEMBER 31, 1995
Current Assets & Current Liabilities Only
(in thousands)

	1996	1995
Current Assets:		
Cash	$ 3,400	$ 2,920
Accounts Receivable	1,825	2,212
Merchandise Inventory	1,170	966
Prepaid Expenses	240	270
Total Current Assets	$ 6,635	$ 6,638
Current Liabilities:		
Accounts Payable	$ 2,321	$ 1,740
Notes Payable	3,100	3,300
Total Current Liabilities	$ 5,421	$ 5,040

REQUIRED:

a.   Calculate Reggie's current ratios for 1996 and 1995.

b.   Calculate Reggie's quick ratios for 1996 and 1995.

c.   Which financial statement users are most interested in
     these two sets of ratios? Explain why the ratios are
     considered important to these users.

d.   Assume that the average company in Reggie's industry has
     a current ratio of 2:1 and a quick ratio of 1.25:1. If
     you were evaluating Reggie's liquidity, what can you
     learn by comparing Reggie's ratios to those of the
     industry average?

601

A12-4   Presented below are partial comparative balance sheets of Halifax Company at December 31, 1996 and 1995:

HALIFAX COMPANY
PARTIAL BALANCE SHEETS
AT DECEMBER 31, 1996 AND DECEMBER 31, 1995
Current Assets & Current Liabilities Only
(in thousands)

	1996	1995
Current Assets:		
Cash	$ 2,110	$ 2,650
Accounts Receivable	1,254	977
Merchandise Inventory	730	856
Prepaid Expenses	127	114
Total Current Assets	$ 4,221	$ 4,597
Current Liabilities:		
Accounts Payable	$ 1,054	$ 1,330
Notes Payable	2,100	1,750
Total Current Liabilities	$ 3,154	$ 3,080

REQUIRED:

a.   Calculate Halifax's current ratios for 1996 and 1995.

b.   Calculate Halifax's quick ratios for 1996 and 1995.

c.   Which financial statement users are most interested in these two sets of ratios? Explain why the ratios are considered important to these users.

d.   Assume that the average company in Halifax's industry has a current ratio of 2.5:1 and a quick ratio of 1:1. If you were evaluating Halifax's liquidity, what can you learn by comparing Halifax's ratios to those of the industry average?

e.   What, if anything can you determine by comparing Halifax's current ratio and quick ratio for 1995 with the same ratios for 1996. Explain your reasoning.

Presented below are the comparative balance sheets for Hogle Company at December 31, 1996 & 1995. Also included is Hogle's income statement for the year ended December 31, 1996.

HOGLE COMPANY
BALANCE SHEETS
AT DECEMBER 31, 1996 AND DECEMBER 31, 1995
(in thousands)

ASSETS:	1996	1995
Current Assets:		
Cash	$ 1,618	$ 1,220
Accounts Receivable	1,925	2,112
Merchandise Inventory	1,070	966
Prepaid Expenses	188	149
Total Current Assets	$ 4,801	$ 4,447
Plant & Equipment:		
Buildings, Net	$ 4,457	$ 2,992
Equipment, Net	$ 1,293	1,045
Total Plant & Equipment	$ 5,750	$ 4,037
Total Assets	$10,551	$ 8,484
LIABILITIES:		
Current Liabilities:		
Accounts Payable	$ 1,818	$ 1,686
Notes Payable	900	1,100
Total Current Liabilities	$ 2,718	$ 2,786
Long-Term Liabilities	2,500	2,000
Total Liabilities	$ 5,218	$ 4,786
STOCKHOLDERS' EQUITY:		
Common Stock, no par value	$ 3,390	$ 2,041
Retained Earnings	1,943	1,657
Total Stockholders' Equity	$ 5,333	$ 3,698
Total Liabilities		
and Stockholders' Equity	$10,551	$ 8,484

HOGLE COMPANY
INCOME STATEMENT
FOR THE YEAR ENDED DECEMBER 31, 1996
(in thousands)

Net Sales		$11,228
Less Cost of Goods Sold		7,751
Gross Profit on Sales		$ 3,477
Less Operating Expenses:		
Depreciation - Buildings & Equip.	$	102
Other Selling & Administrative		2,667
Total Expenses		$ 2,769
Operating Income	$	708
Less Interest Expense		168
Income Before Taxes	$	540
Income Taxes		114
Net Income	$	426

A12-5 continues on the next page

A12-5.   (continued)

Additional Information:

The company had an average of 270,000 shares of common stock outstanding during 1996.

REQUIRED:

Calculate the following ratios for 1996:

a.   Return on Total Assets.

b.   Profit Margin Percentage.

c.   Total Asset Turnover.

d.   Earnings Per Share.

e.   Current Ratio.

f.   Quick Ratio.

g.   Debt-To-Equity.

h.   Times Interest Earned.

A12-6.   Presented below are the comparative balance sheets for
         Brandywine Company at December 31, 1996 & 1995 and the income
         statements for the years ended December 31, 1996, and 1995.

BRANDYWINE COMPANY
BALANCE SHEETS
AT DECEMBER 31, 1996 AND DECEMBER 31, 1995
(in thousands)

ASSETS:	1996	1995
Current Assets:		
Cash	$ 1,292	$ 980
Accounts Receivable	1,068	1,112
Merchandise Inventory	970	906
Prepaid Expenses	88	109
Total Current Assets	$ 3,418	$ 3,107
Plant & Equipment:		
Buildings, Net	$ 3,457	$ 2,442
Equipment, Net	$ 993	945
Total Plant & Equipment	$ 4,450	$ 3,387
Total Assets	$ 7,868	$ 6,494
LIABILITIES:		
Current Liabilities:		
Accounts Payable	$ 998	$ 786
Notes Payable	600	500
Total Current Liabilities	$ 1,598	$ 1,286
Long-Term Liabilities	837	467
Total Liabilities	$ 2,435	$ 1,753
STOCKHOLDERS' EQUITY:		
Common Stock, no par value	$ 2,490	$ 2,000
Retained Earnings	2,943	2,741
Total Stockholders' Equity	$ 5,433	$ 4,741
Total Liabilities		
and Stockholders' Equity	$ 7,868	$ 6,494

BRANDYWINE COMPANY
INCOME STATEMENTS
FOR THE YEARS ENDED DECEMBER 31, 1996 AND 1995
(in thousands)

	1996	1995
Net Sales	$ 9,228	$ 8,765
Less Cost of Goods Sold	6,751	6,097
Gross Profit on Sales	$ 2,477	$ 2,668
Less Operating Expenses:		
Depreciation - Buildings & Equip.	$ 80	$ 56
Other Selling & Administrative	1,667	1,442
Total Expenses	$ 1,747	$ 1,498
Operating Income	$ 730	$ 1,170
Less Interest Expense	98	89
Income Before Taxes	$ 632	$ 1,081
Income Taxes	190	357
Net Income	$ 442	$ 724

A12-6 continues on the next page

A12-6. (continued)

Additional Information:

1) The company had an average of 170,000 shares of common stock outstanding during 1996 and an average of 160,000 shares of common stock outstanding during 1995.

2) Total assets on the balance sheet at December 31, 1994 were $6,281,000.

REQUIRED:

Calculate the following ratios for 1996 and 1995:

a. Return on Total Assets.

b. Profit Margin Percentage.

c. Total Asset Turnover.

d. Earnings Per Share.

e. Current Ratio.

f. Quick Ratio.

g. Debt-To-Equity.

h. Times Interest Earned.

A12-7.   The   chapter   discussed   several   limitations   to   the
usefulness of ratio analysis.   They were:

1)   Using past results to predict future performance.

2)   Using historical cost as a basis for ratios.

3)   Using year-end balances as either the numerator or
     denominator for many ratios.

4)   Industry peculiarities.

5)   Lack of uniformity in defining the numerators and
     denominators used in calculating ratios.

6)   The amount of credence given to ratio analysis.

REQUIRED:

Explain in your own words why each of the six items listed in
the problem limit the usefulness of ratio analysis.

ACTIVITIES WORKBOOK
for
"Introduction to Accounting:
A User Perspective"

Martha S. Doran
Kumen H. Jones
Jean B. Price

Notes to the Student

The activities in this workbook have been designed to provide you with a great deal of experience in using accounting information. The two key aspects of these assignments are EXPERIENCES and APPLICATIONS. Your experience will help you discover and learn from your own attempts as compared to someone else telling you. The applications or uses will help you ponder WHY accounting information is designed and used in the business system. Most of the activities will be organized and presented in the following format:

PURPOSE: This section appears at the beginning of each activity and will explain WHY you are doing the activity.

DIRECTIONS: The next section will explain HOW you should complete the activity.

REQUIRED: The last section will explain WHAT you need to prepare, complete, or produce as the final outcome of the activity. (This may be what your professor asks you to turn in for a grade.)

Many of the activities include articles for you to read. The articles are placed on the pages **following** the activity. In addition, some of the activities require you to read and use the financial statements of an actual corporation. This company is MASCO CORPORATION, and their statements and notes begin on page 128.

Table of Contents

Table of Contents (Continued)

START UP ACTIVITIES

BASIC ELEMENTS OF COOPERATIVE LEARNING
GROUP ACTIVITY

PURPOSE:

To help you comprehend certain basic elements of cooperative learning by becoming an "expert" and teaching your teammates.

DIRECTIONS:

Look at your card and see if you hold a red (hearts or diamonds) or black (spades or clubs) suit.

If you are a Heart or Diamond you are to do the following:

1.   In "Basic Elements of Cooperative Learning" read the sections about Positive Interdependence and Face to Face Promotive Interaction.

2.   In "Cooperative Learning vs. Small Group Discussion..." read the items 1 through 3c. This should give you additional information relating to the basic elements you read.

3.   The adjacent hearts and diamonds should pair up and discuss how to teach the basic elements of Positive Interdependence and Face to Face Promotive Interaction.

4.   When you are comfortable you know how to teach these Basic Elements, pair up with the adjacent spades and clubs and teach them.

5.   When you are done, trade off and let the spades and clubs teach you.

If you are a Spade or Club you are to do the following:

1.   In "Basic Elements of Cooperative Learning" read the sections about Individual Accountability/Personal Responsibility, Interpersonal Skills and Group Processing.

2.   In "Cooperative Learning vs. Small Group Discussion..." read the items 3d through 6. This should give you additional information relating to the basic elements you read.

3.   The adjacent spades and clubs should pair up and discuss how to teach the basic elements of Individual Accountability/Personal Responsibility, Interpersonal   Skills and Group Processing.

4.   When you are comfortable you know how to teach these Basic Elements, pair up with the adjacent hearts and diamonds and let them teach you.

5.   When you are done, trade off and you and your partner teach the hearts and diamonds.

REQUIRED:

Within your group of four, make sure each member is clear on all of the 5 basic elements of cooperative learning. Use these elements as categories to discuss what you feel are the three biggest strengths and weaknesses to using teamwork in the college classroom. Have the team recorder makes notes of your results, so that your team can present your findings to the class.

Cooperative Learning vs. Small-Group Discussions and Group Projects:
The Critical Differences
Joseph B. Cuseo

In the previous issue of this newsletter a taxonomy was proposed to bring some clarity to the myriad forms of learning that have been loosely referred to as Collaborative/Cooperative in American higher education. The present article, continuing this quest for identity, delineates the key differences between Cooperative Learning (CL) and two other forms of small-group learning used in higher education: small-group discussions and group projects.

Cooperative Learning may be defined as a learner-centered instructional process in which small, intentionally selected groups of 3-5 students work interdependently on a well-defined learning task; individual students are held accountable for their own performance and the instructor serves as a facilitator/consultant in the group-learning process.

More specifically, CL can be operationally defined in terms of six procedural elements, which when implemented together, distinguish it from other forms of small-group learning in higher education.

1. Intentional Group Formation

In contrast to traditional methods of small-group learning, such as small-group discussions and group projects, in which students often select their own group members or groups are randomly formed by the instructor, CL typically begins with the intentional selection of group members on the basis of predetermined criteria which have been deliberately designed to potentiate the positive effects of small-group learning. For instance, groups may be deliberately formed to maximize heterogeneity and diversity of perspectives by grouping students with different: (a) levels of academic achievement (e.g., high-low-medium GPAs), (b) learning styles (e.g., deep processors and shallow processors), (c) academic majors, (d) personality profiles (e.g., as measured by the MBTI), (e) ethnic or racial backgrounds, (f) geographical backgrounds, (g) gender, (h) ages (e.g., traditional and reentry students) or (i) class standing (e.g., lower-division and upper-division students), or some combination of these selection criteria.

The criteria for determining group composition may vary depending on the instructor's objectives or the characteristics of students in the class, but the essential factor is that group formation is not left to chance; instead, careful forethought is given to the question of who comprises each learning group in an attempt to create the optimal social-learning environment.

2. Continuity of Group Interaction

In contrast to traditional small-group discussions or buzz groups, which typically group students sporadically for a relatively short period of time, CL groups typically meet regularly over an extended period of time. This allows for continuity of interaction among group members and creates the opportunity for social cohesion and bonding to develop among group members. In this fashion, CL groups are given the time needed to evolve into a tightly-knit social network.

3. Interdependence Among Group Members

Rather than simply allowing students to interact in small groups and then hoping they will do so in a cooperative manner, CL incorporates specific procedures designed to create a feeling of group identity among students and collective responsibility for one another's learning. The following procedures are used to increase the likelihood that this sense of positive interdependence develops within CL groups:

(a) Group production of a common product at the end of the Cooperative Learning experience.

In contrast to the usual discussions, or buzz group which gets together for informal discussion of some course-related issue, each CL group is expected to generate a formal product which represents a concrete manifestation of the group's collective effort (completion of a work sheet; a compendium or chart of specific ideas; an overhead transparency which can be displayed to other groups). The objective of working toward a clearly defined, common goal is essential for keeping individual students on task and focused on a group goal.

(b) Assignment of interdependent roles for each group member.

A sense of individual responsibility to the group may be increased if each group member has a specific and essential role to play in achieving the group's final goal or product. For instance, individuals within the group could be assigned the following interdependent roles: group manager--who assures that the group stays on task and that all members actively contribute; group recorder--who keeps a written record of the group's ideas; group spokesperson--who is responsible for verbally reporting the group's ideas to the instructor or other groups; and group processor--who monitors the social interaction or interpersonal dynamics of the group process. Roles can also be assigned on the basis of different perspectives that group members are expected to contribute to the final product--e.g., historical, ethical, economic, or global, etc. (For further information on this concept of assigning multiple roles for the purpose of achieving multiple perspectives, see "Cooperative Learning: Implications

for Liberal and General Education" in Cooperative Learning &
College Teaching, Winter, 1992.) Such role specialization assures
that each individual has an explicit and well differentiated
responsibility to the group throughout the learning process. A
further advantage of role specialization is that the quality of
each member's contribution can be more readily identified and
assessed by the instructor, thus allowing for individual grading
and individual accountability--which is one critical feature of
CL.

*(c) Team-building activities designed to produce a sense of group
identity and social cohesiveness.*

Such activities would include ice breakers or warm-up activities
when groups are first formed (e.g., name-learning and personal
information sharing); taking team photos; creating team names;
providing explicit suggestions and concrete recommendations for
promoting cooperation and teamwork (e.g., exchanging phone
numbers with other group members; reviewing individual lecture
notes as a group; seeking feedback from group members on
individual course assignments; encouraging group study sessions,
etc.)

The underlying rationale for these team-building activities is to
create a social and emotional climate conducive to the
development of an esprit de corps and a sense of intimacy among
the group's members, thus enabling them to feel comfortable in
future CL tasks that will require them to express their personal
viewpoints, disagree with others and reach consensus in an open,
non-defensive fashion. The key assumption here is that the
potential cognitive benefits of small-group learning are more
likely to be realized in a social context characterized by group
cohesiveness, mutual trust, and emotional security. Furthermore,
such explicit attention to the social and emotional aspects of
small-group dynamics may be instrumental in fostering social
support and emotional ties among peers--which are factors known
to have a significant impact on student retention.

*(d) Provision of individual rewards as an incentive for promoting
group interdependence.*

This has been the most hotly debated CL strategy for creating
group interdependence because it involves extrinsic rewards for
cooperative behavior. For example, if an individual student
improves her score from one exam to the next, then all group
members are rewarded by gaining extra (bonus) points toward their
individual course grades. Or, if each group member's performance
exceeds a certain criterion (e.g., each group member achieves a
score of at least 90%), then all members of the group earn bonus
points toward their individual course grade.

Some practitioners of CL oppose these strategies because they feel it is unnecessary--students will be intrinsically motivated to cooperate and take responsibility for helping others as long as they are given a well-defined task and the opportunity to work together. Other practitioners feel that providing extrinsic rewards for helping others tends to destroy intrinsic motivation for behaving cooperatively and altruistically. However, those who do use these incentives feel that, if group performance rewards are not large (e.g., representing extra bonus points only, rather than a significant portion of the course grade), then such incentives can serve to promote group interdependence and increase academic achievement (Slavin, 1989).

Since the issue of whether or not to use extrinsic rewards for promoting interdependent behavior in CL groups is still unresolved at the precollegiate level and has yet to be investigated at the college level, it is perhaps best to consider this strategy as an optional, rather than essential procedure for promoting group interdependence.

4. Individual Accountability

Though procedures for ensuring interdependence and cooperation among group members are essential elements of CL, students are graded individually, i.e., all group members do not receive the same group grade (in contrast to most group projects). Recent educational research consistently supports the importance of personal accountability and individual grading for realizing many of the positive outcomes of CL. This precollegiate research is reinforced by findings reported by social psychologists on the phenomenon of social loafing--i.e., the effort produced by individuals will decrease when they are placed in a group, unless the output or effort of each individual is uniquely identifiable (Williams, Harkins, & Latane, 1981). These research data are consistent with familiar, anecdotal reports of high-achieving students who often contend that they dislike group projects in which all group members receive the same group grade because their individual effort and contribution to the group's final product often exceeds the efforts of their less motivated teammates--who inequitably receive the same grade for the group assignment.

5. Explicit Attention to the Development of Social Skills

In contrast to the strictly academic goals of most small-group work in higher education, a major objective of CL is the intentional development of students' interpersonal communication and human relations skills. To achieve this objective, CL incorporates the following procedures:

(a) *Explicit instruction on effective skills for communicating and relating to others are given to students prior to, and in preparation for their involvement in small-group learning activities.*

Such instruction may include strategies for encouraging and supporting other group members, active listening, constructive agreement, conflict resolution, and consensus building. Thus, students receive some preparation and guidance for handling the social and emotional demands of small-group work, rather than being left entirely to their own devices.

(b) Provision of opportunities for students to reflect on, and evaluate the process of social interaction.

Meta-social awareness is encouraged by having groups and/or individuals assess the quality of group interaction with respect to already-learned principles of effective interpersonal communication. Furthermore, students are asked to reflect on how the nature of their social interaction in CL groups has affected their individual learning. (For example, by having students answer such questions as: Do you find that you learn more or less when you verbalize your thoughts to other group members? When there is disagreement between yourself and another group member? When you question the reasoning of other group members?) Opportunities to reflect on such questions pertaining to both the group's social process and its impact on the individual's learning may serve to promote students' meta-social and meta-cognitive awareness simultaneously.

(c) Effective interpersonal behavior displayed by students within groups is explicitly noted and verbally reinforced by the instructor, then shared with the entire class--as specific exemplars or models to be emulated in future group interactions.

The instructor is alert not only to the cognitive aspects of group work, but to the social aspects as well. Specific, effective forms of interpersonal communication exhibited by students in their learning groups are praised and utilized by the instructor for educational purposes--as concrete, behavioral illustrations of key human-relations principles.

6. Instructor as Facilitator

In contrast to most small-group discussions and group projects, where students are left on their own to verbalize their ideas and conduct their work, CL involves the instructor as a facilitator and consultant in the group-learning process. Though the instructor does not sit in on individual groups (such intrusiveness might disrupt the student-centered advantage of group learning), he/she will circulate actively among the groups, offering encouragement, reinforcing positive instances of cooperative behavior, clarifying task expectations, catalyzing dialogue, or issuing timely questions designed to promote elaboration and higher-order thinking. Being careful not to be overly directive or authoritative, the instructor functions as a learned peer or collegial coach, interacting with students in a much more personal, informal, and dialogic fashion than would be possible in the traditional lecture or lecture-discussion format.

Moreover, the opportunity to interact with students in small groups may not only benefit the students but may also enable college instructors to better know their students (e.g., know their names, their styles of thinking, and their styles of communicating and relating to others).

Conclusion

The foregoing six features of CL, taken together, distinguish this instructional technique from the methods of small-group discussion and group projects which have been traditionally used in higher education. Faithful implementation of these six features of CL may be essential for assuring that the full spectrum of benefits associated with small-group learning are actually realized.

Research involving large-scale, meta-analyses of hundreds of studies at the precollege level provide overwhelming empirical documentation for the cognitive, social, and affective benefits of CL--operationally defined in terms of the six key procedural elements described herein (Johnson & Johnson, 1989; Slavin, 1990). Research on CL college level is much less extensive, but results thus far are very consistent with those reported in precollegiate settings (Cooper & Mueck, 1990; Johnson & Johnson, 1989; Johnson, Johnson, & Smith, 1992).
If more practitioners in higher education begin to carefully implement the six critical features of CL in their classrooms, then the benefits of CL for college students could be assessed with the same degree of rigor and replication as it has at the precollegiate level. We encourage college faculty to conduct their own assessments of CL in their individual courses. Such local assessments would be consistent with the national call for classroom research (Cross, 1987) and the new scholarship--the scholarship of teaching (Boyer, 1990).

We also encourage high-level administrative support for faculty who attempt to implement and evaluate CL in their classrooms-- e.g., via provision of needed resources, recognition/reward in promotion and tenure decisions, and in the form of incentives such as: small grants, stipends, or released time. Such administrative support would not only stimulate CL practice and research, it may also serve as a stimulus for faculty development and campus-community building. For instance, faculty development workshops or retreats could be offered to bring CL practitioners together for purposes of preparing them for effective implementation and evaluation of CL. It is noteworthy that a recent Carnegie Foundation survey revealed that over 70% of college presidents rated "greater effort to build stronger sense of community" as "very important" for improving the quality of life at their institution (The Carnegie Foundation and the American Council on Education, 1989). CL may be one mechanism for building community among college students--within the context of the classroom teaching, and among college faculty--within the context of faculty development.

Basic Elements of Cooperative Learning

Students working together to get a job done in a classroom where students are concerned about each other's learning in addition to their own is the heart of cooperative learning. Cooperative learning is characterized by five basic elements:

Positive Interdependence exists when students believe that they are linked with others in a way that one cannot succeed unless the other members of the group succeed (and vice versa). Students are working together to get the job done. In other words, students must perceive that they "sink or swim together." In a problem-solving session, positive interdependence is structured by group members (1) agreeing on the answer and solution strategies for each problem (goal interdependence) and (2) fulfilling assigned role responsibilities (role interdependence). Other ways of structuring positive interdependence include having common rewards, being dependent on each other's resources, or a division of labor.

Face-to-Face Promotive Interaction exists among students when students orally explain to each other how to solve problems, discuss with each other the nature of the concepts and strategies being learned, teach their knowledge to classmates, and explain to each other the connections between present and past learning. This face-to-face interaction is promotive in the sense that students help, assist, encourage, and support each other's efforts to learn.

Individual Accountability/Personal Responsibility requires the teacher to ensure that the performance of each individual student is assessed and the results given back to the group and the individual. The group needs to know who needs more assistance in completing the assignment and group members need to know they cannot "hitch-hike" on the work of others. Common ways to structure individual accountability include giving an individual exam to each student, randomly calling on individual students to present their group's answer, and giving an individual oral exam while monitoring group work.

Collaborative Skills are necessary for effective group functioning. Students must have and use the needed leadership, decision-making, trust-building, communication, and conflict-management skills. These skills have to be taught just as purposefully and precisely as academic skills. Many students have never worked cooperatively in learning situations and, therefore, lack the needed social skills for doing so.

Group Processing involves a group discussion of how well they are achieving their goals and how well they are maintaining effective working relationships among members. At the end of their working period the groups process their functioning by answering two questions: (1) What is something each member did that was helpful for the group and (2) What is something each member could do to make the group even better tomorrow? Such processing enables learning groups to focus on group maintenance, facilitates the learning of collaborative skills, ensures that members receive feedback on their participation, and reminds students to practice collaborative skills consistently.

From: Johnson, D. W., R. T. Johnson, and K. A. Smith. 1991. *Active Learning: cooperation in the college classroom*. Edina, MN: Interaction Book Company.

LETTER WRITING ACTIVITY

PURPOSE:
To assist you in reflecting on your personal goals and expectations from this accounting course.

DIRECTIONS:
For this assignment, pretend you have a good friend who graduated from your school in 1990 with a degree from the College of Business. Your friend has asked you to write them a letter about your expectations from your accounting courses.

REQUIRED:
In one typewritten page, share your ideas about what you expect to get from this course. If you are having trouble knowing where to start, you might want to let your friend know:

> Why you're taking this course...

> What you expect to learn to do in this course...

> How any of these skills will be used by you in the future...

"TRANSITIONING" ACTIVITY
ARTICLE BY K. PINCUS AND B. INMAN

PURPOSE:
To enable you to understand and think about changes that are occurring in accounting education, and how these changes may affect you.

DIRECTIONS:
Read the article "Transitioning".

REQUIRED:
Prepare answers to the following questions.

1.   What is the purpose of the article?

2.   What questions/issues does this article raise for non-accounting majors?

3.   The article indicates that it is essential that accountants develop strong communication skills to be successful in the future. Does this surprise you? Why or why not? What are some of the groups with which accountants are required to communicate?

4.   What are the advantages and disadvantages of being a student at one of the eleven schools discussed in the article? How would you feel as a student recently graduated from one of the schools (before the changes) or as a student from a non-change school?

5.   Are you surprised that the changes are occurring across the country? Explain. Which would you prefer, to be at a change or non-change school? Give an example that supports your choice.

6.   The article discusses three principal sets of skills required by accountants in the future: strong interpersonal communication, teamwork and analytical/problem solving skills. Are there elements of this class are which may help you to develop the skills mentioned here?

TRANSITIONING
by Karen V. Pincus, Ph.D., CPA and Brent Inman

Neither accounting curricula--nor students--can afford to stagnate.

Karen V. Pincus, Ph.D., CPA is an associate professor of accounting at the University of Southern California and academic fellow of the California Society of CPAs.

Brent Inman is a partner and national director of recruiting for Coopers & Lybrand.

Almost a century ago, Catherine the Great, Empress of Russia, wrote a letter to a French baron about the enormous changes she saw coming in her country. "A great wind is blowing," she observed, "and that gives you either imagination or a headache." Throughout the past two decades, we've watched the winds of change blowing in the business world in the form of rapidly changing technology, increasingly competitive markets, and new demands arising from the internationalization of business. Now, the winds of change are also blowing on college campuses as the result of a national movement to revamp accounting education. What are these winds of change and how can you cope with them?

Why is accounting education changing?

Given the magnitude and rate of changes taking place in the business world, it was inevitable that change would come, too, to accounting education. In fact, academics and practitioners have been talking about the need for change for many years. For example, in 1989, the then Big-Eight largest international CPA firms joined together to publish *Perspectives on Education: Capabilities for Success in the Accounting Profession*, explaining why and how accountants of the future need to be educated in a different manner than accountants of today. These future employers of today's students called for a broader, more conceptual education that places greater emphasis on analytical and problem-solving skills, as well as increased focus on communications and interpersonal skills.

A broader, more conceptual education, emphasizing analytical and problem-solving skills--Today's students will spend their careers in a world where advanced technology and globalization will be the norm. The emphasis in 21st century careers will increasingly be on creating new types of information demanded by a broader group of users and made possible by technology. Accountants of the past concentrated on tangible measures of "kick 'em and count 'em" physical assets like plant, property and equipment, which were the key economic resources in an industrial society. Accountants of the 21st century must have a broader focus appropriate to information age economies, which depend more heavily on intangible assets and require a greater variety of qualitative and quantitative information. Twenty-first century accountants must help organizations develop and use new measures--such as accounting information about environmental impact--that weren't called for in earlier eras. In this environment, broad-based analytical problem-solving skills become more important than in the past.

The need for increased emphasis on interpersonal and communications skills--Today's students must be ready for a different, more team-oriented work environment than their predecessors faced. Teamwork is critical today--you can no longer forge a successful career being just an individual contributor. In this environment, success depends even more than before on communications and interpersonal skills. The need for these skills is also influenced by technology. Technology has freed today's new accountant of much of the "number-crunching" aspects that were long the hallmark of entry-level accounting jobs. Tax return preparation, for example, once took up many hours of a junior tax accountant's workday, but now is facilitated by software that takes much of the drudgery out of the job. Consequently, today's students will face the challenge of being on the front line of interaction with internal or external clients early in their careers. The accountant's role as a business adviser, always an important aspect of accounting careers, is becoming much more important than ever before.

When will the changes occur?

The Accounting Education Change Commission--a blue ribbon group of educators and practitioners funded by donations from Big Six public accounting firms--has taken on the task of helping academia move beyond discussing the need for change to actually implementing change. Now, only three years after the Commission's birth, AECC-funded curriculum revision is underway at 11 universities and several community colleges. Each of these schools is undertaking a significant revamping of its program.

Other schools have also taken action to change their curricula. For example, the University of Southern California began offering a completely new undergraduate curriculum in January 1991 and will see its first graduates in 1993. The new curriculum, funded initially by a grant from the Coopers & Lybrand Foundation, is organized around broad topics that integrate aspects of auditing, systems, tax, managerial and financial accounting into each course. Teaching methodologies have also changed, moving away from lectures toward a more interactive classroom environment, where students (both as individuals and members of small groups) are more active participants in their own education. Every course includes both domestic and international examples involving business, non-profit and government organizations. From the first course to the last, students are exposed to problem solving in complex, realistically ambiguous situations.

At many other schools, curriculum change is on the agenda for the near future. As one professor noted, "The question is no longer *whether* we are going to change, but *when* we're going to change."

How does this change affect you?

With the winds of change blowing so strongly, you should expect
to feel at least a breeze, no matter where you are in your
education program: a student thinking about becoming an
accounting major, a current student in a changing program, an
"almost graduate" in a traditional program, or a recent graduate.
New students--For the near future, students who are just thinking
about majoring in accounting may face more complicated decisions.
For example, if there is a choice of schools to attend, should
they attend a traditional curriculum school or a new curriculum
school?

Students in programs that are changing--Students now enrolled at
a college undergoing change may find themselves part of the first
group of students to face the daunting task of taking courses
that no one has ever taken before--no grapevine, no ready access
to helpful experienced tutors, no map of what things will be like
next semester or when you enter the job market or take the CPA
exam. Given the lack of role models and historical results, new
program students live with a lot of uncertainty.
"Almost grads" and recent alumni--On the other hand, students who
are close to graduation from a traditional program--or who are
recent alumni--face the tail winds, leading to a lot of looking
over the shoulder behavior. The fear, of course, is that a
traditional accounting education could become "obsolete," leaving
them old (outdated) before their time. Will the new program
students coming up shortly behind have competitive advantages
over them?

How do you cope with the change?

Accounting education is in transition--and, like it or not, you
are in transition with it. We'd like to suggest three practical
steps you can take to help cope with accounting education change:

Expect to feel some anxiety.
Get beyond the anxiety. Take action. Don't react passively.
Focus on the positive.

Step 1-Expect to feel anxiety.

Change--even when we see it coming and even when we want it--is
never really easy. As Eric Hoffer wrote in his 1964 book, *The
Ordeal of Change*, "Even in slight things the experience of the
new is rarely without some stirring and foreboding." When you
consider that we manage to worry about something as simple as a
change in the formula of Coca-Cola, it isn't hard to figure out
that change of great magnitude may be accompanied by more than a
little anxiety.

Consequently, you should expect to feel some anxiety as
accounting education changes around you. Some level of anxiety is
a normal part of the change process. It's not a sign that
anything is wrong; it's just an indication that change is

occurring. Just knowing that some anxiety is a normal reaction is the first step in coping with change.

Step 2-Take action.

Your anxiety level will never go down, and may even increase, as long as you react passively to a changing environment. Remember the one lesson you learned from all those video games you've played: the quickest way to get yourself into trouble--or die--is to stand still and do nothing. Or, as the late Will Rogers put it: "Even if you are on the right track, you'll get run over if you just sit there."

The kinds of actions you can take fall into several categories: keeping yourself well-informed, discussing your concerns with people who can help, participating in the change movement, observing first-hand what is happening, and, if needed, creating your own personal new program.

Keep yourself well-informed--One of the best antidotes to change anxiety is dealing from facts and knowledge, not fears and rumors. Read articles about accounting education change; read about the new programs at schools funded by the AECC; read about the new programs at other colleges. The very fact that you're reading this article is a step toward coping with change. In addition to keeping up with *New Accountant*, other good sources of information include journals for practitioners (such as the *Journal of Accountancy* or *Management Accounting*) and academics (such as *Issues in Accounting Education* or *Accounting Horizons*). For example, in the June 1992 issue of *Accounting Horizons*, an article entitled "The Third Wave Breaks on the Shores of Accounting," by Robert K. Elliott, a partner with KPMG Peat Marwick, provides a detailed discussion of the forces for change in accounting education. If you read an article like this one, you will know more about why you need a different education than your predecessors. The more you know, the easier it is to deal with change.

Discuss your concerns with people who can help--Don't just chew on your own worries or trade worries with other people at the same level that you are. Talk to people who can help. Talk to faculty at your institution, talk to students from other programs that have undergone change, talk to practitioners. Don't feel that asking for help is a sign of trouble or weakness; everyone can use help dealing with change. For example, the Federation of Schools of Accountancy, which actively supports accounting education change, recognizes that even schools who want to revamp their curriculum will experience some natural anxiety about change. So, the FSA set up a committee to gather and share information about how faculty can overcome their own resistance to change.

Participate in the change movement--If your school is undergoing change, take part in the planning, implementation and evaluation process. Whether you are a new student, a current student or a recent graduate, there is something you can do to take part in the process. Volunteer to be part of the advisory boards and assessment committees that are set up as part of the change process. Respond to surveys you are sent. Attend programs discussing planned changes or providing feedback on changes already implemented.

At USC, for example, there's a group of recent alumni (graduates of the traditional program) that volunteered to help evaluate and improve the new program. By volunteering to help, these young professionals are helping themselves as well as the school. Working with the group also gives these volunteers a chance to deal with their own fears or misconceptions and keep their thinking current. When they first came together, for instance, some of the group has reservations about the new program because they had heard many of the assignments were ambiguous, and they feared that this was unfair. When they learned more about the new program, they came to realize that accounting courses now deliberately include some fuzzier problems in more complex settings because that is what employers tell us new accountants need. Our discussions help them tie what is happening in the classroom to things they are already experiencing on the job, where problems are not provided--but must be identified--and where correct approaches to solving problems are not always obvious. From the university's perspective, the recent alumni group is helping the school by providing good ideas and concrete suggestions for improving new courses. For example, the group has come up with excellent ideas to help improve the use of outside speakers in the first course.

Observe firsthand what is happening--Alumni or current students in traditional programs that are just beginning new courses can take advantage of the opportunity to visit some of the new classes. Come with an open mind--not looking to criticize either the old program or the new one, but simply to see what is "new" in the curriculum. At USC, there's been a steady stream of visitors to the new courses and most say they understand the change movement much more clearly when they actually see what is going on in the classroom.

Create your own personal new program--If you are an "almost graduate" at a school that hasn't yet changed its curriculum, how can you take action to be part of the change process? If you read about the reasons for change and the suggested types of changes, you'll find a consistent emphasis on broadening your education and building communications, interpersonal, analytical and problem-solving skills. If you are creative, you can start your own personal new program by a wise selection of elective courses and by the way you approach your traditional accounting courses.

For example, if the new curricula are more internationalized than your school's current program, take a course in international relations or politics. If you want to further develop your own communications skills, take some courses in public speaking, debate, drama--anything that gets you up in front of an audience, large or small. To enhance your analytical skills, take an

A-22

additional philosophy or logic course. If you want to keep up with state-of-the-art technology, don't read the FASB pronouncement from your paper-back book, go to the library and search for guidance on the accounting issue it covers by using an electronic database such as NAARS. While you'll still end up reading the same FASB pronouncement, you will gain valuable skills in formulating questions and creating efficient research strategies.

Step 3-Focus on the positive.

Finally, keep in mind the old saw about viewing a glass as half-empty or half-full. If you focus on the positive, you will find it easier to adapt to change. Don't view it as a curse that you live in changing times, view it as an opportunity. Remember that even the invention of the automobile created change anxiety once, though we couldn't imagine living without the automobile today.

While change brings with it some anxiety, change also keeps your days interesting, your career fresh. As John Fitzgerald Kennedy once noted: "Change is the law of life. And those who look only to the past or present are certain to miss the future."

BOXES ACTIVITY

PURPOSE:

To enable you to experience and use the skills of active listening and questioning, as part of the communication process, and to compare the results from two ways of using these skills.

DIRECTIONS:

Use the blank space provided below to draw a figure (diagram) which one of your classmates will describe to you.

REQUIRED:

Listen to the explanation and description given by the person in front of the class and draw the box shapes they describe.

INTRODUCTION TO BUSINESS IN THE US

A CAMPUS FACE FOR ALL SEASONS

PURPOSE:
To enable you to distinguish various factors of productions by using a campus business idea as an applied example.

DIRECTIONS:
Consider the following scenario:

The local college campus is bountifully endowed with gorgeous guys and gals. Some of the more enterprising students decide to use "local" talent and create a great calendar. The students have named their business Campus Calendars. The first printing is a sell-out within one month, and orders are even coming in from other colleges.

REQUIRED: Respond to the following questions:

1. What are the factors of production in this business?

   Natural resources?

   Labor?

   Capital?

   Entrepreneurs?

2. What kind of economic system is operating here?

3. If the University took over production and used the proceeds to benefit the student union, what kind of system would be in use?

4. Is the "invisible hand" of competition at work in the Campus Calendar? Explain.

5. If another campus in town was doing the same thing, what would be the effect on the Campus Calendar ? What would be the effect on the students (customers)?

BEN & JERRY'S ACTIVITY
SOCIAL RESPONSIBILITY ANALYSIS

PURPOSE:

To enable you to compare and contrast aspects of the sympathetic and mercenary societies as they relate to a present day corporation, Ben & Jerry's.

DIRECTIONS:

Read the article about Ben & Jerry's. As you read, make notes about the policies that support a high level of social responsibility. Identify the primary beneficiary of each policy. Also identify who has to sacrifice something for the benefits to be received.

REQUIRED:

Based on your notes and class discussion, prepare a one page analysis of three policies or programs instituted by Ben & Jerry's and explain why these policies ARE or ARE NOT in the best interest of Ben & Jerry's shareholders.

"To improve the quality of life of a broad community" is this company's social mission both inside and outside the organization.

Not many companies include a "social performance report" right after the president's letter in their annual report. But Ben & Jerry's does. The company's credo, "Turning Values into Value" centers on putting the firm's money where its mouth is--not just to make ice cream and frozen desserts, but also to create a socially responsible firm and place for people to work.

A small company with a big heart, Ben & Jerry's has human resources programs that are just as socially correct as the company's philosophy. The HR function oversees a variety of innovative plans that improve the quality of life for employees. Among them are opinion surveys; tuition reimbursement; flexible spending accounts; evaluate-your-boss polls; paid health club fees; 12 unpaid weeks' maternity, paternity, and adoption leave; child care centers; and a seven-times-salary ratio plan. (No one can make more than seven times the company's lowest paid employee.)

The HR department also administers a wellness plan, in which employees can get such care as free cholesterol and blood pressure testing and even body and foot massages.

"The whole philosophy at Ben & Jerry's is giving back to the community--both internally and externally," says Kathy Chaplin, Ben & Jerry's personnel operations manager. "We're always thinking about ways to improve our benefits, and creating programs that are inclusive of everybody," says Chaplin. For example, Ben & Jerry's covers employees' unmarried domestic partners under its health care plan.

It also created a short-term disability program, in which employees can receive 100% of their salary for six weeks, and 60% of their salary for six months until long-term disability kicks in. "Many plans opt for a 30-day wait before the plan starts paying," says Chaplin. But employees have bills. "We went with the opposite idea."

The firm also reimburses employees' adoption costs, and caps them at the cost of a normal hospital delivery.

The company challenges itself, its employees, *and* its vendors to give something back to the community. Even the company's financial counselor, with whom employees may confer on their personal financial affairs, gives part of her earnings to Parents Anonymous--a not-for-profit, self-help organization.

Ben & Jerry's management reflects a commitment to minority and women representation. Of five senior positions filled in 1990, four were filled by women or minorities. The results of its programs, according to an independent evaluator's statement, indicated "in all measures of work life, Ben & Jerry's people have a more favorable view of their jobs, supervision, and company than do employees from American companies in general."

"BE DATA LITERATE"ACTIVITY
ARTICLE BY PETER F. DRUCKER

PURPOSE:

To enable you to compare and contrast the characteristics of data and information.

DIRECTIONS:

Read the Drucker article.

REQUIRED:

Prepare responses to the following questions:

1. What do you think Drucker means when he says that managers/decision makers need to become "data literate"? *take raw data, convert into useable info*

2. Why is it so important that managers/decision makers become data literate? *Look long term, tap into non customer group, better strategy*

3. According to the article, managers/decision makers don't know what information to ask for in order to do their job properly. If this is true, who is deciding what information decision makers are getting from their accounting and computer systems departments? What are the problems with this arrangement?

4. How does someone become "data literate"?

5. Why did we read this article in an accounting class?

Be Data Literate--Know What to Know
Peter F. Drucker

Executives have become computer-literate. The younger ones, especially, know more about the way the computer works than they know about the mechanics of the automobile or the telephone. But not many executives are information-literate. They know how to get data. But most still have to learn how to use data.

Few executives yet know how to ask: What information do I need to do my job? When do I need it? In what form? And from whom should I be getting it? Fewer still ask: What new tasks can I tackle now that I get all these data? Which tasks should I do differently? Practically now one asks? What information do I owe? To whom? When? In what form?

A "database," no matter how copious, is not information. It is information's ore. For raw material to become information, it must be organized for a task, directed toward specific performance, applied to a decision. Raw material cannot do that itself. Nor can information specialists. They can cajole their customers, the data users. They can advise, demonstrate, teach. But they can no more manage data for users than a personnel department can take over the management of the people who work with an executive.

The First Challenge

Information specialists are toolmakers. The data users, whether executive or professional, have to decide what information to use, what to use it for and how to use it. They have to make themselves information-literate. This is the first challenge facing information users now that executives have become computer-literate.

But the organization also has to become information-literate. It also needs to learn to ask: What information do we need in this company? When do we need it? In what form? And where do we get it? So far, such questions are being asked primarily by the military, and even there mainly for tactical, day-to-day decisions. In business such questions have been asked only by a few multinationals, foremost among them the Anglo-Dutch Unilever, a few oil companies such as Shell, and the large Japanese trading companies.

The moment these questions are asked, it becomes clear that the information a business most depends on is available, if at all, only in primitive and disorganized form. For what a business needs the most for its decisions--especially its strategic ones-- are data about what goes on outside of it. It is only outside the business where there are results, opportunities, and threats.

So far, the only data from the outside that have been integrated into most companies' information systems and into their decision-making process are day-to-day market data: what existing customers buy, where they buy, how they buy. Few businesses have tried to get information about their noncustomers, let along have integrated such information into their databases. Yet no matter how powerful a company is in its industry or market, noncustomers almost always outnumber customers.

American department stores had a very large customer base, perhaps 30% of the middle-class market, and they had far more information about their own customers than any other industry. Yet their failure to pay attention to the 70% who were not customers largely explains why they are today in a severe crisis. Their noncustomers increasingly were the young affluent, double-earner families who were the growth market of the 1980s.

The commercial banks, for all their copious statistics about their customers, similarly did not realize until very late that more and more of their potential customers had become noncustomers. Many had turned to commercial paper to finance themselves instead of borrowing from the banks.

When it comes to the nonmarket information--demographics, the behavior and plans of actual and potential competitors; technology; economics; the shifts signaling foreign exchange fluctuations to come and capital movements--there are either no data at all or only the broadest of generalization. Few attempts have been made to think through the bearing that such information has on the company's decisions. How to obtain these data; how to test them; how to put them together with the existing information system to make them effective in a company's decision process--this is the second major challenge facing information users today.

It needs to be tackled soon. Companies today rely for their decisions either on inside data such as costs or on untested assumptions about the outside. In either case they are trying to fly on one wing.

Finally, the most difficult of the new challenges: We will have to bring together the two information systems that businesses now run side by side--computer-based data processing and the accounting system. At least we will have to make the two compatible.

People usually consider accounting to be "financial." But that is valid only for the part, going back 700 years, that deals with assets, liabilities and cash flows; it is only a small part of modern accounting. Most of accounting deals with operations rather than with finance, and for operational accounting money is simply a notation and the language in which to express nonmonetary events. Indeed, accounting is being shaken to its very roots by reform movements aimed at moving it away from being financial and toward becoming operational.

There is the new "transactional" accounting that attempts to relate operations to their expected results. There are attempts to change asset values from historical cost to estimates of expected future returns. Accounting has become the most intellectually challenging area in the field of management, and the most turbulent one. All these new accounting theories aim at turning accounting data into information for management decision-making. In other words, they share the goals of computer-based data processing.

Today these two information systems operate in isolation from each other. They do not even compete, as a rule. In the business schools we keep the two apart with separate departments of accounting and of computer science, and separate degrees in each.

The practitioners have different backgrounds, different values, different career ladders. They work in different departments and for different bosses. There is a "chief information officer" for computer-based data processing, usually with a background in computer technology. Accounting typically reports to a "chief financial officer," often with a background in financing the company and in managing its money. Neither boss, in other words, is information-focused as a rule.

The two systems increasingly overlap. They also increasingly come up with what looks like conflicting--or at least incompatible-- data about the same event; for the two look at the same event quite differently. Till now this has created little confusion. Companies tended to pay attention to what their accountants told them and to disregard the data of their information system, at least for top-management decisions. But this is changing as computer-literate executives are moving into decision-making positions.

Up for Grabs

One development can be considered highly probable: Managing money--what we now call the "treasury function"--will be divorced from accounting (that is, from its information component) and will be set up, staffed and run separately. How we will otherwise manage the two information systems is up for grabs. But that we will bring them together within the next 10 years, or at least sort out which system does what, can be predicted.

Computer people still are concerned with greater speed and bigger memories. But the challenges increasingly will be not technical, but to convert data into usable information that is actually being used.

INTRODUCTION TO DECISION MAKING

SPRING BREAK ACTIVITY
GENERAL DECISION MAKING

PURPOSE:

To enable you to analyze and apply the process of decision making. This process is an integral part of our day-to-day life and utilizes a cycle of choices and analysis of choices:

- Determine the real problem to be solved.
- Identify the alternative courses of action.
- Analyze each alternative critically.
- Select the best alternative in the circumstances.
- Implement the chosen alternative.
- Re-evaluate the decision as new information becomes available.
- Evaluate the final outcome.

DIRECTIONS:

Think about your plans for spring break. There are many options as to how you might spend that week. The object of this activity is to use the decision process to decide how you are going to spend the week. Please understand that *what you decide is not as important as the process* you go through to make the decision.

REQUIRED:

Respond to the following **five** items (they continue onto the next page).

a. ***What are your options?*** Identify **three** alternative ways you personally could spend the week of spring break.

   Option #1:

   Option #2:

   Option #3

b. ***What factors (criteria) are most important to you in evaluating the alternatives you selected?*** Identify **three** factors and rank them in order of importance (the most important factor being #1):

   Factor #1:

   Factor #2:

   Factor #3:

c. ***Using the three factors you have identified, evaluate each of the three alternatives you listed.*** In this requirement you are attempting to determine:
   1) The potential **benefits** associated with each alternative.
   2) The potential **costs** associated with each alternative. Do not restrict yourself to the costs in terms of dollars.

   Alternative #1:
   Benefits

   Costs

   Alternative #2:
   Benefits

   Costs

   Alternative #3:
   Benefits

   Costs

d. ***What is your decision?*** It should be obvious to you that there is no "correct" answer to this requirement. This is **<u>YOUR</u>** decision.

e. ***What new information in the next 7 days could cause you to re-evaluate your decision?*** Identify <u>**three**</u> pieces of new information and explain ***how*** each of them might cause you to rethink your decision.

   #1.

   #2.

   #3.

PARABLE ACTIVITY

PURPOSE:
To enable you to reflect and ponder the impact of society's rules and values, as well as your own rules and values, in decision making.

DIRECTIONS:
Read "Take Two of These and Call Me in the Morning". Make notes and underline as you read, for meaning and comprehension.

REQUIRED:

1. As a team, discuss the following questions:

   a. What is a parable?

   b. In this parable, who did the society <u>originally</u> look to in order to stay healthy?

   c. How did this change when the doctor arrived?

   d. Compare and contrast this parable to our society's growing dependence on government laws and regulations. What are the **similarities**? What are the **differences**?

   e. Have you ever heard the saying "form over substance"? What does it mean?

   f. Relate the phrase "form over substance"

      to this parable.

      to the reliance on external laws instead of internal values .

TAKE TWO OF THESE AND CALL ME IN THE MORNING

A long, long time ago, in a country far away from here, a group of people banded together to form a community. Their society was, in many ways, not unlike the one in which you live. They married, had families, worked at various occupations, and in general had pretty satisfying lives.

Of particular interest was their system of health care. It had evolved over many years, and consisted mainly of the people being responsible for taking care of themselves. Most of the citizens tried to eat right, exercise regularly, and it was the custom for people to establish health codes for themselves. Of course there were some folks who did not take care of themselves, so they got sick, and in some instances made others around them sick, as well. But all in all, the community was happy with its state of health.

One day, a stranger came into town, and the first person he encountered was a man who had eaten (over eaten, actually) something that had made him very sick. The stranger took one look at him, opened a black bag he was carrying, removed some tiny pills, and said 'Take two of these, and call me in the morning'. The sick man swallowed the pills, and almost immediately felt much better. This was amazing, because nothing like this had ever happened in the community before. Within minutes, the news had spread throughout the entire town.

A crowd gathered around the stranger, and everyone was talking at once, asking him who he was, how he had made the sick man better, and what other kinds of magic he had in the little black bag. The stranger smiled, and when he had succeeded in quieting the crowd, announced simply, 'I am a Doctor. I have spent many years learning how to make sick people well.' He went on to explain that he had been looking for a town just like this one where he could spend his life helping people. 'If you will let me live with you', said the Doctor, 'I will dedicate my life to helping you stay healthy.'

And so, the Doctor came to live in the town, and he was every bit as good as his word. When someone did get sick (which wasn't very often, at first), he or she went to see the Doctor. The Doctor asked some questions about what he called "symptoms", and then performed "an examination". When he was finished, he took down one of the many books he had on his shelf, and read for a few minutes. Then came the part the people really loved. He gave them "medicine"! 'Take two of these', he would say, 'and call me in the morning'. And sure enough, if they did what he told them to do, they got better.

Life in the town could not have been better. At least for a while. As time went on, however, the people began to rely more and more on the Doctor's ability to cure illness, and less and less on keeping themselves healthy. They didn't worry nearly so much about what they ate or whether they got sufficient exercise. In fact, within a few short years, the people of the town came to consider the entire area of their health to be the responsibility of the Doctor.

Unfortunately, there began to be more and more incidence of serious illness in the community. And even more alarming was the Doctor's seeming inability to cope with it. The people began to be suspicious. Maybe this man was not all he had claimed to be. Then one day, a large group of them went to the Doctor's office to confront him. He tried to explain to the people that their health was still primarily their own responsibility. 'That is not what you said when you came here' the people cried. 'You promised that when we got sick you would make us better'. 'But I never said you didn't have to take care of yourself' said the Doctor. The people were angry with the Doctor. Very angry. 'Kill the Doctor' shouted someone in the mob. 'We don't need him anyway. We have his pills and his books. We will use them to take care of ourselves when we get sick'.

So the Doctor was forced to flee from the town. He didn't even stop to pick up his little black bag. The people were glad he was gone. He had proven himself to be a fake. And besides, they had all the things he had used to make them better.

Many years passed, and the town was still, in many ways, not unlike the one in which you live. The people married, had families, and worked at various occupations. Young people loved to hear the old folks tell stories about the olden days, especially the one about the time the phony doctor came to town, how he was discovered for what he was, and how he was driven out.

But there was something dreadfully wrong in the community. The problem was their health. Very few people felt responsible for taking care of themselves. They ate whatever they wanted to, they did not exercise, and they were experiencing a great deal of sickness. In many instances they made others around them sick, as well. The idea of establishing a personal health code was unheard of in the town. All the people living when the doctor had come were now dead, so obviously no one remembered what it was like before he came. All in all, the community was very unhappy with its state of health. Many town meetings were held to discuss the problem, and to try and figure out ways to improve their system of health care.

Here is how the town's health care system worked. When people got sick, they went to the Doctor's office. They had kept it just the way it was the day they drove the phony doctor out. The books were still there and there was always a full supply of pills in the little black bag. These were new pills, of course, because the ones left by the doctor had long since been used up. But they looked just like the originals.

When they got to the Doctor's office, they asked themselves some questions about their "symptoms", and then performed "an examination". Nobody knew exactly what the examination was for, or exactly how to perform one, but they knew it was an important part of the healing process. When they finished the examination, they took down one of the many books from the Doctor's shelf, and read for a few minutes. It didn't really matter which book, or how long they read, because they didn't understand anything written in them anyway. Then came the part the people really loved. They gave themselves "medicine"! 'Take two of these', they chanted, 'and call me in the morning'. Just doing the chant made them feel better. But in the morning they were still sick. In fact, they were sicker than before.

Meetings were held all over the town. 'Maybe we need to do the chant more often', someone suggested. No, somebody else had already tried that. 'Do you think taking more pills will help?' asked someone else. 'Yes, yes, more pills', they cried, 'and more examinations'. Then someone remembered that an important part of the healing process at one time included reading from the Doctor's books. So they decided that in addition to all else, they would begin again to read from those books.

And so they took more of the little pills, and chanted 'take two of these and call me in the morning.' They read from the books; they held meetings; they held training sessions to teach themselves how to do "examinations" (whatever they were) on themselves and on each other. And the more they swallowed pills, did chants, read the books, and trained one another to do examinations, the sicker they got.

Finally everyone in the town had died. Everyone that is, except for one man, and he was very near death. So, with all the strength he could muster, he dragged himself to the Doctor's Office. He asked himself questions about his "symptoms", performed "an examination", and read a few lines from the only book he had the strength to lift. Then, with his last breath, he whispered 'take two of these and call me in the morning', swallowed the two tiny pills, and quietly, but peacefully died, secure in the knowledge that he had done all he could do.

GROUP DYNAMICS ACTIVITY

PURPOSE:
To enable you to brainstorm and then discuss with members of your team the elements necessary to successfully form and then work in a group.

DIRECTIONS:
Use this worksheet to write down your individual ideas or issues about FORMING A GROUP (What's important when your first start a group?), GETTING IT TO WORK (What's important to make everyone work together?), GATHERING IDEAS (What's necessary so that everyone contributes?), and COMING TO A CONCLUSION (What's necessary so that the team can agree on a solution?). When you are finished, discuss your notes with your team members.

REQUIRED:
Prepare a team list of what you have decided are the most important characteristics of a GOOD team member and HOW you would evaluate that characteristic. The outline is provided for you, at the bottom of the last page (A GOOD TEAM MEMBER IS: HOW WE CAN TELL?)

Forming a Group:

Getting it to Work:

Gathering Ideas:

Coming To A Conclusion/Completion:

PREPARE THIS SECTION AS A TEAM

A GOOD TEAM MEMBER IS: **HOW CAN WE TELL?**

1.

2.

3.

4.

ECONOMIC DECISION MAKING &
USEFUL ACCOUNTING INFORMATION

LOAN APPLICATION ACTIVITY I

PURPOSE:

To enable you to use economic decision making skills and experience both the loan applicant's and the banker's perspectives in a loan situation. This activity has you take the role/perspective of the loan applicant.

BACKGROUND:

Not that it should surprise you, but banks are in the business of making money. To do this, banks take in deposits, then lend the funds out to other individuals or businesses. Banks earn money by charging a higher interest rate on loans than they pay on deposits. However, in order for this to work, the banks must **receive back the money they lent out**. The bank's assessment of whether the loan will be repaid is the basis for a decision to grant or deny a loan. In order to help with this decision, banks require that individuals requesting a loan complete a loan application.

DIRECTIONS:

Assume you have been out of school for a few years and have decided to start a small business. In order to obtain the money necessary to start your business, you are applying to a bank for a loan.

REQUIRED:

As part of your loan application, you are required to do the following:

1) Write a short statement detailing: *2 paragraphs*

   a) What type of business you intend to start
   b) How much money you want to borrow
   c) What you would use the money for (ie: computer, delivery van, etc.)
   d) Any other information you think the bank would find helpful in   uating your loan application.

   Note: This statement should be typed, no more than one page.

2) Complete the attached loan application. Note: You may be creative on the numbers here -they don't need to be real, just realistic. The loan application does not need to be typed, but it must be **neatly** hand written.

LOAN APPLICATION FORM

As of _____ 19___

Name _____

Address	Employed by	Years
Home Phone No.	Position
Social Security No.	Business Phone No.
Age	Name of Spouse
	Soc. Security No. of Spouse

ASSETS	DOLLARS	LIABILITIES	DOLLARS
Cash in Bank (where applying for loan)		Notes Payable (this bank)	
ACCOUNT #		Account #	
Cash in other accounts		Notes Payable	
Bank Name & Account #		Account #	
Accounts Recievable-Good		Accounts Payable	
Due from Friends/Relatives		Due to Friends/Relatives	
(Describe)		(Describe)	
Notes Recievable		Contracts Payable	
& Contracts Owned		(To Whom)	
Cash Value Life Insurance		Loans on Life Insurance	
Stocks & Bonds, closely held		Taxes Payable	
Stocks & Bonds, publicly traded		Real Estate Indebtedness	
Real Estate		Other Liabilities:	
Vehicles-Market Value		(Describe)	
(Describe)			
Personal Property			
Other Assets:			
(Describe)		TOTAL LIABILITIES	(B)
		NET WORTH (A - B)	(C)
		TOTAL (B + C)	
TOTAL ASSETS	(A)		

APPROXIMATE ANNUAL INCOME AND EXPENSE

ANNUAL INCOME		ANNUAL EXPENSES (Exluding primary living expenses)	Last Year Actual	This Year Estimate
Salary				
Salary (Spouse)				
Securities Income				
Rentals		Real Estate Payments		
Other (Describe)		Rent		
		Income Taxes		
		Insurance Premiums		
TOTAL INCOME		Property Taxes		
		Installment Payments		
LESS TOTAL EXPENSES		Other (include alimony, child support		
		or separate maintenance payments		
NET CASH INCOME		you are obligated to make)		

TOTAL EXPENSES _____

A-45

LOAN APPLICATION ACTIVITY II

PURPOSE:

To enable you to use economic decision making skills and experience both the loan applicant's and the banker's perspectives in a loan situation. This activity has you take the role/perspective of the bank officer.

DIRECTIONS:

Assume you are now a **bank loan officer** responsible for evaluating a loan application and statement completed in the Loan Application Activity I. It is your responsibility to review the loan application and decide if the loan will be granted. The bank you work for requires that you document your evaluation and decision in a **memo to the file**. The memo should include the following items:

1) The 3 criteria you used to evaluate the loan.

2) Explain what information each of the criteria gives you in deciding whether the loan should be granted.

3) Evaluate the loan application on each criteria.

4) Decide if the loan will be granted or not. (Be sure that your decision is consistent with your evaluation in 3).

   Remember, as a loan officer you need to take <u>some</u> risk that the loan will not be repaid. Alternatively, information can minimize that risk.

REQUIRED:

Prepare a memo as explained in the directions above. This memo must be 1-2 **typed** pages in memo format. (See example below.) The loan application and statement that you evaluated should be attached to this memo.

To: Memo to the file
From: Mr./Ms. Loan Officer
Date: Today's date
Re: Evaluation of Loan Application by (Your name)

In the body of your memo, address the 4 issues outlined in the directions of this assignment.

CHARACTERISTICS OF USEFUL ACCOUNTING INFORMATION

PURPOSE:

To enable the student to evaluate the characteristics of useful accounting information by discovery of the power inherent in these characteristics.

DIRECTIONS:

You are considering several investment opportunities. One of the companies you are considering is the Wooster Company. On February 8, 1993, you requested financial statements from the company for January, 1993. Today is March 5, 1993 and Bertie Wooster (the owner of the company) has provided the company's income statement presented below. Also included were two notes explaining the amounts on the income statement.

```
                      WOOSTER COMPANY
                      Income Statement
            For The Month Ended January 31, 1993


     REVENUES (Note #1)
     Sales.............................................$7,788,000
     EXPENSES (Note #2)
     Cost of Product Sold................$3,680,000
     Salaries & Wages.................... 1,150,000
     Rent................................    50,000
     Advertising.........................    25,000
     Utilities...........................    15,000
     Insurance Premiums..................    10,000
     Total Expenses....................................$4,930,000
     Net Income........................................$2,858,000
                                                       ==========
```

Note #1:   Although the actual cash sales for the month of January totaled only $752,000, our customers have told us they plan to buy an additional $7,036,000 of product later this year. Even though the $7,036,000 has not been received in cash, nor has the product been delivered, we have included them as sales so you would have a better idea as to what our potential really is.

Note #2:   The actual cash paid out for the product totaled $680,000 in January. We are assured by our supplier that with the amount of sales we anticipate, the total product cost for the sales we have recorded will be $3,680,000. The rest of the expenses represent the amount of cash paid out for these items during the month of January, 1993.

CHARACTERISTICS (Continued)

REQUIRED:

1. As a potential investor in Wooster Company, how useful is the above income statement? Support your answer with specific items from the income statement and notes.

2. What characteristics of the income statement make it useful to you as a potential investor? What features decrease its usefulness?

3. Using your responses to the above two questions and other factors you may wish to consider, list the characteristics that you believe accounting information must possess in general in order to be useful to decision makers.

"HOW 2 FLA FIRMS FOOLED AUDITORS" ACTIVITY

PURPOSE:
To enable you to analyze and critique the characteristics of useful accounting information and some of its limitations.

DIRECTIONS:
Read the article entitled "How 2 Florida Firms Fooled Stockholders, Auditors and the SEC". Then answer the question below. **Your answer should be typewritten, double-spaced, and no more than one page in length.** REMEMBER, THIS IS A MAXIMUM LENGTH, NOT A MINIMUM. YOUR ANSWERS MAY BE SHORTER.

REQUIRED:
It is apparent from this article that although accounting information was used by investors and other parties who did business with these two firms, the information may not have been of much value. Pick one of the firms from the article (Cascade or College Bound) and discuss the weaknesses in the accounting information provided to the decision makers doing business with the firm. (In other words, why wasn't the accounting information useful to decision makers?) Your answer should be framed in terms of the qualitative characteristics (and sub-characteristics) of accounting information that were discussed in Chapter 3. Specifically, you should select and discuss the characteristics (and sub-characteristics) of accounting information which have been violated.

HOW 2 FLORIDA FIRMS FOOLED STOCKHOLDERS, AUDITORS AND THE SEC
Daniel Pearl

If a company is largely a mirage, how long should it take for
investors to find that out? With two Florida companies, Cascade
International Inc. and College Bound Inc., it took years. Quarter
after quarter, the two enterprises continued to win the praise of
investors, the loyalty of employees and the approval of auditors, even
though much of their revenue--and all of their profits--apparently
were an illusion.

Their stories are bizarre. Cascade International, a women's clothing
and cosmetics retailer, had a vanishing chief executive, an imaginary
cosmetics division and millions of shares of bogus stock. College
Bound, for its part, kept a secret bank account, and five of every six
dollars it supposedly took in for coaching students for college-
entrance exams were a fiction, according to investors.

Why Nobody Noticed

Still, both companies were able to flourish for mundane reasons--
overburdened regulators, inattentive auditors, and an economic slump
that encouraged struggling companies to resort to fraud and
discouraged employees from blowing the whistle.

"I'm sure there are a lot of similar cases out there," says Howard
Schilit, and American University accounting professor who studied
College Bound and other apparently fraudulent companies. The hot stock
market of the 1980s encouraged small, often struggling companies to
turn to the public markets in unprecedented numbers.

Deltec Securities Corp., a New York firm that invested more than $9
million in Cascade International, has cooled to small growth-
companies. Cascade International is "an ugly example of things that
could happen elsewhere." says John R. Gordon, Deltec's president.

Trying a New Tack

The founders of Cascade International and College Bound started out as
typical entrepreneurs, slavishly devoted to their companies, convinced
they had winning formulas and unwilling to accept defeat.

Victor Incendy had the enthusiasm but not the knack for business. He
and his wife Jeannette launched a company that made lipstick cases in
the early 1970s. After two years, its equipment was repossessed.
Similar start-ups went nowhere, and Mr. Incendy was always late paying
bills, former business associates recall.

Then, in 1985, Mr. Incendy tried a new tack. He gave his creditors
stock in a new public company what would sell Jean Cosmetics--
lipsticks, blushes and nail polishes--designed by his wife. Eager
investors bought in, and Mr. Incendy began buying bankrupt women's
clothing stores that could be an outlet for the cosmetics.

By 1989, the retailing downturn was killing Cascade International. Independent retailers, like Fashion Bug, wouldn't accept the company's cosmetics counters, and the Incendys were having problems turning around their newly acquired Allison's and Diana's women's clothing chains.

Yet analysts, relying mostly on Mr. Incendy's rosy projections, predicted ever-higher earnings. Mr. Incendy, apparently to buy time, claimed to have more and more cosmetics counters--255 by last year. The truth was closer to six. At the same time, Mr. Incendy created and began secretly selling more than six million shares of unauthorized stock, according to lawyers for the company and its creditors.

Mr. and Mrs. Incendy, now divorced, both disappeared last November and haven't turned up. Cascade International's stock is worthless. The company's Chapter 11 bankruptcy trustee recently closed the remaining 29 stores. They are scheduled to be auctioned off later this month.

Demand for a Cram Course

College Bound's founders also started out legitimately. Janet Ronkin, a former schoolteacher, wanted her sons to go to medical school, so she tutored them herself for college-entrance exams. (They ended up going to the University of Miami law school.) Then, friends asked her to tutor their children. By 1981, she and her husband, George, were running a thriving little company out of their Plantation, Fla., garage. The idea was to help students cram for exams, choose extracurricular activities, pick a college, even iron out problems with teachers.

But expanding the concept beyond affluent south Florida was tougher than the Ronkins expected when they began to sell franchises in 1986. By 1988, franchisees were demanding the Ronkins buy them out. Desperate for cash to expand, the Ronkins solved their problem by taking the company public. They raised $30 million from European investors over the years, according to their investment banker.

The Ronkins quickly opened centers through the country. Their goal was 15 a quarter--and they sought immediate results. The Ronkins, whose company had moved into gleaming offices in Crocker Center in Boca Raton, often worked until midnight and were back in their twin offices, separated by a sliding door, at eight in the morning. At some point before the fall of 1990, to mask the poor turnout at many of their new centers, they began concocting revenue by transferring money from one bank account to another, according to the Securities and Exchange Commission, which is suing the company for allegedly defrauding investors. The SEC estimates College Bound overstated its center revenues by $8.9 million, or 489%, last year.

Through their Tampa, Fla., lawyer, John Lauro, the Ronkins deny intentional wrongdoing. Mr. Lauro says they "intend to litigate this case very aggressively." College Bound's centers have all been closed, and the company now is being sold off in bankruptcy court. The highest bid for the test-preparation business is $600,000--less than 0.5% of its value in the Nasdaq market a year ago.

Suspicions Aroused

To some, it was obvious the companies weren't what they purported to be. Thompson McKinnon, a brokerage firm that was one of Cascade International's early boosters, became so suspicious of the company in 1987 that it quietly eased its clients out of the stock. Catherine Hall, hired to be Cascade International's in-house attorney in late 1989, testified in May that she quit after four months. She said a call to the company's insurance carrier showed Cascade had far fewer stores and cosmetics counters than it claimed.

Cosmetics-industry officials say they have never heard of Jean Cosmetics, even though the company said in its 1986 annual report, for example, that "Jean Cosmetics is in the formidable company of Lancome, Estee Lauder, Elizabeth Arden, and other well-established firms." As for College Bound, John Katzman, president of Princeton Review, a leading test-preparation firm, called it the "stealth competitor" because "they don't show up anywhere on the radar map."

Others, however, took the company's SEC filings at face value, including James Bax, who sold his 17-year-old professional-testing firm to College Bound in May 1991 for shares that are now worthless. Mr. Bax, who recently had to pay more than $1 million to get the company back, says, "Most people assume, with the government putting imprimatur on something, that it's certifying that they're OK."

In fact, Cascade International and College Bound's operations flew too low for the government's radar for years. Both companies went public in a way that attracts less scrutiny than an initial public offering: merging into an existing shell corporation. The Incendys, for instance, merged Jean Cosmetics into Cascade Importers, a public company with no operations, and got most of the public company's stock in return. This gambit is popular among entrepreneurs because they can save months of work and hundreds of thousands of dollars by avoiding the formal underwriting of an initial public offering.

Once public, both Cascade International and College Bound did file regularly with the SEC. But the agency's main office gives only about 10% of all annual reports and 7% of all quarterly reports full reviews. And the Miami branch, which has 15 attorneys and one accountant, investigates tips rather than systematically screening for fraud. "Policemen don't stand outside every bank and wait for a bank robbery," said Edward Noakes, the SEC's deputy chief accountant.

Even when the SEC follows up a tip, it can still be slow-going. In the case of College Bound, the SEC at first was sidetracked by charges made by stock speculators that some of the company's centers didn't exist. But College Bound officials produced a box of leases and a scrapbook of photos with managers standing in front of their centers. It took the SEC most of last year to discover the alleged bank-account manipulation. SEC officials won't comment on either investigation.

The SEC says that making sure companies' revenues are real is not its job. "The auditors are there to find material fraud," says Mr. Noakes. "We don't do audits."

The auditor for Cascade International was Bernard H. Levy, and amiable Manhattanite who had prepared Mr. Incendy's personal tax returns for years. He worked mostly from his Central Park South apartment, but the company maintained a private office for him at its headquarters in Boca Raton. Cascade International also leased a car for him, according to a company document.

Accountant's Mission
Mr. Levy won't talk about Cascade International now, but in an interview last November, he explained that Mr. Incendy told him to simply write the SEC reports and not to worry about auditing subsidiaries. That was supposedly done by other Incendy accountants, he said. When Mr. Incendy disappeared, Mr. Levy said he didn't have the name of the accountant for the phantom Jean Cosmetics unit.

Last year, Mr. Levy endorsed financial reports that said the company had $11.1 million in profit in the year ending June 30, 1991. The reality, according to the company's bankruptcy examiner, was more like a $7.0 million loss. "Obviously I didn't do everything I should have done," Mr. Levy said in the November interview. "I'm a trusting person."

Professional standards for auditors prohibit such things as driving a company car and trusting the chief executive about subsidiary results. To enforce these standards, a trade group, the American Institute of Certified Public Accountants (AICPA), requires members who audit public companies to let another firm review their work regularly. But neither the SEC nor the National Association of Securities Dealers, which listed Cascade International and College Bound shares, requires auditors to join the trade group. Mr. Levy didn't.

Gordon K. Goldman, College Bound's auditor until last March, *was* a member of the AICPA. But Mr. Goldman, a close friend of Mrs. Ronkin's twin brother, never did get a peer review. (The trade group says it is investigating why.) The 47-year-old accountant works out of his house in the Queens borough of New York City and didn't bother to attend College Bound's only annual meeting last year.

Nobody has claimed that Mr. Goldman colluded with the Ronkins. But he attested to College Bound's claim last year of $5.5 million in net income. The SEC says the company actually had a loss. One thing Mr. Goldman apparently failed to notice was that expense records had been inflated by adding two digits to the left (a $538.48 furniture invoice was listed on a ledger as a $43,538.48 expense, for example, according to investigators.)

Mr. Goldman's only comment: "If you want to bury something, you can bury it. You can bury it in a way that can't be found by someone who doesn't already suspect it."

Currently, "there's no requirement that an accountant look actively for fraud," says Rep. Ron Wyden. The Oregon Democrat has sponsored three unsuccessful bills aimed at changing that. He believes many auditors, large and small, are more concerned with protecting their client relationship than the public.

Many investors believed the companies' ability to get NASD listing meant they were real. Yale Hirsch, publisher of the Ground Floor Newsletter, touted Cascade International in the fall of 1990 without visiting the company or its stores. He says, "When a company is on Nasdaq and is a fairly decent size, you assume they're doing decent work.

NASD Requirements

But NASD says it doesn't inspect the operations of the 4,000 companies it lists and can't inspect their books. The organization does require each listed company to have at least two "independent" directors on its board, individuals "able to exercise independent judgement." The independence of College Bound and Cascade International's boards was questionable. College Bound was negotiating with one of its two independent directors to buy out his company's 50% interest in 31 Ronkin centers for College Bound stock. Mr. Incendy dominated Cascade International's board and kept it from meeting more than once a year, according to a former director's lawsuit.

In the absence of aggressive auditors and board members, the SEC relies on tips from employees that something is amiss. But both Cascade International and College Bound kept workers well-paid and ill-informed. Maurice Mayberry, who was paid $101,538 last year, had the title of chief financial officer of College Bound. Bud he didn't do much more than pay the company's bills, according to his deposition in bankruptcy court. He said he didn't track the company's revenues or checking accounts--the Ronkins did--and that, one day, he found he could no longer see the company's bank balance because Mrs. Ronkin had changed the computer password.

Center directors didn't know their own profitability, because they deposited checks into shared bank accounts and sent bills directly to headquarters. "I had no idea what my center needed to break even, and no budget to work with," says Mark Bilotta, a former center director in Worcester, Mass. One former College Bound manager recalls asking Mrs. Ronkin for sales reports on the centers, and "she smiled and patted me on the back and said, 'They're doing great out there.'"

At Cascade International, John T. Sirmans was the Incendys' vice president. Mr. Incendy, when questioned about the cosmetics counters, "told me that he would give me the list of his counters when I could give him the list of the Avon ladies from Avon," Mr. Sirmans testified. On other occasions, he said, Mr. Incendy pulled a manila folder from his briefcase and read off figures purportedly from the cosmetics division. "I was fed just enough to satisfy me," said Mr. Sirmans.

Money was enough incentive for some people to keep their mouths shut. Unlike the Defense Department and the Internal Revenue Service, the SEC doesn't pay informants. Bernard Lake, who joined Cascade International as a buying manager in 1988, said he knew within three months that the Incendys were "playing a game" of some kind. But, "I got a good paycheck on Friday. I didn't give a damn what they did."

TOOLS OF THE TRADE PART I - THE BALANCE SHEET: INITIAL FINANCING - INVESTMENT BY OWNERS

MAP GAME ACTIVITY

PURPOSE:
To enable you to begin to discover some of the purposes and limitations of financial statements..

DIRECTIONS:
Study the map of the city of Nashville and jot down answers to the questions below, relating to that map.

REQUIRED:
After you have answered as many questions as you can, work with your team and try to answer all questions. Make sure you can explain WHY your answers are right.

1. Who produced this map?

2. In what year was it produced?

3. How can you tell which way is north, south, etc.?

4. ~~What are the coordinates of~~ where is the Country ~~Museum~~ music Hall of Fame?

5. What additional information might make it easier to find the museum?

6. Can you locate 2011 West End Ave. on this map? If not, why not? (~~Hint: West End Ave. is at B-12~~).

7. Traveling west on I-40 to I-65 and then heading north on I-65, exactly how far is it from Nashville International Airport to the Cumberland River?

8. How long would it take to drive from Nashville International Airport to the Cumberland River?

9. What highway would you use to travel from downtown Nashville to OPRYLAND USA?

10. Approximately how far is it in miles from downtown Nashville to OPRYLAND USA?

MAP OF NASHVILLE

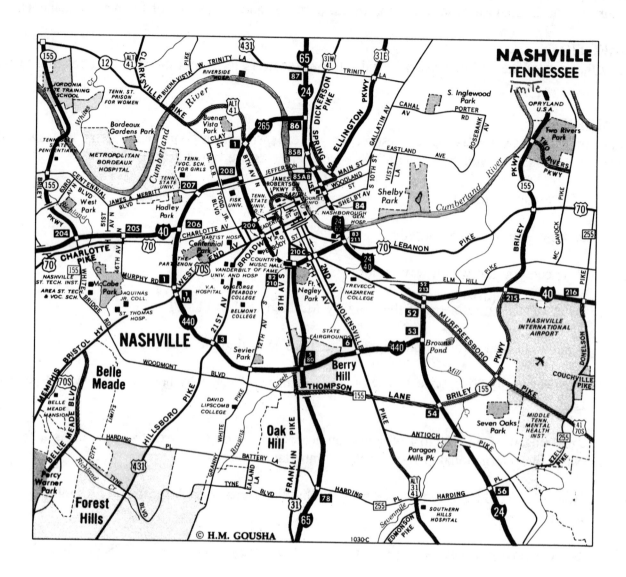

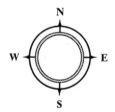

A-58

BARON COBERG ACTIVITY

PURPOSE:

To enable you to compare and contrast data vs. information and to discover how accounting standards can help and hinder economic decision making.

DIRECTIONS:

Read the case "Baron Coberg". Make notes concerning the data in the case. As you read the case, decide 1)What is relevant vs. irrelevant data and 2) What is the best format to present your analysis to someone else.

REQUIRED:

Evaluate the performance of the two farmers and decide who did the best job. Be sure to explain how you define performance. Prepare a report that supports your evaluation.

BARON COBURG
W.T. Andrews

Once upon a time many, many years ago, there lived a feudal landlord in a small province of Western Europe. The landlord, Baron Coburg, lived on a castle high on a hill. He was responsible for the well-being of many peasants who occupied the lands surrounding his castle. Each spring, as the snow began to melt and thoughts of other, less influential men turned to matters other than business, the Baron would decide how to provide for all his peasants during the coming year.

One spring, the Baron was thinking about the wheat crop of the coming growing season. "I believe that 30 acres of my land, being worth five bushels of wheat per acre, will produce enough wheat for next winter," he mused, "but who should do the farming? I believe I'll give Ivan and Frederick the responsibility of growing the wheat." Whereupon Ivan and Frederick were summoned for an audience with Baron Coburg.

"Ivan, you will farm the 20-acre plot of ground and Frederick will farm the 10-acre plot," the Baron began. "I will give Ivan 20 bushels of wheat for seed and 20 pounds of fertilizer. (Twenty pounds of fertilizer are worth two bushels of wheat.) Frederick will get 10 bushels of wheat for seed and 10 pounds of fertilizer. I will give each of you an ox to pull a plow, but you will have to make arrangements with Feyador the Plowmaker for a plow. The oxen, incidentally, are only three years old and have never been used for farming, so they should have a good 10 years of farming ahead of them. Take good care of them, because an ox is worth 40 bushels of wheat. Come back next fall and return the oxen and the plows along with your harvest."

Ivan and Frederick genuflected and withdrew from the Great Hall, taking with them the things provided by the Baron.

The summer came and went, and after the harvest Ivan and Frederick returned to the Great Hall to account to their master for the things given them in the spring. Ivan said, "My Lord, I present you with a slightly used ox, a plow, broken beyond repair, and 223 bushels of wheat. I, unfortunately, owe Feyador the Plowmaker, three bushels of wheat for the plow I got from him last spring. And, as you might expect, I used all the fertilizer and seed you gave me last spring. You will also remember, my Lord, that you took 20 bushels of my harvest for your own personal use."

Frederick spoke next. "Here, my Lord, is a partially used ox, the plow, for which I gave Feyador the Plowmaker 3 bushels of wheat from my harvest, and 105 bushels of wheat. I, too, used all my seed and fertilizer last spring. Also, my Lord, you took 30 bushels of wheat several days ago for your own table. I believe the plow is good for two more seasons."

"You did well," said the Baron. Blessed with this benediction the two peasants departed.

After they had taken their leave, the Baron began to contemplate what had happened. "Yes," he thought, "they did well, but I wonder which one did better?"

TERMINOLOGY GAME ACTIVITY

PURPOSE:

To enable you to practice your knowledge of what the new terms from Chapter 4 relating to corporate organizations mean.

DIRECTIONS:

1. You will be randomly assigned to one of four teams, by your professor.

2. One person from your team will be called on to answer a terminology question. **YOU CANNOT USE ANY NOTES OR BOOKS FOR THIS ACTIVITY!**

3. If the person from your team answers correctly, your team receives a point. If your teammate cannot answer correctly, a person from the next team is asked to respond.

4. This process continues until the question is correctly answered OR all four teams have attempted to answer and could not. Then the point is lost and the class discusses the term.

5. At the end of the question and answer period, the members of the team with the most points will receive a "reward", as specified by your professor.

THE BALANCE SHEET (CONTINUED):
ADDITIONAL FINANCING - BORROWING FROM OTHERS

"SMALL VICTORIES" ACTIVITY

PURPOSE:
To enable you to compare and contrast traditional and nontraditional ways of lending money.

DIRECTIONS:
Read the article "Small Victories".

REQUIRED:
Prepare written responses to the following questions, including actual quotes from the article where appropriate.

1. Is it possible that "conventional" banks view the decision to grant a loan as a routine decision whereas "unconventional" banks view it as a nonroutine decision?

2. To what extent can qualitative information (peer groups, personal character, etc.) be more helpful in answering "Will I be paid?" and "When will I be paid?" than quantitative information (credit history, cash flow, etc.)?

3. What is an audited cash flow statement? What information does it give to help answer "Will I be paid?" and "When will I be paid?"

4. Despite the success of South Shore Bank and WSEP, these loans still appear to be risky. While this is not reflected in their default rate, it is indirectly reflected in their higher administration costs. So overall, is it fair to say they are any more "successful" that traditional banks?

5. How is this higher administration cost passed on to the borrowers?

6. If this is such a profitable way to run a bank, why aren't there more banks like this? Could it be that this "unconventional" lending strategy is situation specific? Under what conditions might it be more or less successful?

7. South Shore Bank's loan losses increased as the recession grew. Is this an indication that their strategy leads to more fluctuations from year to year? If so, why?

8. In the long run, are the banks really aiding social progress by lending to individuals starting businesses with such an uncertain future?

SMALL VICTORIES
David Wessel

Two Unusual Lenders Show How 'Bad Risks' Can Be Good Business

Dorothy Wallace would seem a lender's nightmare. Separated from her husband, she is on welfare with her two teen-agers. She hasn't held a steady job since 1984. She says her credit rating is "ruined by accounts I messed up."

Vivian Wilson wouldn't rank high on the typical banker's list, either. She operates a guard service out of a windowless brick building across from a burned-out storefront on a desolate stretch of 71st Street. When she ran into cash-flow problems, she discovered that the bank where she had kept money for decades was unwilling to lend to someone with hardly any collateral to put up.

But Dorothy Wallace and Vivian Wilson are proving to be flawless borrowers now—thanks to two Chicago institutions that see good bets in gritty neighborhoods where others see hopeless cases. Ms. Wallace borrowed $800 from the Women's Self-Employment Project, founded in 1986 to assist low-income women interested in self-employment as a way out of poverty. It is funded primarily by contributions and loans from foundations and corporations. Ms. Wilson arranged a $250,000 line of credit from South Shore Bank, a bank determined to prove that profit and social progress are compatible.

Credit is the lifeblood of any economy, but in America's inner cities it has largely dried up. Many bankers tend to view inner-city residents as lousy credit risks. But WSEP and South Shore Bank show that's not necessarily true. By putting a new spin on the old-fashioned technique of relying on personal contact rather than impersonal credit evaluations, the two institutions manage to get paid back at enviable rates.

WSEP depends on four other low-income women in Ms. Wallace's "borrowing circle" to make sure she makes her loan payments on time. The gimmick seems to work. In three years of making loans of a few thousand dollars each to circles of low-income women without so much as a credit check—60 loans in all—WSEP hasn't had a single default.

The notion comes from Bangladesh, where the Grameen bank pioneered the use of peer pressure as a way to assure repayment of the small loans it makes to landless villagers, mostly women. Founded in 1983 by a visionary named Muhammed Yunus, the bank has hundreds of thousands of borrowers and a world-wide network of disciples. Although WSEP sticks most closely to the Grameen model, other foundation-backed experiments in "micro-enterprise" lending are under way—with mixed results—in a dozen or so pockets of poverty in the U.S., from a Sioux reservation in South Dakota to South Central Los Angeles.

South Shore Bank is more conventional. It specializes in loans many other bankers shun: loans to buy and renovate small apartment

buildings in a handful of rundown Chicago neighborhoods and loans to
novice minority entrepreneurs. The bank and its affiliates have
financed the rehabilitation of about 30% of the 25,000 apartments in
South Shore, helping to rescue a neighborhood that fell on hard times
about 25 years ago as middle-income whites fled and lower-income
blacks moved in.

Yet the bank has been consistently profitable, and its loan-loss
figures compare favorably with those of similar-sized banks. Last
year's losses were a respectable 0.67% of loans outstanding. It has
been stuck with just one piece of real estate in the past three years.

Part of its secret seems to be a willingness to make loans as much on
character as on collateral. In a market where many other bankers see
only trouble, South Shore has learned to discern the good risks and
also to keep close tabs on them after they borrow. "We spend a hell of
a lot more time . . . working with the borrower one-on-one," says
Richard Turner, senior vice president for lending.

Peddling Perfume

WSEP specializes in much smaller loans. Dorothy Wallace, for instance,
bought perfume with her $800 loan from WSEP. Like door-to-door
peddlers of old, she carries a shoulder bag full of cologne, lotion
and perfume that she sells to steady customers in downtown offices and
to strangers on the Chicago El.

Ms. Wallace began taking orders for the line of additive-free
fragrances two years ago as a way to supplement welfare checks, and
used her loan to buy inventory so she could offer instant delivery.
Since she began attending twice-a-month meetings of her WSEP borrowing
circle--a combination of consciousness-raising and business training--
she has begun to talk of opening an office and working her way off
welfare.

For now, though, she concentrates on making timely loan payments. She
owes $33.22 every other week, but pays $40 to cut interest on the one-
year loan. Ms. Wallace is almost as grateful for the moral support as
for the money, which helps explain why she and other women are so
diligent about making their payments. "They gave me a chance to start
all over again," she says.

No Defaults

As they listen, the four other women in her circle--dubbed "Too
Blessed" by its members--nod in unison. One sells jewelry that she
makes, and borrowed $600 for materials. A retired bank clerk sells
hand-sewn lingerie and linens; she borrowed $700 to buy a heavy-duty
sewing machine. A former Head Start aide, who borrowed $500, is
selling custom gift baskets and peddling fruit on street corners and
parks. A woman with four children of her own and four foster children
hopes to learn to read and to get a day-care license. All five women
live in Englewood, a neighborhood where every block has a boarded-up

building, and two inches of bullet-proof plastic separates workers from customers at Kentucky Fried Chicken.

The "Too Blessed" circle works like all the others that WSEP has established. The five members choose two to get the first loans. The first two borrowers have to be current for six weeks and all five members of the circle have to have attended three meetings in a row before the third is eligible. Peer pressure is supposed to assure timely repayment.

And it does. In the past three years, WSEP has lent about $60,000 to 60 women without a single default; the late payment rate is about 3%. By comparison, the American Bankers Association reports that the current delinquency rate is around 3.75% on bank personal loans and 3% on credit cards. "Peer support and peer pressure really serve as a good way to lower your risk," says Connie Evans, WSEP's director.

Beatrice Lynn Hardy, a budding graphic artist who borrowed $1,500 through another circle in the same neighborhood, recalls the time she bounced a $61.50 loan-payment check. Fearful that her misdeed would hurt another woman who was up for a loan, she frantically called the WSEP office and the would-be borrower to explain. This from a woman who describes her credit record with a silent "thumbs down."

Mixed Results

Results from other experiments with the peer-pressure technique are mixed. In rural Arkansas, a borrowing circle called the Good Faith Fund found it insufficient. In its first two years, the fund had a 40% default rate, and it has since moved away from the classic Grameen model. "Peer pressure isn't as significant as it might be in a place like Bangladesh," says Director Julia Vindasus. "But the peer support is really important. It's a very isolating thing running your own business."

But managers of the Lakota Fund on the Pine Ridge Indian Reservation in South Dakota, who initially shunned the peer-pressure approach, now embrace it. In 1987, Lakota made 68 individual loans. More than half the loan payments were late; 28% of the money was never paid back. So Lakota began forming borrowing circles in 1989. After $26,000 in loans to 13 circles, the default rate is running around 7%. "You don't lose many loans," says Director Elsie Meeks. "Someone always knows where the borrowers are."

Despite the obvious appeal of turning welfare moms into entrepreneurs, some people are skeptical that many poor women can escape poverty through self-employment. "If my sister was on welfare, would I tell her to start a business? No," says David Shryock, South Shore Bank's vice president for commercial lending. "Then why should I tell some poor black woman on
welfare to do it?"

Micro-enterprise funds, something of a fad in economic development circles, are also costly to run. In its circle fund and a separate, more conventional loan program, WSEP has lent a total of $200,000 to 200 women. But it spends more than it lends. Ms. Evans estimates that about $280,000 of its $700,000 a-year budget goes to running the two loan programs, and some of the rest goes for related overhead. In part, this is because WSEP is still experimenting, but it also reflects how costly it is to administer tiny loans.

A $1 Million Contract

That's where South Shore Bank has an edge. Its loans are far smaller than those big banks make, but at least they are in the tens or even hundreds of thousands of dollars. South Shore Bank is owned by foundations, churches and big corporations, the ultimate in patient capital, but it borrows and lends at a profit just like any other bank. Like WSEP, it makes loans to people who often can't get credit anywhere, but its borrowers are typically working- or middle-class.

Like Vivian Wilson. Her successful bid on a $1 million contract to provide security guards to the city of Chicago almost cost her the Star Security & Detective Agency Inc. that she inherited from her father. She hadn't realized how slowly the city paid its bills. After weeks of back and forth in the spring of 1988, the bank in which Ms. Wilson kept her accounts refused to make her a loan. To meet her payroll, she was dipping into her savings and was within two weeks of running out of cash.

She ended up at Mr. Shryock's desk as South Shore Bank. "That kind of receivable is hard to underwrite," he says today. "If there is a problem, you worry that the city will say it's not a valid receivable." The owners of bigger businesses put up personal assets in similar circumstances; Ms. Wilson hadn't much to pledge besides a small apartment building she owned.

But Mr. Shryock was impressed that Star Security had been around since 1923. And he was impressed by Ms. Wilson's daughter, a Chicago police officer who helps run the firm. "We had confidence she could make the city payment system work," he says. Within two weeks, he had arranged the $250,000 line of credit, secured in part by her apartment building. The bank keeps close tabs on Star's cash flow because all of Star's accounts are kept at South Shore, which gets copies of all its bills.

South Shore's Style

The loan illustrates South Shore's style. It didn't demand the collateral, detailed borrowing history or audited cash flow statements that bankers usually get from business borrowers. It found a way to limit its risk--in this instance by getting half the loan guaranteed by a fund established by a purchasing manager's group to help minority-owned business.

South Shore more often relies on the Small Business Administration for guarantees, but it rarely calls on government to make good on them. In three of the past five years, South Shore's loan losses (including losses on loans that were partially guaranteed by the government) were less than half the rate reported by similar-sized banks across the country. The recession took its toll in 1990 and 1991, though, hitting South Shore harder than banks that hadn't been as aggressive. Last year's 0.67% loan loss rate exceeded the 0.42% reported to the government by other small banks. Sour loans to three fast-food franchises and two auto dealers were to blame.

South Shore's lenders offer three explanations for their track record. They stick to neighborhoods and businesses they know, often relying on franchisers to provide borrowers with strategy and advice. They match the borrower to the deal, often steering an overly ambitious novice rehaber to a smaller building. And they are quick to pounce on borrowers who fall behind, and just as quick to locate buyers to get troubled borrowers off the hook. "Our motto is: Knock them down, but help them up," says James Bringley, vice president for real estate and installment lending. He boasts that the bank writes off only about 1/20 of 1% of its real-estate loans annually.

Both Mr. Shryock and Mr. Bringley deny that their bank serves as a behind-the-scenes partner, helping novices to run their businesses. "It's not like we can't do lending in this neighborhood until we teach these 'ignorant people' what to do." Mr. Bringley says.

But particularly in real estate, borrowers say the bank has helped teach them the business. When plumber Leroy Jones and his wife, Josephine, began renovating apartment buildings on the south side, they met twice a month with other landlords at breakfasts sponsored by South Shore. "The one thing I really learned that has really stuck with me is not to be a softie," Mrs. Jones says.

Today, the Jones own five buildings, all financed by South Shore. They say they notice how South Shore keeps close tabs on them. Their first building was purchased with a loan from another bank. "You know, I don't think they ever came by," Mrs. Jones says. "Mr. Bringley is always saying, 'I drive past your building. I see you put up a new tree.'"

MASCO "WARM UP" ACTIVITY

PURPOSE:
To enable you to discover where information about debt and equity is presented in financial statements and to begin to discern the relationships that exist between debt and equity in financing a business.

DIRECTIONS:
Using the MASCO Financial Statements answer the following questions. Work together as a team and utilize the team roles. The RECORDER should read the questions outloud and take team notes, the LEADER needs to make sure everyone is participating and understands the responses, the SPOKESPERSON needs to be ready and able to report the team answers to the class, and the MONITOR needs to decide on the best way to make sure everyone gets the information they need from the team worksheet.

REQUIRED:
EACH TEAM MEMBER needs to perform an active role in solving the questions and taking their own notes for class discussion.

1. Did long term debt increase or decrease?

2. Did common stock increase or decrease?

3. What's the par value of the common stock?   How did you find this out?

4. How much preferred stock has been

   Authorized?

   Issued?

   Outstanding?

5. What is the average sales price on the common stock?   How did you calculate this? $\frac{3250,000 + 64950,000}{3250,000 \text{ # of shares}} = \$21$

   P.A 140

6. Were any dividends PAID in 1991?   How much?

7. Were any dividends DECLARED in 1991?   How much?

A-70

MASCO DEBT & EQUITY ACTIVITY

PURPOSE:
To enable you to further discover the properties of debt and equity financing by comparing and contrasting debt and equity in the balance sheet from an annual report of MASCO Corporation.

DIRECTIONS:
Read through the balance sheet from the annual corporate report of MASCO.

REQUIRED:
Use the balance sheet to prepare written responses to the following questions. Note where you found the information that supports your answer.

1. Examine the liabilities and shareholders' equity section of the Masco Corporation Balance Sheet at December 31, 1990 and 1991. In your own words, briefly describe each category of liability and shareholders' equity listed.

2. Examine the balance sheet of Masco Corporation at December 31, 1990 and December 31, 1991. Does Masco obtain most of its external financing from debt or equity? How can you tell?

3. Examine the liability categories "Notes payable" (current liability) and "Long-term debt". From #1 above, it should be clear that these two categories represent borrowings from third parties. In your own words, explain what you think happened to borrowings from third parties <u>in total</u> during 1991.

4. Based on what appears in the shareholders' equity section of the balance sheet, describe in your own words what happened to affect shareholders' equity during 1991.

5. Read the Note to the Financial Statements on page 48 entitled "Long-Term Debt". How does this affect your answer to #3 above? Besides the Note, is there anywhere else in the financial statements to obtain more information on borrowing by the corporation?

6. Read the Note to the Financial Statements on page 49 entitled "Shareholders' Equity". How does this affect your answer in #4 above? Is there anywhere else in the financial statements to obtain some of this information?

7. Why do you think the company borrowed $425 million with bonds and used the money to repay bank borrowings?

8. Is there anything else in the long-term debt footnote that is of concern to you? Explain fully.

DARLING BICYCLES ACTIVITY

PURPOSE:
To enable you to use decision making skills, in order to compare and contrast debt investments and equity investments.

DIRECTIONS:
Read the case on Darlene Rafferman and make notes of the most important problems facing her bicycle business. As you read, contemplate what you think Darlene needs to do to "save" her business. List any alternatives Darlene could implement.

Now, YOU have an opportunity to put your money where your mouth is. Your Aunt Tillie, a distant relative, has passed away and left YOU $1,000,000 (after-tax, of course). After consuming a large portion of the $1,000,000, you have $100,000 remaining that you are interested in investing for your future.

Darlene is low on cash after the slow start by Darling Bicycles and, as a result, has asked you to make an "investment" in the bicycle business. Darlene has suggested that you either buy 40% of the business for the $100,000 or that you loan the money at 10% interest, with the interest payable once a year. In addition, Darlene suggests that the loan be repaid at the end of five years.

REQUIRED:
Prepare a ONE page response to the following questions. Be sure to take enough time to organize your thoughts before you begin writing so that your answers are well-organized and well-reasoned.

1) Determine the three key questions you, as a potential investor, are trying to answer in order to decide if you want to invest in Darlene's business.

2) What additional information do you want to get to assist you in deciding whether or not to invest in Darling Bicycles? What will the information do for you?

3) Analyze the two investment alternatives critically. Include in your analysis how each of the three questions from requirement #1 are answered under each alternative.

DARLING BICYCLES

Darlene Rafferman has been a biking enthusiast ever since she was in the second grade at Pershing Elementary. Now the mother of three teenagers, whom she is raising alone following the death of her husband, Darlene has decided to take some advice. Childhood chum Eloise MacMahon once said to Darlene: "Why don't you change your avocation into a vocation; open a bicycle shop!" Whether the advice was solid and valid we shall not judge here. Nevertheless, Darlene Rafferman followed it, and on April 11, she held her grand opening for **Darling Bicycles**--a partial incorporation of her own name into a description of her products.

The Darling shop was established in an old building in the center of downtown Clinton--quite frankly a commercially-depressed area ever since the rambling Clinton Hills Mall was erected on the south edge of town. In order to cater to the "whole biking family," Darling had bikes of every possible description, plus a complete array of scooters and tricycles. Her feature spot was to be the "rental island"-- bringing biking health to all of Clinton.

Darlene wanted to open with a few loose ends hanging rather than to wait and lose what she called "precious merchandising moments." One of those loose ends was the shop's repair service. Darlene had already contracted with Arthur Smrill to handle all repairs. Arthur was thorough--and that was good--but since his shop was located eleven miles away in Dorfman, there would be some delay in such service. For example, Darlene would have to truck repair bikes over to Smrill's location at the end of each work day. But it would be done right the first time, Darlene convinced herself. Arthur Smrill's arrangement would kick in on or after June 15.

To paint a more complete picture of the ambiance in which Darling Bicycles would be operating, there should be a socioeconomic sketch of Clinton. Close to downtown Clinton, especially to the north, there were most modest dwellings inhabited by less-than-affluent citizens. Just to the south of the decayed downtown square were several high-rise towers for the elderly, many of whom had their rent funded by government programs, while others were confined to wheelchairs or restricted to walkers. Far out on the southern fringes of the city were to be found the more expensive residential structures and the "exclusive neighborhoods." If there could be a "biking community" anywhere in the Clinton vicinity, it was way south. In fact, the official city biking trails had been established along that southern edge. Shop space for Darling Bicycles was available in the Clinton Hills Mall, but rental and ancillary fees were astronomical. Rent on the downtown location of Darling was very reasonable.

Based on what you have read so far, you can probably guess that sales at Darling Bicycles were low. Some days, nary a soul darkened the door of the shop. The wonderful word-of-mouth "advertising" that Darlene had counted on just never developed.

TOOLS OF THE TRADE PART II:
INCOME STATEMENT AND STATEMENT OF OWNERS' EQUITY

CAMPUS CALENDARS ACTIVITY

PURPOSE:
To enable you to identify and discuss the elements of REVENUES and EXPENSES, and to construct a single step income statement and Statement of Owner' Equity.

DIRECTIONS:
Read the Campus Calendars Reading, underlining important points and making notes of any additional questions you have.

REQUIRED:
1. Prepare a single step income statement for Campus Calendars.

2. Explain to Molly what REVENUES are and show her which deposits she made fit your explanation.

3. Explain to Molly what EXPENSES are and show her which checks she wrote fit your explanation.

4. Prepare a statement of capital for Campus Calendars.

CAMPUS CALENDARS READING

Some enterprising students at a local college campus have started a business of making and selling a calendar which uses "local" campus talent (all the gorgeous students) to pose for each month of the calendar. The first printing was a sell out in less than a month and new orders are coming in from other colleges. The founder of Campus Calendars (CC), Molly Brown, has asked you to help her figure out if Campus Calendars is making any profits.

She wasn't sure exactly what you would need, so she made a list summarizing all the activity in the business checkbook. (Molly's older sister had advised her to open a separate checking account for CC, which Molly did on 9/8/93.)

SUMMARY OF CAMPUS CALENDAR CHECKING ACCOUNT**

Checks Written		Deposits Made	
Film	15.00	from Molly	250.00
Printing	500.00	Loan from Parents	500.00
Development (film)	20.00	Calendar sales	1000.00
Camera rental	25.00	TOTAL	$1750.00
Talent payments	250.00 10 ppl		
to Molly	50.00		
Pizza, etc.	140.00		
Repay parents	500.00		
TOTAL	$1500.00		

**NOTE: Molly rounds her checks up, so the actual balance on her account is $256.43.

You also made the following notes from your first conversation with Molly:

o   The Copy Shop agreed to print the color calendars for $5.00 each, based on minimum orders of 100 calendars per printing.

o   The students who posed for the calendar and the student photographer agreed to payments of $25.00 each for the first edition of the calendar.

o   Molly bought pizza and sodas for the "crew" after some of the photo sessions and planning meetings, which totals to $140.00.

o   When the first printing was a sell out in less than a week, Molly wanted to pay back her parents and show them how profitable the business is.

o   Molly had deposited all of her savings in the business when she opened the checking account in September. Her car broke down in October and she had to use $50 from the business to get it fixed.

PROVIDING ASSISTANCE TO CAMPUS CALENDARS

PURPOSE:

To enable you to construct a multi-step income statement, identify and discuss terminology and classifications on the income statement, and practice using accounting information to make better decisions.

DIRECTIONS:

Read the Campus Calendars Reading, underlining important points and making notes of any additional questions you have.

REQUIRED:

1. Prepare a multi step income statement for Campus Calendars.

2. Explain to Molly
    her Cost of Goods Sold;
    her Gross Margin;
    her Net Profit.

3. Explain to Molly how you recorded the payment she made to herself and why.

4. Explain to Molly how you recorded the payment to her parents and why.

5. Using the multi step income statement, provide Molly with a list of ideas, questions or problems that you have concerning Campus Calendars.

MASCO CORPORATION: CHANGES IN SHAREHOLDERS' EQUITY ACTIVITY

PURPOSE:

To enable you to read and interpret the information presented in the shareholders' equity section of the balance sheet.

DIRECTIONS:

Read the shareholders' equity section of the balance sheet and the related notes for MASCO Corporation., for the years ended December 31, 1989, 1990, and 1991.

A friend of yours bought stock in MASCO and received a balance sheet and the related note entitled "Shareholders' Equity" from the company. He doesn't understand the statements, and has come to you for help, since you are taking a course in accounting.

REQUIRED:

1. Briefly describe for your friend the purpose of the shareholders' equity section of the lance sheet and the related note (WHAT they are and WHY they give the user important information.)

2. Describe for your friend the changes that have occurred in the following accounts during the last two years (1990 & 1991):

   Common Shares

   Paid-In Capital

   Retained Earnings

3. Your friend also wants you to explain the company's "track record" in paying dividends. He wants to know how MASCO can pay more dividends than they made in net income for 1991.

REMEMBER: Your friend is intelligent, but knows nothing about accounting. Make sure your answers reflect this.

KEEPING SCORE: BASES OF ECONOMIC MEASUREMENT

CASH VERSUS ACCRUAL SCORE KEEPING ACTIVITY

PURPOSE:
To enable you to compare and contrast the CASH and ACCRUAL methods of accounting for business transactions.

DIRECTIONS:
Based on your knowledge and comprehension of CASH and ACCRUAL accounting from Chapter 7 and from class discussions, ponder the following questions. Make notes of your responses in the space provided.

	CASH	ACCRUAL

1. What **measurement criteria** does each basis use? *cash* — *when a legally enforceable claim to cash has been established btn the parties involved in the transaction*

2. When is an **expense recognized**? *when its paid in cash* — *when the benefit from the expense is received*

3. When is a **revenue recognized**? *when its received in cash* — *when it is deemed to be earned - when they have a legally enforceable claim to cash associated with that revenue*

4. What is its biggest **strength**? *Simpler keeps eye on cash* — *attempt to show relationship btn expenses and the revenues they help generate*

5. What is its biggest **weakness**? *doesnt recognize expenses created in same period as the revenues they generated* — *takes eye off cash*

6. Under each basis, what can cause a difference between **reality** and **measurement of reality**? *poor prediction of future profitability*

REQUIRED:
1. After completing your individual responses to the six questions, compare and contrast your answers with those of your fellow team members.

2. Develop a chart or grid to present to the class which clearly and concisely explains the differences, strengths and weaknesses of the two bases of accounting.

PROGRESSIVE BALANCE SHEET - CASH BASIS ACTIVITY

PURPOSE:
To enable you to use accounting information in order to diagnose what effect an economic transaction has on the accounting equation and to comprehend what took place in the business .

DIRECTIONS:
Below are four progressive balance sheets, each prepared immediately after some economic event. The cash basis of accounting has been used to account for all of these economic events. Because only the balance sheets are presented, any revenue or expense item will be reflected in *Retained Earnings*.

REQUIRED:
In the space provided below each of the balance sheets, explain what happened to the accounting equation (ie, Assets increased and Liabilities increased) and explain the nature of the economic event reflected in the cash basis balance sheet.

Balance Sheet #1

```
ASSETS:                        LIABILITIES & OWNER'S EQUITY:
Cash              $15,000      Liabilities          $   -0-
                               Owner's Equity
                               Contributed Capital    15,000
                               Total Liabilities and
Total Assets      $15,000      Owners' Equity       $15,000
```

Balance Sheet #2

```
ASSETS:                        LIABILITIES & OWNER'S EQUITY:
Cash              $25,000      Liabilities      $10,000
                               Owner's Equity
                               Contributed Capital 15,000
                               Total Liabilities
Total Assets      $25,000       & Owners' Equity $25,000
```

Balance Sheet #3

ASSETS:		LIABILITIES & OWNER'S EQUITY:	
Cash	$13,000	Liabilities	$10,000
		Owner's Equity	
		Contributed Capital	15,000
		Retained Earnings	(12,000)
		Total Liabilities and	
Total Assets	$13,000	Owners' Equity	$13,000

paid dividend → can't do so unless w have income

net loss of $12000

cash goes ↓ and OE goes ↓

maybe paid the own some $ back, but its not considered a return of share of of the earnings, rather its a return of capital

---

Balance Sheet #4

ASSETS:		LIABILITIES & OWNER'S EQUITY:	
Cash	$33,000	Liabilities	$10,000
		Owner's Equity	
		Contributed Capital	15,000
		Retained Earnings	8,000
		Total Liabilities	
Total Assets	$33,000	& Owners' Equity	$33,000

net increase of $20,000. Have received this as income from sales or other revenue.

cash goes ↑ and OE goes ↑

PROGRESSIVE BALANCE SHEET - ACCRUAL BASIS ACTIVITY

PURPOSE:
To enable you to use accounting information in order to diagnose what effect an economic transaction has on the accounting equation and to comprehend what took place in the business .

DIRECTIONS:
Below are four progressive balance sheets, each prepared immediately after some economic event. The accrual basis of accounting has been used to account for all of these economic events. Because only the balance sheets are presented, any revenue or expense item will be reflected in *Retained Earnings*.

REQUIRED:
In the space provided below each of the balance sheets, explain what happened to the accounting equation (ie, Assets increased and Liabilities increased) and explain the nature of the economic event reflected in the accrual basis balance sheet.

Balance Sheet #1

```
ASSETS:                          LIABILITIES & OWNER'S EQUITY:
Cash                   $21,000   Liabilities      $43,500
Accounts receivable     41,000
Inventory               21,000   Owner's Equity
Buildings & equip.     127,000   Common Stock      10,000
                                 Retained earnings 119,500
Accum. depr.          (37,000)   Total Liabilities and
Total Assets          $173,000   Owners' Equity $173,000
```

Balance Sheet #2

```
ASSETS:                          LIABILITIES & OWNER'S EQUITY:
Cash                   $39,000   Liabilities      $43,500
Prepaid insurance        6,000
Accounts receivable     17,000
Inventory               21,000   Owner's Equity
Buildings & equip.     127,000   Common Stock      10,000
                                 Retained earnings 119,500
Accum. depr.          (37,000)   Total Liabilities and
Total Assets          $173,000   Owners' Equity  $173,000
```

-$24↑ A/R
$18 cash ↑
$6 Prepaid Ins ↑

A-83

Balance Sheet #3

ASSETS:		LIABILITIES & OWNER'S EQUITY:	
Cash	$46,500	Liabilities $33,500	
Prepaid insurance	6,000	Deferred revenue 17,500	
Accounts receivable	17,000		
Inventory	21,000	Owner's Equity	
Buildings & equip.	127,000	Common Stock 10,000	
		Retained earnings 119,500	
Accum. depr.	(37,000)	Total Liabilities and	
Total Assets	$180,500	Owners' Equity $180,500	

Cash $7,500 ↑ } split deferred revenue btn cash + liab.   A and OE ↓

liab $10,000 ↓

deferred revenue $17,500↑

Balance Sheet #4

ASSETS:		LIABILITIES & OWNER'S EQUITY:	
Cash	$46,500	Liabilities $33,500	
Prepaid insurance	5,000	Deferred revenue 13,500	
Accounts receivable	17,000	Rent Payable 1,200	
Inventory	21,000	Owner's Equity	
Buildings & equip.	127,000	Common Stock 10,000	
		Retained earnings 119,600	
Accum. depr.	(38,700)	Total Liabilities and	
Total Assets	$177,800	Owners' Equity $177,800	

Ins $1,000 ↓   Assets + OE ↓

Deferred revenue $4,000 ↓ — have done this much working sevices

rent Payable $1,200↑

Accum. depr $1,700↑ (900,400)

retained earnings $100↑

revenue ($4000)
- expenses (rent, ins, dep $3,900)
= retained earning ($100)

A-84

CHALLENGING ISSUES UNDER ACCRUAL ACCOUNTING: LONG-LIVED ASSETS-A CLOSER LOOK

"RISE IN CAPITAL OUTLAY IS PROJECTED AT 8%" ACTIVITY

PURPOSE:
To enable you to comprehend the relationship between long-lived assets and economic production.

DIRECTIONS:
Read the article "Rise in Capital Outlay is Projected at 8%" and make notes as you read.

REQUIRED:
Prepare answers to the following questions and be ready to present your answers. (HINT: you may want to include specific quotes from the article or references from Chapter 8.)

1. What is "capital outlay"?

2. Why is "increased spending on factories and equipment" related to "strongerdemand from customers"?

3. What effect will Whirpool's new factory have on Tulsa's economy?

4. What effect will the new factory have on Whirlpool's **balance sheet?** income **statement?**

5. A friend of yours has read this article and says "I don't get it. Why would Coca Cola want to spend so much money? I thought it was in business to make money?" How would you respond?

6. "Spending on factories and equipment is expected to advance (increase) 9.8% this year...". Where would a user of financial statements expect to find evidence of this increase on the statements?

7. How could a company's choice of depreciation method affect the **balance sheet? income statement?**

RISE IN CAPITAL OUTLAY IS PROJECTED AT 8% FOR '94
By Bloomberg Business News

WASHINGTON, April 7 -- Businesses plan to increase spending on their factories and equipment by 8 percent this year, the largest gain in five years, as they scramble to meet stronger demand from consumers, the Commerce Department reported today.

The increase, to $633 billion, shows that "the economy is still on a strong footing," said Astrid Adolfson, an economist at MCM Money Watch in New York. "We haven't had any effect from the higher interest rates."

As if to back up the report on capital spending, the Whirlpool Corporation announced plans to spend more than $100 million to build an appliance factory in Tulsa, Okla. Construction is to begin this summer.

The capital-investment figures follow previous Government estimates of a 5.4 percent gain in such spending this year, before adjustments for inflation. In 1993, spending on factories and equipment advanced 7.1 percent.

In a separate report, the Labor Department said today that the number of Americans entering unemployment lines for the first time increased last week--the first gain since the beginning of March.

Initial jobless claims rose a larger-than-expected 6,000 last week, to 337,000, though analysts said the increase did not mean that the economy was weakening. Last Friday, the Government said the economy added 456,000 jobs in March, a figure that surprised the bond market, sending interest rates surging on fear of too-rapid growth.

Greenspan Perplexed

Consumers, though, remain worried about the economy "despite what is obviously solid evidence of economic strength," said Alan Greenspan, the Federal Reserve Board's chairman, in a speech in San Francisco today.

Perhaps reflecting this unsettled mood, consumer borrowing rose in February at about half the pace expected by analysts, according to new Fed figures. Installment credit rose by $3.54 billion in February, the ninth straight increase, after rising $6.38 billion in January.

The Commerce Department's report on capital spending showed that the industries with the largest planned increases included steel works and blast furnaces; stone, glass, and clay producers, and auto and truck makers.

The Roanoke Electric Steel Corporation in Virginia is planning to spend $10 million over the next two years to install a ladle furnace to meet demand. "We can hardly keep up," said Thomas Crawford, the company's assistant vice president and secretary. "We're producing a lot of steel, and it doesn't seem to be enough."

Coca-Cola intends to increase spending by 50 percent, or $400 million, this year, with 75 percent of the money going toward international expansion. Other American businesses are spending more on their international operations,too. On Wednesday, the Commerce Department said foreign affiliates of United States companies planned to raise spending on factories and equipment by 8 percent this year, the biggest gain since 1990.

Interest in U.S. Neighbors

Of the $5.3 billion increase in spending this year, about half the gain is headed for Canada and Mexico after approval last year of the North American Free Trade Agreement.

In transportation, the Burlington Northern Railroad recently announced plans to buy 1,000 more jumbo covered hoppers for its fleet of grain-hauling freight cars.

But aircraft makers plan to trim spending on factories and equipment, reflecting military cutbacks and the financial trouble of airlines.

The Commerce Department's capital-spending statistics, which are revised quarterly, are based on a survey of several thousand businesses.

Adjusted for inflation, spending on factories and equipment is expected to advance 9.8 percent this year after rising 8.6 percent in 1993.

Recent gains may be slower, and higher interest rates could hurt the pace of capital spending in 1995 and 1996. Such spending usually trails off after other parts of the economy have slowed. Analysts said higher rates would restrain housing activity first.

The Federal Reserve has pushed up short-term interest rates twice this year in an effort to prevent twice this year in an effort to prevent inflation from accelerating. Long-term rates rose as an unintended consequence in the process.

Still, Commerce Secretary Ronald H. Brown said the planned increase in capital spending showed that "investment is not being choked off by the recent run-up in long-term rates."

ACCOUNTING ELEMENTS ACTIVITY

PURPOSE:
To enable you to think about (analyze) each accounting element and then create (synthesize) a way to communicate how each element relates to the accounting equation.

DIRECTIONS:
Using your notes and your textbook, make notes of definitions and examples of each accounting element listed below:

1. Assets (Chap. 4) 174 *probable benefits controlled by an entity as a result of previous transactions or events -what a company has*

2. Liabilities (Chap. 4) *The probable future sacrifices of assets arising from present obligations of an entity as a result of past transactions or events -what a company owes*

3. Equity (Chap. 4) 176 *The residual interest in the assets of an entity that remains after deducting liabilities*

4. Revenues (Chap.6) 282 *Represents the inflows of assets as a result of an entity's ongoing major or central operations. The rewards of doing business*

5. Expenses (Chap.6) 181 *Represents the outflow of assets resulting from an entity's ongoing major or central operations. The sacrifices required to attain the rewards of doing bus.*

6. Gains (Chap.8) 392 *Net inflows resulting from peripheral activities of a company.* *EX: Sale of an asset for more than it's book value*

7. Losses (Chap.8) *Net outflows resulting from peripheral activities of a company.* *EX: Sale of an asset for less than its book value*

REQUIRED:

1. Compare and contrast your individual responses with your team members. Come to a consensus for a good explanation of each element.
   2 examples

2. Create a way to visually communicate the articulation (relationships) among and between the various elements. In addition, you can provide written and verbal communication. (You may want to think about making a model, a formula, a chart, an analogy.)

3. Be prepared to present your project to the class.

CHALLENGING ISSUES UNDER ACCRUAL ACCOUNTING: MERCHANDISE INVENTORY AND COST OF GOODS SOLD

"SATURN RETURNS TO FULL OUTPUT OF CARS" ACTIVITY

PURPOSE:
To enable you to comprehend some of the related issues which decision makers must consider concerning inventories, profits and the financial condition of the business.

DIRECTIONS:
Read the article "Saturn Returns to Full Output of Cars" and make notes as you read about each of the phrases listed below.

1. "the tiny auto maker created...to pioneer manufacturing and sales techniques..."

2. "to seek backing from GM for an additional assembly plant in hopes of bolstering profits". (Explain why an additional plant (costs) could bolster profits (revenues).

3. "The industry considers a supply of 50 to 60 days sufficient."

4. ..."sales are lagging because design has grown stale"...

5. "Such incentives would work against Saturn's goal of making a profit."

6. "...that goal (300,000 cars)...is still less than the plant capacity of more than 320,000".

7. ..."how to insure strong profits".

REQUIRED:

1. Discuss your notes explanations and interpretations of the above phrases with your team members.

2. Prepare an individual one page analysis of two or three strengths (positive outcomes) and weaknesses(problems)of Saturn's decision to return to its full output of cars. Then **conclude** with whether or not you agree or disagree with Saturn's plan and why.

Make sure you <u>explain</u> the rationale behind your evaluations of positive outcomes and problems. DO NOT ASSUME the reader of your analysis <u>knows</u> the challenging issues under accrual accounting as they relate to inventories. You would be wise to outline your analysis before you write a draft, as one page will require you to be very clear and concise.

SATURN RETURNS TO FULL OUTPUT OF CARS
By JAMES BENNET
Special to the New York Times

A GM Unit tries to show it can sell all it builds.

DETROIT, April 25 -- The Saturn Corporation, the tiny auto maker created by the General Motors Corporation to pioneer manufacturing and sales techniques, said today that it had return to its prior production level of small cars after its sales rose with the industrywide boom.

The move clearly puts Saturn in a stronger position as it prepares to seek backing from G.M. for an additional assembly plant in hopes of bolstering its profits. Saturn officials have to demonstrate that they can sell everything they can now build before asking for more production capacity.

Saturn cut production a month ago by 29 percent, because unsold cars were piling up on dealers' lots. Last fall, to reach its goal of posting a profit for 1993, Saturn slashed its advertising after it added a new, third crew of workers to raise production at its assembly plant in Spring Hill, Tenn. Partly as a result, dealer inventories soared in January above a 100-day supply.

But a combination of factors including a renewed advertising effort, the production cut, an inexpensive lease deal and a booming auto market, have lowered Saturn inventories to 66 days' supply as of today, Greg Martin, a Saturn spokesman, said.

At the end of March, the average dealer inventory for all cars built in North America was 58 days, according to Ward's Automotive Reports. "Days' supply" expresses the relationship between the number of cars dealers have in stock and the rate at which they have been selling. The industry considers a supply of 50 to 70 days sufficient.

In March, Saturn sales climbed 6 percent in the United States, compared with 19.2 percent for the industry in general. For the first quarter, Saturn sales improved 4.2 percent, compared with 15.3 percent for the industry.

Industry analysts have said that Saturn sales are lagging because the design has grown stale and the cars lack equipment, like passenger-side air bags, found in some competitors.

Indeed, some analysts were surprised that Saturn had resumed full production. "I wonder about that decision to bring back production, because sales and production were pretty well balanced in March," said David Healy, auto industry analyst for S. G. Warburg in New York City. Saturn produced 24,766 cars in March and sold 22,136 of them, he said.

"I wouldn't be surprised if inventories started creeping up again, unless they have some tricks up their sleeves as far as sales are

concerned," Mr. Healy said. Saturn has no plans to offer special
incentives, Mr. Martin said. Such incentives would work against
Saturn's goal of making a profit again this year.

Big Gain in Leasing

Saturn customers are increasingly choosing to lease, Mr. Martin said.
From 4 percent of retail transactions last year, leases rose to 14
percent in the first quarter, he said. In addition, Saturn is trying
to increase the number of sales showrooms, which would help to
disperse the increased production. Saturn hopes to raise the number of
dealers to at least 340, from 285, an increase of 19 percent.

As of today, the Spring Hill plant resumed operating 20 hours a day, 6
days a week. At that rate, the factory produces 1,133 cars daily,
compared with 800 during the cutback, said Bill Betts, a Saturn
spokesman.

With the restored production, Saturn hopes to sell 300,000 cars this
year, Mr. Betts said. While that goal would surpass last year's sale
of 229,356, is still less than the plant's capacity of more than
320,000.

As a result, Saturn's long-term problem--how to insure strong profits-
-remains unsolved. Saturn officials have been preparing to present a
case to G.M. for a second factory. But the presentation has been
repeatedly delayed, and officials have said they need to demonstrate
that they can sell every car they can build at Spring Hill before
asking for more capacity.

MASCO CORPORATION: THE EFFECT OF LIFO/FIFO ACTIVITY

PURPOSE:
To enable you to compare and contrast the effects of choosing different methods of accounting for inventory costs, in the context of an actual corporation.

DIRECTIONS:
Read the balance sheet, income statement and related notes concerning inventories for MASCO Corporation.

REQUIRED:
1. Knowing that the US was in a period of inflation (rising prices) during the last few years, what would have been the effect (increase or decrease) on the two amounts below if MASCO had chosen a **LIFO** method of inventory instead of a **FIFO**?

   a. Net Income_____

   Why?

   b. Value of the Inventory_____

   Why?

2. Which method would best fit each requirement listed below?

   a. To provide the user with an accurate estimate of the most recent purchase prices recorded as part of the assets of the company.

   b. To provide the user with an accurate estimate of the most recent purchase prices recorded as the cost of selling the product.

3. In you opinion, which method is better for the shareholders? Explain why.

TOOLS OF THE TRADE PART III: THE STATEMENT OF CASH FLOWS: BRINGING THE FOCUS BACK TO CASH

"EARNINGS SCHMERNINGS...LOOK AT CASH" ACTIVITY

PURPOSE:
To enable you to compare and contrast the kinds of accounting information provided by the financial statements.

DIRECTIONS:
Read the article entitled Earnings Schmernings - Look at the Cash by Jeffrey M. Laderman.

REQUIRED:

1. Answer each question below. **Your answers should be typewritten, double-spaced, and no more than one page in length.** REMEMBER, THIS IS A MAXIMUM LENGTH, NOT A MINIMUM. YOUR ANSWERS MAY BE SHORTER.

Questions:

a.. When evaluating a potential investment, which do **YOU** think is more important, cash flow or earnings? Support your position.

b. Why do you think for most investors "... net income will remain the handiest snapshot of a company"?

EARNINGS, SCHMERNINGS--LOOK AT THE CASH
Jeffrey M. Laderman

In coming weeks, Wall Streeters will be glued to their video terminals as companies terminals as companies start to report second-quarter earnings. It's a tense time, especially for securities analysts who pride themselves on the ability to forecast profits. But some savvy investors say the singular focus on net income is foolhardy. The bottom line isn't an end in itself but just the beginning of the more difficult, and more rewarding process of tracking a company's cash flow.

Looking past earnings to invest in companies for their cash flow isn't new, but it's finding new popularity. It represents a return to one of the most basic rules in economics: The value of an investment is derived from cash flow. More than anything else, it's the boom in takeovers and leveraged buyouts that has turned investor attention toward cash flow. And scrutinizing it is more feasible now that accountants require public companies to publish more of the statistical building blocks. Some big companies are going further, talking up cash flow in their annual reports or asking Wall Street to look beyond their meager earnings and marvel at their bounteous streams of green.

The problem with cash flow is that not all investors see it quite the same way. Cash flow, in its simplest form, is net income plus items such as depreciation--bookkeeping charges that have cut into net income even though they don't take any cash out of the corporate coffers. Simple cash flow isn't a particularly useful figure by itself--it's just an accountant's way station (box).

Free ride. Takeover artists and LBO operators hunt for "operating cash flow." That's the money generated by the company before the cost of financing and taxes come into play. LBO specialists will take on as much debt as their operating cash flow (OCF) can support--just as home buyers may borrow as much as a lender will approve for their level of income. When the OCF is dedicated to debt payments, there isn't anything left over for taxes. But that's all right. Since there's no profit to declare, there won't be taxes to pay.

[Begin boxed material]

Cash flow? What do you mean by that?

CASH FLOW = NET INCOME + DEPRECIATION + DEPLETION + AMORTIZATION

Net income. It's the bottom line but just the starting point when figuring out a company's cash flow

Depreciation. An accounting charge that writes down the cost of an asset, such as a factory or a machine tool, over its useful life. This charge is made for shareholder and tax reporting, but it does not require cash outlays.

Depletion. When the asset being used is a natural resource, such as oil, gas, coal, or minerals, the write-off is called depletion.

Amortization. A write-down of limited term or intangible assets is called amortization. Acquisitive companies often have an entry on the books called goodwill, the difference between what they paid for a company and the lower book value. Goodwill is amortized over a long period, usually 40 years, and requires no cash outlay.

OPERATING CASH FLOW = CASH FLOW + INTEREST EXPENSE + INCOME EXPENSE

Interest Expense. Add back the interest expense to get the broadest measure of cash flow. If you're a raider, you'll reorder the whole debt scene anyway.

Income Tax Expense. Add back the taxes because they won't have to be paid after a new owner adds so much debt that there is no book profit and hence no tax due.

FREE CASH FLOW = CASH FLOW - CAPITAL EXPENDITURES - DIVIDENDS

Capital Expenditures. Subtract only the capital expenditures necessary to maintain plant and equipment and keep the company competitive but not optional ones such as costly new headquarters.

Dividends. If the company deems the dividend sacrosanct, deduct it here. But if a major recapitalization is underway, the dividend will probably be scratched anyway and need not be deducted.

[End boxed material]

You don't have to be a raider to like OCF. In recent years, investing in companies based on their price-to-OCF multiples has been one of the best strategies around, says Robert C. Jones, and analyst at Goldman, Sachs, & Co. In 1988, a portfolio comprised of the stocks that were cheapest in OCF terms would have gained about 30.5%--nearly double the return of the Standard & Poor's 500-stock index. For the first half of 1989, OCF stocks again beat the market, though only by one percentage point.

While OCF is the broadest measure of a company's funds, some prefer to zero in on the narrower "free cash flow." That measures truly discretionary funds--company money that an owner could pocket without harming the business. Companies with free cash flow, and not all public companies have any, are golden. They can use it to boost dividends, buy back shares, or pay down debt. And businesses that look pricey based on earnings may be bargains when measured by the yardstick of free cash flow (table).

"I will not invest in a company that has no free cash flow," says Kenneth S. Hackel, whose Systematic Financial Management, Inc. picks stocks for their cash-flow characteristics. That choice immediately cuts out many hot-growth companies that consume more cash than they generate and thus depend on external financing. The constraint hasn't cost Hackel much in performance. Since 1980, his portfolio has recorded annual average returns of more than 20%. It was up 29% in 1988 and 17% in the first half of 1989.

Consumer loyalty. A few industries, including real estate and energy, have long been viewed through a cash-flow prism. In real estate, depreciation usually wipes out "profits"--event though the property is actually appreciating. For oil and gas, depletion knocks the wind out of earnings. But increasingly, the cash-flow standard is applied to companies with valuable "franchises" in their markets. Tobacco, food, and media companies are among those where tangible assets matter a lot less than the consumer loyalty they command.

That's what Time Inc. Chairman J. Richard Munro told shareholders at the recent annual meeting: "When it comes to valuing media and entertainment companies like ours, what matters is not profits but cash flow." Munro had good reason for his conversion to the cult of cash flow. If Time succeeds in its bid to acquire Warner Communications Inc. for $70 a share, earnings will disappear for several years to come. Likewise, executives at Paramount Communications Inc. have asked Wall Street to look at it as a company driven by cash flow, rather than by earnings. If Paramount prevails in its quest to buy Time for $200 a share, its profits will vanish.

Are the media moguls trying to deflect investor concern that earnings are going to the dogs? Not really. "Reported earnings are a complete fiction," says Robert L. Wiley III, who follows media companies for brokers Furman Selz Mager Dietz & Birney Inc. "Earnings have nothing to do with what cash flows the company has available to it." In fact, Wiley argues that either deal involving Time would allow ample cash to service debt immediately and would generate enough free cash flow to start paying down the principal by 1991.

The best reason for judging a "franchise" company by its cash flow is that it usually has a lot of goodwill on the balance sheet. That's the difference between what the business paid for an acquisition and the target's lower book value. Accounting rules make companies amortize the goodwill, which reduces reported profit. And since the write-off is not tax deductible, there's no tax savings. Even though the write-off may be spread over as many as 40 years, the impact on reported profits can be substantial. Wiley estimates that annual goodwill write-offs for Paramount could be as much as $257 million, or $2.20 per share, and $313 million, or $5.53 per share, for Time.

The case for cash flow doesn't mean that profits are pass,. For most investors, net income will remain the handiest snapshot of a company. Even so, following the cash as it flows though a company, says Stuart Crane, an analyst with Gruntal & Co., "gives you insight into the quality of earnings." Indeed, if profits are soaring, but the cash flow isn't, a company's good fortunes may prove to be short-lived.

Where Cash Flow Tells a Different Story

Based on the widely-used yardstick of price-earnings ratios, all of these stocks appear pricey. Each has a p-e of at least 19, vs. 13.7 for the Standard & Poor's industrials. For free cash flow, the average multiple is 25.5; on that basis, all these companies look cheap.

Company	Price-earnings ratio	Price-free cash flow ratio
BELO (A.H.)	60.7	16.3
BOWNE	24.5	17.3
CAMPBELL SOUP	23.5	19.6
CORDIS	33.9	8.7
GENERAL SIGNAL	44.5	11.1
HALLIBURTON	47.5	9.2
HUFFY	26.1	18.8
ITEL	38.1	16.6
KNIGHT-RIDDER	20.9	18.6
LOTUS DEVELOPMENT	23.4	13.9
MEREDITH	21.0	10.0
MULTIMEDIA	39.6	14.4
NETWORK SYSTEMS	23.9	15.9
OCCIDENTAL PETROLEUM	25.9	10.8
SANTA FE SOUTHERN PACIFIC	29.3	9.7
TGE FRIDAY'S	20.7	12.1
UNITED ASSET MANAGEMENT	21.2	11.9
VOLT INFORMATION SCIENCES	49.3	9.3
WEINGARTEN REALTY TRUST	25.8	12.4
WILEY (JOHN) & SONS	60.0	12.1

DATA: SYSTEMATIC FINANCIAL MANAGEMENT INC.

USING ACCOUNTING INFORMATION ACTIVITY

PURPOSE:
To provide you with an opportunity to practice and use the skills necessary to read and interpret the "Tools".

DIRECTIONS:
Read the article by Jane Bryant Quinn entitled <u>How to Read an Annual Report</u>. Then read the financial statements and reports from MASCO.

REQUIRED:

1.. Look at MASCO's statements. Under each category listed below, what is MASCO's MAIN account and its dollar amount from the four "tools" (the financial statements). From which "tool" did you find each item?

F/S CATEGORY	ITEM	$ AMOUNT	WHICH "TOOL"?
current asset			
other assets			
current liab.			
long-term liab.			
s/h equity			
revenues			
operating expenses			
other expenses			
cash from operations			
cash from investing			
cash from financing			

2. What are the four "tools"? Describe <u>in your own words</u> what kind of knowledge and data you can get from each specific tool.

3. If you only had a (balance sheet, income statement or statement of cash flows), what information from each statement could you find out about the company using ONLY that tool? What would you still want to know that you would NOT be able to get from that tool?

A-101

HOW TO READ AN ANNUAL REPORT
By Jane Bryant Quinn

International Paper asked Jane Bryant Quinn, business commentator for the CBS-TV Morning News, columnist for Newsweek, and author of Everyone's Money Book, to tell how anyone can understand and profit from a company's annual report.

To some business people I know, curling up with a good annual report s almost more exciting than getting lost in John le Carre's latest spy thriller.

But to you it might be another story. "Who needs that?" I can hear you ask. You do_if you're going to gamble any of our future *working* for a company, *investing* in it, or *selling* to it.

Why should you bother?
Say you got a job interview at Galactic Industries. Well, what does the company do? Does its future look good? Or will the next recession leave your part of the business on the beach?

Or say you're thinking of investing your own hard-earned money in its stock. Sales are up. But are its profits getting better or worse?

Or say you're going to supply it with a lot of parts. Should you extend Galactic plenty of credit or keep it on a short leash?

How to get one
You'll find answers in its annual report. Where do you find *that?* Your library should have the annual reports of nearby companies plus leading national ones. It also has listings of companies' financial officers and their addresses so you can write for annual reports.

So now Galactic Industries latest annual report is sitting in front of you ready to be cracked. How do you crack it?

Where do we start? *Not* at the front. At the *back!* We don't want to be surprised at the end of this story.

Start at the back
First, turn back to the report of the *certified public accountant*. This third-party auditor will tell you right off the bat if Galactic's report conforms with "generally accepted accounting principles."

Watch out for the words "subject to." They mean the financial report is clean *only* if you take the company's word about a particular piece of business, and the accountant isn't sure you should. Doubts like this are usually settled behind closed doors. When a "subject to" makes it into the annual report, it could mean trouble.

What else should you know before you check the numbers?

Stay in the back of the book and go to the *footnotes*. Yipep! The whole profits story is sometimes in the footnotes.

Are earnings down? If it's only because of a change in accounting, maybe that's good! The company owes less tax and has more money in its pocket. Are earnings up? Maybe that's bad. They may be up because of a special windfall that won't happen again

A-102

next year. The footnotes know.

For what happened and why
Now turn to the *letter from the chairman*. Usually addressed "to our stockholders," it's up front, and *should* be in more ways than one. The chairman's tone reflects the personality, the well-being of his company.

In his letter he should tell you how his company fared this year. But more important, he should tell you *why*. Keep an eye out for sentences that start with "Except for . . ." and "Despite the . . ." They're clues to problems.

Insights into the future
On the positive side, a chairman's letter should give you insights into the company's future and its *stance* on economic or policital trends that may affect it.

While you're up front, look for what's new in each line of business. Is management getting the company in good shape to weather the tough and competitive 1980's?

Now_and no sooner_should you dig into the numbers!

One source is the *balance sheet*. It is a snapshot of how the company stands at a single point in time. On the left are assets_everything the company owns. Things that can quickly be turned into cash are *current assets*. On the right are *liabilities*_everything the company owes. *Current Liabilities* are the debts due in one year, which are paid out of current assets.

The difference between current assets and current liabilities is *net working capital*, a key figure to watch form one annual (and quarterly) report to another. If working capital shrinks, it could mean trouble. One possibility: the company may not be able to keep dividends growing rapidly.

Look for growth here
Stockholders' equity is the difference between total assets and liabilities. It is the presumed dollar value of what stockholders own. You want it to grow.

Another important number to watch is *long-term debt*. High and rising debt, relative to equity, may be no problem for a growing business. But it shows weakness in a company that's leveling out. (More on that later.)

The second basic source of numbers is the *income statement*. It shows how much money Galactic made or lost over the year.

Most people look at one figure first. It's in the income statement at the bottom: *net earnings per share*. Watch out. It can fool you. Galactic's management could boost earnings by selling off a plant. Or by cutting the budget for research and advertising. (See the footnotes!) So don't be smug about next earnings until you've found out how they happened_and how they might happen next year.

Check net sales first
The number you *should* look at first in the income statement is *net sales*. Ask y ourself: Are sales going *up at a faster rate* than the last time around? When sales increases start to slow, the company may be in trouble. Also ask: Have sales gone up faster than inflation? If not, the company's *real* sales may be behind. And ask yourself once more:

Have sales gone down because the company is selling off a losing business? If so, profits may be soaring.

(I never promised you that figuring out an annual report was going to be easy!)

Get out your calculator

Another important thing to study today is the company's debt. Get out your pocket calculator, and turn to the balance sheet. Divide long-term liabilities by stockholder's equity. That's the *debt-to-equity ratio*.

A high ratio means that the company borrows a lot of money to spark its growth. That's okay_if sales grow, too, and if there's enough cash on hand to meet the payments. A company doing well on borrowed money can earn big profits for its stockholders. But if sales fall, watch out. The whole enterprise may slowly sink. Some companies can handle high ratios, other can't

You have to compare

That brings up the most important thing of all: *One* annual report, *one* chairman's letter, *one* ratio won't tell you much. You have to compare. Is the company's debt-to-equity ratio better or worse than it used to be? Better or worse than the industry norms? Better or worse, after this recession, than it was after the last recession? In company-watching, *comparisons are all*. They tell if management is staying on top of things.

Financial analysts work out many other ratios to tell them how the company is doing. You can learn more about them from books on the subject. Ask your librarian.

But one thing you will *never* learn from an annual report is how much to pay for a company's stock. Galactic may be running well. But if investors expected it to run better, the stock might fall. Or Galactic could be slumping badly. But if investors see a better day tomorrow, the stock could rise.

Two important suggestions

Those are some basic for weighing a company's health from its annual report. But if you want to know *all* you can about a company, you need to do a little more homework. First, see what the business press has been saying about it over recent years. Again, ask your librarian.

Finally, you should keep up with what's going on in business, economics and politics here and around the world. All can_and will_affect you and the companies you're interested in.

Each year, companies give you more and more information in their annual reports. Profiting from that information is up to you. I hope you profit from mine.

GENERALLY ACCEPTED ACCOUNTING PRINCIPLES & OUTSIDE ASSURANCE

"NEW RULE HURTS PROFITS" ACTIVITY

PURPOSE:
To enable you to read an article dealing with a recent change in GAAP and to analyze the effect of the change.

DIRECTIONS:
Read the article "New Rule Hurts Profits" and make notes about the meaning of each phrase listed below

1. "a floodgate of red ink"

2. "bite the bullet and record the charge as one big hit"

3. "amortize the expense over 20 years"

4. "FASB 106 requires a company to **recognize** certain employee-retirement obligations while its workers are still employed...".

REQUIRED:

1. Discuss your notes and explanations of the phrases from the article with your team. Make sure you come to a consensus on each phrase.

2. Prepare answers to each of the following questions :

a. Which companies will make bigger profits **over the 20 year period**, ones that bite the bullet or ones that amortize? Explain.

b. Which companies will make bigger profits **each year during the 20 year period**, ones that bite the bullet or ones that amortize? Explain.

c. Which GAAP assumption provides the rationale behind FASB 106? Describe the assumption and the basis of accounting which would support the assumption.

d. What effect (increase or decrease) does the implementation of FASB 106 have on a company's assets, liabilities, revenues and expenses? HINT: Use the accounting equation to analyze the effect and make sure the equation stays in balance.

e. When the expenses discussed in the article are recognized, net income will be reduced. Yet the article states that cash flows will not be affected. Explain.

NEW RULE HURTS PROFITS
Some key state firms affected by accounting change
By Russ Wiles

The Arizona Republic

A new accounting rule that has opened a floodgate of red ink at General Motors Corp., Ford Motor Co., American Airlines and other corporate giants also is hurting the bottom-line results of several leading Arizona companies.

Phelps Dodge Corp., Pinnacle West Capital Corp. and Dial Corp. are among Arizona firms that have or soon will be reporting lower profits because of rule 106 from the Financial Accounting Standards Board, or FASB, a group empowered with setting national accounting guidelines.

At Dial, for example, the new rule was responsible for a one-time charge of $115 million, resulting in a net loss of $81.5 million for 1992.

But that's pocket change compared with an anticipated $7.7 billion charge Ford says it will take because of rule 106, or a possible $20.8 billion expense facing General Motors.

The GM charge is expected to result in the largest yearly loss ever for corporate America, at around $23 billion.

AMR Corp., the parent of American Airlines, last month announced a 1992 loss of $935 million, with a 106-related charge of $595 million.

What's more, the rule_technically known as Statement of Financial, Accounting Standards No 106_likely will translate into higher prices for at least some goods and services, more confusion for investors and reduced retirement benefits at certain corporations.

"It's realistic to assume that some benefits programs will be cut back," says Robert Fenimore, a partner at the accounting firm of KPMG Peat Marwick in Phoenix and president of the Arizona State Board of Accountancy. "At the least, companies will want to re-evaluate what benefits they wish to provide."

In short, 106 requires a company to recognize certain employee-retirement obligations while its workers are still employed, rather than when the firm actually pays the benefits years later. The impact shows up both as an expense on the income statement and a liability on the balance sheet.

"FASB is saying that it's more appropriate to recognize these costs during the period an employee provides the service rather than later on," says Jim McAuliffe, a partner at the Deloitte & Touche accounting firm in Phoenix.

The change pertains to a variety of retirement benefits including life insurance, housing subsidies, tuition assistance and, especially, health-care coverage, Fenimore says. Pension payouts are not affected.

The rule gives companies a choice of how to handle accumulated liabilities for past years.

Some, like Ford, General Motors, American Airlines and Dial, decided to bit the bullet and record the charge as one big hit.

Either ways, firms will face an annual charge for each future year's obligation.

Although 106 did not become effective until January 1993, some corporations such as Dial applied the charge against 1992 income to get the depressed results behind them, accountants say.

One thing the rule doesn't do is force companies to set aside money now to meet those future obligations.

"It doesn't change cash flows, just the way they're recorded," says Thomas M. Foster, vice president and controller at Phelps Dodge, which took a $66.4 million, one-time charge against its 1992 results.

Foster adds that he thinks the new rule is "proper accounting."

Because the 106 standard doesn't require that money be set aside now to pay for future costs, there's no guarantee all firms will be able to meet these obligations, McAuliffe notes.

This is especially true when you consider that health-care costs have exploded and people are living longer than ever in retirement.

"As the population continues to age, this will be an increased expense," he says.

Not all firms will be influenced to the same degree by 106.

The greatest impact will be felt by older, established companies with unionized work forces operating in mature industries, since these are the firms that offered such generous post-retirement benefits in the first place, Fenimore says.

Because this doesn't describe the typical Arizona company, he doesn't expect the impact to be felt so strongly here.

Developer Del Webb Corp., for example, is one prominent Arizona firm that doesn't anticipate that it will be affected by 106.

The impact on consumer prices will likely vary by company. Firms able to pass the retirement costs along to customers won't hesitate to do so, while others facing stiff competition or regulatory pressure might have less leeway.

Pinnacle West Capital, the parent of Arizona Public Service Co., said in its 1991 annual report that it intends to seek regulatory approval in the form of electricity-rate increases for the recovery of benefit costs, estimated a $200 million.

However, the relevant annual amortized charge_about $12 million a year before taxes_is not sufficiently large in and of itself for the utility to seek a rate increase, says Bill Hemelt, APS treasurer.

"This item is just one of a set of costs that go into the determination of a rate increase," he says, noting that APS has agreed not to seek any rate hikes until December at the earliest.

Employees and consumers aren't the only ones likely to feel an impact from rule 106. Investors also will notice a difference because of the considerable influence it will exert on company profits, book value and the like.

The rule will change some financial ratios that investors use to analyze stocks and bonds. McAuliffe says.

For example, he anticipates investors will increasingly pay more attention to cash flow, which isn't affected by the rule, and less attention to net income, which is. That could result in a ratio like price/earnings dropping in stature, while another such as price/cash flow rises.

It's also possible that the accounting rule will lead to lower ratings on bonds issued by corporations saddled with reduced profits yet greater liabilities.

When a firm's rating gets downgraded, the firm is considered a greater credit risk and consequently, must pay higher yields on its bond to attract investors.

But more than anything standard 106 will focus attention on company-provided benefits, particularly in the health-care area.

"Rule 106 has spotlighted the high costs of medical benefits." Hemelt says.

LEVELS OF ASSURANCE ACTIVITY

PURPOSE:
To enable you to comprehend the meaning of various phrases used in accounting reports and then to compare the kinds of assurance with different management needs.

DIRECTIONS:
Reread each of the sample reports provided in your textbook (AUDIT report, REVIEW report and COMPILATION report. Use the worksheet for this activity (next page) and make notes about what each of the following phrases means in terms of the **assurance** provided to the user of each kind of report.

REQUIRED:
1. Discuss your notes and explanations of each of the phrases on the worksheet.

2. Prepare answers to the following questions and be prepared to present your answers to the class:

a. Which report provides the highest level of assurance to the user of the financial statements?

b. Which kind of report would cost the most to prepare?

c. Are there any circumstances when a lower level of assurance would be acceptable to a user of the statements? Provide an example of the circumstance for each kind of report.

d. A friend of your father knows you are taking accounting and starts a conversation with you at a recent family event. He has occasionally purchased stock and always tries to read the annual report sent by each company. "They get harder to read each year, but as long as I can find the auditor's report, then I'm OK. Because then I know who to sue if the books don't balance to the penny." How would you respond?

WORKSHEET FOR LEVELS OF ASSURANCE

AUDIT report

    a. reasonable assurance

    b. material misstatement

    c. examining on a test basis

    d. in our opinion

    e. present fairly

    f. in conformity with generally accepted accounting principles

REVIEW report

    a. representation of the management

    b. inquiries of company personnel and analytical procedures

    c. substantially less in scope than an examination in accordance with GABS

    d. we do not express such an opinion

    e. we are not aware of any material modifications that should be made

COMPILATION report

    a. representation of the management

    b. we have not audited or reviewed the accompanying statements

    c. we do not express an opinion or any other form of assurance on them

    d. elected to omit substantially all the disclosures required by GAAP

    e. limited to presenting in the form of financial statements

"BATTLE OF THE BEAN COUNTERS" ACTIVITY

PURPOSE:
To enable you to become familiar with both sides of an issue relating to GAAP and to appreciate the complexities involved in financial reporting.

DIRECTIONS:
Read the article "Battle of the Bean Counters" and make notes on the following issues:

   a. List the two factions or sides of the argument over using fair value or current value reporting on financial statements.

   b. List each group's reasons for why FASB 107 **helps or hurts** the users of financial statements.

REQUIRED:
   1. Form pairs (teams of 2) within your team. Decide which pair is PRO and which is CON on the new FASB 107.

   2. With your partner, PREPARE what you consider to be your best case for the side you are representing.

   3. PRESENT your case to the other pair.

   4. Switch and let the other pair PRESENT.

   5. DISCUSS the other pairs's comments with specific facts or arguments which point out why their best case is not correct.

   6. Switch and let the other pair DISCUSS why your best case is not correct.

   7. Change your PERSPECTIVE and take the other side's position. Take turns and each pair needs to present/argue for the opposite side.

   8. As a team of four (no longer two pairs), pull together the best synthesis of all the facts and arguments presented. Be prepared to present your best reasoned judgement on the use of FASB 107.

THE BATTLE OF THE BEAN COUNTERS
Ford S. Worthy

In this battle of regulatory titans, Richard Breeder, head of the
Securities and Exchange Commission, weight in at seven pounds, zero
ounces. Alan Greenspan, chairman of the Federal Reserve Board and
Breeder opponent in a fierce debate that could lead to sweeping
changes in the way companies measure financial performance, tips the
scales at a few pounds more--or less. Ludicrous? Not according to
generally accepted accounting principles, or GAAP (pronounced *gap*).
GAAP calls for recording and maintaining most corporate assets and
liabilities based on their original cost--a practice akin to measuring
a person's size by his birth weight (as we just have).

Should anything be done about this kind of gross distortion of
financial reality? Yes, says Breeder. He is campaigning vigorously for
a new approach that could ultimately shelve the use of historical
costs in favor of current, or market, values. In his camp are
Comptroller General Charles Bowsher, who heads the General Accounting
Office; Edmund Jenkins, a partner at Arthur Anderson & Co., who chairs
a high-level accounting industry group that is studying financial
reporting standards; and a number of influential economists. Squared
off against them is a powerful crowd that includes Greenspan, Treasury
Secretary Nicholas Brady, Federal Deposit Insurance Corp. Chairman
William Taylor, and, it seems, virtually every banker and bank
regulator in the country.

The stakes in this seemingly esoteric argument over the bean counter's
art are potentially large and wide-ranging. Greenspan and other
defenders of the status quo argue that jettisoning established
accounting conventions for new, untested rules depending upon highly
subjective estimates of market values would undermine investors' and
depositors' confidence in banks. Such a change could also encourage
bankers to abandon their traditional roles as providers of long-term
credit and holders of long-term securities.

Those risks must be taken seriously. But the risks of inaction may be
even greater. Exhibit A in the case for change: the collapse and the
bailout of the savings and loan industry, now expected to cost
taxpayers at least $150 billion before it's over. Though different
accounting rules might not have averted this disaster, greater
reliance on market values would have signaled impending doom far
earlier and could have forced regulators to shut down thrifts while
their losses were still manageable. Says Edward J. Kane, a finance
professor at Boston College and an authority on the S&L fiasco:
"Misleading accounting practices allow zombie institutions to conceal
the depth of their insolvency."

Even now, traditional accounting may be allowing banks, which finally
seem on the mend, to delude themselves, regulators, and investors
about their true health. On average, banks' financial statements show
them holding capital equal to about 7% of the historical value of
their assets. But Emory University economist George J. Benston, and

expert on bank capitalization, maintains that if their balance sheets, which are still burdened with bad real estate loans, were marked to their current market value, many banks and thrifts would appear insolvent or close to it.

The task of deciding how best to reform GAAP falls to an unusual organization, the Financial Accounting Standards Board. Its rulings effectively have the force of law. That power is bestowed upon it by the SEC, which has statutory authority over the accounting practices that companies must follow. Yet FASB's seven members are chosen by a private foundation and its bills are paid in part by its main constituents, which are large corporations and accounting firms. Its stated aim is to devise "neutral" accounting standards that provide information without regard for any particular policy result. In fact, FASB's dry, academic-minded deliberations, conducted in public in a classroom-like space at its offices in Norwalk, Connecticut, sometimes lead to pronouncements that profoundly affect society (see box, pp. 87 & 88).

So far FASB appears inclined to side with market value proponents, though just how far it will go remains uncertain. Late last year it finalized a rule, Statement 107, that will require companies with more than $150 million in assets to disclose the "fair value" of securities, loans, and a wide range of other financial instruments that they hold, beginning with reports issued from fiscal years that close after December 15, 1992. Smaller companies will have three extra years to comply. (Fair value as defined by FASB is the amount at which an asset or a liability can be exchanged in a current transaction between a willing buyer and a seller who is not under duress.) Because the forthcoming disclosures are to appear as footnotes to financial statements, they won't alter earnings or the values reported on balance sheets, which will continue to be produced on the basis of GAAP.

Even so, the new disclosure rule was strenuously opposed by banks and many nonfinancial companies. They fear it is merely the first step in a radical overhaul of the GAAP system, which already contains some projections about the future alongside its historical-cost foundation. At Breeder urging, FASB is hashing through a proposal that would go beyond Statement 107 and require companies to recognize--either on their income statements or on their balance sheets--fluctuations in the market values of certain securities and related liabilities.

Also on its agenda: possible changes in when and how loans are written down once they are deemed impaired and new rules for the accounting treatment of plants, equipment, and real property whose value seems to have permanently fallen. GAAP now gives companies considerable leeway in each of these situations--leeway they often use to manage the earnings they report. Says Donald Nicolaisen, Price Waterhouse's national director of accounting: "These proposals are all related. They reflect the same gnawing concern that historical cost accounting doesn't work anymore."

Bankers, the group most directly affected by these new notions, concede that a few current practices need reform. The most notable of these is known as "gains trading," the practice of selling your winners (bonds on which you have paper gains) while holding your losers (bonds with unrealized losses) in order to boost reported earnings. Such cherry picking is made possible by rules that allow bonds to be accounted for at a cost rather than market value as long as the company claims it intended to hold them until they matured.

But the moneymen argue vehemently that trying to mark assets and liabilities to market is a cure far worse than the original disease. Their first line of defense: It is virtually impossible to come up with verifiable estimates of what many financial instruments are worth. The assumptions and guesstimates required, bankers contend, make the end result meaningless.

Take commercial loans, which account for about a third of the assets on many banks' balance sheets. "Our portfolio has tens of thousands of highly customized loans, mostly to small and midsize companies," says Susan Bies, chief financial officer for First Tennessee National, a Memphis bank holding company with $7.9 billion in assets. If such loans traded on a well-developed secondary market, determining their value would be a snap. But most trade infrequently or not at all.

So calculating each loan's present value depends on how you answer a battery of tough questions. Will a borrower pay off the loan early if interest rates go up by two (or three or four) percentage points? Under what conditions might he convert from an adjustable-rate loan to a fixed-rate one? How vulnerable is his collateral to an economic downturn? Says Bies: "In good conscience, different banks can come up with different forecasts and arrive at vastly different estimates of value for similar loans."

Valuing other crucial items on a bank's balance sheet is even slipperier. Banks profit by lending money held in low-interest checking and savings accounts to other customers at far higher rates of interest. The stability and long-term nature of these so-called core deposits endow them with considerable worth beyond their face value. But they don't trade; nor is there any good way to forecast future cash flows, because they can always be withdrawn at any time. Economist Benston, who is a market value enthusiast, admits no one has come up with a satisfactory way to value core deposits.

Others raise an even more basic objection to market value accounting. They argue that showing the price a 20-year loan could fetch were it sold today is simply not an appropriate way to measure the performance of a bank that fully expects to be around 20 years hence when that money is due to be repaid. Weighing in last year against what became FASB's Statement 107, Lester Stephens Jr., Chase Manhattan's corporate controller, wrote: "These values represent a 'fire sale' valuation that will gyrate up and down as interest rates and credit factors change. This doomsday portrayal can be very damaging to the uneducated user."

Or perhaps even to educated users. For Stephens and other bankers, the doomsday scenario is built upon a belief that Wall Street--and maybe regulators as well--will severely penalize them if the more volatile earnings that market value accounting would bring show up on their income statements. "A 1% change in interest rates would cause a 3% flip-flop in the value of our bond portfolio. That would have a significant impact on our earnings," says P. Michael Brumm, chief financial officer for Cincinnati's Fifth Third Bancorp. In that case he predicts banks will try to dodge such swings by stuffing their investment portfolios with far more short-term bonds whose market values are less susceptible than long-term securities to big up and down movements.

Banks might also be far less apt to hole bonds issued by small municipalities, speculates Gary Anderson, CFO at Zion Bancorp. in Salt Lake City. This debt is often relatively risky, not actively traded, and thus more prone to wide swings in value. Since banks are major buyers of municipal bonds such a shift would make it harder and costlier for cities to raise capital for urgent needs such as rebuilding bridges and up-grading schools.

Treasury Secretary Nick Brady contends that market value accounting "could even result in more intense and frequent credit crunches." In an insistent letter to the chairman of the FASB, Brady maintained that temporary declines in the market value of assets, if recognized in the balance sheet, "would result in immediate reductions in bank capital and an inevitable retrenchment in bank lending capacity."

Now here's the case for making a change, despite these worries. It is undeniable that interest rate shifts send the value of a bank's loans, say, spiraling up and down though current accounting practice allow such changes to remain undisclosed to the outside world. While no one can be certain how investors and creditors might respond to a clearer picture, it seems doubtful that the reality hidden by GAAP would come as a complete surprise to Wall Street analysts who supposedly earn their big salaries by parsing balance sheets in search of the truth-- and who presumably find, if not the whole truth, at least a good deal of it.

True, some banks with unexpectedly spikier earnings probably would get punished. But a former Fed economist, who asks not to be identified because he remains part of the banking industry, maintains that, on a whole, Wall Street will accept with equanimity financial statements that look more volatile. Another closet market value enthusiast, a respected economist at a major bank, agrees and adds, "If you're not sufficiently capitalized to withstand the true volatility inherent in your balance sheet, taxpayers are better of knowing that unsettling fact sooner rather than later."

Consider again the lessons of the S&L mess. In 1981 the S&L industry's collective balance sheet showed $28 billion in capital, according to retrospective figures gathered by Richard Pratt, former chairman of the Federal Home Loan Bank Board, the main overseer of thrifts in the

1980s. Yet, on a market value basis, the industry's liabilities exceeded assets in 1981 by a staggering $178 billion. If financial statements had given off even a whiff of such gross insolvency, regulators--and legislators too--would have had little choice but to force sick institutions to find additional capital, or, failing that, to close them before their difficulties multiplied.

Three years ago the Office of Thrift Supervision, the successor to the Home Loan Bank Board, began requiring the thrifts it supervises to submit detailed cash flow and interest rate information about their loan portfolios and other balance sheet items. OTS feeds the data through an elaborate model that estimates how sudden changes in interest rates might affect the market values of assets and liabilities.

The model was designed primarily to help thrifts better understand and manage their interest rate exposure. As a by-product it also produces approximations of the market value of an institution's capital, the crucial margin of safety for uninsured creditors and the federal deposit insurance fund. Though OTS officials remain harshly critical of shifting to market value accounting, some grudgingly admit this new information could prove useful. Says one: "It's potentially an important red flag."

While FASB ponders how far to push market value accounting, a few companies are moving ahead on their own. Two years ago Roosevelt Financial Group, a St. Louis-based thrift holding company with $2 billion in assets, began including in its financial statements what it calls net market value, in essence the difference between the market value of its assets and the market value of its liabilities. Interestingly, Roosevelt's most recent net market value is 9% *lower* than the company's book value according to GAAP.

Despite such negative tidings, CEO Stanley Bradshaw praises market value accounting with the fervor of a preacher delivering the gospel. He gives the back of his hand to the argument that such calculations are impractical, acknowledging that might have been true when interest rate swaps, mortgage-backed securities, financial futures, and other innovations didn't exist or were not widely traded. But the proliferation of such products over the past decade, he says, along with the development of complex mathematical pricing models, now makes it feasible to estimate market values for most financial instruments. Though this depends on a lot of assumptions, Bradshaw argues that the judgment required is no more extensive or imprecise than what GAAP currently expects of bankers in estimating, say, loan loss reserves.

Some investors also see big benefits from publishing market value estimates. Says Thomas Jones, chief financial officer at Teachers Insurance and Annuity Association, which provides retirement and insurance plans for colleges and universities: "Policy holders and regulators will have more insight into whether liquidity and safety concerns are warranted, and investors will get a clearer fix on possible hidden values." One such financial Spindletop burbles on the books of SunTrust Banks, a $35 billion bank holding company headquartered in Atlanta. SunTrust has long disclosed market value information for its investment securities, though not its loans. The annual eye popper: the revelation that its vaults contain shares of Coca-Cola Co. that a subsidiary received as an underwriting fee when Coke went public in 1919. That stock, which remains on SunTrust's balance sheet at its original value of $110,000, is now worth almost $1 *billion*.

Among companies committed to market value accounting, none is more sold on the idea than the Federal Home Loan Mortgage Corp., a New York Stock Exchange-listed company created by Congress to buy home mortgage loans from banks and other vendors. Freddy Mac first began experimenting with market value management concepts in the mid-1980s and since 1989 has issued a full-fledged market value balance sheet as a supplement to its regular quarterly financial statements. It is probably the only company whose present disclosures satisfy the requirements of FASB's Statement 107, which all big companies will have to start complying with eight months from now.

Freddie Mac Chairman Leland Brendsel believes the real appeal of market value accounting lies in the managerial insight it provides. He insists, for example, his company's computerized market-value model gives managers more realistic guidance about how to limit exposure to interest rate changes that could ever be gleaned from historical numbers.

How is FASB likely to proceed? Slowly, if the past is a guide, and that's probably not a bad speed. While the value of the insight offered by market value accounting is compelling, the nitty-gritty of adopting such a new approach on a comprehensive scale will require a lot more hard work and thought.

John Spiegel, chief financial officer at Atlanta's SunTrust, strikes what seems the right balance on this contentious issue. He recognizes the power of analyzing balance sheets through a market value lens, an exercise that he and his colleagues perform regularly for the better "feel" it gives them in hedging interest rate risks. And unlike most bankers, he doesn't object to FASB's Statement 107, which limits market value information to footnotes. But before going further, Spiegel argues, it's important to find out whether such information will really help users of financial statements make better decisions. In other words, let the disclosures FASB has already decreed serve as a laboratory to test the feasibility, and the ultimate value, of market values.

[Begin Boxed Material]

What Else FASB Will Hit You With

Retirement Benefits

Talk about big numbers. Between now and the first quarter of 1993, corporate America's reported net income--and, in turn, its stockholders' equity--will shrink by an estimated $225 billion thanks to a new FASB rule now being phased in. The product of a nearly 11 years' work, Statement 106 requires large public companies to begin taking charges for the cash they expect to pay out one day for medical and other nonpension benefits promised to retired employees and their families.

Up to now, such costs have been recognized as expenses as they were paid each year. In shifting from pay-as-you-go to accrual accounting, companies must acknowledge a huge "catch-up" liability--the total present value of future commitments already made to present retirees and employees. They may account for this burden by taking a single big bath--as IBM ($2.3 billion) and General Electric ($1.8 billion) did last year--or they may spread the cost over 20 years, as General Motors (estimated catch-up obligation: $16 billion to $24 billion) is likely to do. Nonpublic companies whose pension plans cover fewer than 500 people have until 1995 to comply.

The new rule is a prime example of FASB's influence on the real world. By forcing managers to take account of the huge costs of retirement programs, costs that in many cases were poorly understood, "FASB has done companies a real service," says Harold Dankner, a partner with Coopers & Lybrand. Already the new rule is prompting some stunned employers to begin exploring ways to reduce the benefits of future retirees.

Income Taxes

With its recent adoption of Statement 109, FASB will make the byzantine realm of income tax accounting slightly less incomprehensible. The new rule, which all companies must begin following by the end of the first quarter of next year, is the result of years of intense lobbying by companies seeking to overturn a highly complex and restrictive income tax standard that FASB issued in 1987 but never enforced. Companies henceforth will be able to recognize in current financial statements tax benefits such as loss carry-forwards, as long as they expect eventually to be able to realize a benefit in the tax returns they file with Uncle Sam. Previously they were not permitted to recognize a tax benefit from a loss carry-forward in financial statements until they actually produced income against which the carry-forward could be offset.

Stock Options

Despite unremitting opposition, FASB recently renewed its effort to find a way to recognize the cost of the incentive stock options that so many companies use to compensate key executives. Right now most options to buy shares in the future are not deemed by generally accepted accounting principles to be an expense for the companies that hand them out, even though they unquestionably have value--oodles of it--to the managers on the receiving end. Trouble is, reasonable people cannot agree on a method to determine the value. If FASB's rulemakers don't come up with an answer soon, says Paula Todd, a principal and compensation consultant at Towers Perrin, "there's a risk that Congress may enact something worse than the current rules."

[End Boxed Material]

FINANCIAL STATEMENT ANALYSIS

"READING BETWEEN THE LINES" ACTIVITY

PURPOSE:
To enable you to comprehend some areas of concern for a user of financial statements.

DIRECTIONS:
Read the article "Reading Between the Lines" and make notes about the meaning of each phrase listed below:

1. "extracting the most value from (reading the financial statements) is somethingelse again"

2. "the challenge is learning how to translate this verbiage"

3. "the ultimate outcome of this litigation is not presently determinable"

4. operations "were drastically ahead of last year's results"

5. "you can gauge the company's ability to control its costs"

6. "owning stock in a company where rhetoric matches results"

REQUIRED:

1. Compare and contrast your explanation of each of the phrases with your team members and come to a consensus.

2. Prepare answers to the following questions:

    a. According to the article, what is the first thing you should look at? Why?

    b. Why are the footnotes to the financial statements important?

    c. Does an increasing trend in earnings per share signal that a firm is successful?

    d. Do you agree with the author's discussion of ratios? Explain.

    e. Why do you think the author says not to count on the letter from the Chairman to give you valuable insight into the company's condition?

READING BETWEEN THE LINES OF AN ANNUAL REPORT
Gary Weiss

"To our shareholders." An innocent enough beginning, but what follows those three words can try the patience of the most savvy investor. Sure, reading a corporate annual report is easy_but extracting the most value from the experience is something else again.

At the beginning there is a "message from the chairman" that doesn't always give a brutally frank version of the year's events. Ignore it for now. Part of the challenge is learning how to translate this verbiage_as we've done in the accompanying illustrations on these pages.

In their quest for higher earnings, more companies are resorting to accounting changes, pension-plan terminations, and other controversial techniques. "There are lots of tricks to make things less obvious in annual reports," observes Douglas W. Kurz, a partner at accountants Coopers & Lybrand.

You needn't be an accountant to do a solid analysis of a company's report. With the tips that follow, you can sift out enough facts to decide whether a company is a good or a shaky investment.

REVEALING GLANCE. A general rule: Look at the back pages of the report first. That's where you find the opinion of the independent auditor that the company hires: Even a glance can be revealing. "Generally the auditor's statement is two paragraphs. Anything longer can be significant," notes Norman Strauss, regional director at accountants Ernst & Whinney in New York. So if the statement's long, better take time to read it.

It's possible that an extra paragraph or two may simply be a note that the company has changed its accounting practices i some minor way. But the additional material also may focus on serious stuff. In Texaco's 1985 annual report for instance, the auditors at Arthur Andersen added a paragraph mentioning the $11.1 billion judgment against the company in a suit brought by Pennzoil. It noted that the "ultimate outcome of this litigation is not presently determinable." Andersen could endorse the financial statement only "subject to the effect . . . of such adjustments, if any, that might have been required had the outcome of the litigation . . . been known." (It still isn't although one Texas court has shaved $2 billion from the judgment).

That kind of cautionary note_or "qualified opinion"_rarely tells the observant stockholder anything that's terribly surprising. Indeed, the initial Pennzoil judgment was old news when the annual report came out. But to skip the auditor's statement risks overlooking a bombshell. At least, it can confirm earlier hints of trouble.

Next, look for the section labeled "Management Discussion and Analysis of Financial Condition and Results of Operations." Undoubtedly, management does a considerable amount of discussing and analyzing throughout the report. But this section has to meet standards set by the Securities & Exchange Commission and the Financial Accounting Standards Board. "The auditors review it to make sure that it's factually consistent with the financial statement," notes Kurz.

STRAIGHT TALK. You can expect the section to present a reasonably straightforward analysis of the company's operations. Let's say that the report says earnings went up and your wonder why. IN U.S. Shoe's 1985 annual report for instance, readers learned that the company's specialty retailing operations were "dramatically ahead of last year's depressed results." Note that word "depressed." It's significant. If the prior year hadn't been so weak, 1985 wouldn't have look so good.

For more details, turn to the footnotes to the report. Among them, you'll find a breakdown of the company's lines of business, and how much each unit contributes to sales and earnings. You can also learn if the company has been making heavy use of tax benefits. The new tax law wipes out many such provisions, including the investment tax credit for equipment purchases, so the future might not be as bright.

The footnotes also indicate the health of the company's pension plan. If it's underfunded, coming up with the money to meet future pension liabilities could be a strain. But if the plan is overfunded, the company may be able to terminate the plan and institute a new one, shifting the excess into its own coffers. As an example, knowledgeable readers of the 1985 annual report of U.S. Steel (now USX) were pleased to see that the company's pension plan held 26% more assets_about $2 billion_than would be required to pay its pensioners in the future. Exactly how much the pension plan is overfunded is a matter of controversy, but the footnote was an indication that the amount may be considerable, and could be a possible source of future cash for the corporation.

Your next step: Examine the report's income statement and balance sheet. The income statement tells you how the company has been doing recently. It shows revenues, costs, and earnings for the past three years. Here you can see if the company has been able to sustain or increase the market for its products and services, and you can also gauge the company's ability to control its costs. Further down is the proverbial "bottom line"_earnings per share based on the average number of commons shares outstanding during the year. If the company has issued bonds convertible into stock, or if executives have a lot of stock options yet to be exercised, the statement will show the earnings per share "fully diluted"_as if all the potential shares were in existence.

If earnings per share have been increasing steadily, stockholders have reason to be happy. But don't rejoice if the statement shows that significant income has been derived from one-time events, such as selling of the corporate headquarters. Similarly, don't be too apprehensive if the company's earnings have been penalized during the year by the cost of shutting down facilities. Earnings may benefit in the long run.

RIPE FOR RAIDS. Then there's the balance sheet, a snapshot of the company's capital structure. It shows the assets, liabilities, and the common shareholders' equity in the company at the end of the year. That's the same as net worth, or book value: the amount that the common stockholders would get, at least in theory, if the company were liquidated. The balance sheet also tells you how much cash the company has on hand. Too little, and it may have trouble expanding; too much, and it may tempt a raider to move_which could be bad for management but good for the stock's price. You'll also see the degree to which the company relies on borrowed funds to finance its operations. A heavy debt isn't always bad, if the company's rate of return on its assets in above the cost of borrowing.

With the balance sheet and earnings statement before you, pull out your calculator. Divide common shareholder equity by the number of shares outstanding to get book value per share. If the company's shares are selling at book value or less, they may be a bargain. Generally, shares sell well above book value.

To measure how well the company is using its resources, divide net income by the company's assets, taking the year's average instead of the yearend figure. What you get is the percentage return on assets. And divide net income by average equity to see h ow well the company is doing for its stockholders. Is there adequate cash? You can find out by dividing the current assets by current liabilities. That's the current ratio.

By deriving these ratios for the previous and current years, you can tell if the company's financial position is improving or worsening. It also helps to compare your results with the numbers prevailing in the particular industry. A profit margin, of course, is the difference between the price a company gets for its products and the cost producing them. But retailers commonly have margins as low as 1% or 2%, while 15% isn't unusual among newspaper publishers. To find average ratios, turn to Dun & Bradstreet's annual compendium of 14 key business ratios for all major industries, available at most public libraries. And BUSINESS WEEK's annual ranking of the top 1000 companies, appearing in April, will handily allow you to compare the profitable of the nation's largest companies. A worthwhile reference: *Understanding Financial Statements*, part of the Investor Information Kit available for $4.00 from the New York Stock Exchange, 11 Wall St., New York, N.Y. 10005.

Have you mused over the earnings statement and balance sheet? And crunched numbers to your heart's content? Now, finally, you can read what the chairman has to say (or, more precisely, what the chairman's public relations person has to say), You may get some valuable insight into the company's condition. But don't count on it. If the chairman's words jibe with your analysis of the data in the annual report, you will feel more confident as an investor. If not you may be happier owning stock in a company where rhetoric matches results.

Gary Weiss

WHEN THEY SAY THIS:
The uncertain regulatory climate poses challenges for our business.

THAT MAY MEAN THIS:
(The SEC has subpoenaed our records and our lawyers are scared to death.)

We can prosper only by being better managed than our competitors.
(If we can sell below cost long enough we'll have the field to ourselves.)

Your company is now poised for earnings growth.
(We lost so much money earnings can't get worse.)

We're seizing the growing opportunities for global out-sourcing.
(We're moving production in the Far East, where wages are dirt-cheap.)

Last year we substantially strengthened the ranks of our senior management.
(After the latest series of indictments, heads rolled.)

We are vigorously seeking creative techniques to bring our costs in line.
(We are going to slash salaries by 20% and cash in our pension plan.)

MASCO CORPORATION: RATIO ANALYSIS
BALANCE SHEET ACTIVITY

PURPOSE:
To enable you to analyze an actual corporation using liquidity and leverage ratios, and to alert you to inherent limitations in ratio analysis.

DIRECTIONS:
Read through MASCO Corporation's **Consolidated Balance Sheet** and then use it to answer the following questions:

    a. What is MASCO's current ratio for 1990? 1991?

    b. What does this trend (increase or decrease) tell you about the company?

    c. What's in inventory? Why did it decrease from 1990 to 1991?

    d. Describe the shareholders' stake in MASCO in terms of how much is contributed and how much is earned. What does this tell you?

    e. As a potential investor, what do you think about MASCO's dividend policy?

REQUIRED:

1.   Calculate the following ratios and explain what they mean:

        a. Debt to equity ratio   *$2.5*

        b. Times interest earned ratio   *1.77* $\frac{97600+126580}{126580}$

        c. Quick ratio   *1.1*

2.   Do any of these ratios give you more information on the trends you found in the current ratio? Explain.   *All look good*

3.   Describe MASCO's **liquidity** and **leverage.**   *Okay bcz current ratio above 2. Leverage is poor bcz below*

4.   What are some possible limitations to your analysis?   *4:1*

MASCO CORPORATION: RATIO ANALYSIS
INCOME STATEMENT ACTIVITY

PURPOSE:

To enable you to analyze an actual corporation using profitability ratios and to alert you to inherent limitations in ratio analysis.

DIRECTIONS:

Read through MASCO Corporation's **Consolidated Statement of Income** and then use it to answer the following questions:

[handwritten: gross profit not sales]

a. What is the trend (increasing or decreasing) of MASCO's gross profit percentage? Is the percentage trend more important then the actual numbers?

[handwritten: decrease .311 to .298]

b. What is the trend of MASCO's selling, general and administrative expenses percentage? Is the percentage trend more important that the actual numbers?

[handwritten: increase in expense decrease revenue + gross profit]

c. What is the largest component in "Other Income (Expenses)"? How does this compare with prior years?

REQUIRED:

1. Calculate the following ratios and explain what they mean:

    a. Return on total assets   *[handwritten: $\frac{44900 + 126580}{3785810 + 3760740} = 4.5\%$]*   *[handwritten: How much you get back from what you invested]*

    b. Profit margin percentage   *[handwritten: $\frac{171480}{3141000} = .055$ or 5.5%]*

    c. Total assets turnover   *[handwritten: $\frac{3141000}{3773275} = 83\%$]*

    d. Earnings per share   *[handwritten: $\frac{44900}{153210} = .293$ or $.29 per share$]*

2. Do any of these ratios give you more information about the trends you found in a and b? Explain.

3. Describe MASCO's **profitability** based on your ratio analysis.

4. What are some possible limitations to your analysis?

A-127

MASCO CORPORATION:
FINANCIAL STATEMENTS AND NOTES

Corporate Development

While no major acquisitions occurred in 1991, acquisitions have contributed significantly to Masco's long-term growth, even though generally the initial impact on earnings is minimal after deducting acquisition-related costs such as interest and added depreciation and amortization. The important earnings benefit to Masco arises from subsequent growth of acquired companies, since incremental sales are not handicapped by these expenses.

In December 1991, Masco Capital Corp., an affiliated company, sold its most significant asset, junior subordinated discount debentures of Payless Cashways, Inc. These debentures, originally acquired for approximately $168 million in 1988, were sold for their approximate accreted value of $290 million, with Masco Capital then retiring its outstanding long-term indebtedness. The Company then acquired the remaining 50 percent ownership in Masco Capital Corp. from Masco Industries, Inc. for approximately $50 million. The principal remaining assets of Masco Capital are convertible preferred stock of Payless Cashways, Inc. and other long-term investments.

Profit Margins

After-tax profit margins were 1.4 percent, 4.3 percent and 7.0 percent of sales in 1991, 1990 and 1989, respectively. After-tax profit return on shareholders'equity was 2.5 percent, 7.5 percent and 12.7 percent in 1991, 1990 and 1989, respectively.

The margin declines in the last three years were primarily the result of: lower levels of consumer spending resulting in product sales below expectations, unfavorable results and write-downs related to equity investments, increased interest expense, and significant costs related to new product expansion and profit enhancement programs. These programs are expected to contribute to improved margins in the future.

Liquidity and Capital Resources

At year-end 1991, current assets were approximately 2.7 times current liabilities.

Over the years, the Company funded its growth through a combination of cash provided by operations and long-term bank and other borrowings.

During 1991, cash was provided by $251 million from operating activities, and by $64 million from the issuance of common stock; cash decreased by $113 million for the purchase of property and equipment, by $50 million for the acquisition of Masco Capital Corp., by $85 million of cash dividends, by $30 million for a net decrease in debt, and by $26 million for other net cash outflows; the aggregate of the preceding items represent a net cash inflow of $11 million in 1991. Cash provided by operating activities totalled $251 million, $201 million and $224 million in 1991, 1990 and 1989, respectively; the Company has generally reinvested a majority of these funds in its operations.

In April, 1991 the Company issued $250 million of 9 percent nonredeemable notes due April 15, 1996 and strengthened its balance sheet by issuing 3 million shares of its common stock for approximately $64 million. In October, 1991 the Company issued $175 million of 9 percent nonredeemable notes due October 1, 2001. The proceeds from these debt and equity offerings were used to reduce outstanding bank indebtedness.

In January, 1992 the Company redeemed at par its $300 million of 9.25 percent five-year notes due 1993 with borrowings under its $750 million bank revolving-credit agreement.

The Company's anticipated internal cash flow is expected to provide sufficient liquidity to fund its near-term working capital and other investment needs. The Company believes that its longer-term working capital and other general corporate requirements will be satisfied through its internal cash flow and, to the extent necessary, future borrowings and equity offerings in the financial markets.

32

Inventories and Receivables

In 1991, the Company's receivables increased by $13 million. This increase is primarily the result of increased fourth quarter sales in 1991 compared with the same period in 1990.

In 1991, the Company's inventories decreased by $18 million. As compared with the average manufacturing company, the Company maintains a higher investment in inventories, which relates to the Company's business strategies of providing better customer service, establishing efficient production scheduling and benefitting from larger, more cost-effective purchasing.

Capital Expenditures

Capital expenditures totalled $113 million in 1991, compared with $166 million in 1990. These capital expenditures primarily pertain to building, machinery and equipment costs for new products, expected future increased demand for Company products and profit enhancement programs. New products include wood veneer flooring, new cabinet product lines and the creation of a complete line of furniture products. Capital expenditures for profit enhancement programs include a complete manufacturing facility for builders' hardware, building and equipment costs to implement just-in-time manufacturing for the kitchen appliances operations, machinery and equipment costs to implement just-in-time manufacturing and improved inventory management at other operations, and a new plant to manufacture cabinet doors that were previously purchased from unaffiliated vendors.

The Company continues to invest in automating its manufacturing operations and increasing its productivity, in order to be a more efficient producer and improve customer service and response time.

Depreciation and amortization totalled $103 million in 1991, compared with $93 million in 1990. This continued high level is primarily the result of recent acquisitions and the Company's capital expenditures programs.

Equity and Other Investments in Affiliates

Equity loss from affiliates was $12.6 million in 1991, compared with an equity loss of $8.8 million in 1990 and equity earnings of $29.1 million in 1989.

The Company's equity earnings from Masco Capital, prior to its being acquired by the Company in late 1991, were approximately $4 million in 1991 and $7 million in 1990.

In the fourth quarter of 1991, the Company recorded approximately $32 million in non-operating charges attributable to write-downs of the Company's carrying value of investments in certain affiliated companies and other long-term investments.

Cash Dividends

During 1991, the Company increased its dividend rate 7 percent to $.15 per share quarterly. This marks the 33rd consecutive year in which dividends have been increased. Dividend payments over the last five years have increased at an 11 percent average annual rate.

General Financial Analysis
1991 versus 1990

Net sales in 1991 decreased 2 percent to $3,141 million. Cost of sales remained relatively unchanged, while increased promotional, advertising and other selling expenses contributed to selling, general and administrative expenses increasing 3 percent. Operating profit declined 25 percent. The sales decrease was primarily due to continued lower levels of consumer demand. This trend is expected to continue in the near-term.

38

The Company's Building and Home Improvement Products sales in 1991 decreased 1 percent while operating profit declined 8 percent. The operating profit was negatively impacted primarily by lower sales as well as expenses related to profit enhancement programs.

Sales and operating profit in 1991 of the Company's Home Furnishings Products decreased 3 percent and 60 percent, respectively. The significant decline in operating profit was primarily attributable to start-up costs of major new product lines, lower sales and market share improvement programs.

Unfavorable operating results from the Company's equity affiliates contributed to the 1991 earnings decline. Masco Industries reported a net loss, after preferred stock dividends, of $18.6 million in 1991 compared with a net loss of $16.2 million in 1990. The results of Masco Industries were negatively impacted by the economic recession, particularly the significant depressed levels of automotive production. Emco Limited, a Canadian affiliate, had a net loss of $16.8 million (U.S.) in 1991 as compared with a 1990 net loss of $25.8 million (U.S.). The results of Emco Limited were negatively impacted by the economic recession in Canada.

Included in other income and expense for 1991 is approximately $32 million of non-operating charges attributable to write-downs of the Company's carrying value of investments in certain affiliated companies and other long-term investments.

Included in other income and expense for 1990 is an approximate $20 million reportable portion of the gain from the sale of three subsidiaries to TriMas Corporation in January 1990.

The Company reported declines in net income and earnings per share of 68 percent and 67 percent, respectively, in 1991 as compared with 1990.

1990 versus 1989

Net sales in 1990 increased 2 percent to $3,209 million. Cost of sales increased 2 percent, while increased promotional, advertising and other selling expenses contributed to selling, general and administrative expenses increasing 13 percent. Operating profit declined 14 percent. The softening in demand in a number of consumer markets in 1989 continued through 1990, resulting in only modest sales increases for 1990.

The Company's Building and Home Improvement Products sales in 1990 increased 3 percent while operating profit declined 2 percent. The operating profit decline was primarily the result of plant start-up and relocation costs at certain of the Company's operations.

Sales and operating profit of the Company's Home Furnishings and Other Specialty Consumer Products increased 1 percent and declined 32 percent, respectively. The significant decline in operating profit was primarily attributable to major growth initiatives undertaken in 1990, such as: consolidating operations, implementing "just-in-time" manufacturing technologies, introducing sophisticated computerized marketing programs, and initiating new product lines.

Unfavorable operating results from the Company's equity affiliates contributed to the 1990 earnings decline. Masco Industries reported a net loss of $16.2 million in 1990 compared with net income of $56.6 million in 1989. Masco Industries incurred significant charges, primarily within the automotive vehicle conversion business; in addition, recessions in most major markets resulted in lower product sales and reduced operating margins. Net income of Masco Industries in 1989 included $57 million and $13.6 million of pre-tax gains from the sale of a subsidiary and the sale of TriMas common stock holdings, respectively. Emco Limited, a Canadian affiliate, had a net loss of $25.8 million (U.S.) in 1990 as compared with a 1989 net loss of $11.2 million (U.S.). Emco's results were severely impacted by the depressed conditions in the Canadian housing market, as well as costs related to inventory write-downs and branch and plant closures.

39

The Company reported declines in net income and earnings per share of 37 percent and 36 percent, respectively, in 1990 as compared with 1989. In addition to the foregoing, the earnings declines were caused by significant costs incurred related to new product development and profit enhancement programs.

General Information For Shareholders

Masco Corporation has approximately 8,700 registered shareholders, and 39,900 employees with approximately 150 manufacturing facilities located in 21 states and 19 countries. The Masco Group (including affiliated companies in which the Company owns at least a 40 percent equity interest) in 1991 had aggregate sales of almost $6 billion, and 61,000 employees with 302 manufacturing facilities located in 34 states and 20 countries.

Executive Appointment

During the last 12 months Masco Corporation made the following executive appointment:

Robert H. Schirmer was appointed to the newly created position of Vice President—Marketing.

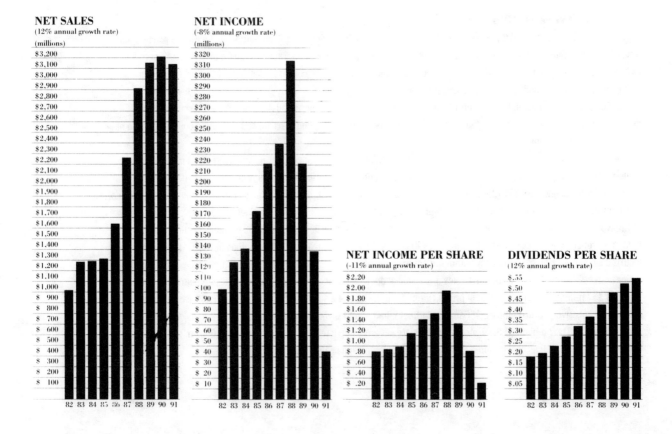

NET SALES (12% annual growth rate) (millions)

NET INCOME (-8% annual growth rate) (millions)

NET INCOME PER SHARE (-11% annual growth rate)

DIVIDENDS PER SHARE (12% annual growth rate)

40

CONSOLIDATED STATEMENT OF INCOME
for the years ended December 31, 1991, 1990 and 1989

	1991	1990	1989
Net sales	$3,141,000,000	$3,209,000,000	$3,150,500,000
Cost of sales	2,206,460,000	2,209,510,000	2,174,650,000
Gross profit	934,540,000	999,490,000	975,850,000
Selling, general and administrative expenses	686,210,000	667,990,000	591,930,000
Operating profit	248,330,000	331,500,000	383,920,000
Other income (expense), net:			
Re: Masco Industries, Inc.:			
Equity earnings (loss)	(9,170,000)	(7,700,000)	26,120,000
Interest and dividend income	17,100,000	12,000,000	12,120,000
Equity earnings (loss), other affiliates	(3,470,000)	(1,060,000)	2,940,000
Other, net	(28,610,000)	26,930,000	14,830,000
Interest expense	(126,580,000)	(125,770,000)	(112,830,000)
	(150,730,000)	(95,600,000)	(56,820,000)
Income before income taxes	97,600,000	235,900,000	327,100,000
Income taxes	52,700,000	97,100,000	106,200,000
Net income	$ 44,900,000	$ 138,800,000	$ 220,900,000
Earnings per share	$ .30	$ .91	$1.42

See notes to consolidated financial statements.

42

MASCO CORPORATION and Consolidated Subsidiaries

CONSOLIDATED BALANCE SHEET
December 31, 1991 and 1990

ASSETS	1991	1990
Current Assets:		
Cash and cash investments	$ 62,100,000	$ 51,110,000
Marketable securities	8,200,000	17,780,000
Receivables	497,000,000	480,530,000
Inventories	738,940,000	753,420,000
Prepaid expenses	69,660,000	62,310,000
Total current assets	1,375,900,000	1,365,150,000
Equity investments in Masco Industries, Inc.	238,740,000	263,850,000
Other investment in Masco Industries, Inc.	130,000,000	130,000,000
Equity investments in other affiliates	78,810,000	174,930,000
Property and equipment	1,000,070,000	970,140,000
Excess of cost over acquired net assets	630,880,000	641,320,000
Other assets	331,410,000	215,350,000
	$3,785,810,000	$3,760,740,000

LIABILITIES and SHAREHOLDERS' EQUITY

	1991	1990
Current Liabilities:		
Notes payable	$ 132,050,000	$ 199,780,000
Accounts payable	128,410,000	126,670,000
Accrued liabilities	253,380,000	225,360,000
Total current liabilities	513,840,000	551,810,000
Long-term debt	1,369,290,000	1,334,300,000
Deferred income taxes and other	103,770,000	100,590,000
	1,986,900,000	1,986,700,000
Shareholders' Equity:		
Common shares authorized: 400,000,000; issued: 1991–153,210,000, 1990–149,960,000	153,210,000	149,960,000
Preferred shares authorized: 1,000,000	—	—
Paid-in capital	64,950,000	—
Retained earnings	1,596,180,000	1,638,390,000
Cumulative adjustments	15,120,000	16,240,000
Treasury shares (2,200,000) related to merger, at cost	(30,550,000)	(30,550,000)
	1,798,910,000	1,774,040,000
	$3,785,810,000	$3,760,740,000

See notes to consolidated financial statements.

MASCO CORPORATION and Consolidated Subsidiaries

CONSOLIDATED STATEMENT OF CASH FLOWS
for the years ended December 31, 1991, 1990 and 1989

CASH FLOWS FROM (FOR):	1991	1990	1989
OPERATING ACTIVITIES:			
Net income	$ 44,900,000	$138,800,000	$220,900,000
Depreciation and amortization	102,690,000	93,490,000	89,080,000
Equity (earnings) loss, net	38,090,000	10,540,000	(27,070,000)
Write-down of long-term investments	31,800,000	—	—
Deferred income taxes and other	(3,550,000)	13,290,000	2,760,000
Gain on sales of subsidiaries, net	—	(16,690,000)	—
Total from earnings	213,930,000	239,430,000	285,670,000
(Increase) decrease in receivables	(13,180,000)	32,120,000	(36,510,000)
(Increase) decrease in inventories	17,560,000	(48,710,000)	(39,030,000)
Increase (decrease) in accounts payable and accrued liabilities	32,480,000	(22,250,000)	13,620,000
Net cash from operating activities	250,790,000	200,590,000	223,750,000
INVESTING ACTIVITIES:			
Proceeds from sales of subsidiaries	—	93,670,000	—
Proceeds from redemption of Masco Industries debentures	—	36,000,000	—
Investment in Masco Industries preferred stock	—	(30,000,000)	—
Acquisition of Masco Capital Corp.	(49,450,000)	—	—
Capital expenditures	(112,990,000)	(165,570,000)	(163,710,000)
Other, net	(25,840,000)	(29,800,000)	(75,690,000)
Net cash (for) investing activities	(188,280,000)	(95,700,000)	(239,400,000)
FINANCING ACTIVITIES:			
Issuance of stock	63,600,000	—	—
Increase in debt	449,690,000	247,040,000	204,060,000
Payment of debt	(479,660,000)	(78,070,000)	(42,390,000)
Cash dividends paid	(85,150,000)	(81,120,000)	(74,830,000)
Repurchase of Company common stock	—	(188,120,000)	(109,800,000)
Net cash (for) financing activities	(51,520,000)	(100,270,000)	(22,960,000)
CASH AND CASH INVESTMENTS:			
Increase (decrease) for the year	10,990,000	4,620,000	(38,610,000)
At January 1	51,110,000	46,490,000	85,100,000
At December 31	$ 62,100,000	$ 51,110,000	$ 46,490,000

See notes to consolidated financial statements.

44

A-135

ACCOUNTING POLICIES

Principles of Consolidation.   The consolidated financial statements include the accounts of Masco Corporation and all majority-owned subsidiaries. All significant intercompany transactions have been eliminated. Corporations in which Masco has a voting interest from 20 to 50 percent are accounted for by the equity method.

Prior-Year Reclassification.   Prior years have been reclassified to conform with 1991 presentation.

Average Shares Outstanding.   The average number of common shares outstanding in 1991, 1990 and 1989 approximated 149.9 million, 152.6 million and 155.6 million, respectively.

Cash and Cash Investments.   The Company considers all highly liquid investments with a maturity of three months or less to be cash and cash investments.

Receivables.   Accounts and notes receivable are presented net of allowances for doubtful accounts of $13.7 million at December 31, 1991 and $13.0 million at December 31, 1990.

Property and Equipment.   Property and equipment, including significant betterments to existing facilities, are recorded at cost. Upon retirement or disposal, the cost and accumulated depreciation are removed from the accounts and any gain or loss is included in income. Maintenance and repair costs are charged to expense as incurred.

Depreciation and Amortization.   Depreciation is computed principally using the straight-line method over the estimated useful lives of the assets. Annual depreciation rates are as follows: buildings and land improvements, 2 to 10 percent, and machinery and equipment, 5 to 33 percent. Depreciation was $70.2 million, $61.3 million and $59.4 million in 1991, 1990 and 1989, respectively. The excess of cost over net assets of acquired companies is being amortized using the straight-line method over periods not exceeding 40 years; at December 31, 1991 and 1990, such accumulated amortization totalled $93.3 million and $73.8 million, respectively. Purchase costs of patents are being amortized using the straight-line method over their remaining lives. Amortization of intangible assets was $32.5 million, $32.2 million and $29.7 million in 1991, 1990 and 1989, respectively.

ACQUISITION

Masco Capital Corp., which was jointly owned by the Company and Masco Industries, became a wholly owned subsidiary of the Company in late 1991 when the Company acquired Masco Industries' 50 percent interest in Masco Capital. The Company paid Masco Industries $50 million for its ownership in Masco Capital. At December 31, 1991, the principal assets of Masco Capital are preferred stock of Payless Cashways, Inc. and other long-term investments. Prior to the Company becoming the sole owner of Masco Capital Corp., Masco Capital sold its most significant asset, debentures of Payless Cashways, Inc., at approximate carrying value of $290 million, and thereby retired its outstanding long-term indebtedness.

INVENTORIES

	(In Thousands) At December 31	
	1991	**1990**
Finished goods	$272,130	$323,160
Raw material	269,100	252,380
Work in process	197,710	177,880
	$738,940	$753,420

Inventories are stated at the lower of cost or net realizable value, with cost determined principally by use of the first-in, first-out method.

45

A-136

EQUITY INVESTMENTS IN AFFILIATES

Equity investments in affiliates consist primarily of the following common stock and partnership interests:

	At December 31		
	1991	**1990**	**1989**
Masco Industries, Inc.	47%	47%	49%
Emco Limited, a Canadian co.	44%	44%	44%
Mechanical Technology Inc.	49%	49%	49%
Hans Grohe, a German partnership	27%	27%	27%
TriMas Corporation	8%	8%	8%
Masco Capital Corp.	—	50%	50%

Excluding Masco Industries and TriMas Corporation, the Company's carrying value of the above investments at December 31, 1991 approximates the Company's equity in the underlying net book value in these affiliates.

The Company's carrying value in the common stock of Masco Industries exceeds its equity in underlying net book value by approximately $44 million at December 31, 1991. This excess, substantially all of which resulted from the repurchases by Masco Industries of its common stock, is being amortized over a period not to exceed 40 years. The Company's carrying value in the common stock of TriMas Corporation exceeds its equity in the underlying net book value by approximately $15 million at December 31, 1991.

In late 1990, the Company exchanged 10 million shares of its Masco Industries common stock and $30 million for $77.5 million of Masco Industries' newly issued 12 percent preferred shares. The Company did not realize any gain or loss in connection with this exchange. In part, this transaction was pursuant to the Company's right to require Masco Industries to repurchase shares of its common stock from the Company under a long-standing stock repurchase agreement.

Excluding the preferred shares of Masco Industries and the partnership interest in Hans Grohe, for which there is no quoted market value, aggregate market value, in U.S. dollars, of the Company's equity investments at December 31, 1991 (which may differ from the amounts that could then have been realized upon disposition), based upon quoted market prices at that date, was $176 million, as compared with the Company's related aggregate carrying value of $220 million.

Approximate combined condensed financial data of the above companies, excluding December 31, 1991 data of Masco Capital, are summarized in U.S. dollars as follows, in thousands:

	1991	**1990**	**1989**
At December 31:			
Current assets	$ 1,190,160	$ 1,149,310	$ 1,266,300
Current liabilities	(509,770)	(494,900)	(673,070)
Working capital	680,390	654,410	593,230
Property and equipment	882,530	876,140	802,920
Other assets	816,340	1,156,820	1,131,080
Long-term liabilities	(1,880,060)	(2,088,250)	(1,922,280)
Shareholders' equity	$ 499,200	$ 599,120	$ 604,950
Net sales	$ 2,907,660	$ 3,101,390	$ 3,011,340
Net income (loss)	$ (2,070)	$ (16,130)	$ 60,490
The Company's net equity in above income (loss)	$ (12,640)	$ (8,760)	$ 29,060
Cash dividends received by the Company (including $21.1 million from Masco Capital in 1991)	$ 25,450	$ 1,780	$ 1,990

Equity in undistributed earnings of affiliates of $105 million at December 31, 1991, $144 million at December 31, 1990 and $154 million at December 31, 1989 are included in consolidated retained earnings.

46

Summarized unaudited financial information related to Masco Capital, prior to its becoming a wholly owned subsidiary in late 1991, is as follows, in thousands:

	1991	1990	1989
At December 31:			
Current assets	—	$ 1,210	$ 620
Current liabilities	—	(62,320)	(212,830)
Working capital	—	(61,110)	(212,210)
Other assets	—	330,280	278,860
Long-term liabilities	—	(150,000)	—
Shareholders' equity	—	$ 119,170	$ 66,650
Net income	$ 11,500	$ 14,020	$ 9,650

OTHER INVESTMENT IN MASCO INDUSTRIES, INC.

	(In Thousands) At December 31	
	1991	1990
Convertible debentures, 6%, due 2011	$130,000	$130,000

The 6 percent debentures are carried at cost and are convertible into Masco Industries' common stock at any time prior to redemption or maturity at $18 per share. The debentures are redeemable at par, plus a redemption premium, at the option of Masco Industries.

PROPERTY AND EQUIPMENT

	(In Thousands) At December 31	
	1991	1990
Land and improvements	$ 75,420	$ 73,460
Buildings	556,520	476,570
Machinery and equipment	828,220	824,960
	1,460,160	1,374,990
Less accumulated depreciation	460,090	404,850
	$1,000,070	$ 970,140

ACCRUED LIABILITIES

	(In Thousands) At December 31	
	1991	1990
Salaries, wages and commissions	$ 58,970	$ 53,860
Insurance	32,040	17,860
Interest	28,960	25,640
Dividends payable	22,750	20,790
Income taxes	14,390	12,080
Pension and profit-sharing	14,230	14,960
Advertising, sales promotion and other	82,040	80,170
	$253,380	$225,360

47

A-138

LONG-TERM DEBT

	(In Thousands) At December 31	
	1991	**1990**
Notes, 9.25%, due 1993	$ 300,000	$ 300,000
Notes, 8.75%, due 1996	200,000	200,000
Notes, 9.0%, due 1996	250,000	—
Notes, 9.0%, due 2001	175,000	—
Convertible subordinated debentures, 5.25%, due 2012	177,930	177,930
Notes payable to banks	210,000	615,000
Other	82,570	92,900
	1,395,500	1,385,830
Less current portion	26,210	51,530
	$1,369,290	$1,334,300

The 8.75 percent ten-year notes due March 1, 1996 are redeemable after February, 1993 at par.

In April, 1991 the Company issued $250 million of 9 percent nonredeemable notes due April 15, 1996. In October, 1991, the Company issued $175 million of 9 percent nonredeemable notes due October 1, 2001. The proceeds from these debt offerings were used to reduce outstanding bank indebtedness.

The 5.25 percent subordinated debentures due 2012 are convertible into common stock at $42.28 per share.

The notes payable to banks relate to a $750 million revolving-credit agreement, with any outstanding balance due and payable in November, 1995. Interest is payable on borrowings under this agreement based upon various floating rates as selected by the Company.

In January, 1992, the $300 million of 9.25 percent five-year notes due 1993 were redeemed at par with borrowings under the Company's bank revolving-credit agreement.

Certain debt agreements contain limitations on additional borrowings and restrictions on cash dividend payments and common share repurchases. At December 31, 1991, the amount of retained earnings available for cash dividends and common share repurchases approximated $109 million under the most restrictive of these provisions.

The maturities of long-term debt during the next five years are approximately as follows: 1992–$26.2 million, included in current notes payable; 1993–$5.1 million; 1994–$8.9 million; 1995–$513.7 million; and 1996–$453.8 million.

At December 31, 1991, the Company had shelf-registration statements on file with the Securities and Exchange Commission for up to $425 million of debt securities as well as up to 3.5 million shares of its common stock.

Cash payments for interest were $127 million, $123 million and $110 million in 1991, 1990 and 1989, respectively.

48

SHAREHOLDERS' EQUITY

	1991	1990	(In Thousands) 1989
Common Shares, $1 Par Value			
Balance, January 1	$ 149,960	$ 157,820	$ 158,120
Shares issued	—3,250	1,160	3,830
Shares repurchased	—	(9,020)	(4,130)
Balance, December 31	153,210	149,960	157,820
Paid-In Capital			
Balance, January 1	—	85,320	108,570
Common shares issued	— 64,950	31,510	84,820
Common shares repurchased	—	(116,830)	(108,070)
Balance, December 31	64,950	—	85,320
Retained Earnings			
Balance, January 1	1,638,390	1,641,340	1,498,840
Net income	44,900	138,800	220,900
Cash dividends declared	(87,110)	(81,890)	(78,400)
Common shares repurchased	—	(59,860)	—
Balance, December 31	1,596,180	1,638,390	1,641,340
Cumulative Adjustments			
Balance, December 31	15,120	16,240	4,500
Treasury Shares Related to Merger			
Balance, January 1	(30,550)	(30,550)	(30,070)
Shares repurchased	—	—	(480)
Balance, December 31	(30,550)	(30,550)	(30,550)
Shareholders' Equity			
Balance, December 31	$1,798,910	$1,774,040	$1,858,430

In April, 1991, the Company issued 3 million shares of its common stock for approximately $64 million. The proceeds from this offering were used to reduce outstanding bank indebtedness.

During 1990 and 1989, the Company repurchased and retired approximately 9.0 million and 4.1 million of its common shares in open market transactions at an aggregate cost of $185.7 million and $112.2 million, respectively.

On the basis of amounts paid (declared), cash dividends per share were $.57 ($.58) in 1991, $.54 ($.55) in 1990 and $.50 ($.51) in 1989.

Included in cumulative adjustments are equity adjustments from foreign currency translation and, at December 31, 1990, unrealized losses on long-term securities.

49

A-140